Southern Illinois University Press

Carbondale and Edwardsville

Selected

Writings of

James Hayden Tufts

Edited
with an Introduction by

James Campbell

Library of Congress Cataloging-in-Publication Data

Tufts, James Hayden, 1862–1942.
    [Selections.   1992]
    Selected writings of James Hayden Tufts / edited with an
introduction by James Campbell.
        p.   cm.
    Includes bibliographical references and index.
    1. Ethics.   2. Social ethics.   I. Campbell, James, 1948–   .
    II. Title.
    BJ1011.T762   1992
    170—dc20   91-3193
    ISBN 0-8093-1714-1   CIP

Frontispiece: James Hayden Tufts (Courtesy Special Collections, Morris Li-
            brary, Southern Illinois University at Carbondale)

The paper used in this publication meets the minimum requirements of American National Standard for Information Sciences—Permanence of Paper for
Printed Library Materials, ANSI Z39.48-1984. ⊗

Contents

Preface

The following selections were chosen with the intention of representing the full range of the thought of James Hayden Tufts (1862–1942). With this in mind, I have chosen pieces from across the length of his career and the breadth of his interests. With the exception of the largely autobiographical essay "What I Believe" with which these selections begin, the pieces appear in chronological order. The selections are presented in their original form, except where noted by ellipses or brackets, although I have silently regularized spelling, punctuation, and typography, and occasionally corrected quotations or improved citations.

I have been working on this volume for several years, and, along the way, I have accumulated a number of debts. I am grateful for the assistance of the staffs of the three libraries that hold archival materials by and about Tufts: the Amherst College Library, the Regenstein Library of the University of Chicago, and the Morris Library of Southern Illinois University at Carbondale. Closer to home, I have been greatly assisted in my efforts to obtain copies of all the materials listed in the Bibliography by Joanne L. Hartough of the Carlson Library of the University of Toledo; in the preparation of the Bibliography by Nancy C. Kolinski of the Philosophy Department of the University of Toledo; and in the preparation of the text itself by my wife, Linda M. Campbell. I am most grateful to all three of them.

Other debts, to teachers and colleagues, are obvious to me but must go unmentioned here—except for my spiritual debt to Harold Zyskind (1918–1990), whose efforts to continue working under circumstances that others would have found impossible were an inspiration to all. It is to his memory that this volume is dedicated.

Introduction

It is comforting to believe that intellectual figures about whom we know little deserve their relative obscurity. James Hayden Tufts is such a little-known figure. Few are familiar with any of his work; and, among those who are, Tufts is usually thought of only as the individual who helped John Dewey write his *Ethics*, a misconception that recent commentary on the volume has done little to dispel.[1] In addition, the secondary literature in American philosophy has not treated Tufts any better.[2] Moreover, most of his books other than the *Ethics* are long out of print, and his shorter pieces are scattered throughout scores of journals. Given this situation of general anonymity, why would anyone encountering this obscure philosopher's name, or the mention of one of his works, think it necessary to inquire further? What incentive could be offered for being more careful?

The main reason to be cautious is that, in our haste and intellectual overconfidence, we might overlook an important figure. Objectively, Tufts has all the earmarks of potential importance. Thinkers whom we respect thought very highly of both Tufts and his work. He was a prolific writer, producing during his lifetime nine books and other major studies, well over one hundred articles, and nearly two hundred reviews and sixty-nine dictionary entries. He also served as editor of *The School Review* for three years, and of *The International Journal of Ethics* for seventeen years. Tufts was a major figure at the University of Chicago, present from the day it opened in 1892 until his retirement at the end of 1930, serving as chair of the philosophy department for over twenty-five years, as dean three different times for a total of over nine years, as vice-president for over two years, and briefly as acting president in 1925. Tufts was also well respected among his philosophy colleagues, who elected him president of the Western Philosophy Association (1906 and 1914), of the American Philosophy Association (1914), and, after the unification in 1926 that he helped to bring about, of the Pacific Division of the American Philosophy Association (1934). And, somehow he managed to set aside enough time to engage in extensive social reform activities. Maybe such a figure merits a second look.

From the point of view of the history of American thought, Tufts and his work played an important role on the philosophical scene for many years. He would seem to have earned some place, even if a minor one, in our sense of its history. Our lack of familiarity with his work leaves a blank space in our understanding of the history of American philosophy, and this fact alone would justify reevaluating his perspective. However, there may be more. Since Tufts was not working to earn such a historical place, but rather to advance the common good through intelligent social reconstruction, a recovery of an organic sense of his work might serve us as a means to something more than simply the rediscovery of a lost intellectual hero. Readers will find in his work, I think, an important perspective on the nature of the social process that we will do well to study and to adapt for our current situation. They will find in his work a clear demonstration of the need to rethink our inherited intellectual tools to satisfy the demands of ongoing social life. They will find in his work a compelling vision of the role of education and the educator in the process of human growth and social betterment. And they will find much more. The purpose of this volume is to give Tufts a second chance.

TUFTS'S LIFE

James Hayden Tufts[3] was born in Monson, Massachusetts, on July 9, 1862, barely two months after Henry David Thoreau's death on May 6 in Concord. He was the only surviving child of James Tufts and Mary Warren Tufts. (An older child, James Frederic Tufts, died suddenly after a brief seven months of life in 1860.)

The elder James Tufts (1812–1901) came from a religious background. He had originally intended to follow his father into the pulpit, and, with this vocation in mind, he attended Yale College (A.B., 1838) and Andover Theological Seminary. He suffered, however, from a severe problem with his voice, and was forced to give up hope of a life of preaching. As a substitute, he returned to teaching, which had helped pay for his studies. In 1852, the elder Tufts became the principal of the Monson Academy. Because of a recurrence of his throat problem, he was forced to give up this post after seven years. He turned to farming and to conducting a 'home school' in Monson.

Mary Elizabeth Warren (1823–1910) grew up in Wardsboro, Vermont, as did her future husband, sharing with him the same preacher—his father—and the same physician—her father. She studied at the Mount Holyoke Seminary and Castleton Seminary and taught school in a variety of contexts. Included among these were her own private school in New York City prior to her marriage in 1855, the Monson Academy, and the later home school with her husband.

James Hayden Tufts received his initial education at the home school of his parents, following an academic regime inclined more to the particular needs of the various students who passed through the home than to some general outline for his own education. He also worked on the family farm, recalling even late in life his pride in his control of a team of oxen. He attended Monson Academy, but only briefly. His own teaching experience began with a class of students ranging in age from four to the midteens in one the schools of the Monson School District in the spring of 1878, when he was himself not yet sixteen. He taught at various locations in the Monson area, earning money to continue his education, until he matriculated at Amherst College in September 1880.

While at Amherst, Tufts was an active student, cherishing the comradeship of a diverse group of men of his own age. He relished the friendly competition of the mind (for example, winning the Hardy Prize for debate) and of the body (he was a 'rusher', that is, a lineman, for the college football team). By far the most memorable of his instructors was the professor of philosophy, Charles Edward Garman (1850–1907), who impressed upon Tufts both the importance of the craft of teaching and the centrality of the spiritual role of the college instructor in the developing moral lives of the students. Tufts was the class president during his junior and senior years at Amherst, and he graduated Phi Beta Kappa at the age of twenty-one in the spring of 1884.

In the fall of that year, Tufts became the principal of the newly opened Staples High School in Westport, Connecticut. There, in addition to performing his teaching and administrative duties, he met his future wife, Cynthia Whitaker. Cynthia Hobart Whitaker (1860–1920) was one of thirteen children born to Augustus Greenleaf Whitaker and Caroline Hobart, eight of whom survived to adulthood. She worked while a young girl as a seamstress and began teaching district school at the age of fourteen. Financial difficulties ended her attempts at a high school education and put her to work in a silk mill. However, she was able to return to school teaching, the initial profession of both of her parents, and, when offered a teaching position by Tufts at Staples High School, she accepted. She stayed in Westport for two years (1884–1886) before enrolling at Smith College (1886–1888). She was prevented, again by financial troubles, from completing her studies, and she returned to school teaching until her marriage to Tufts in 1891.

Tufts left Westport at the end of the 1884–1885 school year to return to Amherst College as the Walker Instructor in Mathematics and to study philosophy further with his mentor, Garman. He held the mathematics position for two years (1885–1887), apparently with great joy. During the intervening summer he worked, as he had worked every summer, on the family farm in Monson, taking off enough time to enroll at the Concord School of Philosophy in July to attend lectures by William Torrey Harris and Thomas Davidson. During his second year as mathematics instructor at Amherst, Tufts continued to study philosophy and to ponder his unsettled future.

In the fall of 1887 Tufts entered the Yale Divinity School to prepare for a life in the ministry, although, as Garman—who also had earned a divinity degree at Yale—had shown, such preparation did not lead necessarily to the pulpit. Because of his general intellectual and religious background, Tufts was able to enter immediately into the second-year class, thus cutting his stay in New Haven from three years to two (1887–1889). His studies there were much broader than simply divinity work. They included philosophy and psychology with George Trumbull Ladd, political economy and anthropology with William Graham Sumner, and Semitic languages and 'Higher Criticism' with William Rainey Harper. He also became engaged to be married to Cynthia Whitaker in February of 1888, although the wedding was not to occur for three and a half years.

At the end of his first year at Yale, Tufts won the Porter Prize of $400 for an essay entitled "The Growth of the Love of Nature in English Poetry." During that summer, after being certified as sufficiently orthodox and being licensed to preach, he served as a replacement pastor in the Congregational church in the town of Inkster, in Grand Forks County of the Dakota Territory, under the auspices of the American Home Missionary Society. During his second year at the divinity school, he spent many weekends preaching around the Connecticut River Valley, honing his sermons and earning some badly needed money. He received his B.D. degree in the spring of 1889.

Tufts was still uncertain of his 'calling' to the ministry. Fortunately for him another calling came. President James Burrill Angell of the

University of Michigan offered him a position beginning that fall as instructor of philosophy assisting John Dewey, who was returning to Ann Arbor from the University of Minnesota. Tufts stayed at Michigan for two years (1889–1891), teaching courses in ancient and medieval philosophy, modern philosophy, elementary logic, and psychology (using Dewey's *Psychology* as the text).[4]

During his time in Ann Arbor, Tufts received his M.A. degree from Amherst, using the Porter Prize essay as his thesis. In spite of his general happiness at Michigan, Tufts recognized that if he and Cynthia were ever to marry, he would need a substantial increase over his instructor's salary. He recognized as well that if he was to continue on in higher education, a doctorate would be necessary. And, in spite of the example of Dewey whose Ph.D. was from Johns Hopkins, a doctorate for Tufts meant study in Germany.[5] The direct impetus for this German study came in the winter of 1890–1891 from his former teacher at the Yale Divinity School, William Rainey Harper, who was then assembling a staff for John D. Rockefeller's new university in Chicago. Armed with the promise of a better-paying position at a growing institution, Tufts and Cynthia Whitaker married on August 25, 1891, and sailed almost immediately for Europe.[6] He studied during the fall semester in Berlin, attending lectures by Hermann Ebbinghaus and Friedrich Paulsen. He left Berlin for Freiburg im Breisgau for the spring semester, in part because the faculty in Berlin would not count his two years of study at the Yale Divinity School toward the requirements for his degree. At the Albert-Ludwigs-Universität, he studied with Hugo Münsterberg and Alois Riehl. The latter directed and accepted his dissertation, "The Sources and Development of Kant's Teleology." With his Ph.D. in hand, Tufts and his wife returned to the United States in time for the opening of the University of Chicago in the fall of 1892.

During that first year in Chicago, the university itself, with a faculty studded with world-famous scientists and former college presidents, lurched into gear in a growing city that, besides its normal industrial and transportation activities, was preparing to host the World's Columbian Exhibition of 1893.[7] Tufts himself was kept busy with classes, primarily in the history of philosophy, seeing to the publication of his dissertation [1892:01] and the translation of Windelband's *Geschichte der Philosophie* [1893:01]. Family matters were important for the young couple as well. In the fall of their second year in Chicago, their daughter Irene was born; in the spring of their third year, their son James Warren.

In between these two highly important personal dates came the fateful year 1894. In that year, Tufts was promoted to associate professor of philosophy; but, more importantly, that was the year that the shape of the department was forever changed. With the arrival of John Dewey to head the philosophy department and George Herbert Mead to share the teaching load, a new school of philosophy was born—as William James wrote, "a *real school*" with "*real Thought*."[8] With the inclusion of James Rowland Angell, and the later additions of Addison Webster Moore and Edward Scribner Ames, 'The Chicago School' proceeded to develop a powerful and compelling social pragmatism that drew upon the psychological bases and ethical fervor of James, and the social orientation and scientific rigor of Charles Sanders Peirce.[9]

Tufts was appointed dean of the Senior Colleges at the University of Chicago in 1899, a position he held until 1904, and again during the academic year 1907–1908. In 1900, he was promoted to the rank of professor. During these years, he was also teaching his classes, translating the second edition of Windelband's *History* [1901:01], and working on his two small volumes on the relation of the individual to society in the history of British thought [1898:01 and 1904:01]. In 1904 he was awarded an honorary doctorate by Amherst College. When Dewey left the University of Chicago in 1904, Tufts became head of the Philosophy Department, a position he held until just before his retirement in 1930. He served as president of the Western Philosophical Association in 1906 [1906:10], and was an editor of *The School Review*, a journal of secondary education housed in the department from 1906–1909. During these years, Tufts was also working on an ethics text with Dewey.

Ethics, by Dewey and Tufts, appeared in 1908 [1908:01]. Tufts had originally had the idea for the book around 1900 and he had little trouble interesting Dewey in the novel project, but carrying the project through to fruition took far longer than they anticipated.[10] The novelty of the volume was in its presentation of the historical and anthropological examination of the growth of Western morality (written by Tufts) in combination with a theoretical examination of the conscious experience of an inquiring moral agent (written by Dewey) and then the application of this dual examination to a series of specific political, economic, and familial problems of the current social situation (written by both of them).[11] The text succeeded in its effort "to awaken a vital conviction of the genuine reality of moral problems and the value of reflective thought in dealing with them"[12] for nearly a quarter century until it was replaced by the revised version in 1932 [1932:01].

Tufts's interest in the problems of society, demonstrated in the *Ethics*, can also be seen in his direct efforts at improving the social conditions of Chicago. Interest in social reform was not unusual at the new university, and the philosophy department of Dewey, Mead, and the others was connected to such efforts through its Laboratory School and through such institutions as Jane Addams's Hull House and the Chicago City Club.[13] Tufts himself served on the Committee on Housing Conditions of the City Club beginning in 1908, becoming its chair in 1910. During this same time, he did research for the Illinois State Conference on Charities and Correction on housing in various other cities in Illinois [1909:13]. In 1912, he became president of the Illinois Association for Labor Legislation, and early in 1913 he was named chairman of the Illinois Committee on Social Legislation.

At the end of 1909, Tufts was in Portland, Oregon, considering the position of president of the soon-to-be-built Reed Institute, a position that he declined. In 1914, he served as president of both the Western Philosophical Association and its younger eastern cousin, the American Philosophical Association, in their pre-unification days [1915:05]. He became editor of *The International Journal of Ethics* in the fall of 1914 and held the post, with increasing amounts of help from T. V. Smith after 1924, until the middle of 1931.

During the Great War, Tufts published three major works. One, *The Real Business of Living* [1918:01], on which he had been at work since 1912, was an attempt to help students in the final years of high school to develop a fuller sense of public morality and the duties of a citizen by examining the long process of social progress. Another volume, *Our Democracy* [1917:01], published the year before, presented some of the same material, this time organized as a summary for the general reader of the principles that undergirded America's recent entry into the war. In the third volume, *The Ethics of Cooperation* [1918:02], Tufts explored the forms of social organization that might be possible in the postwar world.

The war years found Tufts, in addition to his regular scholarly, university, and editorial duties, serving as the district director for Illinois, Wisconsin, and Michigan of the war issues course for the Student Army Training Corps. His personal life during and shortly after the war included both happiness and suffering. His daughter, Irene, returned from a six-month period of work as a nurse in France for the American Fund for French Wounded and later married George Herbert Mead's son, Henry Castle Albert Mead, in May of 1919. His son, James Warren, served overseas in France as an enlisted man in the army's Signal Corps, working as a meteorologist. He returned to Chicago and married Gertrude Dickinson White in January of 1921. Most significant of all, however, was his wife Cynthia's final illness and death in January of 1920, three months short of her sixtieth birthday.

Beginning in January of 1919, Tufts had undertaken the position of chairman of the Board of Arbitration that implemented the agreement between the owners of the Hart, Schaffner and Marx clothing company and the local unit of the Amalgamated Clothing Workers of America. This position expanded in December of 1919 when Tufts undertook to fill the same position under an agreement that encompassed the approximately forty thousand workers of the entire men's clothing industry for the Chicago area. During his service, he rendered numerous formal decisions and learned a great deal about the possibilities of industrial arbitration.[14] He continued in this position until he moved to New York City in September 1920 to teach at Columbia University during the final year of Dewey's sojourn in the Orient.

During his year at Columbia, Tufts began work on a study of the preparation of students for the developing field of social work that appeared as *Education and Training for Social Work* [1923:01] only after his return to the University of Chicago. Back at Chicago, he assumed the newly created position of Dean of Faculties in April of 1923. His administrative duties were dramatically expanded in January of the next year when he was appointed vice-president of the university with a special purview over matters academic. When President Ernest DeWitt Burton died in the spring of 1925, Tufts became acting president of the university, a position he held for five months until the accession of President Max Mason in October of that year. Among his happier duties during this time was his awarding of a medical diploma on his daughter, Irene Tufts Mead, at the June graduation. In April of 1926 Tufts resigned these administrative duties to return to the philosophy department, of which he was still Head.

In June of 1923, Tufts had remarried. His second wife, Matilde Castro (b. 1879), earned her Ph.D. in philosophy at Chicago in 1907 and had taught philosophy and education at Mount Holyoke, Vassar, Rockford, and Bryn Mawr. As the decade of the 1920s wore on, Tufts, now in his late sixties and in failing health, began slowly disengaging from the university. Rumors that he was to return to Amherst College

as president surfaced but proved false. Back in Chicago, serious conflicts developed between the philosophy department and the new
president of the university, Robert Maynard Hutchins, and Tufts re-
tired to the West Coast at the end of 1930. He had initially planned
to return to Chicago to teach half-time as professor emeritus, but
conditions proved so unattractive, especially after the death of his in-
law, colleague, and friend George Herbert Mead in April of 1931, that
he never returned to teach.

Tufts and Matilde lived initially in Santa Barbara, California, where
he was able to teach one day a week at the University of California
at Los Angeles for a few years, until Depression-mandated budget
reductions eliminated the position. In the fall of 1936 they moved
north to Berkeley. He served as president of the Pacific Division of the
American Philosophical Association in 1934 [1934:02], and he was
awarded a second honorary doctorate in 1937, this time by UCLA.

During his retirement, Tufts continued to write. His primary works
from this period were two. The first was the revised, second edition
of *Ethics* [1932:01] that he wrote jointly with Dewey. The second significant volume was a portrait of the moral life of the country that
he called *America's Social Morality* [1933:01]. During these years, he
corresponded widely. He also spent a good deal of time on his memoirs, only parts of which have ever been published [1942:01 and
1943:02], and on his hobby of genealogical research.

Events surrounding America's entry into the Second World War—
the tidal wave of anti-Oriental prejudice, conservation efforts, black-
outs and air raid drills—crowded their way into Tufts's last year. Just
before American marines landed at Guadalcanal, Tufts died of heart
failure on August 5, 1942, at the age of eighty years and twenty-six
days in the Alta Bates Hospital in Berkeley.

TUFTS'S INTELLECTUAL PERSPECTIVE

In this section, I will try to sketch out Tufts's viewpoint in a general
way. While I would not suggest that his position is a particularly
obscure or difficult one to comprehend, I would still maintain that
what follows is no more than simply an introductory sketch. The fuller
elaboration of his intellectual perspective is to be found—although in
a less systematic fashion—in the following selections and in his other
writings, and a full-scale critical study of Tufts would be necessary to
place and evaluate his writings. For the purposes of display, I have
organized this section under the general headings of pragmatism,

religion, evolution, conceptual change, institutional change, the common good, democracy, education, and meliorism. There is no section devoted specifically to his ethical thought because the ethical theme is present in virtually every sentence Tufts wrote.

Tufts and Pragmatism

Any attempt to elaborate on the intellectual perspective of Tufts must consider at some point the question of the extent to which he was a pragmatist. In light of this necessity, is it perhaps best to simply begin with the question of his relation to pragmatism. Van Meter Ames has reported that, during his own years of study at Chicago, Tufts "stepped around pragmatism like a cat avoiding a pool of water."[15] In an attempt to determine what this avoidance might have meant, especially with regard to Tufts's own possible pragmatism, we can consider a few occasions when Tufts writes explicitly about pragmatism. In the course of this consideration, the fact that Tufts was indeed a pragmatist, and the sort of pragmatist he was, will become clear.

When working in the broad field of social ethics, for example, Tufts's position towards matters pragmatic is uniformly favorable. In his essay "Recent Discussions of Moral Evolution" [1912:03] in the *Harvard Theological Review*, for example, Tufts emphasizes various points about the "pragmatic" or "evolutionary" approach to ethics— the intellectual attempt to address moral problems, the deliberate recognition of responsibility for our choices, the willing acceptance of the limitations imposed by the common good—that demonstrate that in his view it is a moral stance worthy of respect. And, while apparently trying his best not to alienate the more traditional readers in his theological audience, Tufts writes further that the emphases of evolutionary ethics are more appropriate to the new social conditions of our current situation than "absolutist" attempts to "stand still." "Ethical theory," he writes, "must rise to meet these new conditions, or be left on one side as scholastic theology was left by the world of the Renaissance."[16] Yet, in spite of all of the favorable comments that he has to offer about pragmatism in this piece, Tufts nowhere conceded his own adherence to the perspective.

To consider another example, in his review of Roscoe Pound's *Interpretations of Legal History* [1924:03], Tufts clearly discusses the distinction between the pragmatic philosophy of law—he calls it "functional" or "experimental" or "engineering" or "pragmatic"—and the "historical" philosophy of law, and writes glowingly of Pound's recognition of the primacy of the question "What theory best serves our purpose?" over the question "What theory does history establish?" In a later piece, Tufts again returns to the theme of the pragmatic philosophy of law and defends it from charges of ignoring "the wisdom of the past, or the value of system" in its recognition of "social consequences."[17] But again, in neither of these pieces does Tufts acknowledge his own adherence to the perspective.

Another generally pragmatic theme in Tufts's work is his emphasis upon the embodiment of human life, the seamless connection between the animal and the spiritual elements of our existence, and the rootedness of any adequate self-understanding in "the stimulating effect of practical needs." He writes that "[i]n this world of living beings, every organ or faculty has been developed, or at any rate selected and maintained, because it has been of use." The eye, the hand, the brain, and nervous system all have had their origin in the school of natural need. "Finally, the mind itself has emerged and grown in response to the same demands of work to be done, food to be gained, enemies to be thwarted, offspring to be sheltered and protected." Thus, for Tufts, even "the beginnings of moral conduct" are rooted in our natural embodiment.[18] In this case, however, although Tufts clearly admits holding the view in question, he does not describe it as being pragmatic.

We thus find Tufts defending pragmatic positions that he does not explicitly admit to holding, and holding positions that he does not explicitly admit are pragmatic. This "avoidance" of pragmatism, to recur to Ames's term, would seem to require some explanation. The explanation that I would suggest is that Tufts's avoidance was rooted in his beliefs about the pragmatic futility of purely intellectual controversy. This explanation is based upon an interpretation of some of his more personal writings.

If we ask whether Tufts wished to be considered a member of the pragmatic 'school,' for example, the answer seems to be strongly negative. When the cooperative volume *Creative Intelligence* was in the final preparatory stages, Horace M. Kallen sent to the various contributors a one-page list of principles or doctrines about the nature of reality, experience, mind, value, and so on that he thought he found underlying all the submitted chapters and therefore common to the perspectives of all the members of the group. He requested their comments on these various pragmatic principles with the intention that these themes, suitably revised, were to form the core of John Dewey's introduction to the volume. Although the eventual unsigned prefatory note did not contain the anticipated pragmatic 'platform,' and in fact stressed that the purpose of the volume was "cooperation" rather than "unanimity" or "uniformity," Tufts's preemptive response to Kallen is instructive. Tufts wrote that he personally did not agree with most of what he found in the list of principles. In itself, however, this is no indication that Tufts did not consider himself a pragmatist, since he also wrote that as far as he could tell some of the supposedly pragmatic principles were anything but pragmatic. But, perhaps most telling for the interpretation I am suggesting is Tufts's closing comment that the inclusion of such a manifesto would likely be counterproductive and diminish the attractiveness of the volume to the general public.[19]

To cite another instance, Tufts returned to the theme of his uncomfortableness with 'schools' in a letter written in 1941 to Dagobert D. Runes, who was at that time editing a volume to be called *Living Schools of Philosophy* for which he had solicited a piece from Tufts. In this letter, Tufts writes that he is uncertain as to his own 'school' and simply states what he understands as his philosophical perspective in terms of three emphases: the importance of the study of the history of humankind to uncover the origins of the moral ideas and practices, the study of the mores of society and their development over time due to various social pressures, and moral inquiry into the problems of social institutions rather than into theoretical or metaethical issues.[20] The value of our considering this letter is dual. On the one hand, it demonstrates again Tufts's reluctance to become part of a potential controversy over philosophical schools, and, on the other, it affirms his position within the general pragmatic perspective.

As a final piece of evidence, we can consider a passage contained in his unpublished memoirs in which Tufts strongly defends the value of the experimental method while at the same time expresses his own reluctance to defend pragmatism from charges of expediency and materialism. He is reluctant not because he believes that such charges are founded, but simply because, he writes, after the failures of the ringing defenses of pragmatism by James and Dewey and Moore, further defense seems futile.[21]

My general conclusion from this examination of Tufts's work is that, although he deliberately avoided involvement in what he saw as the futile logical and epistemological controversies surrounding the pragmatic movement,[22] he was indeed a pragmatist, a social pragmatist. Tufts, along with Dewey and Mead and the others at Chicago, was interested in social reconstruction. It was this stream of pragmatism that H. S. Thayer has described as "a critical response to the widening cleavage between economic expansion and powerful and elaborate technological advances on the one side, and on the other, deepening divisions between the laboring classes and the owners and directors of business: an increasing separation between the realities of social and political experience and the traditional ideals of American democracy."[23] The intellectual themes that we have sampled in Tufts's work so far—embodiment and the relationship between thought and action, experimentalism and reconstruction—are all fundamentally pragmatic in nature. In what is to come, we will see further development of Tufts's social pragmatism.

Let us consider just one more aspect of Tufts's rejection of what he saw as primarily intellectual controversy. He began his career working mostly in the history of philosophy, as both his own comments and an examination of his early publications will demonstrate. But as he later writes in his essay "What I Believe" [1930:01], in the volume *Contemporary American Philosophy: Personal Statements*, his view began to change as he continued on in philosophy. "I began my work in philosophy with studies in its history," he tells us. "I changed to ethics because, as I came to gain a clearer view of the important tendencies of the time, I thought the ethical changes the most significant." Tufts was reacting in part to his increasing familiarity with the squalor and misery of much of the Chicago situation, and in part to the increasing professionalization of philosophy. Just as the powers of cooperative social inquiry were developing, it seemed that philosophy, which he had described as "the most concrete and vital of all departments of human thought," was moving away from this engagement with life.[24] Philosophy, he writes, "has suffered by its progressive withdrawal from field after field of broadly human interest." Its developing emphasis upon metaphysics and epistemology, on logic and language, were drawing philosophy out of the social mainstream. As he wrote in 1938, "during the past forty years extraordinary changes have been taking place in industry and social classes, in government and the family, in science and education. But philosophy, as if to justify the ancient tradition of Thales, has for the most part calmly ignored such events and devoted its energies to the question, How is knowledge possible?" Tufts attributed much of the trouble in philosophy to an analysis of its role, and to an understanding of its progress, that were both divorced from the life of the society.[25] Thus we can interpret his avoidance of the pragmatism issue as a refusal to be drawn away from his social pragmatic interests. This refusal was grounded, of course, in moral rather than intellectual reasoning. What he saw as primarily intellectual controversies were not false or mistaken, but to a social pragmatist like Tufts they were unimportant.

The Nature of the Religious Life

It is simple thing to say that Tufts was a deeply religious person; it is much harder to explain what this means. He writes compellingly, for example, of the role that religion played in the lives of the young when he was growing up, and of how at Amherst College religion was "the principal field of interest and concern, aside from our subjects studied in the classrooms." Yet, Tufts never demonstrated any recognizable theological interest. We encountered above his own indecision about a career choice between the life of teaching and the life of preaching. His indecision was borne not of two conflicting desires, but rather of his belief that these two possible professions were viable options in his attempt to live a life of service, to do "useful work of some sort." He speaks at one point, for example, of the ministry and teaching as being "allied" professions. If they were allied, however, Tufts increasingly came to believe that they were not of equal promise for the future. "In the eighties and nineties the profession of college or university teacher began to be increasingly effective," he writes, in large part because, unlike the minister, the "thoroughly trained teacher . . . seemed to embody in concrete form the power of ideas."[26] Commitment to the pulpit would thus mean the restraints of an outdated ministry; commitment to the classroom, the liberation of a progressive ministry.

This general development on Tufts's part was not, of course, an abandonment of religion, but rather the logical conclusion of his understanding of the nature and social role of religion. "In its deepest root," he writes,

> religion springs from a certain divine discontent. Man is, on the one hand, limited; he is a very tiny part of the world he sees; his powers are puny; his glimpses of meaning are fragmentary; the good he would, he does not; he encounters pain and death. Yet just as truly, he refuses to recognize or accept limits to his enterprise of knowledge, his control of nature, his achievement of good. . . . He does not rest in any partial version of the total meaning of things; he seeks somehow, if not to know, at least to feel life and the universe in all their wholeness.

For Tufts, then, the import of religion is in its attempts to understand the meaning of life and to renew hope about future possibilities and faith in future actions. Religion functions, potentially at least, to renew "the spirit of service to mankind," and thus to facilitate the development of the human family through the recognition that "the ties which bind mankind" are "but manifestations of the larger life in which we share."[27]

If we consider, however, what the institutionalization of religion has meant in the historical path of human life, and if we consider what religion might still contribute, Tufts emphasizes two points. First, religion was primarily a means of the organization of communal beliefs and practices around some traditional spiritual or transcendent core. Secondly, as society progressed, the religious possibilities of the life of his day were being strangled by religion's unnecessary connections to these outdated intellectual symbols and customary morals. The religion that had been inherited contained "a whole view of life," he writes,[28] but it was no longer a viable view of life.

Tufts emphasizes that the modern world is an intellectually new world. "My generation has seen the passing of systems of thought which had reigned since Augustine," he writes.[29] To say that these systems had 'passed' did not mean to Tufts that they had been proven *false*, however. It meant, rather, that we had finally come to understand the context of these historical systems as *symbolic*. "The religious community of today is beginning to be aware of the gap between the facts which early religion sought to interpret and the symbolism which was used in this effort at interpretation." As Tufts continues, "The symbols which men have hitherto framed to convey what they have deeply felt, or ardently aspired to, or in great moments envisaged, were all for the most part conceived in imagery of long ago. . . . They inevitably come into conflict with advancing thought. But the symbols are not the spirit."[30] With a recognition of the rootedness of our inherited symbols, and their ultimate inappropriateness to our lives, comes the necessity for reconstruction. The old symbols must be recognized as such and be assisted to change.

The modern era is, Tufts writes, "an era of transition between the imagery, doctrines, and conceptions which served to interpret man's deeper life in days past, and those as yet unframed symbols and conceptions which shall both interpret and inform the deeper life of the future." Of course, Tufts did not anticipate that this attempt at the resymbolization of life would be a simple matter. He notes that finding "an imagery for spiritual needs and values, comparable in power and tenderness with the symbolism of the ages, is not easy," and that "no new symbolism has yet proved adequate to embody the profounder experiences which religion has included."[31] Moreover, the organized religions themselves had become entangled in the defense of the inherited set of symbols—theological doctrines, textual interpretations, biblical inerrancy—that mistakenly tied the intellectual life of the religious communities to the literal defense of lyrical and imaginative narratives.

Tufts had seen some progress in resymbolization occur in the initial shifting of intellectual focus from the minister to the teacher. In the hands of early philosophy instructors like his mentor Garman, for example, the "great spiritual meanings and values of life which had found previous formulation in theological terms" had managed to change "their formulation without losing their power."[32] Tufts also saw in contemporary social ethics the attempt "to bring about in more intimate fashion that supremacy of the moral order in all human relations for which the church was theoretically contending."[33] Because of these possibilities of reconstruction, he believed that it was worthwhile to attempt to rescue the religious element in life.

In Tufts's eyes, the inspirational power of the religious perspective was more compelling than that of nonreligious perspectives for understanding "life and the universe in all their wholeness"[34] and for fostering the development of virtues like hope in the future, faith in our cooperative activities, and charity toward others. Tufts saw in some humanist perspectives, particularly those that approached materialism, a kind of hedonistic nihilism that rejects duty and concern with the future for the blind pursuit of present pleasure. He found in Bertrand Russell's thought, for example, a "philosophy of self-expression" that demands "liberty from external restraint . . . [and] . . . from inner restraints likewise," and a blurring of what is desired with what ought to be desired that he saw as a kind of "moral anarchy."[35] Unlike the religious perspective that he saw as allowing for the possibility of overcoming our "partial version of the total meaning of things," he understood this materialistic kind of humanism to be claiming that its views on ultimate human finitude had been proven. Tufts, on the other hand, thought that much more is still in doubt and as yet undetermined. "Over against facts which can be demonstrated and measured," he writes, religion "has asserted possibilities in man and in the universe which cannot be completely demonstrated."[36] In parallel with Dewey's view expressed in *A Common Faith* that "there are forces in nature and society that generate and support" our moral ideals,[37] Tufts asserted these possibilities and called for cooperative efforts to advance these ideals.

Tufts himself maintained his church membership throughout his life. He was interested in maintaining his membership because, as he wrote in his late seventies, "Religion would be a lonely struggle without the church"; and he was able to maintain his membership because he could divorce what he saw as the spiritual core of religion from its intellectual and moral difficulties, avoiding the consideration of "its truth or error" to concentrate on its role "in securing a better world-order." He writes that "[m]ore than most, perhaps, who have aimed to think through these problems honestly, I have continued a relationship with the Church, for I have considered the common purpose and the common feeling more important than the credo." This common purpose and feeling, salvaged from the outdated symbols of inherited religions, Tufts believed, can still help lead us to spirituality. "The Church has, on the whole, and in spite of its failures, borne witness to the existence of other than material aims."[38]

The Role of the Evolutionary Perspective

The examination of Tufts's understanding of the religious life clearly indicates the fundamental commitment on his part to an evolutionary world-view, a view that he considered to be at the core of the intellectual climate of his time. "We are living today," he writes, "in the century of Darwin." For further evidence, let us consider the following warning he gives us in 1903: "The future historian of philosophy who should attempt to give an intelligent account of present philosophic thought would fail completely to grasp its significance unless he took account of the determining influence of the conception of evolution." It is here that Darwin's work was essential because, as Tufts writes, before him no theory of evolution had brought home so vividly "the continuity of the whole organic world" or portrayed so successfully the human as "one link in a chain all forged of one metal and in one fire."[39] It was Darwin's work that finally shifted the intellectual climate to evolutionary thinking.

One of the key aspects of this shift to evolutionary thinking is a changed understanding of the nature of education and the role of the scholar. Under the old system, Tufts writes, the scholar "was the man of learning and culture. He knew many things and knew them exactly." This conception of scholarship "suggested a world complete rather than a world in the making." It fit quite well into the larger world of its time: "If the world of religion, of morality, of commerce, of government stood still, scholarship as learning would be a sufficient ideal." Our current ideal of scholarship, however, is "the ideal of

investigation and reconstruction."[40] Our aim as scholars should be
on developing, and our aim as educators should be on inculcating,
methods for bringing the shared wisdom of the past and present to
bear upon new situations.

With this shift to evolutionary thinking in education and scholarship, the importance of the study of the past is retained even though
the past itself gains a new role, different from its prior one of amassing
information largely for display. As Tufts writes with Dewey in the
Ethics, in the study of any process of life, it is "a great aid for understanding present conditions if we trace the history of the process and
see how present conditions have come about." The study of the past
is thus a necessary component in our attempts at contemporary understanding. "To understand anything of a process or idea it is not sufficient to describe it," Tufts writes, "so far as possible we seek to
discover the factors that have contributed to make it what it is."[41]

Commitment to the evolutionary world-view undergirds Tufts's
view that it is necessary for us to adapt to the new world that we are
facing. This adaptation involves an understanding of the past and
its development into the present. In the practical realm and in the
intellectual realm, changes have been profound; and much of our
current troubles, he writes, is due to the fact of "the carrying over
into present civilization of methods that worked well under simpler
conditions."[42] That is, our social life remains based upon an understanding of community organization, institutions, power, and so on,
that is no longer appropriate. This understanding fit quite well in an
earlier and more open time; but, now that we were becoming a more
complex and integrated country, Tufts believed that we needed to
develop a new self-understanding.

Life on the Frontier—whether on the Atlantic seacoast, or in western Massachusetts, or in Texas or Idaho, or in the Dakota Territory—
had been the key to the American democratic mind-set. Tufts writes
that the Frontier has been "a continual school of democracy in American life."[43] Frontier life was savage and frustrating, but its lesson was
neither brutality nor despair. Rather, Frontier life reinforced in the
settlers the need for hope in future possibilities, for faith in the efficacy
of cooperation to advance the common good, and for democracy as
the method for organizing this cooperation. Moreover, in a nation
of small farmers, under conditions of "practical economic equality,"
cooperation was simpler. Land meant personal security, not economic
power: "Property was for the many a means of security against want,

not a provision for luxuries, to say nothing of being a power over the lives of others."[44]

By Tufts's day, of course, the situation was greatly changed. The growth in population, industrial development, urbanization, and finally the closing of the Frontier meant that the country was leaving behind its defining past. "Equality, opportunity, and independence are no longer secured by free land," he writes in 1933. "Most workers now work for an employer, and opportunity to work lies in conditions beyond the worker's control. The industrial system is anything but a system of equality." Gone was "a nation of small farmers with unlimited land for those who would work it"; gone, a nation of factory workers who "when wages were low . . . had the possible alternative of free land."[45] Before we could face this new world effectively, Tufts, along with many others, saw that we needed to institute serious social changes. Populist movements of various sorts had hesitantly and haltingly begun to take action. In the words of Frederick Jackson Turner, "the defenses of the pioneer democrat began to shift from free land to legislation, from the ideal of individualism to the ideal of social control through regulation by law." In adopting these changes, the American people had begun the process of making itself into a new people. They were closing, again citing Turner, "the first period of American history."[46]

Changes in our understanding of ourselves and our shared lives could not be expected to come about easily. The heart of the difficulty with instituting such changes is that our institutions have inertia and our concepts have roots. Passing over the former at present, we can concentrate on the concepts. Our ideas about what is fair and proper are not "independent of time and place and human bias," Tufts writes, but are "shaped under the influence of economic, social, and religious forces" and then used as "patterns for action" in future situations.[47] How we understand the limits of freedom or the fullness of equality at any time is actually a selection—although it is seldom experienced as such—from among a number of possible interpretations of each term. And, because of the social role of education, these conceptions are largely historically rooted. These historically derived concepts used to make sense, Tufts writes: "Our conceptions of honesty and justice, of rights and duties, got their present shaping largely in an industrial and business order when mine and thine could be easily distinguished; when it was easy to tell how much a man produced; when the producer sold to his neighbors, and an employer had also the relations of

neighbor to his workmen." However, he continues, "Such conceptions are inadequate for the present order."[48] This inadequate relationship between our ideas and our lives calls for attempts at conceptual
reconstruction.

The point of this reconstruction is not that we are to uncover what
these terms 'really' mean through historical and analytic study. Efforts
along these lines, Tufts believed, would at best only indicate the terms'
possibilities as conceived by those who lived long ago. Rather, what
is necessary in ongoing conceptual reconstruction is to keep the formulation of these concepts connected with the basic human values to
which the terms point while at the same time not allowing the traditional understanding of these basic values to prevent development to
satisfy the new situations. We seek a society that is fair, for example;
but, as Tufts writes, "what was fair yesterday may be so unfair today
that the thoughtful mind feels the need of a new conception of
fairness."[49]

Tufts saw a large part of the responsibility for this conceptual reconstruction to fall upon the shoulders of the philosopher. It is the job of
the philosopher "to keep perpetually tinkering with his ideas"; it is
his or her job to explore what our values might mean in our current
situation. Tufts's use of the term 'tinker' may perhaps lead to some
confusion, especially if it is interpreted to mean engagement in a
pleasant distraction—an interpretation that we must reject based upon
his prior demonstration of seriousness—or that we are just fabricating
a new meaning. The second interpretation must be rejected as well
because of his stressing that we must be true to the core of a basic
value like fairness as preserved through historical changes. What the
term 'tinker' is particularly good for, however, is to emphasize that
the new conception we are attempting to reach is constructed, tested,
and revised in our attempts to solve our contemporary problems:
"[W]e do not merely watch ideals unfold; we have to construct them.
And we have to construct them not as dogmatic standards, but as
working hypotheses."[50]

We attempt to construct a conception of 'justice' or 'freedom' or
'equality' that will be able to carry forward the value that the ideal has
traditionally borne while at the same time satisfying the new situation.
The mind of today, the "scientific mind," Tufts writes, "seeks for a
conception which will preserve what was important and true in the
old and at the same time incorporate the new. It does not expect to
find an ultimate solution all at once." We suggest and evaluate and
rethink our ideas, with particular attention to what is new and devel-

oping; for the philosopher, "the growing points of the concept are the most significant."[51] Our old conceptions must be reworked to satisfy new possibilities. As Tufts writes, "[G]ood and right stand for nothing which can be exactly defined and envisaged once for all. They symbolize rather the progressive ideals and standards of a growing moral life, and are constantly taking on new meaning as man knows more fully his powers and kindles more deeply in sympathetic response to his fellows."[52] This progressive aspect of conceptual reconstruction, rooted in new possibilities resulting from human cooperative efforts and constantly facing new problems, will continue, Tufts believed, as an ongoing need of our lives together.

Justice, Freedom, and Equality

If we examine Tufts's discussion of just a few of these fundamental values more carefully, we will be able to understand his position on conceptual reconstruction better. Justice, for example, is a value that is essential to society. Tufts in fact thought that justice is the primary social value. Speaking of the origin of the term millennia ago in Egyptian society, he writes:

> It may be doubted whether any of the words since framed to express human values takes so strong a hold as "justice." It embodies the claim of personality, of the aspirations and expanding life of the human spirit. In disclosing the rights of each as the concern of all it bears constant testimony to the essentially social nature of man's higher development. Denial of justice stings because it is virtually a denial of humanity.

Justice is thus the key value for leading community life in harmony. Among other basic human values that Tufts stresses are liberty and equality, but he sees them as "notes" in "the chord of justice."[53]

Although justice is our primary value, Tufts recognized that there is no universal agreement as to its content. That justice "meant different things to different persons and different groups" was brought home repeatedly to Tufts in his social reform activities. This lack of agreement results in part from the origins of the various conceptions of justice in particular patterns of living. It also results in part from the fact that no particular formulation of the meaning of the term itself is perfect. Or, as Tufts once phrased this latter point in more religious language, "Our justice is in part the divine principles, but it is also in part the work of barbarous times and selfish men."[54] Because of the power of the cry of injustice, however, Tufts emphasizes in such volumes as the *Ethics* and *The Real Business of Living* the ongoing importance of the serious study of the differing approaches to justice.

Tufts writes that the value of the "genetic account of legal philosophies is that it tends to weaken our confidence, that we know what justice is."[55] We can broaden our scope to include more than legal philosophy, but his point about the value of intellectual dislocation is the same. The unsettlement of our intellectual assurance is the first step, he believed, toward recognizing that attaining justice is a complex problem. This doubt serves as well as an opening to the recognition that many of our current social ills are not the result of fundamentally evil or malicious people. He writes that "generally speaking, the [present] inequities are due to the system for which we are all in a measure responsible, and to practices which are simply the carrying-over of the methods—and even the virtues—of one age into the changed conditions of another." We thus need to overcome the historically based sense of justice that has failed us, and to create, Tufts writes, a new sense of justice:

> Justice might still mean the guarantee of rights. But there is a change going on which calls for more fundamental reconstruction. The closer interweaving of all our interests, the deepening interdependence of all our lives, the growing power of public opinion and public sentiment, the gradually forming social consciousness, all these lead us to seek somewhat blindly and uncertainly as yet a 'social' justice.[56]

We know that this social justice will take us beyond the demands of our inherited, individualistic sense of justice.

This reconstructed conception of course will take time and effort to develop: "We have to test, bit by bit, our proposed conceptions of justice." Still, the general content of this new sense of justice may be sketched out. Prominent in this new sense of justice should be, Tufts believed, the recognition that we are attempting to build, not a minimally just society, but a society with a full sense of justice for all. "The principle of justice is based upon the worth of every person, of every member of society."[57] In addition, our sense of justice must be more than narrowly legal and include economic elements. "Like the old justice, it must protect all members of society—even the least—from violence and fraud, but it seeks to distribute more fairly the burdens and gains."[58] These economic elements in justice are an expansion upon the former understanding of economic justice: "The old justice in the economic field consisted chiefly in securing to each individual his rights in property or contracts. The new justice must consider how it can secure for each individual a standard of living, and such a share in the values of civilization as shall make possible a full moral life."[59] Tufts believed that this expansion of the economic element in justice is but a further continuance of the long historical process of expansion of justice in civilization. We must recognize, he tells us, that "new claims" will be made for "new rights,"[60] and we must attempt to evaluate these claims fairly. Tufts emphasizes the role of education in our attempts at fairness in *The Real Business of Living*, where he writes that we have a duty to try transcending our own situation and "looking at a matter from the other man's point of view, and hearing his side."[61] To foster the willing engagement with the unsettlement of such attempts requires also the educational means of family and community life.

A second important fundamental value that stands in need of reconstruction is 'freedom' or 'liberty.' The value is, of course, absolutely essential to a full and growing human life. Freedom is, as Tufts writes, "the only school in which a man can learn to be fully a man." It is only by making choices for oneself, by selecting from options and fulfilling consequential obligations, that a person can attain responsible adulthood. Moreover, Tufts writes that on the national level, that is, in terms of political liberty or independence, "self-government . . . [is] . . . in itself a power which gives dignity and worth to men and trains them to responsibility."[62] However, as with justice, indicating the importance of freedom does not help us to determine its meaning.

Again, as with justice, Tufts believed that we have inherited an older meaning of freedom that needs to be reconstructed. The older sense of freedom was a sense of freedom *from the government*. "Oppression by the government," Tufts writes, "was what the men of '76 feared most." When they adopted the rhetorical fictions of the state of nature and natural rights, he continues, the Founders were "trying to say in the strongest way possible that men *ought* to be free, that governments *ought* to be for the people, and not for their own advantage, and that they *ought* to be responsible to the people and controlled by law." But their emphasis was so strongly upon opposing governmental power because of their own situation. We, on the other hand, face a different situation and "we are not necessarily tied to an eighteenth-century conception of freedom."[63]

At present, we need to recognize in particular the existence of powers of other sorts, Tufts writes, that "[d]angers to liberty may come from sources other than government." The power that he has most clearly in mind is economic. "For the common man," he writes, "the perils of unemployment and the constraints of price are more real and more keenly felt than perils and restraints from government." And, as a consequence, the role of government no longer has to be severely limited to protect freedom. In fact, Tufts writes, in the modern world exactly the opposite is necessary: "In the face of such power over the living conditions of the common man, government is forced to interfere to preserve liberty. . . . A considerable share of the increased functions of government is due to the necessity for meeting the demands to preserve liberty in the presence of a new power."[64] The stronger government that Tufts is advocating should not be conceived of as a distant state with massive, impersonal, bureaucratic powers. Rather, what he has in mind is a series of public institutions that would focus and inform cooperative activities and thus be a means to the achievement of the responsible lives that Tufts advocates. "The twentieth century calls for a higher emphasis upon the goods achieved through association," Tufts writes. "Government is the instrument for securing and protecting these goods."[65] It is thus, for Tufts, a means to achieving the value of freedom.

A similar reconstruction is necessary in our conception of 'equality.' Tufts writes:

[E]quality in 1776 meant that no one is so superior by birth and privilege that he has a divine right to rule another; it was in a certain sense negative. Today the point which needs emphasis is not that no one else is superior to us. It is rather that we must if possible make every citizen as nearly equal to the best as we can. We cannot successfully carry on democratic government except by this constant leveling-up, this constructive ideal.

Democracy in fact meant to Tufts that "all people should share as largely as possible in the best life," that "every one so far as ability, and character, and the common weal allow, should share in the fuller life which human genius, through its conquests over nature, and human will, through cooperation in organized institutions, are making possible."[66] We thus cannot be satisfied with only "formal phrases of equality" that are not translated into actual equality, or with equality before the law that may mean inequality in practice "because of inability to provide a good lawyer." The ideal of equality in our society also means a special commitment on our part to equality in the classroom since, as Tufts writes, equal education "holds out to the common man and his children the one sphere of equality in the conditions that enter into every citizen's life, which is open under our system."[67]

The Reconstruction of Institutions

Tufts emphasized that this conceptual reconstruction is not an activity to be taken simply for its own sake. It is rather part of a larger task of social reconstruction to overcome social ills, a process that integrates contemporary institutional reconstruction as well. We reorganize our ways of thinking so that we can see more clearly our own situation and better measure our achievements against our possibilities. We reorganize our ways of acting so that we can approximate more closely and more generally these possibilities. Our ways of acting are our institutions.

Institutions were essential to Tufts's understanding of human existence. He writes that "the individual's span is at best short. His working years are soon counted. He can accomplish little alone. But man has learned to build institutions."[68] The main characteristics of these institutions are, for Tufts, three. First, institutions are human creations, developed out of simpler and less effective ones. Our evolving family structures and health care systems, our religious groups and accepted ways of settling disputes, are all modes of cooperative action to address recurring difficulties in our shared lives. And all of them have been developed in "the same school of practical necessity" that has been responsible for the development of the hand and the eye. Secondly, our institutions are deliberately modifiable over time to deal with change. "A characteristic of an institution is that while conserving a large measure of what experience has taught it also faces new situations and conflicting interests or forces under a necessity of partial readjustment." The third characteristic of institutions that Tufts emphasized is that they have an aim: They are means devised to approach more closely our ideal of a good society. He writes at one point, for example, that "a good society should aim to secure justice, should keep a right perspective as to the various goods which are desirable, should take account of all the human relations, and should move toward raising all men toward that measure of equality and democracy which has been the ideal and aspiration not only of the finer spirits but of increasing multitudes in the modern world."[69] It is part of our job as citizens to develop and maintain the political institutions that will move us toward such an ideal.

It is also part of our job as citizens to develop institutions of publicity and discussion to test these ideals. Our ideal of a good society cannot be a priori or rigid. Neither can it be monistic. Tufts writes that we need to recognize that there will continue to be "divergence between what different groups hold to be right and desirable."[70] He further writes that, even when there is a large measure of popular consensus about the goods to be pursued, there is still a question of their value. For example, he writes, "there is bound to be frequent divergence between what the expert in a scientific age believes to be better, and what the mass of the people are willing to support." This divergence compels us to a "more careful consideration of the agencies for forming public opinion, and of education in respect to both the ends and the means of good government."[71]

A clear example of Tufts's understanding of institutional reconstruction can be found in his discussions of our system of law, an institution created to bring order and stability to our shared lives. It is important to have stability, he writes, to make it "possible for citizens to rely upon certain general rules in charting their courses of action."[72] Moreover, a certain caution is especially desirable in our legal procedures. The law "is necessarily conservative," he writes, "for it uses compulsion and therefore may well hesitate to move in advance of general moral clarity."[73]

Sometimes, however, legal thinkers go beyond this recognition of the value of legal stability, Tufts believed, and they assert the desirability of, and even the necessity for, legal rigidity. Tufts recognized two major types of problems with this position, which he called above the "historical" philosophy of law. The first is simply that determining the historically 'correct' answer is not easy. Tufts agreed with Roscoe Pound that those who appeal to history too often use, in Tufts's words, "the name of historical method in order to discover in legal history that particular view which they more or less consciously sought." Of course, Tufts recognized that simply because serious historical scholarship has not been done does not mean that it cannot be; and he argues further, in good Jeffersonian fashion, that the historical records should not be decisive anyway. We should not be trapped by our past records, Tufts believed, since the historical legislation being consulted was not directed at the ills that we are facing. Our Constitution, he writes,

> was made for a people largely rural and agricultural. It was made before railroad, automobile and airplane had reduced state boundaries for purposes of commerce and crime to imaginary lines. It contemplated no factory problems, or problems of child labor or women's labor. It took no account of race conflicts, of labor unions, of gigantic corporations, of food adulterations, or the control of drugs and intoxicants.[74]

Moreover, because the law is "the great conservative agency of life and society," he writes, "it is bound to embody remnants of past prejudice, along with past wisdom." Thus, because of both its inappropriateness and its inherent flaws, we should not anticipate that the mechanical application of old law in new situations will bring justice in any full sense.[75]

The historical approach to the law, Tufts writes, satisfies only half of "the twofold purpose of law: It must protect stability; [and] it must adjust to change." Thus, "Law as the conservative principle needs constant supplementation by a principle of progress." We need to consider in our deliberations "not merely the principles recognized in the seventeenth and eighteenth centuries, but the emerging principles of the twentieth."[76] Tufts's recognition of the need for institutional reconstruction in our legal system is thus not a call for radical change but rather a call for ongoing change. "We have bent our Constitution several times," Tufts writes in 1912, "and just now it is believed by many that there must be much more bending if it is to serve as a supreme standard of justice in the changed conditions of modern commerce and industry."[77]

This "bending" emphasizes legislative action; but it also includes Tufts's recognition and acceptance of the "tentative and gradual change" brought about by "the process of judicial interpretation." We must abandon, he writes, our pretense that "judges do not make law, but only declare or interpret law." Although such a stance may seem to be of some value in preserving "the seeming immutability of law while actually admitting change," in practice it hampers our efforts to address social ills intelligently because it denies that judicial decisions are rendered by judges based upon their "differing philosophies."[78] It is the various ideals of a good society contained in these differing judicial philosophies, and in differing legislative philosophies, that must be recognized and tested on an ongoing basis if our legal system is to continue its own reconstruction and to contribute to the advance of society. And it is our broader system of institutions that must undergo continual reconstruction as well if the advance of society is to occur.

Cooperation for the Common Good

Tufts writes that we are fundamentally social in nature and that our basic moral goods are social as well. "Man without friendship, love, pity, sympathy, communication, cooperation, justice, rights, or duties, would be deprived of nearly all that gives life its value."[79] He writes further of a kind of social debt that we all acquire through the social nature of our existence. "The great difference between early men and civilized men today is not in their brains," he writes, but in that we have "inherited so great a stock of ideas and ways of doing things." We have benefited "by the labors of countless 'unknown soldiers' of the common good." We have done nothing to deserve this gift of the collective efforts of centuries, but it certainly makes our lives better. As Tufts writes, "a large part of the life of all of us consists in just walking up the stairs which our forefathers have built ready for us. Many of us never build a single new stair. The best of us build only a few stairs." Tufts believed that, because of these benefits, we are in debt to the past and obligated to our fellows and to the future. To be moral, we must act upon our recognition of this social debt and willingly benefit the common good.[80]

"Civilization, after all, is a garden," Tufts writes. "No one may consider his own needs apart from his dependence upon all and the dependence of others upon him. Many a branch which might grow in a forest must be cut in a garden."[81] Of course, he is not suggesting that we must willingly sacrifice ourselves for the benefit of others. Rather, he is expressing a plea that with suitable social assurances we should subordinate our good to the common good. In this regard, Tufts considers the case of some factory workers who are to be displaced by a new labor-saving machine or process. His view is that "society cannot refuse to accept inventions on the ground that some men will lose their employment in tasks for which they have acquired special skill." But he is not asking these individuals for self-sacrifice because he also maintains that society cannot expect those who are suffering the negative effects of some generally beneficial social policy to pay the costs of the benefit: "Individual workers ought not to bear the burden of readjustment."[82] Our recognition of our social debt should lead us to contribute our share to the common good, but it cannot, except under the most extreme circumstances, require us to sacrifice our well-being.

Tufts saw himself as living in an industrialized country that was reluctant to put the political machinery in the hands of the economically powerful as in communism, or vice versa as in fascism.[83] Therefore, we find embedded in his emphasis upon the common good his recognition of the necessity of dealing with ongoing economic conflicts. These conflicts will occur among the three classes or interests in society that he variously characterizes as producer, laborer, and consumer; "capital and labor organizations . . . [and] . . . public welfare"; "the owner-employer . . . the workman, and . . . the general public"; and so on.[84] However, Tufts does maintain that these conflicts, real though they may be, can be managed in the interest of the common good if we continue to learn how to use the power of our legal and governmental institutions "as an agency for cooperation." If, on the other hand, we give up these efforts at cooperation and conciliation, the result will be ruinous. "For the public simply to form a ring and let the parties fight it out," he writes, "is obviously to abandon justice and revert to barbarism."[85]

This discussion of social conflict indicates that Tufts accepted the ongoing existence of class society, although if we survey a few examples of his writing we can get a sense of his reluctance in this compromise. He writes of the ongoing costs of the bifurcation in class society and of the limited possibility of mutual understanding when "the two classes do such different things that they do not understand each other. . . . Neither half knows how the other lives."[86] He writes of the ongoing costs of inequality in class society and of the difficulty inherent in our requirement "for the underdog in a fight to remember the rules of the game" and avoid violence.[87] And when he writes that "[w]e are not attempting just here to say how far either side is right or wrong in all these points," we need to understand that his unwillingness to dictate answers does not indicate an unswerving support of class society.[88] All of these examples indicate, rather, the desire on his part to move toward greater economic equality without the danger to freedom that he saw in the Soviet system. As he writes very late in life, "we have been wise not to sacrifice freedom entirely to gain equality."[89] The common good is more likely to advance, although slowly, in a society where the economic and political forces are not in the same hands.

If we turn from the question of the nature and potential of the common good to the question of the means of its attainment (or at least its nearer approximation), Tufts's underlying theme is that "[n]o individual counts much through his own resources" but that "men can achieve by common effort what they cannot accomplish singly."[90] To move toward a higher level of social existence requires working in consort with one another. Tufts here explicitly rejects the view of Adam Smith, whom he sees as suggesting the spontaneous advance of the common good if only "everyone sought his own good." Tufts continues, "If an 'invisible hand' is guiding all things so that each man is unconsciously promoting the social weal, however self-centered his intention, why should anyone concern himself about his neighbor?"

He believes that Smith's view can thus be reduced to "the economic philosophy which held that the airship would automatically steer itself and land its passengers in safety at the desired haven of prosperity, and that the pilot in charge need think only of maintaining full speed ahead." Tufts, on the other hand, asserts that "common welfare comes not without common intention."[91]

Both the recognition of the need for cooperation, and the ability to cooperate itself, Tufts saw as social lessons. Earlier people, he writes, "had not yet learned how to cooperate in a large way." Families, cities, and nations are for Tufts, as we have seen, "ways of uniting and cooperating which men have gradually worked out."[92] From the development of football on the most mundane level to that of warfare on the most significant,[93] Tufts found instances of learned cooperation.

The goal of this increasing cooperation is to enact the kind of fundamental social reconstruction that would make possible a better life for all. "The most effective remedy for this insecurity of life," Tufts writes, "seems to be a general provision by which the group stands back of the individual." Working with our ideal of the common good and our recognition of the legitimate needs of our fellows—which Tufts broadly considered to exist whenever there is "a definite gap between the actual conditions of men in education, comfort, health or other good, on the one hand, and the available means for a better condition, on the other"[94]—we ought to try to insure our fellows' well-being. A decent society, one which aspires to justice and humanity, is compelled to try to help. Tufts recognized and admitted that attempts to build a decent society would require a more powerful and responsive government, "the assumption of positive tasks of collective action."[95]

So, for example, when the people acting through their government undertake action to combat the Depression, he writes that it is justified: "Government could not see its citizens starve because through no fault of theirs the processes of business and industry had ceased to fulfill their normal functions, and the farmer was threatened with ruin." This is a clear rejection on his part of the negative conception of government: "The conception often held today seems to be that of a fixed number of powers and functions, which are to be divided between person and community but are incapable of increase. Whatever is added to the one is regarded as necessarily subtracted from the other. Every function assumed by the community is believed to leave the person poorer in person and powers."[96] Tufts, on the other hand, believed that some human possibilities only come into fruition when there is an institutionalized system of organization—like a government—to facilitate cooperation. How extensively the people should use their government to assist in solving their problems is an open question. Tufts writes that we cannot determine finally what government is to be "irrespective of time and place, of race, culture, and education." Government has a formal function that can be specified as that of "mediating between stability and change"; but as to determining at any given time what specifically it should be doing, he writes, "Probably for a considerable time to come, the pragmatic test of experiment and testing by results will be the only test that can be applied."[97]

Democracy and Service

This cooperative attempt to reconstruct society so as to advance the common good is what Tufts saw as the democratic message. "The finest and largest meaning of democracy," he writes, "is that all people should share as largely as possible in the best life." For Tufts, consequently, democracy meant more than "merely sharing political power—it means the widest possible sharing in all good things." Democracy also means the sharing of other sorts of decision-making power. "If citizenship is a good principle in political life," Tufts wonders, "is there no application for it in industry?"[98]

Enacting this broad sense of democracy thus requires a cooperative approach to industrial and commercial life, with an emphasis upon a consciousness of the relationship between the economic core of life and the common good. "The controlling forces in our present-day system," Tufts writes, "are dominantly economic to an extent hitherto unknown in the world's history."[99] Among the results of this development were the undermining of the restraints and the disregard for the responsibilities that had to be taken for granted by the small-town merchant. With growth and competitive imbalances come possibilities for exploitation. "In neighborhood life and industry," Tufts writes, "a man hesitates to sell his neighbor bad eggs, nor would he work his help seven days in the week with a twenty-four hour shift at the end while he himself attended divine service."[100] But operating in an anonymous national or international market decreases the danger of effective consumer or employee resistance and weakens any responsibility that is based upon face-to-face relationships.

We need to recover the sense of a deliberate commitment to the common good, and Tufts believed that it can be done in a number of ways. The initial step is that we rethink our understanding of justice, freedom, equality, and other key moral values to make them more

appropriate to our current situation. The primary economic requirement is that we make public service to the common good, rather than
individual profit, the aim of business. "We no longer allow rulers or
judges or soldiers to collect indefinite wealth through their positions,"
he writes. "I can see no reason why it should be thought unworthy
of a statesman or a judge to use the political structure for his own
profit, but perfectly justifiable for a man to exploit the economic structure for private gain." In a system in which service to the common
good remained a powerful ideal, such exploitation would not be accepted. Tufts continues: "A physician is measured by his ability to
cure the sick, an engineer by the soundness of his bridge and ship;
why not measure a railroad president by his ability to supply coal in
winter, to run trains on time, and decrease the cost of freight, rather
than by his private accumulations? Why not measure a merchant or
banker by similar tests?"[101] When will we bring these, and other,
individuals under the requirement of deliberate service to the common
good?

These questions demonstrate Tufts's belief that the economic core
of the society belongs to the community. "Mankind has built up a
great economic system," Tufts writes. "Pioneer, adventurer, inventor,
scientist, laborer, organizer, all have contributed." It is thus essential
that we take the necessary steps together "to adjust profits to services,"
and treat capital, just as we regard political power, "as a public trust
in need of cooperative regulation and to be used for the general
welfare."[102] With our greater economic integration and our new levels
of cooperation, Tufts believed that this model of business as service
is becoming a possibility. What is necessary is further efforts to make
it a reality.

Turning this examination of the possibilities of commitment to the
common good to the political realm, Tufts recognized that there were
many problems with the contemporary practice of democracy. Perhaps his most telling indictment of a people who claim to be engaged
in true self-government appeared in 1935:

> We may perhaps be correctly called a nation of a hundred million
> guinea pigs for exploitation by business schemers that count on our
> credulity and our liking to be humbugged. We may be subject to such
> emotional spasms as the Ku Klux Klan. . . . We may deify the Consti-
> tution and endow it with all the taboos of the primitive mind. Or in a
> blind rage engage in lynching orgies intensified by race prejudice.

Howevermuch his repeated use of "may" indicates that these criticisms are not the whole story, they are biting. Combined with this

indictment of the populace is Tufts's recognition of the corruption and ineffectiveness of the political system itself, especially the problem of its inability to engage "the great number of citizens who are too busy with their private affairs to take part in government."[103]

These two problems—a political system that neither works nor educates, and a citizenry that is neither prepared nor preparing— were related in Tufts's mind. "A democratic government is a splendid government in many ways, but it will not run itself," he writes; on the other hand, he believed that the process of the active participation in self-government itself leads to growth. He continues, "[W]e believe in democracy as rule by the people" because we believe that participation in the democratic process "makes people more intelligent, free, and responsible."[104] In the deliberate attempt to advance the democratic process by greater involvement, we have the possibility of learning how to govern ourselves. And, as he hinted in his indictment above, Tufts believed that we have made some progress: "Those who can look back over half a century can see . . . a very genuine and rational movement in our institutions toward meeting the changing conditions that call for new measures."[105]

The Importance of Education

Tufts, who was as we have seen a broadly experienced teacher, was quite explicit with regard to the importance that he placed in the study of the philosophy of education and in education itself. In contrast to 'training,' he writes, education suggests "an emphasis upon the full meaning of situations and experiences with which we deal . . . wide acquaintance with all aspects, and sensitiveness to all elements, of culture and life."[106]

It is important when attempting to analyze Tufts's understanding of education to approach those aspects of education that we normally associate with schooling through the larger context of social life. Education is the process of integrating our social heritage with the growing individual, of developing a working relationship between the still-forming person and his or her social inheritance. Only in this way can the young come to take an active role in social life. As Tufts writes, "The world of science, art, commerce, law, morality, and religion is a social world. The individual may try to ignore certain aspects of these facts; but if he lives in any of these spheres, he can no more escape the social than he can escape his own person." If we pay insufficient attention to this social element in education, we will fail in our duty to attempt to lead students to fuller social participation.[107]

The primary unit of socialization is the family, but the impact of this socialization is on all the family members. Tufts's focus upon the family is thus not directed toward the adoption of the parents' values by the children. Such adoption is an aspect of his view, especially in the negative sense that he warns that parents should not attempt to inculcate absolute and unchanging truths. Tufts's primary interest in the socializing role of the family is rather in the family as an institution in which individuals learn and grow through the ongoing experience of parenting. Part of this parental growth is intellectual: "The interchange of question and answer which forces the parent to think his whole world anew, and which with the allied interchange of imitation and suggestion produces a give and take between all members of the family, is constantly making for fluidity and flexibility, for tolerance and catholicity."[108] But Tufts's greatest interest in the role of the parent is moral. Family life, he writes, is "life's greatest experience . . . its greatest moral opportunity." Family life is "a school of kindness and sympathy." It "enlarges affection" and "compels thought of the future." Thus the ultimate moral meaning of family life extends beyond the family. As Tufts writes, "the need of eliciting and directing right conduct in the young is one of the most important agencies in bringing home to the elders the significance of custom and authority, of right and wrong." Parents can thus learn from their encounters with the new, and attempt to inculcate in the young a sense of openness and inquiry.[109]

If we shift our focus to schooling, one of the central themes in Tufts's work is that the aim of education should be the growth of students into the fullness of life, broadly defined. "It is a larger and more difficult thing to *live* than to earn a living," he writes, "and it is for this larger end that schools are founded." We should aim at developing students who will seek "not only a living, but a noble life," who will seek work in some field of endeavor that "has some human value other than merely paying a wage."[110] For many of the students, Tufts writes, this distinction itself may be a new one and one that will need emphasis: "Am I free to prefer Beethoven to 'rag time'? Certainly not, unless I have heard Beethoven. Is the boy of the slums free to think of things pure, noble, and of good report?" Freedom in this sense requires at least familiarity with potential choices. Our educational system must then function as "an agency for giving the common man and woman and child a share in those goods of the mind which are our social inheritance."[111] The centrality of the role of the teacher in the process of intellectual expansion, on through higher education, becomes clearer in an early address to an audience of graduate students when Tufts emphasized, "You are now planning to teach language or history or science. I feel confident that you will come to place the emphasis rather on teaching *men* and *women*."[112]

Colleges and universities have shared in this vision of the possibilities of education, and they also have a role to play in social advance. "A university is not fulfilling its largest function," Tufts writes, "unless its investigations somehow get into the actual life of men and institutions so as to make a difference."[113] Colleges, on the other hand, should place their focus not so much upon research and discovery as upon the more direct role of the teacher, a role that Tufts saw as offering "the possibility of personal influence—the immortality, as Plato calls it, of living on in other lives."[114] The reasons for this educational commitment to social advance are many. Tufts believed, as we have seen, that we all have a general social debt to those who have gone before and that we have an obligation to our contemporaries and to those who are to follow. There is also a particular debt of those who are socially supported that they do something socially useful with this opportunity. "No one can justify a freedom purchased at others' expense," Tufts writes, "unless he is somehow making a contribution to the common weal."[115]

This duty of service is another example of the social pragmatism that was at the foundation of Tufts's thought. As we saw above, he decried philosophers' primary concern with what Dewey, writing in the 1917 cooperative volume *Creative Intelligence,* called "the problems of philosophers" and their progressive withdrawal from "the problems of men." We also find Tufts suggesting about that time that there would be a great benefit from a period of work in which philosophers attempted to "follow the tradition of Plato and Aristotle, Locke, Descartes and Kant, not by discussing their problems, but by attacking the most vital public questions of our day."[116] The life of the scholar was not a private life for Tufts, but a life of service.

Returning to the question of the growing students in a democracy, we find in Tufts a deep interest in the broad political implications of education. It was, for example, his interest in helping high school students prepare for participation in the democratic process that led to his volume *The Real Business of Living.* Unlike other countries that are committed to the education of loyal followers or of the elite few, Tufts writes that the United States is, at least in ideal, committed to "the education of voters." This commitment forces upon the American system a recognition of the need for equal education, of "[t]he moral right of every child to have an education, measured not by his parents' abilities, but by his own capacity." In this regard, Tufts was fond of repeating the message of President Angell of the University of Michigan that "every child in every home in the state should see an open door before him to the opportunities of higher education and larger usefulness."[117]

Our educational system, Tufts writes, "aims to include all children on an equal basis, and relies for support upon all members of the community." To say that we *aim* at equal education is, of course, not to say that we have attained or even approximated it. Moreover, efforts to reach our goal of equal education can never be relaxed as long as society remains in process: "[T]o say that men are equal doesn't make them so. The great task of the present day is to *make good in fact* what our fathers claimed in words or cherished as an ideal."[118] But Tufts believed that the central fact to keep in mind is that our moderately successful public education system "is the only means of making workable an economic system which produces extremes of inequality and a political system based on equal suffrage." We are attempting to prove, he continues, that all persons are fundamentally equal and that they can live in cooperative intercourse; we are attempting, that is, "to prove that democracy is possible."[119] And, in attempting to do this, education is the key.

Tufts was also convinced of the importance of moral education in the schools, in conjunction with other institutions of moral education like "family, church, law, and public opinion."[120] We have seen above Tufts's belief that our conceptions of moral ideas stand in need of ongoing reconstruction if they are to remain adequate to growing moral life in a changing society. We have also seen his emphasis upon the current harm of the unquestioned continuance of habitual institutions. Moral education is an important aspect of the necessary reconstruction, and, Tufts believed, the schools have a major role to play.

In his discussions of the relationship of formal instruction to moral growth, Tufts (as might be anticipated) was not primarily interested in what he called "the personal standpoint" of morality, the standpoint of "preacher and moralist that if we make individuals honest and upright society will be secure." This approach to developing moral character, he believed, is overemphasized in many programs of moral instruction and can lead to the development of students who are "introspective and priggish."[121] Tufts's interest was rather in the study of "the interrelation between man and society" or in developing a conscious understanding of "the mutual interdependence between society and its members." Tufts called this area of inquiry "public morality," an area where the emphasis is not "that of training a boy to follow already established traditions or of forming good habits. The problem is rather of discovering and setting up better standards, of framing ideals which will meet our present changed conditions."[122]

Following this public morality approach, Tufts believed that the emphasis of moral education in the primary grades should be upon using what he called "the indirect agencies" of moral training like cooperative work and the literary and artistic communication of the higher ideals of the society.[123] In the high school, the emphasis should gradually shift to more deliberate study of how society attempts to carry on the cooperative life of these ideals, emphasizing intellectual attempts to understand "the great constructive forces of civilization" like communication and technology, government and law, property and business. It is this sort of inquiry for which Tufts wrote *The Real Business of Living*. We adults should carry on this sort of moral education in the light of our recognition of "the constant remaking of society for better or for worse by the men and women who compose its membership" and in the light of "the social life into which [the students] are to enter."[124] When the adolescents of high school move on to higher education, because they come to the study of ethics "with greater intellectual maturity, and usually with some previous work in psychology and the social sciences," Tufts believed that "we need not forget the constructive side, but we may well bear more heavily upon critical analysis than is possible with younger students."[125] It is at this level that a textbook like the *Ethics* is appropriate.

Tufts and Meliorism

After all we have considered in Tufts's work of a generally hopeful and uplifting nature, it might come as a surprise to some to encounter such remarks as, "With every increase of opportunity and efficiency for good there is a corresponding opportunity for evil."[126] Such a reminder is, however, an essential if less emphasized part of Tufts's viewpoint and of social pragmatism in general. As such, it is fundamentally mistaken to consider Tufts to be an optimist. He is rather, in Dewey's terms, a 'meliorist.' As Dewey writes, "Meliorism is the belief that the specific conditions which exist at one moment, be they comparatively bad or comparatively good, in any event may be bettered."[127] The key differences between this view and optimism are that the meliorist emphasizes the importance of contributory actions and the lurking reality of potential failure. The optimist lives in a passive world of milk and honey; the meliorist, in an active world of chance and peril. But the meliorist stresses the importance of human potentialities, especially if we act in common, to forestall or address our problems.

Tufts writes frequently of the importance of cultivating faith in our fellows and in the possibilities of cooperative action. One point of his view to be considered is the extent to which he believed such faith is justifiable; another, our lack of alternatives to living with faith. If we begin with the former topic, we recognize that Tufts believed that action to advance the common good is not fruitless. In this regard, he challenges Reinhold Niebuhr's position expressed in *Moral Man and Immoral Society* that we are irretrievably trapped in insecurity and bound by instincts of individual and collective egoism. Niebuhr asserts further that human rationality, in which thinkers like Tufts place so much hope, actually contributes to our troubles. "The will-to-power uses reason, as kings use courtiers and chaplains to add grace to their enterprise," Niebuhr writes. "Even the most rational men are never quite rational when their own interests are at stake."[128] But Tufts believed that, whatever the study of past life indicates, with reason we can overcome our inherited selfishness. We can learn broader values. This means that, for Tufts, human nature can change. "Human nature is in certain respects at least the most changeable thing, the most flexible and adaptive thing in the universe, so far as we know," he writes. "It apparently would not survive at all were it not flexible and adaptive." Because of this adaptability, he believed, we can increasingly improve our lives together: "[M]ankind in general has learned law and right, as well as the arts of use and beauty, in the school of life in common."[129] The implication for the future is that, aided by reason and fortified with effort, we can continue to learn to cooperate.

Tufts placed this faith in our rationality because he does not believe that we are irredeemable prisoners of egoism as Niebuhr maintains. Niebuhr writes that, whatever power for charity we might develop, "there are definite limits in the capacity of ordinary mortals which makes it impossible for them to grant to others what they claim for themselves."[130] Tufts, on the other hand, believed that there are no such set limits to the possible growth of cooperation. When we work together toward a common good, we will come to be less selfish. He writes, "Mutual understanding will increase with common action. When men work consistently to create new resources instead of treating their world as a fixed system, when they see it as a fountain, not as a cistern, they will gradually gain a new spirit. The Great Community must create as well as prove the ethics of cooperation." If we can come to recognize our part in the human family and to "think of our life as an opportunity not merely for enjoyment or even for liberty but for creative work," Tufts believed that we will be able to commit ourselves to "cooperation with others to accomplish what no individual can accomplish by himself."[131]

There can be, of course, no antecedent proof or guarantee that reflective and cooperative actions will impartially advance the common good. There is just faith, an element that Tufts considered essential to living. "Faith in the possibility of regenerating society," Tufts writes, "not by miracle, but by the great and profound agencies of larger vision of life's true values and of love to mankind, has a place in a better world-order." Such a faith remains religious, in Tufts's sense if not in more traditional senses, because it goes beyond the material and the provable and recognizes "possibilities in man and in the universe which cannot be completely demonstrated."[132]

The meliorism that Tufts advocates thus emphasizes that "it will make a great difference whether we believe that as things have been, so they must always continue to be, or whether we have faith that human nature can improve, that nations as well as individuals may have a change of heart."[133] Tufts is not suggesting that we will have an easy path to follow, or that eventually all our problems will be worked out. To do so would be optimistic. What he *is* suggesting, however, is that if we allow ourselves to be trapped by a 'realism' like Niebuhr's, without hope of change, we will be able to generate little effort for change. We cannot go on without a melioristic faith in the possibilities of the future. Tufts lived with such a faith and urges us to adopt it and work with it as well.

THE IMPORTANCE OF TUFTS

This introduction has been an attempt to offer an understanding of Tufts and his place in the philosophical world through an examination of his life and thought. A broader and clearer understanding will come from the study of the selections that follow, and a balanced assessment of his historical and philosophical importance waits upon extensive critical evaluation.[134] Still, I believe that a careful study of his work will demonstrate that Tufts is a figure who has been unjustifiably overlooked and forgotten. Our sense of the history of American philosophy, and our own philosophizing, will benefit from the careful reconsideration of his work.

In a world of libraries and reprints and copiers, it is interesting to speculate why a figure like Tufts would drop almost completely from sight. The simplest answer—and the silliest—would be that he was 'wrong,' or that his ideas were 'judged wrong,' or that his philosophy was 'proven wrong.' There are many other possible explanations to consider. Perhaps Tufts's disappearance was due to changes in the philosophy profession from the time that he entered it, when it could be likened to the ministry, to the current day. Perhaps it was due to the replacement of his broad model of philosophical inquiry, that grounded works that even as supportive a commentator as Rucker describes as "more sociological-historical than philosophical in tone,"[135] with narrower standards of philosophical excellence and narrower types of philosophical expertise. Perhaps it was due to his being in Chicago rather than somewhere on the East Coast. Perhaps it was due to the fact that Tufts spent much of his energy in pragmatic activities like administration, social reform, teaching, reviewing, and editing, rather than in the analysis and defense of the pragmatic movement. Perhaps it was due to Tufts being typed as a derivative thinker, a 'minor Deweyan,' rather than as a contributor to the advancement of a mutually reinforcing social pragmatism.

My own view would include all of these reasons and add one more: Tufts was forgotten, just as most once-important philosophers have been forgotten, because our procedures for passing on traditions are accidental and inadequate. Both points deserve consideration. The first is that, in our sifting and evaluating of philosophers to study and pass on, we normally focus too narrowly upon figures who are, for whatever reasons, of immediate interest to the current generation of scholars, and we normally pay insufficient attention to those whose earlier importance seems unjustified.[136] Other figures, however important they might be in some 'objective' sense, if they are unable to pass through this type of accidental evaluative screening, will be lost at least for the near future. The second point is that, because of our intellectual limitations and in the interest of transmitting a wieldy story of our philosophical past, we simplify. Such simplified philosophical histories are eminently more manageable than accurate ones. We settle, for example, upon the 'major' figure(s) of the Metaphysical Club, or the Common Sense tradition, or the Idealist movement, or the Chicago School, and the others—now 'minor' figures—drop from sight as unnecessary complications. The inadequacy of such procedures is only too obvious.

Thus, in contradistinction to the popular Darwinian view that those thinkers who drop from sight do so because they have no ongoing merit, I would suggest that we do not know enough about the vast majority of them to tell whether their current obscurity is justifiable or not. Tufts is, I think, a good example of this process. There are many others.[137] We cannot find value in thinkers that we do not know; and, for intellectual and temporal and numerous other reasons, we tend not to try to find out about them. We rest comfortably in the belief that intellectual figures about whom we know little merit their relative obscurity.

James Hayden Tufts deserves a chance to regain a place in our collective philosophical memory, both for the role that he played in the history of American thought and for the intellectual perspective that he developed. If given such a chance, I think that he will again be seen as an important figure with important ideas. Tufts could also be of particular value in our current academic situation because he recognized long ago that wisdom is more important than erudition, and that the good academic life integrates the life of the mind with broader experience. "The interpretation of the world and of life through both learning and investigation is necessary for the creation of ideals that can really work," he writes, and "the struggle with the conditions of life evokes interpretation." In this way, as inquirer, teacher, citizen, neighbor, and family member, the scholar can become the "servant of all."[138] We need to keep such figures in our pantheon.

NOTES

1. Let us consider just three examples. In 1960, Arnold Isenberg published an edition of parts of the introduction and all of part 2 of the 1932 version of the *Ethics* under the title *Theory of the Moral Life*. In his foreword, Isenberg does not discuss JHT's co-authorship of the Introduction; and, although he denies that JHT's contributions in parts 1 and 3 are outdated, he maintains that the heart of the volume is part 2 (New York: Holt, 1960), iii–vi. In 1978, Charles Stevenson introduced the critical edition of the 1908 version that was appearing in *The Middle Works of John Dewey*, but he restricted his discussion to sections of Dewey's contribution in part 2 (*The Middle Works*, ed. Jo Ann Boydston, 15 vols. [Carbondale: Southern Illinois UP, 1976–1983] 5:ix–xxxiv). In 1985, Abraham Edel and Elizabeth Flower introduced the critical edition of the 1932 version that was appearing in *The Later Works of John Dewey*. They

recognized that the *Ethics* is an integrated volume that should be considered in its entirety and they discussed JHT's contribution here and there; but their primary interest is Dewey's development from 1908 to 1932 (*The Later Works*, ed. Jo Ann Boydston, 17 vols. [Carbondale: Southern Illinois UP, 1981–] 7:vii–xxxv). The overall import of these three instances has to be that JHT's role in the *Ethics* was an unimportant, or at least a minor, one.

2. JHT plays no role, or the role of a minor Deweyan, in such generally excellent studies as: Herbert Wallace Schneider, *A History of American Philosophy*, second ed. (New York: Columbia UP, 1963); Joseph L. Blau, *Men and Movements in American Philosophy* (Englewood Cliffs: Prentice, 1952); H. S. Thayer, *Meaning and Action: A Critical History of Pragmatism*, rev. ed. (Indianapolis: Hackett, 1981); Elizabeth Flower and Murray Murphey, *A History of Philosophy in America*, 2 vols., (New York: Putnams, 1977).

3. The sources of this biographical information include JHT's biographical and autobiographical writings, especially 1902:01; 1912:01; 1920:01; 1930:01; 1930:03; and 1942:01 (for full citations, see the Bibliography below), and archival material located in the Special Collections of the Amherst College Library, the Joseph Regenstein Library of the University of Chicago, and the Morris Library of the Southern Illinois University at Carbondale.

4. For a listing of the course offerings at the University of Michigan during these years, cf. *The Early Works of John Dewey*, ed. Jo Ann Boydston, 5 vols. (Carbondale: Southern Illinois UP, 1969–1972) 3:90–92.

5. Josiah Royce, who studied in Leipzig and Göttingen in 1875–1876 before completing his doctoral studies at Johns Hopkins University in 1878, wrote in 1891 that a generation of budding American scholars "dreamed of nothing but a German University. . . . German scholarship was our master and guide. . . . [O]ne returned an idealist, devoted for the time to pure learning for learning's sake, determined to contribute his *Scherflein* [little bit] to the massive store of human knowledge, burning for a chance to help build the American University" ("Present Ideals of American University Life," *Scribners Magazine*, 10 [1891]: 382–383).

For a further consideration of the role of the German Ph.D. in late-nineteenth-century American academic life—its importance for the career of an aspiring academic; the relative intellectual ease of its attainment; and, most importantly, the meaning of German *Wissenschaft*, *Lehrfreiheit*, and *Lernfreiheit* for the spirit of scholarship in America—see Merle E. Curti, *The Growth of American Thought*, third ed. (New York: Harper, 1964) 564–569; Jurgen Herbst, *The German Historical School in American Scholarship: A Study in the Transfer of Culture* (Ithaca: Cornell UP, 1965) 1–22; Charles F. Thwing, *The American and the German University* (New York: Macmillan, 1928) 40–77.

6. The best source of information about JHT's life from the time he left Westport to the departure for Germany is the collection of over 250 of his letters to Cynthia Whitaker (Tufts Papers, Southern Illinois University at Carbondale, box 2, folder 11-box 7, folder 2).

7. For the beginnings of Harper's University, see Thomas Wakefield Goodspeed, *A History of the University of Chicago: The First Quarter-Century*

(Chicago: U of Chicago P, 1916); *The Story of the University of Chicago, 1890–1925* (Chicago: U of Chicago P, 1925); and Richard J. Storr, *Harper's University: The Beginnings* (Chicago: U of Chicago P, 1966).

8. Henry James, ed., *The Letters of William James*, vol. 2 (Boston: Atlantic Monthly Press, 1920) 201–202; cf. James, "The Chicago School," *Psychological Bulletin* 1.1 (1904): 1–5; Ralph Barton Perry, *The Thought and Character of William James*, vol. 2 (Boston: Little, 1935) 501–502, 523–524.

9. For a thorough examination of the full range of the thought of the Chicago School, see Darnell Rucker, *The Chicago Pragmatists* (Minneapolis: U of Minnesota P, 1969).

10. JHT reports on the beginnings of the *Ethics* project around 1900 in his memoirs on the early years in Chicago ("Chicago III," 5, Tufts Papers, University of Chicago, box 3, folder 16). He later announces and describes the volume in a letter to his mentor, Garman, in March of 1901, adding that the book was to appear by the fall of that year (JHT to Garman, 30(?) Mar. 1901, Charles E. Garman Papers, Amherst College, box 6, folder 5).

11. The division of effort, along with their indication that "each has contributed suggestions and criticisms to the work of the other in sufficient degree to make the book throughout a joint work," is to be found in the preface (1908:01, 5–6) and in the preface to the first edition (1932:01, 7). (All references in this introduction to the *Ethics*, in either the 1908 or 1932 versions, will be to the Carbondale edition cited above in note 1.)

12. 1908:01, 3; 1932:01, 5.

13. The social reform activities at the University of Chicago are discussed by Rucker in *The Chicago Pragmatists*, and explored more thoroughly by Steven J. Diner, *A City and Its Universities: Public Policy in Chicago, 1892–1919* (Chapel Hill: U of North Carolina P, 1980).

14. Cf. 1919:19; 1920:02; and 1921:09.

15. Van Meter Ames, rev. of *The Chicago Pragmatists*, by Darnell Rucker, *Journal of the History of Philosophy* 8 (1970); 499.

16. 1912:03, 176–179.

17. 1924:03, 328–329; 1940:01, 334.

18. 1904:03, 13; cf. 1917:02, 357–361. For further discussions of the theme of embodiment, see William James, *The Principles of Psychology* (1890; Cambridge: Harvard UP, 1981); James Rowland Angell, *Psychology*, fourth ed. (New York: Holt, 1908); John Dewey, *The Middle Works*, vol. 14; George Herbert Mead, *The Philosophy of the Act*, ed. Charles W. Morris, John M. Brewster, Albert M. Dunham, and David L. Miller (Chicago: U of Chicago P, 1938).

19. H. M. Kallen to JHT, 24 Feb. 1916; JHT to H. M. Kallen, 26 Feb. 1916, Tufts Papers, University of Chicago, box 2, folder 7. The volume appeared with only a brief, unsigned prefatory note ([New York: Holt, 1917] iii–iv).

20. JHT to D. D. Runes, 21 Jan. 1941, Tufts Papers, University of Chicago, box 2, folder 11. The volume, containing JHT's essay "Ethics" [1943:01], eventually appeared with the title *Twentieth Century Philosophy: Living Schools of Thought* (New York: Philosophical Press, 1943).

21. JHT, "Chicago III," 4, Tufts Papers, University of Chicago, box 3, folder

16. For the defenses that JHT had in mind, see William James, *Pragmatism: A New Name for Some Old Ways of Thinking* (1907; Cambridge: Harvard UP, 1975) and *The Meaning of Truth: A Sequel to "Pragmatism"* (1909; Cambridge: Harvard UP, 1975); John Dewey's various essays in the years 1907–1911 gathered in vols. 4 and 6 of *The Middle Works*; and Addison Webster Moore, *Pragmatism and Its Critics* (Chicago: U of Chicago P, 1910). See also H. S. Thayer, *Meaning and Action*.

22. Rucker offers a more favorable interpretation of these controversies: "[W]hile [Tufts] was applying pragmatic principles to various problems, he did not further the philosophic development of those ideas to the extent that some of his colleagues did" (*The Chicago Pragmatists* 23).

23. Thayer, *Meaning and Action* 445; cf. Richard Hofstadter, *Social Darwinism in American Thought*, rev. ed. (Boston: Beacon, 1955) 140–141.

24. 1930:01, 333 (this volume: p. 1); 1901:04, 96; cf. 1910:01, 141 (p. 117).

25. 1933:03, 629; 1938:02, 433.

26. 1942:01, 60; 1930:01, 337 (pp. 4–5). Further consideration of the theme of the relation of philosophy and religion in JHT's context can be seen in John Dewey, "From Absolutism to Experimentalism," also in *Contemporary American Philosophy : Personal Statements*, ed. G. P. Adams and W. P. Montague, vol. 2 (New York: Macmillan, 1930) 13–27, and reprinted in *The Later Works* 5:147–160; Max C. Otto, review of *Contemporary American Philosophy: Personal Statements*, ed G. P. Adams and W. P. Montague, *International Journal of Ethics* 41 (1931); 230–234; Thomas LeDuc, *Piety and Intellect at Amherst College, 1865–1912* (New York: Columbia UP, 1946); Robert M. Crunden, *Ministers of Reform: The Progressives' Achievement in American Civilization, 1889–1920* (New York: Basic Books, 1982).

27. 1926:01, 451, 454 (pp. 270, 273).

28. 1911:03, 151.

29. 1930:01, 333 (p. 1); cf. 1926:01, 452–453 (p. 272); 1930:05, 187.

30. 1930:01, 352 (pp. 17–18); 1926:01, 450 (p. 270); cf. 1939:01, 54 (p. 345); 1911:03, 151; Dewey, *The Later Works* 9:40–58.

31. 1922:03, 126 (p. 266); 1930:01, 352 (p. 18).

32. 1918:03, 281; cf. 1907:08; 1909:01; LeDuc, *Piety and Intellect* 101–118.

33. 1908:01, 139.

34. 1926:01, 451 (p. 270).

35. 1930:05, 191–193; cf. 1922:03, 120–121 (pp. 261–262).

36. 1926:01, 451 (p. 270); 1922:03, 118 (p. 260).

37. Dewey, *The Later Works* 9:34; cf. Mead, *Mind, Self, and Society from the Standpoint of a Social Behaviorist*, ed. Charles W. Morris (Chicago: U of Chicago P, 1934) 281–298; Walter F. Willcox, "A Message from 'Eighty-Four,'" *Amherst Graduates' Quarterly* 32 (1943); 119–120.

38. 1939:01, 52 (p. 344); 1922:03, 115 (pp. 257–258); 1930:01, 352–353 (p. 18). For a fuller discussion of the reconstruction of religion at Chicago, see Rucker, *The Chicago Pragmatists* 107–131.

39. 1914:05, 457 (p. 162); 1903:01, 28; 1909:07, 201 (p. 112). In the last-mentioned piece, JHT emphasizes that what is often called 'Social Darwinism' is not Darwin's own message (cf. 1909:07, 195, 205 [p. 106, 115]).

40. 1914:08, 4–5 (pp. 168–170); cf. 1909:06, 407–410 (pp. 95–100); Dewey, *The Middle Works* 4:3–14; Mead, *The Philosophy of the Act* 45–62.

41. 1908:01, 8–9 and 1932:01, 11; 1933:01, 11–12.

42. 1913:03, 635 (p. 144); cf. 1910:01, 142–143 (p. 118).

43. 1918:01, 343; cf. 1921:03; cf. Mead, "The Philosophies of Royce, James, and Dewey in Their American Setting" [1930], in *Selected Writings*, ed. Andrew J. Reck (Indianapolis: Bobbs-Merrill, 1964) 371–391.

44. 1909:06, 408 (p. 96); 1919:19, 592; cf. 1934:02, 144 (p. 336).

45. 1933:01, 367 (p. 302); 1936:01, 256, 270–271; cf. 1929:01, 394 (p. 281); 1919:01, 413.

46. Frederick Jackson Turner, *The Frontier in American History* (1920; New York: Holt, 1962) 277, 38; cf. JHT, 1921:03; Dewey, *The Later Works* 14:224–230.

47. 1930:01, 342, 340 (pp. 8–9, 7); cf. 1932:01, 85; Mead, "Natural Rights and the Theory of the Political Institution" [1915], in *Selected Writings* 159.

48. 1908:01, 443–444; cf. Dewey, *The Later Works* 5:86; Mead, "Natural Rights and the Theory of the Political Institution" 151.

49. 1915:04, 189.

50. 1915:04, 190; 1912:02, 267 (p. 138); cf. 1910:01, 142 (p. 118).

51. 1930:03, 7; 1915:04, 189; cf. 1923:01, 1.

52. 1914:08, 6 (p. 171); cf. 1915:04, 189; 1918:02, 55–57 (p. 224).

53. 1913:04, 186, 188 (pp. 146, 148); cf. 1922:03, 124–125 (pp. 264–265); 1908:19, 396; 1914:08, 7 (pp. 171–172).

54. 1930:01, 340 (p. 7); 1915:01, 101 (p. 184).

55. 1913:02, 280.

56. 1908:06, 184 (p. 85); 1917:03, 42.

57. 1912:02, 267 (p. 138); 1908:06, 184 (p. 85); cf. 1906:10, 362 (p. 65).

58. 1917:03, 42; cf. 1930:01, 344 (pp. 10–11); 1933:02, 194 (pp. 306–307); 1936:01, 254–255; 1919:19, 594.

59. 1908:01, 444.

60. 1918:02, 21 (p. 215); cf. 1906:01, 25–27; 1917:02, 389–392; Mead, "Natural Rights and the Theory of the Political Institution."

61. 1918:01, 262.

62. 1918:01, 103, 111.

63. 1918:01, 357–358, 353; 1933:01, 216; cf. Dewey, *The Later Works* 13:99–100.

64. 1918:01, 361; 1936:01, 254; 1933:02, 195–196 (p. 308).

65. 1933:01, 216.

66. 1914:04, 332–333; 1918:01, 413; 1912:02, 267 (p. 137).

67. 1915:10, 14 (pp. 208–209); 1933:02, 196 (p. 309). For a further examination of the question of conceptual reconstruction, see my *The Community Reconstructs: The Meaning of Pragmatic Social Thought* (Urbana: U of Illinois P, 1992) esp. 59–70.

68. 1939:01, 52 (p. 344); cf. 1943:01, 13; 1935:02, 139.

69. 1904:03, 13; 1935:02, 139; 1932:01, 436.

70. 1933:02, 194 (p. 306). JHT notes that it is one of the values of federalism that it enables people to "unite into one nation without losing enthusiasm and pride in their local neighborhood and in their own ancestral stocks" (1917:01, 196). Let us set aside the question of federalism and consider his use

of the term 'stock.' However uncomfortable to current ears, 'stock'—and related terms like 'race,' 'savage,' and 'primitive'—was frequently used not that long ago. Most of JHT's uses of 'stock' carry the neutral meaning of something like 'background' or 'culture.' For example: "In another respect, of much importance in recent history, all stocks were alike: all were accustomed to use alcoholic beverages" (1933:01, 16). Other of his uses of such terms are ironic and quite telling, for example: "Among civilized people a family may starve while the man next door wastes enough daily to feed the first family for a month" (1918:01, 28). Occasionally, however, we find passages like the following: "In fact at the present time many thoughtful students believe that the problem of maintaining the best stocks is one of the most serious which confronts us" (1932:01, 454). Although such passages indicate that careful, contexted study of his uses of these eugenic and orthogenetic terms will be necessary, JHT's general social perspective would suggest that there is no major racial or ethnic controversy to be anticipated.

71. 1933:02, 194.

72. 1940:01, 334; cf. 1913:05, 518; 1913:04, 191 (pp. 151–152); 1915:04, 189–190.

73. 1934:02, 151 (p. 342); cf. 1933:01, 261.

74. 1924:03, 328; 1932:02, 171; cf. 1917:01, 262; 1933:02, 193 (pp. 305–306). For Jefferson's views on legal reconstruction, see Jefferson to James Madison, 6 Sept. 1789; Jefferson to Samuel Kercheval, 12 July 1816, in *The Life and Selected Writings of Thomas Jefferson*, ed. Adrienne Koch and William Peden (New York: Modern Library, 1944) 488–493, 673–676.

75. 1904:03, 18; cf. 1932:01, 395; 1933:01, 241.

76. 1934:02, 140 (p. 332); 1904:03, 18; 1913:04, 192 (p. 152).

77. 1912:03, 179.

78. 1912:06, 460–461; 1932:02, 171; cf. 1932:01, 397. JHT also emphasizes that our recognition of the actual bases of judicial interpretation explains why such great concern has long been placed in the question of the makeup and the powers of the judicial branch of government. (Cf. 1924:03, 329; 1936:01, 266, 270.)

79. 1908:01, 439; cf. 1906:10, 362 (pp. 64–65); 1908:01, 32, 129, 144, 156; 1930:05, 185; 1932:01, 31.

80. 1918:01, 9–10; 1932:01, 454; 1918:01, 10; cf. 1914:08, 5 (p. 169); Dewey, *The Later Works* 9:57–58; Mead, "Bishop Berkeley and His Message," *Journal of Philosophy* 26 (1929): 430.

81. 1915:02, 31; cf. 1918:01, 251.

82. 1918:05, 308 (p. 238); cf. 1921:09, 412–414 (pp. 251–253).

83. Cf. 1933:02, 197 (pp. 310–311); 1943:01, 28–36.

84. 1908:01, 441, 453; 1932:01, 388; cf. 1914:05, 457 (p. 162); 1918:01, 269, 388; 1919:19, 595; 1921:01, 249; 1932:01, 408; 1933:01, 173, 180, 214; 1936:01, 264–266.

85. 1933:02, 198 (p. 311); 1913:04, 194 (p. 155); cf. 1933:01, 174.

86. 1918:01, 346–347. JHT recognizes, of course, that the two classes in no way represent 'halves.' (Cf. 1921:10; 1921:15.)

87. 1918:01, 387. JHT also recognizes that "in the game of the industrial process there is no option. One must play or starve. And usually there is no

chance to consent to the rules" (1906:10, 373 (p. 74); cf. 1918:01, 255, 290). He writes further that "[t]he ethics of violence in a strike is essentially that of self-defense" (1933:01, 172).

88. 1918:01, 386; cf. 1908:01, 125. We do find Tufts's writing on occasion indicating some of the blind spots of the middle-class intellectual. Consider, for example, his use of the following reason as part of an argument for equality: "No one in a club is permitted to give tips to servants, because this would tend to give some members better service than others" (1918:01, 423; cf. 1908:01, 519; 1933:01, 102; 1907:12, 374; 1915:02).

89. 1943:01, 27; cf. 1933:01, 6; 1932:01, 426–427; 1930:05, 184; 1933:02, 197 (p. 310–311).

90. 1921:16, 400; 1918:02, 19 (p. 214).

91. 1930:01, 348 (p. 14); 1923:01, 16; 1933:02, 195 (p. 308); 1918:02, 44 (p. 221); cf. 1934:02, 145–146 (pp. 336–337).

92. 1918:01, 27, 16; cf. 1906:10, 375–376 (pp. 75–76).

93. Cf. 1917:01, 249; 1942:01, 54–56; 1918:01, 36–37.

94. 1919:01, 413, 408.

95. 1933:02, 198 (p. 311); cf. 1908:01, 484; 1918:01, 65; 1932:01, 414, 433.

96. 1933:02, 199 (p. 313); 1934:02, 150 (p. 341).

97. 1933:02, 193, 198 (pp. 305, 306, 311); cf. Dewey, *The Later Works* 2:259–281; Mead, "The Working Hypothesis in Social Reform" [1899], in *Selected Writings* 3–5.

98. 1918:01, 413; 1919:01, 416; 1932:01, 391; cf. 1908:01, 152.

99. 1930:03, 4; cf. Dewey, *The Later Works* 4:225; 5:90–98.

100. 1913:03, 634 (p. 143).

101. 1923:01, 208; 1918:02, 41, 40 (p. 220); cf. Mead, *Mind, Self, and Society* 298.

102. 1918:02, 41–42 (p. 220). JHT placed great hope in the progressive income tax because it made possible "in principle . . . a far more just distribution of burdens" for the running of the government (1932:01, 422; cf. 1929:01, 395 [p. 282]). But his hope was moderated by his recognition of the important difference between income and wealth (cf. 1921:10; 1921:15); and, because of the way that it was actually being used, he finally describes the progressive income tax more guardedly as "a moral conviction" and "at least a gesture" toward justice (1933:01, 9, 189).

103. 1935:07, 73–74; 1918:01, 405.

104. 1918:01, 405, 394; cf. Dewey, *The Later Works* 13:294–303.

105. 1935:07, 74.

106. 1923:01, 91.

107. 1906:10, 365 (p. 67); cf. 1917:02, 383; Dewey, *The Middle Works* vol. 14; Mead, *Mind, Self and Society*.

108. 1908:01, 520.

109. 1915:02, 29; 1908:10, 121 (p. 90); 1932:01, 40; 1908:01, 520.

110. 1904:03, 13; 1913:03, 633 (p. 142).

111. 1906:10, 367 (p. 69); 1929:01, 397 (p. 284).

112. 1898:02, xxi–xxii (p. 21).

113. 1916:13, 440–441.
114. 1912:02, 268 (p. 139).
115. 1914:08, 2 (p. 166); cf. 1908:01, 152.
116. Dewey, *The Middle Works* 10:46; JHT, 1919:05, 92.
117. 1908:01, 157; 1909:08, 438; cf. 1921:16, 394; 1933:01, 212–213; Dewey, *The Middle Works* 9:87–106.
118. 1929:01, 398 (p. 285); 1918:01, 440; cf. 1918:01, 323; 1918:02, 47–48 (p. 222); 1933:01, 213–214.
119. 1929:01, 397 (p. 284); 1918:01, 441; cf. 1933:01, 367–368 (pp. 302–303).
120. 1914:05, 456 (p. 161); cf. 1908:10, 121 (p. 90). On the general theme of moral education, see Dewey, *The Early Works* 4:54–61, 106–118; 5:54–83; *The Later Works* 5:289–298; Rucker, *The Chicago Pragmatists* 99–104.
121. 1908:11, 551; 1913:03, 632 (p. 142).
122. 1908:10, 124 (p. 93); 1908:11, 552; 1913:03, 632 (p. 141); cf. 1921:01, 415–416; Dewey, *The Later Works* 7:171, 347–348; Jane Addams, *Democracy and Social Ethics* (New York: Macmillan, 1905) 1–12.
123. 1908:10, 123 (p. 92); cf. 1927:01, 205–207.
124. 1914:05, 458 (p. 163); 1908:11, 552–553; cf. 1908:08, 476–477; 1927:01, 207–209.
125. 1914:05, 454, 459 (pp. 159, 164).
126. 1908:01, 160.
127. Dewey, *The Middle Works* 12:181–192. For a general discussion of the themes of this section, see my *The Community Reconstructs*, esp. 91–109.
128. Niebuhr, *Moral Man and Immoral Society: A Study of Ethics and Politics* (1932; New York: Scribners, 1960) 44. For JHT's direct response to this volume, see 1933:01, 349–358 (pp. 289–296).
129. 1914:08, 11 (p. 175); 1918:02, 72 (p. 228).
130. Niebuhr, *Moral Man and Immoral Society* 3.
131. 1918:02, 73 (p. 229); 1932:01, 453.
132. 1922:03, 123, 118 (pp. 263, 260); cf. 1908:06, 187–188 (pp. 88–89).
133. 1922:03, 123 (p. 263); cf. Dewey, *The Middle Works* 11:40–53; *The Later Works* 5:267–278.
134. For example, questions about his speculative anthropology, his use of the Turner thesis, his emphasis upon cooperative efforts to advance the common good, his beliefs about the ultimate compatibility of democracy and science, his meliorism, and other aspects of his work, all need careful study.
135. Rucker, *The Chicago Pragmatists* 23.
136. This theme of 'presentist' bias is explored more fully in Murray G. Murphey, "Toward an Historicist History of American Philosophy," *Transactions of the C. S. Peirce Society* 15 (1979): 1–18; Bruce Kuklick, *Churchmen and Philosophers: From Jonathan Edwards to John Dewey* (New Haven: Yale UP, 1985).
137. To list just another dozen neglected figures: Hartley Burr Alexander, John Elof Boodin, Edgar S. Brightman, Mary Whiton Calkins, Irwin Edman, William Ernest Hocking, Elijah Jordan, Alain Leroy Locke, Arthur E. Murphy, Dewitt H. Parker, Edgar A. Singer, Jr., and Wilbur Marshall Urban.
138. 1914:08, 12 (p. 176).

Selected Writings of
James Hayden Tufts

1   What I Believe

My generation has seen the passing of systems of thought which had reigned since Augustine. The conception of the world as a kingdom ruled by God, subject to his laws and their penalties, which had been undisturbed by the Protestant Reformation, has dissolved. We watch the process, but as yet are scarcely awake to its possible outcome. The sanctions of our inherited morality have gone. Principles and standards which had stood for nearly two thousand years are questioned. The process goes on among us in methods which are perhaps no less radical because they are not violent. In Russia the change is both radical and violent. It is seen at work in our great institutions of law, politics, business, industry, and philanthropy. To understand and interpret the origins of moral life and the complex relationships between moral ideas and the great social institutions has seemed to me a fascinating field of work. I began my work in philosophy with studies in its history. I changed to ethics because, as I came to gain a clearer view of the important tendencies of the time, I thought the ethical changes the most significant.

I was born and received my early education in western Massachusetts. My ancestry along all its various lines, with the exception of the paternal Tufts strain, had come to Massachusetts in the Puritan migration of 1630 or shortly afterwards. My great-great-grandfather, John Tufts, had come to western Massachusetts in the considerable company of Scotch-Irish about a hundred years later. One of the emigrant ancestors, the Reverend Ralph Wheelock, is said to have been enrolled in Clare College, Cambridge; but with this exception all my ancestors in both lines were farmers until my grandfather, James

From *Contemporary American Philosophy: Personal Statements*, ed G. P. Adams and W. P. Montague, vol. 2 (New York: Macmillan, 1930) 333–353 [1930:01].

Tufts, went to Brown University (then Providence College) as a preparation for the ministry, graduating in 1789; and my maternal grandfather fitted himself for the practice of medicine by attendance upon
lectures in Dartmouth College. Both settled in a pioneer town of
southern Vermont, high on the Green Mountains. My clerical ancestor
remained in this, his first parish, until his death, and in accord with
what seems to have been a not uncommon usage, was known as
'Priest Tufts' through all the county, and indeed beyond. He was in
his theology a follower of Nathaniel Emmons, with whom he had
studied after graduation from college. It was a stern doctrine which
he preached; yet for forty years he was a commanding influence as
the spiritual ruler of the community. Very probably it was the ambition
of the alert-planning mother, who was quite as influential in family
decisions as the more formally educated father, that encouraged the
second James Tufts, my father, to set out from home across the mountain, forty miles on foot, his outfit in a small satchel, to begin preparation for Yale College. My father never lost the atmosphere of this
Green Mountain town in which the church was the center and circum-
ference of the community life, and in which no one thought of questioning the minister's declaration of the counsels of God. The Yale
College of that day was a group of very serious young men, many of
them expecting to enter the ministry. The atmosphere of the parsonage
was repeated in New Haven and further found in Andover Theological
Seminary, to which my father went from Yale. Sudden loss of voice
prevented my father from preaching as he had intended, but he maintained throughout his long life his theological interest, and this was
an element in the environment of my early years.

My father was fond of discussion. On week days the morning
newspaper, on Sunday the subjects of the morning sermon were
invariably discussed, and the boys of our family were expected to
remember at least the minister's text and to state the principal 'heads'
of the discourse.

My mother was also an important influence in my education, although during the formative years of my childhood she was a nearly
helpless invalid. She had received a good education according to the
standards of that day for women, and had been a successful teacher
previous to her marriage. She had inherited from both father and
mother a refinement of spirit; her religious experience of conversion
had given scope and purpose to her life. To meet her ambitions and
standards was a goal to be striven for.

My early education was of a somewhat irregular sort. After my father had remained for some years without definite occupation, owing to the loss of his voice, he was induced by his old college friend to become principal of one of the New England academies. After a few years he resigned from this position and took into his home a small number of boys for private instruction. Some of these boys were fitting for college, and my own preparation was hitched on somewhat casually to the work which chanced to be under way. If a boy came along who wished to begin algebra, I began or reviewed algebra, and when other boys began Latin or Greek, I formed one of the beginning class in that subject. My father was an excellent drill master, and I had thorough preparation in the classics with a minimum of hours devoted to study. It was a relatively easy and enjoyable journey that I traversed through Caesar and Cicero and Virgil, Xenophon and Homer. At fourteen I had covered the ground prescribed for college entrance, although in many other lines my education was grossly deficient.

Meanwhile, I was getting another sort of education for which I have always been thankful. My father's homestead included a small farm whose dairy and garden supplied the family table with a large share of what hungry boys ate and drank. The manual labor was in the charge of a capable hired man, but there seemed to be a large amount of work which was within the powers and duties of a boy. In the winter, the care of the cattle after the morning's milking; in the summer, the work of planting and haying and harvesting—all offered strength and health and fellowship with other workers. From being a rather delicate young child I became well and strong. I acquired a constitution that knew little fatigue and seemingly no limits of endurance, during my years of study and early teaching. What was, perhaps, almost equally valuable was my acquaintance with the point of view of the man who works with his hands, and my ability to meet many sorts and conditions of men on common terms. During the four years after I had traversed the preparatory studies for admission to college, and before the actual date of my entrance upon my college course, I had read a considerable amount of history, had reviewed and extended my reading of the classics, and had (unwisely) taught a district school for two years. I had also become a member of the Congregational Church. So far as I can recall, I accepted even the somewhat comprehensive creed. While I do not think that doctrines relating to the future life occupied relatively a large part in actual worship and preaching, I presume that if asked I should have given them assent. At eighteen I entered college and a new stage of my intellectual life began.

The New England college of those days has now completely vanished. The curriculum, indeed, had been partially liberalized by the introduction of a considerable number of elective courses. But the spirit of the college remained much as it had been in the days of its founders, sixty years earlier. We studied the classics, mathematics, the basal natural sciences, the modern languages and literature. In the senior year, all students had the course in philosophy. But the outstanding feature of the college, as I now picture its atmosphere and its influence, was the religious seriousness. The impressive figure of President Seelye made morning chapel and Sunday church service the most characteristic exercises of the week. I elected typical courses in language, literature, natural science, and philosophy. Professor Garman began his work as teacher in our freshman year, as our instructor in mathematics. In our senior year he taught us philosophy, but he had not yet worked out the course which gave him such a conspicuous position among American teachers of philosophy. Yet even so, his sympathetic grasp of the undergraduates' somewhat bewildered state of mind in traversing Hickok's texts and his illumination of the deeper issues in religion and society left a leaven at work.

A conviction of the influence of ideas was one of the chief reasons for the selection of a career. The atmosphere of my home was almost compelling. I recall vividly my mother's report of a conversation which she had with the mother of a classmate at the time of my graduation from college. The two mothers were comparing notes as to the plans and prospects of their sons. The mother of the classmate said, "I don't know what X will do, but his mind is filled with plans for making money." She spoke in a tone of disappointment, and my mother repeated the conversation as though such disappointment was the most natural thing in the world. For women of their antecedents some professional career was the only thinkable line of work. I had never discussed seriously the question of a career, but my own interest in this case coincided with the expectations of my parents. My father, although he had himself expected to enter the ministry, until loss of health compelled him to change to the allied profession of teaching, was more scrupulous than might have been expected in attempting to influence my choice, although I knew he would be greatly disappointed if I did not choose a career which had in it the opportunity for useful work of some sort. In the Amherst College of the eighties a transition was in progress. Until that period a large proportion of the able students among the graduates had entered the ministry. In the eighties and nineties the profession of college or university teacher began to be increasingly effective. President Seelye and Professor Garman did much to encourage this tendency. President Seelye spoke frequently and with pride of the numbers of Amherst men upon the faculty of Columbia and the recently organized Johns Hopkins. It was the conviction of President Seelye and Professor Garman that in the days of transition in religious and political views which was then in progress, the opportunity of the thoroughly trained teacher was greatest of all. He seemed to embody in concrete form the power of ideas. It was hard for one who had passed four years in the study of ideas and their relationships to life and institutions to think in any other terms than in those of the opportunity for influence thus afforded. Reports reached us, through Garman's course, of new industrial organizations, of the beginnings of the struggle of the government with corporate wealth. But to all except a few of the students of the college these reports seemed to be from a world which did not concern us. If we took them seriously we thought of our function in society as that of understanding and discussing rather than of actually plunging into the world of affairs. At any rate, to understand what was going on and to teach young people seemed to many of us at that time one of the genuinely worthwhile lines of effort.

Two years spent in the college as an instructor in mathematics helped to define my problem further. I was still somewhat hesitant between teaching philosophy, as advised by President Seelye and Professor Garman on the one hand, and entering the ministry. During my college course I had taken an active part in student activities from football to debating. I enjoyed speaking to an audience, and thought it probable that the executive opportunities in the ministry might appeal to my interests in that direction. I entered Yale Divinity School with the question still undecided, and divided my time nearly equally between the divinity course, on the one hand, and studies in philosophy with Professor Ladd and anthropology under William G. Sumner on the other. It was an invitation from President Angell to become an instructor in the University of Michigan, coming in the summer after my graduation from the Divinity School, which was the decisive factor in my career. Henceforward I gave myself to the life of the scholar, although at intervals I have taken on administrative work as dean of the colleges; and when in 1925 President Burton, of the University of Chicago, felt the need of assistance in his large plans for a new creative epoch, I found a fascinating though extremely difficult field in the office of vice-president.

The University of Michigan in 1889 was a stimulating place. President Angell was surrounded by a faculty comprising some of the older generation, and some men fresh from Johns Hopkins and other schools of graduate work. Many who have since achieved the highest eminence in their fields were then on the staff. The university was undoubtedly the most active center of research west of the Alleghenies. Professor Dewey had already made himself known by his *Psychology* and his *Leibniz*. The tradition of philosophy, as this had been built by Professor George Morris, was that of a commanding and enriching subject. The ablest students elected it. A young instructor could have had no more favorable conditions.

But at Yale I had studied with Professor W. R. Harper and had been greatly impressed by his tireless energy and far-reaching ideas. When, therefore, he invited me to join the faculty which he was assembling for the new University of Chicago I reluctantly decided to leave my attractive position at Ann Arbor and to cast in my lot with the new enterprise. Believing that study in Europe would be important for effective work in the new institution, I spent a year at Berlin and Freiburg, taking my doctor's degree at the latter university under Alois Riehl with a thesis upon Kant's Teleology. My years of academic training had reached an end. I was eager to join the body of scholars which assembled on October 1, 1892, and with the exception of the year 1920–1921, spent as visiting professor in Columbia University, I have continued in my position in the University of Chicago.

Stimulating and absorbing as it was to take part in the making of a new university, I can now see that this was, perhaps, less crucial for my development in the long run than the contacts with the city of Chicago, and the challenge to all my previous philosophy which the unaccustomed conflicts of forces presented. At the outset I devoted myself to the history of philosophy, and during the first year translated Windelband's *History*. But I began almost from the first to feel the impact of an environment very different from that of my New England scheme of the political and economic order. On the one hand, Chicago was then, and continued to be, a city of power. The center of marketing, transportation, finance, for the great Middle West, it had been a school for forceful leaders. In the building of vast industries, of establishments for wholesale and retail trade, and of substantial banking organizations, it was a city of opportunity. It was a city still in the making, and with ambitions not limited by ordinary bounds. The beauty of its World's Fair augured well for its future support of a university.

Power and the attitude of brooking no resistance to great plans gave rise in some cases to a disposition which, if not arrogant, was at any rate little disposed to submit to restraint or dictation from any opposing body of opinion, whether from labor unions, or from politicians, or from courts. Least of all, perhaps, was it inclined to seek wisdom from academic opinion or social reformer. The tendency was rather toward fighting out controversies than toward compromise. The contrast between dwellings upon the Lake front and those back of the Yards, or in South Chicago, evidenced the sharp division of wealth from poverty.

What place could the university be expected to fill in such a turbulent, swift-moving stream? Would the city dominate the university? Would the university in time supply new interests and contribute toward new standards of individual and civic life? Coming closer to my own field, the many threads which had been thus far weaving no definite pattern beyond that of the traditional systems and methods seemed gradually to fit into an order which for me, at least, was a new structure. The making of ideas and the reaction of ideas upon the forming and reforming of moral and civic trends became the focus of attention.

Ethics must begin by understanding our ethical conceptions. It came home to me that these could not be adequately understood by purely intellectual analysis. Justice, I found, meant different things to different persons and different groups. Perhaps similar ambiguities lurked beneath other concepts. I determined to ask whether history would throw any light upon their formation. I was not definitely challenging Lotze's distinction between origin and validity. In fact, I had been taken by it when I had first heard it applied to the field of religion. Rather I was following a line which had always been fascinating to me and which had been strongly reinforced by my studies in anthropology and folkways under Professor William G. Sumner. But as time went on I came incidentally upon difference in ethical premises, in what we like to think of as our common morality, which could apparently be accounted for only by the attitudes of mind begotten by status or occupation. I found myself impelled in the direction of the thesis: (1) Moral ideas are shaped under the influence of economic, social, and religious forces; (2) and ideas in turn do not remain as objects of contemplation or scientific analysis only, but become patterns for action, emerging, it may be, in a Russian revolution.

Opportunities for more specific testing of both phases of the above thesis were not wanting. For example, I found myself chairman of a committee of the social agencies of the city, which had been appointed to keep track of all legislation, proposed or enacted, that might concern the civic, philanthropic, and protective work of these agencies. We framed a number of bills, some of which passed the legislature and became laws. The subsequent fate of a proposal for providing health insurance by the state was very instructive. A commission was authorized for the investigation of the proposal, a competent expert was engaged, and an excellent study made, but the report which came from the committee to the legislature bore no relation to the data of the experts' inquiry. The combined opposition of labor unionists, physicians, and those opposed to any new and unusual plan killed the measure. It is not easy to pass a law which is likely to interfere with a vested interest.

My closest contact was made possible through an invitation to act as chairman of the Board of Arbitration in the Hart, Schaffner and Marx clothing industry—a responsibility which later came to cover the clothing industry in Chicago. It was of the essence of this function that the arbitration was a continuous process. The board was like a court in that it recorded all its decisions and followed precedents if these seemed to be the best ways of meeting changing situations, but differed from a court in having no necessary rules except those jointly agreed upon by the firm and the union. As the Board of Arbitration met, not as is frequently the case in arbitration proceedings, to settle a particular strike, but rather as a permanent body to make a substitution of reason for force and determine such policies as would promote peace and efficiency in the industry, the conditions called for adjustment, not on the basis of compromise, but rather on the basis of finding, so far as is humanly possible, what was the right thing and what would give permanent satisfaction.

I served for two years in this work and found it very difficult, but also very much worthwhile. For nearly every moral principle which I had been reaching by study of industry from the outside was called upon in the settlement of the questions which were presented to the board. Fortunately, my predecessor had laid well the foundations for subsequent procedure, but every contest for appeal tested the method which I had been following. I repeatedly found that to know the whole history of the situation put a controversy in a different light. I learned at first hand how certain of our basal conceptions are affected by origins.

The thesis that moral ideas are subtly colored or infected by particular circumstances is opposed to the doctrine that such ideas are independent of time and place and human bias; that right is right, and may be discovered and fixed by rational intuition unaided and unaffected by feeling or nonrational factors. In the study of this thesis, I had been particularly struck with the obvious derivation of many moral concepts from class distinctions. 'Honor,' 'nobility,' are obviously the qualities required or found in a superior class; 'mean' and 'villain' are correlates. The military class, the sporting class, the trading class, the working class, each has its term of class approval, and some of these ultimately get recognition as good ethical concepts. But with some of the fundamental ethical concepts, the subtle influence of class is less commonly recognized. Let us examine certain influences that work in fixing the meaning of honesty and justice. These are conceptions which Sidgwick treats as lacking in clearness and certainty, when used by common sense.

One day, as chairman of the Board of Arbitration in a local industry, I had been listening to a rather severe complaint on the part of the management. The charge was made that in a certain workroom the standard of efficiency was low. The particular part of the manufacturing process which was performed in this room had not been placed upon a piece-work basis, nor yet had it been so thoroughly standardized as to give a fairly accurate measure of the work of each man. It was claimed by the management that some of the workers took advantage of the situation and shirked or slacked. "We pay a fair wage; these men do not give a fair day's work in return; they are not honest." Whereupon one of the workers' representatives, not so much in reply to the charge as in genuine uncertainty, exclaimed half under his breath, "What is 'honest'?" I thus had forcibly presented the doubt of the worker as to the standard employed. For when one considers the process of gradual speeding up which has been the accompaniment of constantly improved machinery and constant division of labor, one is forced to recall that the wage cost per hour of product has greatly diminished, while the wage, although increasing, has often increased far less than the total gain from improved processes would seem to warrant. How can we determine what would be the honest share of labor in the increased efficiency of the machine process? Should all the profit go to the manufacturer, or should a part go to the workman? And if the latter, then how much will be an honest share? Can we say that the bargaining of the market will yield a standard of division which can claim moral sanction, or are we forced to say that if the standard is set purely by the market, then the amount of labor given in return should be set likewise by a purely market pace? In other words, honesty under such circumstances is no longer an unambiguously moral conception.

A slightly different aspect of the ambiguity in the conception of honesty is presented by the so-called double standard of business and industry. The workman in industry is expected to perform some service and to receive a wage which represents as nearly as can be determined a fair payment therefor. But in many business transactions the only limit of profit is what you can get. The successful business man is he who can reap the largest profit with the least expenditure of effort. It is, of course, not unknown to the worker that profit is justified on the basis of risk which is a feature of speculation. Nevertheless the obstinate fact remains that in many specific cases huge profits are the result of accident, or of sudden demands for real estate, or of general business trends, and do not imply any useful service on the part of the man who profits. The less expenditure in time and effort which he makes the greater the praise for his shrewdness and business capacity. Certainly it is somewhat awkward to have these two standards side by side, especially since it has been customary to shift a considerable part of risk to the shoulders of employees by reducing the force when times are slack.

Conceptions of justice afford a peculiarly complex example of the mingling of rational and nonrational factors. Justice, together with its allied conceptions of what is fair, or equitable, or reasonable, may plausibly claim to be a conception reached by rational analysis. It seems to disclaim any sociological, or economic, or political warping. The appeal of the Hebrew prophet to do justly, no less than the philosophic conception of the Roman jurisconsult, to live honorably, to injure none, and to give every man his own, or the principles of natural law laid by down by Blackstone, may plausibly claim to be a fixed standard. From the prophetic revival in ancient Egypt unto the present day the scales have been the symbol of justice, and the cry of the 'eloquent peasant,' "Can the scales weigh falsely?" seems to deserve but one answer. Nevertheless to one who traces the history of the concept in law and morals two strands are evident: On the one hand justice seeks equality through its principle of equality before the law; on the other it is tender to vested interests or existing status; on the one hand it magnifies permanence and fixity; on the other it leans toward giving some place for change; on the one it is the ideal of reason; on the other it is the decree of authority. And according as this authority takes the form of precedent or that of the will of the sovereign or of the people, we have the basis for the divided attitude of our poets and the divided conceptions of justice which prevail among our different social classes. Or if we take the mode of defining justice which conceives it as securing and protecting rights, we have still more apparent the influence of class and status. To the property-owning class, rights of property seem fundamental to the established order and good of society. On the other hand, the alleged right of a workman to his job seems a fantastic and fully unjustifiable claim. And a second article in the creed of union labor, "Thou shalt not take a fellow-workman's job," is likewise incomprehensible to an employer, for whom labor is a commodity to be bought and sold in the open market as is any other unit necessary for production. The thinking of the workman naturally starts from what seems to him the most fundamental of all rights—namely, the right to live. How can one live unless he can get a living? And how can he get a living except as he has a job? And to the man who knows but one craft, what job can he claim if not the one which he has learned and practiced?

To the employer, on the other hand, especially if he has built up a business largely through his own organizing ability, the workman has no claims beyond the close of the day or week or month for which he is hired. There may be a place for kindness to the workman who is ill, but there is no requirement of justice.

A head-on collision between conceptions of justice is presented by recent controversy between mineowners and miners. In the Hitchman cases the mineowner required the applicant for a job to sign a contract by which he agrees not to join any labor union while working for the company. On the basis of prohibiting interference with these contracts, the Miners' Union is enjoined by the court from inducing or persuading any of the contracting miners to join the union.

Here, then, is a conflict of fundamental rights which to each party respectively appear absolute. The workman regards the contracts, the signing of which is a necessary condition of getting a job, as depriving him of his natural rights to combine with others in order to improve his conditions. If he is deprived of all help from association, what is left to him? The fact that he has signed a contract does not, in his view, alter the main fact, viz. that he has signed away his one phase of freedom which was most important to him. On the other hand, the mineowner conceives the business as his business and his property. In his view the union is an outside organization which is interfering with the conduct of his business. He does not ask anyone to work for him. He accepts men who apply. He requires a contract which prevents them from joining a union, but he places no coercion upon any man to compel him to sign this contract. The right of property and the right to combine are here in flat contradiction. Which set of rights is favored by courts will evidently depend upon which, in the opinion of the court, are most important to preserve.

In other words, justice is in certain hard cases dependent upon the standard set by the court.

The theory is, of course, that the courts decide cases according to law and not according to bias. No doubt this is true in many types of cases, but in the cases which involve fundamental conceptions, where it is often the decision of the court that will make the law not vice versa, we see the complex influences at work.

The conclusive evidence that the judges are expected to make the law in a given direction is seen in the weight attached in a presidential campaign to the appointing power of the president. When a strong argument for the election of a given candidate for the presidency is found in the probability that he will appoint safe or radical members of the court, no further evidence is needed that the Supreme Court is expected to follow the elections.

The logic which underlies such facts as we have quoted is highly instructive for the procedure in pronouncing judgments in new situations. On the one hand, we attack a situation, bringing to bear previous judgments, which have been more or less consolidated into a rule. But the new situation presents stubborn facts which are not easily brought under the rule. To abide by the rule as a definite standard satisfied one demand; it yields the formula for equality of treatment which is certainly one of the factors in justice. But as Professor Pound has so clearly shown, the opposing demand is equally strong, viz. that we should not be influenced by abstract reasoning in such fashion as to lead us to ignore the actual circumstances of the specific case. "General propositions," says Mr. Justice Holmes, in his famous dissenting opinion in the case of *Lochner v. New York*, "do not determine concrete cases." The logic of the whole process of idea formation and reconstruction could scarcely be better suggested than by the above statement and its implication.

The uncertainty which Sidgwick found in the concept of justice as it functions in the morality of common sense is not surprising when we consider the origins and developments of court rulings. The standard will swing this way or that according as influences of class, or profession, or individual temperament come in to decide which rights ought to prevail.

If, now, it be asked what effect this habitual mode of seeing problems in their concrete and institutional settings has had upon my
attitude toward the great historical problems of philosophy, I think I
should answer somewhat as follows: I had been easily persuaded by
the many arguments by which Plato endeavored to prove that pleasure
could not be considered as the only good. A health of the soul, a life
guided by reason, and fulfilling a function in society, a balanced or
measured life in which thought and feeling, intelligence and pure
pleasures, should all have a place—this seemed and still seems a fair
picture. It appeals to the young; it has a permanent message for each
new generation.

Nevertheless the picture does not include the greater issues of our
day. To interpret these Kant had projected his concepts of duty,
universal law, worth of personality, freedom through autonomy. It
was an interpretation which sought to include the sacredness of the
Hebrew-Christian divine law to which had been added the rational
basis of the Stoic-Roman conception of law of nature. When the authority of this universal law was transferred from external power to
the legislative self, and when such a self was declared to have ultimate
worth, it might appear that Kant summed up the twofold outcome of
the process which culminated in the American and French Revolu-
tions. At least, it presented an approach to a moral problem which
had a fair claim to be set beside the Greek picture.

As I sought to adjust these two rival systems, centering respectively
in the concepts of the good and of right and duty, I thought I found
in my genetic studies a more valuable clue to the problem as to which
concept should be taken as primary and which made subordinate,
than an attempt to solve the problem by analysis. For if we look at the
origins of these ideas we find they are distinct. The idea of good is the
correlate of desire. It finds its birth in a civilization in which values of
various kinds—economic, political, religious, aesthetic—are present;
in which wealth, power, delight of sense, or imagination, at once
stimulate and satisfy. Wherever, through competition and comparison, the various impulses and suggested objects of desire, which
give promise of satisfying some urge or interest, come into a field of
intelligent choice, choice that involves in the last analysis the determination of a new self at the same time with the preference of the object,
we have the category of the good emerging.

The categories of right and duty belong rather to a world of personal
relations. Both right and duty speak the language of a principle emerging with the dawning consciousness of personalities in relationship to

one another, of a social order which speaks of both permanence and change. It is not strange that a culture, such as that of Greece, made the conception of good central. It was not strange that the interpreter of religion, law, and freedom, should make the conceptions of right and duty fundamental.

But the great ethical question of today is not precisely that of Plato, nor that of Kant. It is the question of the ethical principles which are now on trial in our social-economic-political system. It is not a question of imagining a perfect state laid up in heaven, but rather of watching the forces and ideas at work in the societies of America, of Europe, and in the not distant future of Asia. If anything was needed to sharpen our interest, Russia has supplied the lack. Capitalism and communism stand over against each other, while fascism holds itself proudly above both.

Capitalism, as interpreted by Adam Smith, combines three ethical principles. It was based on freedom—freedom to do what one likes; freedom to control one's own property; freedom to buy and sell and exchange as one pleases; freedom to adjust prices by bargaining rather than have them adjusted by guild or government. It was opposed to the medieval doctrine of status. Such a doctrine was welcomed in Europe, but it seemed even more at home in America, for it had no vested rights to fetter it.

In the second place, capitalism made strong appeal to self-interest. The natural right of property, or of the pursuit of happiness, seemed already to put the individual into the center of his world of affairs. Adam Smith held that a man could look after his own affairs better than another. If each man could look forward to profit from his activity he would have the strongest motive to production. The whole motivation of capitalism has it focus in self-interest. In other words, capitalism rests for its second support upon egoism.

In the third place, however, the egoism of capitalism is harmonized with the universal and democratic principle of utilitarianism. If everyone sought his own good, he would contribute in the most effective way toward the happiness of all. Certainly a system which could combine egoism with general welfare, freedom with equality, might claim to be the work of divine wisdom and divine benevolence as Smith declared. But as the system developed in full force, as it employed not merely the new forces of steam and machines, but the cooperation of great numbers of men, the accumulation of credit, the control over transportation, the fixing of prices, it created huge organizations of capital and threatened complete control over the laws of debt and credit, of supply and demand, of price and valuation. On the one hand, the power of wealth with its extraordinary inequality of distribution, on the other, the power of the people expressed through legislation. On the one hand, the masters of our economic life, selected by the competition of the market; on the other hand, the masters of our political life, selected by votes. It is a conflict upon a grand scale. On the one hand, capitalism is immensely profitable; it makes possible a general level of comfort such as had not been known before. On the other hand, is it not probable that to rely upon egoism as the great motive for the world's work is to foster a certain hardness of temper on the part of masters of industry, and to make material wealth the highest value in the scheme of life? I fear that it is. I believe that we have, on the whole, reason to be content with our culture and civilization in proportion as we have found a balance for the naked principle of capitalism. This balance is found, not so much in the attempted legislative control of trusts and monopolies, of huge fortunes, of railroads and banks, as in the policy of public education for all children and young people, which has become increasingly the pride and the serious enterprise of American life. The equality of opportunity, which is afforded in education, stands over against the inequality of property and income, and is in the long run likely to be at least equally significant for liberty of soul.

Capitalism is on trial as to its ability to secure decent living conditions for all members of society. It is worthwhile to have an experiment which seeks to make sure of a minimum of necessities for all its citizens. Brutal as the rule of the Bolshevik has been in its methods of control, it has one principle which it may be well for the world to see tried under fair terms. The principle that all should share in at least the necessities is worth trying. At any rate, it is likely to have a considerable trial. The philosopher may be permitted to watch it, although he may expect in some quarters condemnation for his temerity. When the great world conducts a gigantic experiment, the philosopher may at least watch and learn.

My experience in college teaching, which will complete its fortieth year this coming spring, has been highly fortunate in the contacts which I have made with young men and young women. Very few of them, so far as I have been able to follow their careers, have failed to be useful men and women, and many of them have become distinguished in the world of scholarship and the world of affairs. I differ strongly from the opinion of many writers upon educational subjects who condemn our American system of college education and would confine the work of universities to graduate and professional schools, and who regret the increased tendency on the part of young people to seek a college education.

With the highest respect for men in the professions, they are not, on the whole, the most influential members of the commonwealth. If the college and the university fail to give education to the men of affairs who are the strongest power in American life, they are missing a great opportunity and forsaking a trust. With all due respect to the importance of devoting time and funds to research, through which the causes of natural and social processes can be brought to light, it may be questioned whether any process is more important than the process of education, and whether college and university can afford to omit from their program the education of those who are probably for some generations still to come likely to be the leaders in the commonwealth. It may be that a different college system may give better results than the apparently wasteful methods now in vogue. It seems that our colleges, like our cities, have outgrown the village form of organization and government which gives rise to grossly defective administration. Yet it ought to be possible to maintain for college students the ideals of scholarship and the union of freedom with responsibility which have marked our best institutions. Having taught in an endowed small college for men, in a coeducational state university, and finally for most of my life in an endowed university in which research has been a prominent feature, I believe that the small college will continue to have a place in education; that the state universities in the greater states will probably be forced to divide their numbers in some fashion, especially their undergraduates, or else find in the organization of junior colleges a measure of relief; and that endowed universities may wisely experiment along a variety of types of organization, but will, in my judgment, make a mistake if they disclaim all interest in the education of men of affairs. At present, one of the most serious questions is the somewhat mediocre type of student who presents himself for graduate work. It is a common complaint that numbers of candidates for the master's degree are increasing in quantity without any corresponding improvement in quality, and that even a considerable proportion of those who receive the doctor's degree prove unable or disinclined to carry on scholarly production after their doctor's thesis. In other words, the caliber of those who are candidates for positions as college and university teachers is by no means what is to be desired, if American scholarship is to occupy an appropriate place in the field of world scholarship.

So much concerning the general problem of education I have ven-
tured to put forth as an article of faith to which I have come to subscribe
during my administrative experience as dean and vice-president.

Thus far my more reasoned beliefs. I add certain reflections—perhaps they do not merit the term beliefs—which have a place in my
total attitude. These concern art and religion.

My early life was not particularly adapted to cultivate a taste for
art. A country village provided no art except music, and Amherst in
the eighties, although one of the world's choice places for its natural
beauty, offered likewise meager opportunities in the fine arts other
than literature. Yet in this college period two windows were opened
which have never ceased to afford calm and refreshment—namely,
Greek tragedy and modern literature, especially English and German.
Travel has enabled me to enter into the ideals and constructions of
Western Europe, and I have found much material for instruction and
appreciation in the cultures and products of our American Indians. I
have found in the teaching of aesthetics to successive classes of young
people an opportunity to afford some aid in appreciating both natural
beauty and the forms through which the human spirit has found
expression. I believe strongly that our young people need in their lives
at just the college age the control and poise and sublimation which
are found in the best types of art and literature. I have found interest
and satisfaction in aiding them to see nature and art and to listen to
music with more intelligent appreciation, and to recognize that the
values of life are not exhausted by knowing and doing. I look at the
decorations, patterned from the lotus flower, which beautify many
of our buildings, and wonder whether anything which we are now
thinking or doing or creating will last five thousand years and find
itself as perennially a source of joy. I believe that it helps to give
students a juster view of the worth of different cultures and the
capacities of other peoples, to become familiar with the patterns which
these folk of past ages and wide areas of earth have devised. To follow
sympathetically the expressions of beauty, to be lifted by the sublime,
to confront calamity and catastrophe with tragic depth of comprehension, and to look upon all human efforts and good or ill fortune
with the sympathy and detachment of friendly good humor—all this
belongs to the philosophy of life.

I began this sketch with a reference to the changes in religious
doctrines which I have seen and in a sense felt to be vital. The religious
community of today is beginning to be aware of the gap between the
facts which early religion sought to interpret and the symbolism which

was used in this effort at interpretation. But no new symbolism has
yet proved adequate to embody the profounder experiences which
religion has included. Liberally minded members of the great community are seeking new imagery, but to find an imagery for spiritual
needs and values, comparable in power and tenderness with the
symbolism of the ages, is not easy. Meanwhile, those for whom religion is a spirit rather than a doctrine may at least find themselves
united in the desire to bring about a better order in human society,
and as such may feel, if they cannot know, a unity with whatever
makes for good.

More than most, perhaps, who have aimed to think through these
problems honestly, I have continued a relationship with the Church,
for I have considered the common purpose and the common feeling
more important than the credo. The Church has, on the whole, and
in spite of its failures, borne witness to the existence of other than
material aims. How the future will meet the change in symbolism and
preserve the spirit which has declared the abiding values to be faith,
hope, and love, I am content to leave for coming generations to disclose.[1]

1. Ed. note: JHT follows this piece with a brief bibliography that mentions
1893:01; 1901:01; 1908:01; 1917:02; 1918:01; 1918:02; 1923:01.

2 The Relation of Philosophy to Other Graduate Studies

The theory that certain subjects are indispensable to a liberal education has suffered much in recent times, and there are no signs that it will again receive the unquestioned acceptance of former years. It may, therefore, seem inopportune to advocate the claims of any subject to a place in all university education. For the past few years the need of thorough scholarship in special fields has been rightly emphasized. We became restive under the standards which obtained when classical scholarship showed activity by re-editing German editions and translating their notes, and when controversies in other fields were waged by citing German authorities. We demanded that our instructors should not merely know what others are doing, but do something themselves. We have recognized that to do this men must devote their entire energies to specific subjects until they are masters of some small corner on which they can speak with authority. Specialization has been the great movement of the past twenty years, and we can not question either its necessity or its value.

But in this advance one fact has been left temporarily in the background. A large proportion of these graduate and special students are to do their work, not primarily as investigators in universities, but as teachers in colleges and secondary schools. College authorities have frequently expressed their disappointment with the results of this special study. Men who come armed with the doctorate from the university often prove, it is maintained, not to be teachers at all in the proper sense. They may lack in breadth and cultivation, or in the ability to interest and the patience to instruct. While a Doctor of Philosophy is theoretically a teacher of philosophy, that is, of science in the most inclusive sense, practically he is often neither a teacher

From *Graduate Courses, 1898–99: A Handbook for Graduate Students*, ed.
George Wyllys Benedict (Chicago: U of Chicago P, 1898) xix–xxxi [1898:02].

nor philosophic. Of course, there are certain causes for failure which are palpable. Where there is neither enthusiasm nor method, success cannot be expected. And unless he is a born teacher, the graduate student's interest in the pedagogical aspects of his special study needs constant stimulation—perhaps needs actual experience in teaching for its adequate motivation—so that the teacher may not assume that his college students will be interested at the outset in the special problems which now engage his own research.

But the trouble with the young Doctor of Philosophy is not solely a lack of pedagogical instinct and training. I do not think it entirely fanciful to say that some fail because they have lost from view too entirely that aspect of their work which is suggested by the second word in their title. It seems to me that there is a real basis to the preference which is generally felt for the title *Doctor of Philosophy* as compared with the formerly equal title *Master of Arts*, or even with the nominally equal grade of *Doctor of Science*, and that this basis—aside from the facts of relative advertising power, and of the actual require-ments made for the degrees—consists in this: that the teacher of any subject ought to grasp and present that subject in what we properly call a philosophic manner. I should go farther and say, using the word philosophic in no technical or pedantic sense, that the teacher of men and women should bring to his work a philosophic consideration of life itself, its end and significance, its ideals and values.

It may be that the candidate may disclaim any aspiration to be a guide, philosopher, and friend. He may profess that he claims and desires to do nothing more than teach Greek or chemistry, and that he does not consider himself responsible for anything else. It is none the less true that the college looks and ought to look primarily to the applicant's fitness to be a teacher in the larger and fuller sense.

It is, moreover, for the teacher's own advantage that this larger ideal be maintained. The insignificant commercial value placed by the community upon the services of the teaching profession in comparison with that placed upon the services of the doctor or lawyer, not to speak in the same breath of the managers of business enterprises, must tend to cheapen the profession in the public eye, unless there are counteracting influences. Further than this, if a profession is largely depreciated in public opinion, the most vigorous minds will be natu-rally attracted elsewhere, and the profession will suffer accordingly. Discussions last summer showed how prone the man of affairs is to think that the college president or professor, whom he hires as cheaply as he would a clerk for his office, should of course presume to have no opinions of his own unless authorized by his employer, and it was the protests of men who showed that they were more than mere specialists, and of others in all occupations who stood with them for the larger function of the teacher, which prevented the threatened degradation of the teacher's work.

In Germany the teaching profession has certain external supports in maintaining its dignity and power which are lacking here. There the mere title of *Herr Professor Doktor* gives social station and commands respect even in political affairs. The expert, the specialist, is as such held in honor. In this land of equality a professor is regarded with some degree of suspicion or condescension, the theorist is sneered at, and the specialist has no sanctity attaching to his person. I do not mean to imply that the work of the American teacher is less attractive, but I do assert that in this country there are few or none of the external attractions which obtain in Germany for the professor *an sich*. If the American teacher is to retain self-respect, he must find it in the intrinsic value of his work. If he would have the compensating satisfaction of influence, he must seek it, not as doctor, but as man. And while the doctor and professor count less among us than elsewhere, I believe the man counts more. The militarism and centralization which are so dominant in church and state in the land of the kaiser are not so favorable for the teacher's personal influence as the democratic condition where public institutions, though less well administered, are yet constantly educating the people and remain in touch with them; where the value and standards of life are not absolutely fixed in advance for the young by all the traditions of a continuous past; and where, amid all the crudity, the materialism, and sometimes even the vulgarity, there is yet life, pulsing with energy and responsive to the quickening touch of the real man or woman.

It is the opportunity to stir and in some degree to shape this life which gives greatest value to the teacher's work, and any curtailment of capacity for this work must inevitably react disastrously upon the profession. You are now planning to teach language or history or science. I feel confident that you will come to place the emphasis rather on teaching *men* and *women*. For you know perfectly well, though you may ignore it, that most of your students will not remember the language or the science or the history, and if you have done nothing more for them, if you have been nothing to them but a textbook and an examiner, you will inevitably become as obsolete as your lectures, and sink into oblivion with your subject, where not even the consciousness of having produced a thesis or a book will be a wholly adequate compensation.

Four-fifths or nine-tenths of college students are in training, not for a life of investigation, but for a life of activity in other lines. And while it goes without saying that training for efficient work of any kind is to be secured only by thoroughness and scholarship in the various subjects studied, it is none the less certain that the man behind the desk ought always to be larger than his subject, that he should know how to invest his theme with all the interest which attaches to it from its relations to other fields, and that he should be keenly alive to that supreme interest which directly or indirectly may belong to every department, to wit, the significance of the special problem for the great whole of science, and the value of this whole of science in the yet larger whole of humanity's weal and progress.

It is far enough from my purpose to claim that these great aims of philosophic, scholastic breadth of culture and personal power will be attained by the mere attendance upon a course of study in any subject. I attempt the more modest task of showing that philosophic study is fitted to perform an important function in the attainment of all these ends.

And first as to the bearing of philosophy on the comprehension of the special field of investigation. It may be our most direct course to take an apparently devious route and look first of all at the nature and motive of all scientific study. Science is knowledge; but what is it to know? Knowing has been variously defined as apprehending causes, discovering laws, classifying and systematizing facts, but in all these processes it will be found that we are relating, we are viewing a part in the light of some larger whole which we call a law or a historic unity. If you will pardon a more technical expression, knowing is a discovery of some general or universal and an interpretation of the particular in terms of the universal thus discovered. It must, of course, be understood that by universal is not meant an absolute, fixed whole, but the constantly growing background of relations and law by which the mind illumines each new fact or event, and which is in turn modified and enlarged by its application to the inexhaustible richness of the material interpreted. This is the essence of all knowledge, and there are two general ways in which this process is employed, giving rise to two general groups of sciences, with their respective methods. We may view the particular fact in the light of an abstract law, as in physics or economics; or we may view the fact as constituting part of a concrete whole, and seek its relations to past and future, as in history. But in either case, whether we seek laws of light, laws of production, or laws of syntax, or whether, on the other hand, we trace the history of a planet, of a nation, or of a literature, we are always relating; and relating means discovering the identity in variety, the unity in difference.

If, further, we ask for the motive for science and are not satisfied by the wise word 'curiosity,' or 'wonder,' I suppose we shall have to find our ultimate answer in the statement that the mind seeks to know, to interpret, because the mind itself is just such a unity in variety as it would find in its world of science, and only as it finds unity in variety can it come to birth and develop. Intelligence grows by organizing what it finds, and it organizes that it may grow.

If all this is very trite, it is nevertheless true that the significance of these principles as to the nature and motive of study is often lost sight of in our scientific work, and especially when we turn from our special research to the work of the teacher. For the growth of science has brought with it inevitably the division and subdivision of the territory to be possessed, and in the execution of the command which has gone forth to divide and conquer it not infrequently happens that the victorious companies seem to forget what purpose sent them forth, or in whose name and interest they are taking possession. In other words, division of labor means that each department considers some one aspect of reality. Its work is, therefore, necessarily abstract. And this has important consequences both for the science itself and for the teacher's problem of awakening interest in the science.

For the science itself this abstractness exhibits itself in the conceptions which it postulates as fundamental units to be used in the explanation of all the processes with which it deals. Thus physical science in general postulates a mechanical theory of energy and takes for its task to express all natural processes in terms of energy. Economics postulates desire for wealth, and formulates the laws of human action in terms of this unit of value. The biological and other sciences which employ the great principle of evolution all postulate that the later is to be explained by the earlier, the more complex by the more simple. Now all these postulates are valuable for the sciences which employ them, but the student who knows merely his own special field is in danger of supposing these postulates are not merely useful or possibly indispensable points of view for the study of *certain aspects* of experience, but are axioms of absolute validity for the interpretation of the world.

It often strikes the student as a reversal of the true relation, when he is told that all sciences except philosophy are in some sense abstract, but it is nonetheless true, because they all by necessity deal with *parts* of reality. The crude materialism sometimes professed by those who deal with the mechanical aspects of the universe, the sentimentality sometimes shown by those who consider only its aesthetic aspects, the indifferent aloofness sometimes laid to the charge of those concerned with the commercial aspect of human relations, are all the natural results of taking the part for the whole, the abstract for the concrete. Matter apart from mind, literature and art apart from life, supply and demand apart from sympathy and justice, are all abstractions, and need continual reference to the whole from which they are separated.

Such a narrowness as this is not merely injurious to one's *Weltanschauung*, it is most unfortunate for the development of the special science. We have but to mention Riemann and Helmholtz, Darwin and Huxley, Comte and Mill, to note how often the men who have been most stimulating in the investigation of special sciences have been those who have stood enough outside their science to realize the abstract and hypothetical nature of its fundamental postulates, and to seek to illumine it afresh by more searching criticism and a more central point of view.

I am well aware that the modern theory of specialization is not so much a division of territory as a division of problems, and that any problem may take the student through a wide range of pursuit—that to study the nerve cell may call for anatomy and physiology and chemistry and physics and psychology—but this, it seems to me, calls all the more for a philosophic standpoint and method. The botanist of today might conceivably quote to the philosopher the lines of Tennyson, and say

> I study not the plant alone,
> But the mystery of the universe;
> For if I could know yon little flower
> Root and all, and all in all,
> I should know what God and man is.

But the philosopher can reply in turn, "True, indeed; but the converse is just as true. You will know the little flower, root and all, and all in all—when? When you know what God and man is, and not until then." No aspect of reality will be completely known until it is interpreted in relation to the whole.

I have taken the above illustrations chiefly from the natural sciences, but it would be easy to show that literature, language, and history suffer as severely from the abstractness of their standpoint, unless the student is conscious of this abstractness. How easy it is for literary criticism, for example, to become gush of sentimentality because beauty and imagination are used as ultimate categories, without psychological analysis and without reference to that development of human life and thought which has sought expression in artistic form. How history has suffered at the hands of those who have made it the annals of kings and the record of battles!

Professor Stephens, of Cornell, in a charming informal talk on the aim of the modern historian, reiterated the statement that it is the aim of the scientific writer of history, not to be interesting, but to tell the truth. This doctrine was doubtless in point for the audience which he was addressing, but I am confident that Professor Stephens is too good a historian not to be fully aware that no historian tells the whole truth, and that a recital of facts is anything but history. He must tell the truth, but what truth shall he tell? The facts of a single day, if all recorded, would occupy more volumes than have ever yet been written. The historian's special task is quite as truly in the selection of his material and the perspective of his survey as in the verification of facts. And the great historian is surely he who apprehends most profoundly the great interests of humanity, and selects what is of greatest import for human progress, who has the keenest insight into the forces of character, and portrays institutions, laws, politics, in the light of human nature as a whole.

I repeat, then, that every science must inevitably suffer as a science, unless its abstractness is recognized, its postulates criticized, and its one-sidedness corrected by frequent consideration of its relation to intelligence as a whole.

If it is true that any science suffers in its own development from isolation, it is even more true that every department of study, when taught in college or secondary school, will suffer, unless every effort is made to illumine it by making it a part in the whole of human interest. This, it seems to me, is the root of the difficulty in the early teaching of many graduate students. They are themselves intensely interested in some very special problem. Their own horizon has been advanced, their own interest has gone with it so far that this problem seems vital. On it may depend a whole group of other problems which perhaps are now most under discussion in the journals and reviews. But the average young man (or even young woman) is not exclusively absorbed in knowledge per se. He may at first be quite careless as to the significance of the latest theories about the subjunctive. He may be willing to remain in ignorance as to whether a given fossil is eocene or miocene. He does not feel it to be of the greatest importance to know whether Kant was "roused from his dogmatic slumber" by Hume in 1763, or 1769, or possibly not until 1773. Perhaps it is just as well, on the whole, that he does not, and it will be not be safe to dub him stupid on that account. At any rate, if we wish to gain his attention, we must start with *his* interest, and not with our own, and this will involve that the subject should be presented in something of the order in which every science has struck root and grown, first the more general, then the more special.

It would be as natural to expect a tree to grow by collecting leaves or branches, as for the mind to develop by the pursuit of facts not kept in vital relation to the unity of conscious intelligence. Science has been a constantly branching trunk. We cannot expect the individual student to begin at the ends and grow in.

Moreover, the graduate student is apt to forget that he is himself, so to speak, an abnormal product of civilization. He is interested in knowledge for its own sake. He forgets that this is not universal in the race. Or at least he assumes that every college student certainly should find this a sufficient spring to toil, and a sufficient joy in labor. Taking college students as we find them, however, we must confess that love of knowledge per se is not the all-absorbing passion of their lives. It is such for the scientist, because he has staked all his weal or woe on success in this field. His scientific self is his deepest, most real self. Self-assertion, self-development, life itself, for him consequently takes the form of scientific interest. But the self of the average undergraduate is not so. He is to find his true self in commerce or politics, as preacher or reformer, and where his treasure is there will his heart be also. Now, whether he is to be interested in the problems which are so dear to the heart of the scientific man will depend largely on the mode of presentation. If they are presented in an isolated way, it will require extraordinary personal enthusiasm to stir any interest at all. But if the teacher has constantly in mind the actual self of his student, and makes that his point of departure; if, further, he grasps his subject in all its relations to the activities of thought and of life, and presents it at the outset with constant regard to these relations, he is far more likely to gain a hearing. Then he may proceed to widen his hearers' horizon until it stretch off indefinitely with increasing interest, perhaps to reach his own.

Nor is it, as some may think, derogatory to the dignity of a science that it should rest to some degree on foreign support. It is difficult to suppose that the day will ever dawn when the highest interest of any science will not properly lie in the light it sheds on the universe as a whole. But the universe of knowledge will always center in the mind of man and find its worth estimated in the aspirations and appreciations of human activities and human feeling. The sooner that this is recognized in our educational plans, the better it will be, both for the particular sciences and for the work of education as a whole.

It may seem that I have thus far sedulously and with considerable success avoided the topic which was announced as the subject of the paper. But I have really had it constantly in mind. The thesis has been maintained that the specialization in science needs to be supplemented from the standpoint of science as a whole; that this is necessary for the sciences themselves that the abstractness of their concepts and postulates may not be lost sight of, and necessary especially for the college teacher that he may supply to the special all possible significance and interest. Philosophy aims to do just this work of criticism and relation. Philosophy has no disposition to aspire to construct a universe, to create a moral life, to prescribe canons to art. It finds more than enough in the task of understanding the world as it is, of interpreting the actual, moral, and artistic activities. In this it is at one with all science. But whereas science, in the ordinary usage of the term, is not one, but many, philosophy aims above all never to lose from sight the unity of knowledge and the unity of life. For the abstractness of the special sciences consists not merely in their division of the field, but even more in the fact that they are obliged to leave out of account the relation of all knowledge to the mind which knows, and of all principle of explanation to the intelligence which gave them birth. To the scientist, space and time, law, energy, and cause are ultimate and objective. But the philosopher cannot rest there. He sees that these are ultimately just the mind's way of explaining. The student of law or history or literature may assume personality, right, or beauty as ultimate; the philosopher will see that these, too, are but concepts for interpreting forms of inner experience, and will push back his analysis to discover these experiences themselves. Harnack has said that we study history to free ourselves from the past. I conceive that we are not really educated men unless we so study as to free ourselves from the dogmatism of any science which does not criticize its own fundamental assumptions, or from the barrenness of an art or literary criticism which treats any form as ultimate, and does not seek its principles in the inexhaustible interests of the human spirit.

Philosophy, then, aims first of all to overcome the abstractness of the special sciences by showing their relation to the mind itself. Such in part is the work of psychology, of logic, of ethics, of aesthetics, and, finally, of metaphysics. It further aims to relate science, literature, politics, as varied forms of human activity, to human thought and progress as a whole, and thus to correlate all these expressions of man's advancing life. This forms in part the task of the history of thought.

The question may now be asked, What special work could be recommended to the candidate for the doctor's degree? Psychology is so generally recognized today that it is perhaps scarcely necessary to speak of its importance. Its study should properly come, as is the case in most institutions, as a part of the undergraduate work. Coming now to graduate study, two general lines of work seem indicated. Students of natural science would find most help in a study of the methods and conceptions involved in their own problems. Such a course might be in part historical and in part critical, showing the development of scientific thought and the relation of the scientific view of the world to other aspects. The student of literature or history would find his needs better met by a study of the history of thought, supplemented in the one case by aesthetics and in the other by political ethics. Such courses would naturally be less technical than courses designed exclusively for philosophical specialists; but this would perhaps be for the good of the instructor. Philosophy may be pursued as one-sidedly and technically as any other subject, and if it would be true to its function, it must ever maintain the most intimate relations with the sciences that have gone out from it.

Nor would I be understood as implying that philosophy is taught only by its professors. The masters in all the sciences bring to their work a philosophic spirit, but the average student should find much aid and suggestion from the work of those who by necessity are forced to give their whole attention to the lines of work described. It ought at any rate to aid in gaining something of a philosophic attitude toward the problems of a special field.

I have left until the last the question as to the value of philosophy for the conduct of life, and for the teacher's personal power. I must assume that every teacher has something of this, however vaguely, in his plan. Every investigator may well ponder the words of a man who was not merely a philosopher, but was among the most rigid and profound investigators, who is known not merely as the expounder of the categorical imperative, but as the promulgator of the nebular hypothesis, to whose name and genius every scientific man in Germany does homage.

"I am myself," wrote Kant,

> by bent and inclination an investigator. I feel his whole thirst for knowledge, and the eager anxiety to push farther, or, again, the satisfaction which waits on every step in advance. There was a time when I believed that this constituted the true honor of man. I despised the ignorant common herd. Rousseau set me right. This illusory pre-eminence vanishes. I learn to honor men, and should find myself much less useful than the common laborers if I did not believe that my work could give worth to all others, by establishing the rights of man.

The teacher who would fill the place of a human being as well as that of a lecturer must certainly aim to "see life steadily and see it whole." If he would feel that he, too, is in some measure a force in human progress, a helper toward the "larger life that is to be," he must certainly look thoughtfully and broadly upon the end and meaning of human life. He must weigh its current values, and question its present standards. His may not be the swift blood which stirs the reformer, or the eloquence which lifts the multitude. But the world needs candor and sanity as well as conviction and fervor, light as truly as heat; and the teachers of the country, though they may not be able to solve the deeper problems of life and society, cannot be called liberally educated unless they can show their students and the public an example of a candid and sympathetic attitude toward these problems. They may show that the broadening of vision does not necessarily mean the loss of enthusiasm. They may show that education stands neither for a radicalism that would lose the ideals, the standards, the goods of the past, nor for a dead conservatism that would remain in unchangeable allegiance to them; neither for a zeal that outruns judgment and so brings on reaction, nor for a cold-blooded aloofness which has no sympathy with the struggling humanity outside the schools. If they can do this, they will contribute their especial part in human progress. They will retain self-respect and the respect of those whose respect is worth having, and no teacher ought to be satisfied without some measure of such influence. For the attainment of such a standpoint philosophy ought to contribute much. Ever since the declaration of Socrates that a life without examination is not a life worthy to be led by man, ethical science has sought to bring its disciples to a consideration of life's ultimate standards and values, and in this is found the fitness of the motto of the Phi Beta Kappa Society: "Philosophy the guide of life." In proportion as philosophy can do this, it may be recommended to the consideration of all students and teacher, whatever the special field in which their task may lie.

3 Contributions to *Baldwin's Dictionary*

A. SCHOOLS OF GREECE: Ger. *Philosophenschulen der Griechen*; Fr. *écoles philosophiques de la Grèce* Ital. *scuole filosofiche dei Greci.*

(1) In a looser sense, the various groups of Greek thinkers, allied by race, locality, or opinion, e.g., Ionics, Sceptics.

(2) In a stricter sense, the more or less definitely organized groups which had personal relationship as a more or less fundamental element, and carried on joint labors under a recognized head or 'scholarch.' The ideas of some founder, such as Plato or Epicurus, were thus defended and elaborated by successive generations of the school.

I. The most important schools in the narrower sense may be grouped under three periods, Pre-Socratic, Socratic, and Post-Socratic. To the first belong (1) the Milesians, located at Miletus, comprising Thales, Anaximander, and Anaximenes, of the 6th century B.C. Heraclitus of Ephesus (about 536–470 B.C.) is often grouped with them under the general term Ionic school. (2) The Pythagoreans, of Crotona in Italy, founded by Pythagoras of Samos (born about 580 B.C.), and having Philolaus of the next century as the most prominent philosopher. (3) The Eleatics, of Elea in Italy, together with Xenophanes (of Colophon, born about 570 B.C.; his connection with Elea is doubtful), Parmenides (who wrote about 470 B.C.), and Zeno (about 490–430 B.C.); Melissus of Samos shared Eleatic views. (4) The Atomists, of Abdera in Thrace, of which Leucippus and Democritus (about 460–360 B.C.) are the leading members, although Protagoras (about 460–410 B.C.) went out from this city also. All the above, as well as Anaxagoras of Clazomenae (about 500–430 B.C.), who founded a school at Lampsacus, were Ionians. For their theories see PRE-SOCRATIC PHILOSOPHY [below]. In the second half of the 5th century B.C. the schools or

From *Dictionary of Philosophy and Psychology*, ed. James Mark Baldwin, vol. 2 (New York: Macmillan, 1902) 495–498, 334–337, 549–552 [1902:02].

philosophical societies, with the exception of the Pythagoreans and
the school of Abdera, gave place to the freer and more public discussion which characterized the teaching of the SOPHISTS (q.v.) and of
Socrates.

II. The second period is that of Socrates (469–399 B.C.) and the
Socratic schools. Socrates himself conducted his discussions in so
public a manner that he could hardly be said to have a school. But his
disciples founded several, each claiming to represent the teaching of
the master. For Plato and his school, the Academy, as well as Socrates,
see SOCRATIC PHILOSOPHY [below], and below.

The other Socratic schools were: (1) the school of Megara (the
Megarians or Eristics), founded by Euclid, which applied the Eleatic
metaphysics to the Socratic principles, maintaining the good to be the
only being, and asserting that the actual and the possible are one.
Eubulides, Alexinus, Diodorus Cronus, and Stilpo were members of
the school, which was famous for its skill in 'eristic' or polemic, with
a use of catch-questions and logical subtleties. Little is known of (2)
the Elean-Eretrian school founded by Phaedo of Elis, which lasted but
a short time, and had Menedemus as another member. (3) The Cynic
school (named from the gymnasium Cynosarges, in which it was
conducted) was founded by Antisthenes. Starting from the principle
that virtue is the only good, the school argued that virtue must therefore make man independent of fate and fortune. It must then consist
in freedom from wants—in living in a 'state of nature.' Diogenes is
the famous representative of this. (4) The Cyrenaic school, founded
by Aristippus of Cyrene, maintained that the good is to be found in
pleasure. The Socratic element manifests itself in the doctrine that the
completest pleasure can be gained only by intelligent insight and
appraisal. This led to a preference of mental over bodily pleasure by
later members of the school (Anniceris). Hegesias drew a pessimistic
conclusion. The Epicureans were the heirs of the Cyrenaic teaching.
See HEDONISM.

III. In the third period are included the most celebrated schools: (1)
The *Academy* (from a grove and gymnasium named from the hero
Academos), at first, as (a) the 'Older Academy,' developed Plato's
teaching, especially on the ethical side, and combined with it the
Pythagorean number theory; then, as (b) the Middle Academy, under
Arcesilaus (about 315–241 B.C.) and Carneades (214–129 B.C.), was an
exponent of SCEPTICISM (q.v.); and finally, in (c) the New Academy,
under Philo of Larissa (about 100 B.C.) and Antiochus, turned to
dogmatism and eclecticism. Plato's doctrines were later studied and

developed in the form know as NEO-PLATONISM (q.v.) at Alexandria by Ammonius (A.D. 175–250) and Plotinus (A.D. 204–269), and also in a Syrian school founded by Iamblicus (died about A.D. 330). Neo-Platonism at Athens was represented by Plutarch (died about A.D. 120) and Proclus (A.D. 411–485). Damascius was head of the Academy when it was closed by the Emperor Justinian in A.D. 529.

(2) The *Peripatetic* school, founded by Aristotle (384–322 B.C.) was located in the Lyceum, a gymnasium sacred to Lycaean Apollo (Lycaeus, a mountain in Arcadia). The school was named from the shady walks (περίπατοι) in which Aristotle talked with his disciples. Theophrastus (370–287 B.C.) and Strato, his successor, as head of the school, maintained and developed Aristotle's theories, but the school was especially active in literary, historical, and scientific studies. In ethics the school maintained a less extreme view than either the Stoics or Epicureans, holding that external goods are necessary for the attainment of complete well-being, although, on the other hand, virtue is worthy to be sought for its own sake, and other goods without virtue are valueless.

(3) The *Stoic* school, founded at Athens by Zeno of Cyprus (about 340–265 B.C.), was so named from the porch (Στοὰ Ποικίλη) where Zeno taught. Of Zeno's successors, Cleanthes is known as the author of a hymn to Zeus, and Chrysippus (died 206 B.C.) for his extraordinary productiveness, and for the ability with which he systematized and defended the Stoic principles. The Stoic principles proved especially congenial to Roman thinkers, to whom they were presented especially by Panaetius (cir. 180–111 B.C.), with more or less of an eclectic adoption of ideas from other schools. Seneca (A.D. 4–65), Epictetus (cir. A.D. 100), and Marcus Aurelius Antoninus (emperor A.D. 161–180) represent a Stoicism modified by religion. The doctrines of the school will be treated below in connection with those of the Epicureans.

(4) The *Epicurean* school was founded by Epicurus (341–270 B.C.) and conducted in the garden of the master. Many works of Philodemus, a contemporary of Cicero, were found at Herculaneum, but the best known literary representative of the school is the Roman poet Lucretius (98–54 B.C.). The school was noted for the personal friendships which it fostered, and for the strictness with which it adhered to the founder's doctrines. It continued as late as the 4th century, and its principles were taken up and reproduced for the modern world by Gassendi (1592–1655).

The Socratic philosophy had (a) grown out of an attempt to interpret the life of Greek culture at its height. (b) It was given a dualistic development by Plato under the influence of the cult of Dionysus. It was partially restored to the philosophy of 'this world' by Aristotle, but the Platonic influence remained manifest in the very conceptions through which reality was conceived. (c) In this development the theoretical interest was always present, and in Aristotle assumed the commanding position. The Stoic and Epicurean schools represented a different attitude in each of these three respects. (i) Greek civic life had disintegrated. The rich artistic and political activity of the citizen had given place to the quest for a measure of happiness for the individual. (ii) The Stoic harked back to the more primitive animistic view of the world, especially in the form in which this was presented by Heraclitus (see PRE-SOCRATIC PHILOSOPHY [below]), and the Epicureans took up a negative attitude towards all religious conceptions. (iii) The dominant aim in both Stoic and Epicurean schools was practical. Theoretical interests were kept entirely subordinate.

(a) The common problem of both schools was, How can the individual lead a happy life? The Greek demand for intelligence, especially as formulated in the philosophy of Socrates, led both schools to give a common formal answer to their problem in their ideal of the sage— the wise man who knows the true good. Further, the political uncertainties, and the change from an attitude of boundless hope and thirst for achievement to an attitude of accepting certain limitations as inevitable, found expression in both systems in certain qualities of the ideal sage. He must above all be independent of the world's fortunes. This meant that he must be master of his own emotional life, for it is only through the feelings that we are at the mercy of events. Repose, imperturbability, apathy are the conditions most prized. But in defining how this shall be attained, the ways part. The Epicureans, following the Cyrenaics, seek this peace by a choice of the calmer pleasures, especially those of friendship and culture, by avoiding political or other responsibilities, and by freeing the mind from superstitious fears of the gods and the future. Far from teaching a coarse sensualism, Epicurus maintained that a wise man would not allow himself to become the slave of violent desires or passions; he will remain master of himself. The Stoics, on the other hand, maintained that the sage shows his wisdom, not in distinguishing *between* pleasures—as if feeling were after all the only good—but in maintaining the supremacy of reason as *against* feeling. The controlling or ruling faculty is the most important part of man. To obey reason is to 'follow nature'; to keep reason ever supreme is the chief excellence or virtue, and virtue is the only good; to overcome the world means to be completely free from passions or emotions. This is 'apathy.'

(b) The Stoic and Epicurean views of nature stood in close connection with their ethical ideas. Epicurus found in the atomic theory of Democritus a view of the cosmos which offered a purely mechanical theory, and was hence adapted to banish superstitious dread of the unseen. The only important deviation from the earliest atomism was the assumption that to form the first complexes, the atoms deviated voluntarily from a straight line of fall. 'Voluntarily' here means 'without cause,' and the same conception of uncaused action was applied by Epicurus to the choice of the will (see FREEDOM). The Stoics, on the other hand, developed the primitive animistic theory of the cosmos in such a way as to make their conception capable of being characterized at once as pantheism and as materialism. This was effected through the conception of the PNEUMA (q.v., see also PSYCHE), which was on the one hand the all-pervading and animating spirit or life of the universe, and on the other was still a material substance, a finer air or fiery breath. In this pneuma each individual shares. Accordingly, to follow nature means not merely to follow human nature's highest principle of reason, but to conform to the all-pervading and controlling principle of the world, to the divine law or LOGOS (q.v.) which characterizes the pneuma in this its rational aspect.

Resignation to destiny, voluntary conformity to the ongoing of the world, was thus given a rational motive, and with many took on the distinctly religious aspect of submission to the divine ordering of events. The early emphasis upon the control over the individual by some system or authority had retreated into the background in the presence of the search for a principle which should be first good and therefore binding. In the Stoic system this emphasis is restored in the conception of 'duty.' Further, this conception of participation in a common world-reason favored the conception of man as a social being and a citizen of a world-state—a philosophic ideal which Cicero and later Roman thinkers applied to the Roman Empire. The law of this universal state is the 'law of nature,' i.e., of the universal reason. The Epicureans consistently held an individualistic view of the state, regarding it as formed by a 'compact' to supply human wants. Finally, in defending their view of the world as controlled by reason, the Stoics developed the leading arguments of TELEOLOGY (q.v.), while the Epicureans refused to admit their validity.

(c) As respects the problems of logic and epistemology, the Stoics

and Epicureans were forced to assert some criterion as against the
SCEPTICS (q.v.). Both schools assume that all knowledge comes from
sense perceptions. The Epicureans made the clearness or vividness of
these the test. The Stoics found a further basis for the value of certain
general conceptions in their metaphysical theory that the various human spirits or pneumata are emanations from the one world-pneuma.
Ideas common to all men—*communes notiones*—may be presumed to
be true. This theory as transformed into the doctrine of 'innate ideas'
long remained influential. The Stoics also asserted the distinction
between ideation and JUDGMENT (q.v.), and recognized in this latter a
volitional element. [JHT added a brief bibliography here.]

B. PRE-SOCRATIC PHILOSOPHY: Ger: *vorsokratische Philosophie*; Fr.
philosophie présocratique; Ital. *filosofia presocratica*.
Philosophy in Greece prior to Socrates.

This may be properly considered under one topic, because it was
mainly devoted to one problem, the study of nature. The Sophists
form a transition to the Socratic philosophy. The earlier thinkers of
the period (see under SCHOOLS OF GREECE [above] for the names of
the individual philosophers) are frequently called the Ionics; but as
practically all Greek philosophy until the time of Aristotle was the
work of the Ionians (either in Asia or in Italy or at Athens), the term
is liable to mislead. Two subperiods may be distinguished in the period
before the Sophists. The earlier thinkers stand in closer relation to
previous religious or mythical views, and seek to substitute an intelligible hypothesis, based on real things or events, for the myths of the
poets. In doing this they usually fix upon some one conception of
seemingly fundamental importance and maintain it in a one-sided
manner. The later thinkers of the period are freer from the mythical
conceptions, and aim to adjust or construe the valuable elements in
the earlier views. A distinction in the religious views which were
influential at successive periods may also be noted. The earlier thinkers
were most in touch with the Olympian religion, which concerned
chiefly the deities of the sky, earth, and ocean. The worship of chthonic
deities, Dionysus, Demeter, etc., among the Orphic sect and in the
Eleusinian mysteries, on the other hand, emphasized the immortality
of the soul and its need of purification, this directing the thought
within, and introducing a dualism which had important ethical and
metaphysical consequences. This religion influenced especially the
Pythagoreans and Plato.

The myths which described the generation of the gods and the origination of worlds implied at least a view of a single, connected process, and of an inclusion of all in the universe within that process. The detached phenomena of sea or sky, or of successive days and seasons, were given unity and relation in such beings as Uranus (heaven) and Gaia (earth), or Dionysus. The work of the first philosophers was to substitute for these personifications actual concrete substances. They found ready to hand the conception that the world is one. They asked, "From what did it come? What is the primal substance?"—calling their writings Περὶ Φύσεως (concerning the origin, or primal substance, or essential nature of things). These three connotations were probably all more or less involved in the term, though not as strictly distinguished until later.

The first answers selected, at least, actual substances, when Thales said "water," and Anaximenes "air"; Anaximander's "boundless" or "infinite" suggests the chaos of the myths. All three of these Milesians regarded the world naively as animate, and its processes of change as spontaneous movements, hence they were called Hylozoists (regarding matter as animate).

Another religious and social conception found conspicuous recognition in the thought of the Ephesian Heraclitus (about 470 B.C.). Like the Milesians, he names a primal substance, fire, of which all things are transformations; but to say that fire is the ultimate 'nature' of things and of the world is to emphasize a process, a flux, with a 'way downward' in which the change is from fire into things, and a 'way upward' in which things are becoming fire. The most fruitful conception in this thought was, as intimated, the principle of rational law (λόγος) or justice (δίκη), which controls this process and regulates the allotted (εἱμαρμένη) changes. The decree of Zeus, the destiny (μοῖρα) of the gods, the social and religious law of justice, have become the central conception for viewing a physical process, with implications which cling to the terms even in modern science. This law of changes gave a union of the 'one' and the 'many'—an antithesis which continually challenged the attention of the Greeks.

The characteristic of the Eleatics was a one-sided emphasis upon the first factor of the antithesis, the 'One.' Xenophanes, the religious satirist, criticized anthropomorphic conceptions of gods as born like mortals, and said that the One was God. Parmenides made this conception of oneness and permanence of determining and exclusive importance. What *is* must always have been and must always be: Change is impossible, for this would imply that something could arise out of nothing, or pass into nothing, and both suppositions are absurd.

This was not an abstractly logical principle, nor did it refer in the mind of Parmenides to the conservation of energy. 'What is' meant 'what occupies space.' The principle would then mean nearly the indestructibility of matter, except that matter had not yet been so abstractly conceived.

The earlier teaching of the Pythagoreans was religious and ethical rather than speculative. Like the Orphic religious societies, they emphasized the immortality of the soul (see PSYCHE) and the necessity of purifying it, thus preparing the way for a later, more complete separation between soul and body, and between the true being of the 'other world' and present world of change. See SOCRATIC PHILOSOPHY [below], NEO-PYTHAGOREANISM, and NEO-PLATONISM. The astronomical and musical studies of the school reinforced the general demand for 'measure' or 'limit,' so fundamental in all Greek thought, and a later member of the school, Philolaus, regarded measure and number as the most important aspect of things. Taking the speculative position that wholes are made up of simple parts, and regarding the units reached by numerical analysis as the proper units, he held that things are made up of numbers (i.e., not of abstract numbers, but of simple units, as a line is made up of points). The fact that mathematical analysis, as in the successive bisection of a line, never gives an absolute unit, made possible the celebrated criticisms of Zeno, the Eleatic, upon pluralistic theories. These at once seem to explain the real as made up of simple units, and yet are unable to provide the units. If a line is made up of points, we ought to be able to say how many. But the fact that we can never reach an end of our bisecting proves that we cannot assign any number. Similar criticisms were applied to pluralistic views of time as made up of instants, of which 'Achilles and the Tortoise' is the most famous.

The one versus the many—permanence versus change—formed the problem of the thinkers mentioned thus far, and usually with a one-sided insistence on one term of the antithesis. Empedocles of Sicily (about 490–430 B.C.), Anaxagoras of Klazomene (about 500–428 B.C.), and the Atomists combined these two terms in their mediating theories. All maintain the permanence of certain elements, and attribute the apparent arising and disappearing of things to re-arrangements of these elements. Empedocles named four 'roots' of things—earth, air, fire, and water (selected, perhaps, partly on mythological grounds). Anaxagoras hit upon the standard of modern chemistry, and treated as elements substances which resisted analysis into heterogeneous materials. Later writers termed them ὁμοιομερῆ (homogeneous particles). The Atomists conceived their permanent elements more abstractly as ATOMS (q.v.), which they regarded as differing only in shape and arrangement—quantitative as contrasted with qualitative difference. The atoms were therefore each like the One of Parmenides, in that they were conceived as filling space, but, in addition to the atoms, the school postulated also the 'existence' of the void, of 'what is not.' To explain the rearrangements of elements, which cause changes in things, Empedocles and Anaxagoras introduced auxiliary elements which did the work of forces, although not considered as purely abstract forces. These were, for Empedocles, love and strife. The survival of the combinations produced was decided in his view by natural selection, while his conception of the cosmical process is quite similar to modern evolutionary theories in general outline. The combining and disposing element for Anaxagoras was the NOUS (q.v.), which ordered things intelligently, although it was not conceived as mind (distinct from matter) in a modern sense. Leucippus did not introduce another element, but supposed the atoms to be always in motion, and the various worlds to be the complex structures formed by atoms impinging upon each other. A mechanical theory of natural processes thus reached a clear formulation, and was developed in the hands of Democritus (who properly belongs to a later period) to a comprehensive system of MATERIALISM (q.v.).

For views of the soul in these earlier thinkers see PSYCHE. The problem of knowledge was not made the direct object of inquiry, and yet the discrepancy between theoretical conceptions and common opinion forced several thinkers to note the distinction between reflection and sense perception. The usual solution was to charge the senses with deception. Heraclitus based the charge on the fact that the senses find permanence in objects; Parmenides, on the ground that they report change.

The Sophists represent a shifting of the center of interest and study from the cosmos to man, and an emergence of science from closed schools or societies into public discussion. The growing democracy made knowledge valuable to the citizen as well as to the scholar. Teachers of every subject, and especially teachers of rhetoric, found eager hearers. The study of the art of persuasion, especially upon political themes, led naturally to the study of politics itself. This was favored also by the decay of older religious beliefs, and the series of political upheavals in which laws and justice seemed to become the sport of despots. The same problem as to the φύσις (the primal nature or essence) is raised again. But this time it is the 'nature' of justice and institutions, not of the cosmos. And as in the former period, so now, it is a process of transition from the older religious ideas and controls. The older Sophists—Hippias, Protagoras, Gorgias—are not represented by Plato as holding radical views on these questions. Younger Sophists are, however, depicted as maintaining that 'might is right,' or that laws are merely the invention of the 'many weak' against the 'natural law.' Individualism is thus the prevailing note, and this found expression in the saying attributed to Protagoras, "Man is the measure of all things," which is the classic formulation for the doctrine of RELATIVISM (q.v.). It is not known that Protagoras himself applied his principle to ethics. He developed it rather with reference to sense perception. He affirms that knowledge is perception, and that all perception is based on a two-fold motion—motion from the thing, and motion from the percipient organ—which forms a peculiar product that is neither the thing itself nor the organ itself, but a joint product different from either of its sources. He infers that what we perceive is an appearance and not the thing. See PHENOMENALISM, and SUBJECTIVISM.

Whether Democritus of Abdera, the city of Protagoras, was directly stimulated to his theory of knowledge by Protagoras [JHT added a brief bibliography here], he at least made a distinction between 'true' knowledge and that which is not genuine, and a corresponding distinction between the subjective character (νόμῳ) of perception, on the one hand, and the real existence of atoms and the void (ἐτεῆ) on the other. Perception yields phenomena; rational thought (λόγος) gives things as they are in truth. This same principle determines the ethical principle of Democritus. No φύσις or permanent reality can be found in bodily pleasures. True happiness is found rather in repose and quiet that wait on knowledge. [JHT added a brief bibliography here.]

C. SOCRATIC PHILOSOPHY: Ger. *Sokratische Philosophie*; Fr. *philosophie socratique*; Ital. *filosofia Socratica*.
The philosophy which was determined as to its method, and in part as to its aims, by Socrates. In the broadest sense this would include the so-called 'Socratic Schools' (see SCHOOLS OF GREECE *[above]) and their successors. The Stoic Epictetus, for example, constantly appeals to Socrates. In this article the term will be restricted to the philosophy of Socrates and his two most distinguished and all-sided followers, Plato and Aristotle.*

In these three we may distinguish (1) a thorough appreciation of the social, political, and moral life of the Greek city, and an increasingly successful effort to analyze this and give its theoretical statement. (2) Springing out of this and developing in connection with it, a growing consciousness of the necessary *method* to be pursued—at first in the discovery of ethical principles, then, more generally, in any scientific investigation. The way here lies from the discussions of Socrates with his teachers and the man on the street, through the more comprehensive and subtle divisions and dialectic of Plato, to the clear consciousness of method formulated in the systematic logic of Aristotle. (3) In Plato and Aristotle the construction of a theory of reality, based, in Plato's case, jointly upon his ethical and methodological views, and, in the thought of Aristotle, upon methodological and physical considerations. (4) An analysis of the aesthetic life in its appreciations and creations. (For these see ART THEORIES, and BEAUTY.)

The thought of Socrates has been preserved mainly in the writings of his two disciples, Xenophon and Plato. In the latter's Dialogues it is sometimes difficult to say what is purely Socratic and what is Plato's own, but in general it is considered that the more distinctly metaphysical discussions, the more elaborate dialectical investigations, and the doctrines connected with the belief in the preexistence and immortality of the soul (see PSYCHE) fall under the latter class. The problem of Socrates was set by his conviction, on the one hand, that a merely habitual and conventional morality no longer sufficed—"an unexamined life is not worthy of man"—and on the other, that underneath moral codes and political laws lay a basis for a theory which could justify itself fully to the reason. In the first of these convictions he shared the free thought of the Sophists (see PRE-SOCRATIC PHILOSOPHY [above]), and was accordingly classed with them by the popular mind and by the conservative Aristophanes, who represented Socrates as the arch-Sophist, teaching irreverence, substituting natural agencies for the ancient gods, and training his disciples "to make the worse appear the better reason." But whereas the Sophists either did not seek or did not find a new authority to replace the old, an inner law to replace the external code, Socrates both sought and found such a new standard. The Sophists were mainly wandering teachers, with the freedom of life and thought frequently found in the man who has no civic or family responsibilities. For such a life individualism is a natural position. Socrates was above all the citizen of Athens, whose conception of life meant life as a member of a city-state. In seeking to discover what is 'good,' the younger Sophists particularly meant 'good for the individual,' and found as their answer 'the full, uncramped development of the impulses and desires.' Socrates sought '*the* good,' which must commend itself as such to the public-spirited citizen, and which had found expression in laws and institutions. True to the genius of Greek life, he found it in knowledge, in insight. Excellence (ἀρετή), which in Homer's day had been mainly valor, is now declared to be knowledge; and since it is not to be supposed that a man will intentionally injure himself, as he must do if he misses the good, no one can be regarded as doing wrong (i.e., as pursuing evil) voluntarily. All wrongdoing is due to ignorance. Many, if not most, are ignorant of the true good, and need to be stung into a consciousness of their ignorance. Socrates conceived it to be his duty to enlighten his fellow citizens, to convince them of their ignorance, and in the fulfillment of this task he incurred that personal resentment which combined with the more general grounds noted above in causing his trial and conviction on the charge of "corrupting the youth and introducing strange deities."

It was in the effort to discover the good which is not determined by individual desire, but is universally valid, that Socrates developed his *method*. Assuming that there is such a general good, it ought to be discovered as the common element in all particular instances, and in the ideas of different men. Socrates therefore endeavored to elicit the opinions of all whom he met, to criticize and compare the views presented, and finally to gain a definition, a general concept. The method of delivering others of their opinions Socrates called his art of 'maieutic' or mental midwifery, and the accompanying profession of his own ignorance was made with a sometimes playful, sometimes satirical 'irony' (see Plato's *Theaetetus* and *Gorgias*). This confidence in the objectivity of the general conception is an illustration of the general Greek position that the mind can apprehend only what already exists objectively—a position which found further illustrations in Plato's doctrine of ideas (below). The method, however, contained the fundamental principle of all scientific inquiry insofar as this analyzes facts to find laws or general concepts.

In the Dialogues of Plato we have religious, ethical, theoretical, and artistic interests combining to give a view of the world and of life which has exercised permanent mastery in the world of thought, and furnished apparently inexhaustible suggestion, largely because of this comprehensive inclusion and interpretation of human experience. The ethical, logical, and aesthetic problems develop side by side. The religious conception of immortality and the 'other world' comes in to give definite imagery to the demand for a distinction between the relative and the absolute, between the changing and the permanent, and a metaphysics frames a theory of reality embodying all these elements.

Plato's early ethical inquiries raise the question whether there can be a science of conduct. If all the various virtues may be reduced to one, and this one wisdom, it is apparent that some single principle underlies all the recognized 'goods.' The next question is, What content is to be assigned to the good thus analyzed? The Cyrenaics (see SCHOOLS OF GREECE [above]) had suggested 'pleasure.' If this be accepted (cf. the *Protagoras*), wisdom will find its part simply in measuring the more and the less. But there are several reasons why this identification of the good with pleasure cannot be admitted. (a) Pleasures cannot be weighed objectively. Their respective values will depend upon who is judge. It is therefore the character or wisdom of the man which determines the value of the pleasure, and not the quantity of pleasure which determines the good. Education aims to teach the young to find pleasure in the right objects—not to find the greatest quantity of pleasure, no matter how or where. (b) Knowledge is not merely an agency for measuring values; it is itself a value, an element in the perfect life. (c) The aesthetic demand for a complete, harmonious life requires a normal fulfillment of functions, not an intemperate intensification of desires and their gratifications. (d) 'The good' is a social category. If it is absurd to call a man good because he is experiencing pleasure, it is because the true good for man is discovered to lie only in the fulfillment of his function in the state. (e) Finally—and here the religious conception of the PSYCHE (q.v.) enters to give a new turn—the immortal life of the soul introduces quite another set of values, which are not relative, like the exchange of one pleasure for another, but absolute. Union with God, assimilation in character to God—this is the absolute good.

Plato's logical discussions led to the same culmination. The RELATIV-ISM (q.v.) of Protagoras (see PRE-SOCRATIC PHILOSOPHY [above]) was admitted to apply to perception by the senses, but declared suicidal if applied to reflective thought (cf. the *Theaetetus*). Knowledge is impossible without the use of such conceptions as those of likeness, difference, and equality. These cannot be discovered by perception. "The soul discovers the universals of things by herself." But the soul cannot discover these universals in the particulars of experience. It cannot find a 'one' in the 'many.' There is no absolute equality or absolute goodness in this world. Whence then does the soul obtain such universals? The Greeks did not recognize a creative activity of thought, but the religious dualism already noted afforded an answer. The psyche has seen these universals in its previous existence, where it has beheld truth, beauty, and goodness absolute—separate from any particulars. The experiences of this world suggest, but do not contain universals. They *remind* the soul of its former vision (cf. the *Meno*, *Phaedrus*, *Phaedo*). Some of the difficulties implied in this theory, according to which particulars which contain no true universal are yet to be known by an external universal, were recognized by Plato (in the *Parmenides*, if this is Plato's) and further developed by Aristotle. The doctrine of 'recollection' or 'reminiscence' is not always emphasized or even mentioned, and may not have been regarded by Plato at all periods of his thought as a necessary element in the system. But the distinction between two kinds of knowledge was fundamental. Perception can give only opinion; reason or reflective thought may give scientific knowledge.

To these two kinds of knowledge correspond two spheres or worlds of reality. The object apprehended through perception is a world of change, of generation and corruption. The reality apprehended through rational thought is the world of true being (οὐσία). This world of true being has its characteristics determined by all the *motifs* stated above. As the true home of the soul it has the qualities which Orphic and Pythagorean had embodied in their ideal of the 'other world.' As the world of absolute knowledge it must be the world of universals, separate from particulars of sense, of the changeless 'IDEAS' (q.v.). As the world which is of supreme value, it must be a world in which that intelligence and measure are expressed which belong above all to the good. The 'Idea of the Good' is of controlling significance (*Republic*, *Philebus*), and even in the world of change it finds some manifestation (*Timaeus*). For the maker or Demiurge (δημιουργός) of this world looked to the eternal pattern and made the world good and fair. The good, through this mediating conception of a Demiurge or Deity, becomes not merely a static universal, but a dynamic agent, i.e., a causal as well as a conceptual relation is sought. Cf. also WORLD-SOUL, which is another mediating conception. The things of this world are also sometimes regarded as 'participating' in the Ideas, or as copying them as ectypes copy archetypes.

It follows therefore that he who would know the true good, even for human life, must lift his consideration beyond the particulars of sense and study the ultimate good. The ideal state will be governed by the 'philosophers' who seek the absolute good, and their education will be directed to this end (*Republic*).

What Plato had thus sharply contrasted in the two worlds of 'becoming' and 'being' Aristotle attempted to bring together. But he aimed to preserve the values of the universal, and of that other world which Plato had separated from the particulars of experience in his effort to bring out its values. That knowledge involves the reference of every particular to some universal, a deduction from some general, Aristotle asserts in his LOGIC (q.v.). His doctrine of the SYLLOGISM (q.v.) exhibits one form of such a use of the universal to explain a particular brought under it by some middle term. But he insists that the general which is to explain the particular cannot be a separate, abstract universal. For in that case the particulars would still remain particulars, unrelated to it or to each other. And so in conceiving reality, instead of the two unrelated or scarcely related worlds—the one of particulars, the other of universals, the one of changing process, the other of changeless substances—Aristotle substitutes one world of individuals, each of which is neither mere particular nor yet abstract Idea—neither wholly unrelated to its preceding state, nor yet a static, changeless entity. Reality is conceived as DYNAMIC (q.v.). Aristotle's terminology for this conception (see GREEK TERMINOLOGY) is that everything in nature is both FORM (q.v.) and MATTER (q.v.), both ACTUALITY (q.v.) and POTENTIALITY (q.v.). Motion is the transition from the potential to the actual. The true substance is the individual as thus constituted, and is at once a realization of one form and a potentiality of another. The seed is an actual organization of its material up to a certain stage; at the same time it is potentially a plant. Another analysis or explanation of the individual is that by the four causes (see CAUSE): material, formal, final, and efficient. These four may be distinguished in the case of a work of art. In an organic product of nature the last three are not distinct. One qualification must be added to the above statements. While there can be no matter without form—nothing merely potential with no actuality—there may be Pure Form, complete actuality or energizing. This Pure Form corresponds to Plato's 'Idea of the Good.' Its activity is to be conceived as *νόησις νοήσεως*, self-conscious reflection. This corresponds to the religious ideal, the deity. This Pure Form is the prime mover, the first cause of all motion, but it operates as a final cause, through the intrinsic longing of matter to take on form. In other words, while the transcendence of the Pure Form is asserted, Aristotle seeks also to avoid reducing the world to the abstract matter of the materialists. It should further be noted that in addition to the conception of matter (*hyle*, *ὕλη*) as the potential and as the correlate of 'form,' Aristotle employs the term with a more positive connotation. It is the substratum, the subject of growth and decay, the source of inherent qualities. It is an accessory cause (see IDEALISM).

Aristotle's conception of reality as organized or formed matter found illustration in his view of the soul as the entelechy of the body (see PSYCHE). His aim to unite the elements which Plato separated is well shown in his *Ethics*. The good of man cannot be determined by any 'absolute' idea of good; it must be sought rather in human well-being (*eudaimonia*). But on the other hand this well-being is to be sought in the complete development or realization of the part of man which is most peculiarly human, to wit, the rational nature. The 'practical' virtues involve a rational control of habit or impulse—the fundamental Greek principle of 'measure' or 'limit' here finds its place—and may be regarded as each a 'mean' between extremes; but still higher than the practical virtues stand the intellectual. The highest ideal is found in contemplation of the truth.

The general change in emphasis towards a more completely intellectual conception of the meaning of wisdom, which is disclosed in the development from Socrates to Aristotle, finds expression not only in this ethical ideal, but in the whole scope of Aristotle's investigations. The whole field of existing knowledge was surveyed; new investigations were undertaken in such widely diverse provinces as those of comparative politics, literary criticism, psychology, and comparative anatomy; many sciences were practically organized *de novo*. Finally, the increasing theoretical trend from Socrates is illustrated in the respective attitudes toward the state. Socrates was eminently a citizen of Athens, caring not to live unless he could live in Athens and influence its life by his teaching. Plato, in disgust with the actual city which could put to death its teacher, constructed in the *Republic* an ideal state whose pattern was "laid up in heaven." The philosopher's citizenship is in this better city. Aristotle is at one with Socrates and Plato in recognizing the social and political nature of man, but the changed political situation which had one type of expression in the individualism of the Stoics, Epicureans, and Sceptics, favored in Aristotle a scientific and theoretical rather than a reforming or idealizing temper. His work on *Politics* is largely a historical and comparative study of the various forms of polity. Plato's *Republic* has been the inspiration of religious and social ideals. Aristotle's *Politics* furnished conceptions for secular theories of the basis of institutions. [JHT added a brief bibliography here.]

4 On the Genesis of the Aesthetic Categories

The purpose of this article is to consider some of the generally accepted aesthetic categories in the light of social psychology. The thesis to be maintained is that the distinctive characteristics of aesthetic feeling or of the aesthetic judgment (aesthetic value) are due, in part at least, to the social conditions under which the aesthetic consciousness has developed. This thesis may be presented in three parts:

I. The aesthetic consciousness in its beginnings is connected with art rather than with nature.

II. The relation of the aesthetic (appreciative) consciousness to art is not that of cause, but that of effect. Art has not arisen primarily to satisfy an already existing love of beauty. It has arisen chiefly, if not wholly, from other springs, and has itself created the sense by which it is enjoyed.

III. Art has its origins, almost without exception, in social relations; it has developed under social pressure; it has been fostered by social occasions; it has in turn served social ends in the struggle for existence. In consequence, the values attributed to aesthetic objects have social standards, and the aesthetic attitude will be determined largely by these social antecedents. Or, in other words, the explanation of the aesthetic categories is to be sought largely in social psychology.

Before considering the propositions *seriatim*, it will be convenient to note briefly what the characteristics of the aesthetic consciousness are. In this the aim will be, not to present an exhaustive list, but rather to indicate categories which have been generally and widely recognized as distinguishing the aesthetic from other values, such as the ethical, logical, or economic, or from other pleasures, such as the agreeable. And amid the seeming multiplicity of such marks or

From *The Decennial Publications of the University of Chicago*, First Ser., vol. 3, part 2 (Chicago: U of Chicago P, 1902) [1902:03].

differentia which have been put forth by writers on aesthetics there is, after all, a considerable degree of uniformity. They may be grouped under three heads:

1. The aesthetic judgment (a) expresses a value, and hence implies a subjective element; but (b) this value is not apprehended *as* subjective, private, and relative, but rather as objective, independent of personal states or conditions, and hence as appealing actually or normally to others.

This characteristic has found various terms. Volkelt denotes it as a fusion of feeling and contemplation (*schauen*), or as the association of an element besides sense-impression, or as the unity of form and content corresponding to percept and feeling respectively.[1] Santayana defines it as "objectivity," or "pleasure regarded as the quality of a thing."[2] Home uses the phrase "spread upon the object." Kant employs the terms 'universality' and 'necessity.' By 'universality' he has sometimes been supposed to mean that all agree in their aesthetic judgments. This is analogous to supposing that when Kant asserts the universality of a priori judgments in pure physics he means that a savage and a Newton would agree on the causes of eclipses. Kant means rather that the judgment, "This is beautiful," as contrasted with the judgment, "This pleases me," implies an elimination of the subjective attitude, just as in the judgment, "This body is heavy," there is an elimination of the subjective as contrasted with the statement, "If I carry this body, I feel the pressure of its weight." That such is the correct interpretation, and that by 'universality' Kant is giving in terms of the critical philosophy the equivalent of Santayana's 'objectivity,' is evident from Kant's own words: "He will speak of the beautiful as though beauty were a quality of the object."[3] To avoid the misunderstanding to which the term 'universality' is liable Cohn would substitute *Forderungscharakter*.[4] The aesthetic value appeals to us with a demand for recognition. It may be actually realized by few, but this does not detract from its imperative character. It is 'super-individual.' Further, when Bain names 'sharableness' as characteristic of aesthetic feelings, we have a recognition of the same attitude. It implies that

1. Johannes Volkelt, "Die psychologischen Quellen des ästhetischen Eindrucks," *Zeitschrift für Philosophie und philosophische Kritik*, 117 (1901): 161–189.
2. George Santayana, *The Sense of Beauty* (New York: Scribners, 1896) 44–49.
3. Immanuel Kant, *The Critique of Judgment* (1790) Section 6.
4. Jonas Cohn, *Algemeine Ästhetik* (Leipzig: Engelmann, 1901) 37–46.

my attitude toward the aesthetic object is not individual, but is possible for any of my fellows.

2. A second widely recognized characteristic of the aesthetic attitude is expressed negatively as a detachment, or freedom from desire, and positively as an immediacy, or purely intensive quality, in the pleasure experienced. The value does not call us to go farther for its full attainment, and hence that deepest feeling of reality is absent which arises in the actual strain of effort, or in the clash of conflicting wills and egoistic appropriation. This characteristic appears under diverse names: in Plato as the pure pleasures independent of desire; in Schopenhauer as the stilling of the will; in Kant as disinterestedness, or a contemplative attitude; in Schiller as play. In recent writers who, I think, tend to magnify one of the means of this detachment—it is semblance, imitation, conscious self-illusion, or make-believe. Cohn prefers the term 'intensive' or 'immanent' value; the former as opposed to the 'consecutive' value of the useful which is valued as a means to an end; the latter as opposed to the 'transgredient' value of the true and good which point beyond themselves for significance or achievement. The work of art is a closed unity. The frame of the picture has an important function. The aesthetic object or world is a world apart.[5]

3. A third characteristic of the aesthetic is that stated by Volkelt as "widening of our life of feeling toward the typical, comprehensive, and universal." This characteristic may not be equally evident in all grades of aesthetic feeling. It is more conspicuous in the art of poetry than in that of architecture. Aristotle and Hegel emphasize the universality of the aesthetic object. It expresses the idea. It gives the human and not merely the particular. An allied principle appears in Tolstoy's requirement that art shall stimulate human sympathy. Kant does not admit it among the marks of formal, i.e., formal, as contrasted with dependent beauty, but it is widely recognized.

There are other marks which have been held to characterize aesthetic value; but as the purpose of the paper is not to enumerate these categories exhaustively, but to explain certain of the more generally accepted of them, the three already mentioned will suffice.

Assuming, then, that universality or objectivity, disinterestedness or detachment from reality, and a widening of sympathy or an apprehension of the broadly significant, characterize the aesthetic, can we

5. For a forcible illustration of this in the principles of tragedy see Theodor Lipps, *Der Streit über die Tragödie* (Hamburg: Voss, 1891).

go back of these categories to seek any explanation for their genesis? Such an explanation may be sought in three fields: (a) in biology; (b) in psychophysics; (c) in social psychology.

A convenient illustration of (a) is offered by the theory of [Karl] Groos regarding play and the arts which grow out of play. Play, with the psychological attitude of make-believe, is a practice by the young of activities which are to be of use in the struggle for existence later on. Illustrations of (b) are furnished by the usual explanations for universality and objectivity. In many cases aesthetic pleasure is due to ease of adjustment, which, in turn, is favored by unity, symmetry, rhythm, etc. Hence, as the minds of men are similarly constituted in this respect, it may be presumed that objects in which these qualities are conspicuously present will give pleasure to all. As regards objectivity, it may be pointed out that the eye and the ear are the preeminently aesthetic senses. But these are just the senses which objectify all their qualities—color, form, sound—and do not demand private appropriation of the object.

Santayana offers a more detailed psychogenetic explanation. The tendency to regard our emotional reaction as the quality of a thing "is the survival of a tendency, originally universal, to make every effect of a thing upon us a constituent of its conceived nature." Emotions, pleasures, pains were thus all regarded as objective by an animistic and primitive consciousness. We have now transferred most of these elements to the subjective side of the account, but the aesthetic pleasures are still objectified. The reason for this survival is easy to discover. For whereas in eating or touching we may first perceive the object, and then later, when we taste or manipulate it, get a new and distinct sensation of pleasure, in the case of the purely aesthetic pleasures, on the other hand, the pleasure arises right in the act of perception, and hence is naturally regarded as inseparable from the object.[6]

It is not necessary, for the purpose of this paper, to deny that each of the explanations cited may furnish elements toward a complete account. But there is a fact not explained by them, and it was reflection upon this which led in the first instance to the theory presented in this paper. The fact in question is this: *Aesthetic pleasure is not always objectified, but under certain conditions wavers between the subjective and the objective.* When I see a new picture, or hear a new piece of music, or attend the presentation of a drama, particularly if I distrust my judg-

6. Santayana 44–49.

ment in the special field in question, I am very apt to express my first judgment in the form, "This pleases me," or, "I like it." What kind of pleasure does it give me? It would seem very difficult to maintain that the pleasure is not aesthetic. And yet it is not objectified. But, as I continue to look or to listen, if I find that the work not only gives a superficial and momentary thrill, but rouses a deep and lasting emotion; if it appeals, not merely to a passing mood, but to the wider reaches of thought and feeling; in a word, if it appeals, not to the more particular, but to the more universal within me, my attitude changes. Instead of, "I like it," it becomes, "This is fine!"; instead of, "It impresses me," it becomes, "This is sublime!"; instead of, "I admire that character," it becomes, "That is heroic!" How is this process of wavering and final fixation of attitude to be interpreted? It cannot be explained upon the basis that eye and ear are the universally objectifying senses, for it is not possible to make my judgment as to color waver between the subjective and the objective attitude. Upon Santayana's hypothesis, we should be obliged to say that in passing from "I like it" to "It is beautiful" we are falling back into a more naive attitude. The explanation which I desire to submit is that in making this change we pass from a private or individual to a social standard of value. The elimination of a personal and subjective attitude is equivalent to the substitution of a social and objective attitude, and, so far as I can analyze my own processes, the universalizing or socializing of the standard is the ground, rather than the consequent, of the objectifying. I do not mean by this that I look around to see how the rest of the company are affected. I may do this. But it might be that, while all the company approved, I should yet fail to sympathize with them or vice versa. The community of sentiment to which my standard refers may not be that of my actual spectators. It is, of course, that of real or supposed experts. It is this which gives it the normative or imperative character. The basis for this social reference, and for the distinction between the numerical and a really social universality will be shown in the exhibition of the three parts of the thesis announced at the outset of the paper, which we may now consider.

I. That the aesthetic consciousness is at the beginning connected with art rather than with nature requires no proof here. Admiration of natural scenery is relatively late in the development of child or race. Even the art which 'imitates nature' by reproducing animal or plant form in carving or color, by no means presupposes an aesthetic appreciation of the objects reproduced. The animal or plant may be the ancestral totem, or the prized article of food, or the religious emblem. Nor does the impulse to imitate or reproduce depend upon the discovery of beauty in the object. It is in its beginnings quite independent.

II. The second proposition may receive fuller statement, although the evidence on which it rests has appeared in print. The proposition is that art production is prior to art appreciation, and is its cause rather than its effect. This is a reversal of the usually assigned or implied order. Textbooks on aesthetics generally begin with the analysis of beauty or aesthetic appreciation, and treat art production as subsequent, or at least as not determining the sense of beauty. This is probably due to the fact that until recently the art which was studied was the art of peoples at the period of the highest artistic development. Recent work on the origin and history of art affords the basis for a different interpretation. It has been shown that art has its origin, not in any single impulse, much less in any desire to gratify an already existing aesthetic demand for beauty, but rather in response to many and varied demands—economic, protective, sexual, military, magical, ceremonial, religious, and intellectual. Some illustrations of these varied origins may be briefly considered.

The geometric patterns found extensively on pottery might seem to be evidently intended to gratify the aesthetic sense by the 'ease of apperception.' But Holmes has shown these to be due to the conservatism of the savage, who preserves thus the pattern of the basket in which his clay pottery was formed and 'fired.'[7] Another illustration of conservation of technical motive which becomes aesthetic in another stage of art is seen in the survivals in Greek architecture of the forms of wooden rafter-ends as ornamental features of the stone construction.

Another slightly different motive appears clearly in the drinking vessels of the early American Indians, which are exhibited in the Field Columbian Museum, Chicago. The Indians naturally used as drinking vessels the various forms of gourds which were ready to hand. When they began to make pottery vessels, these were at first made in imitation of the gourds. The series of forms on exhibition shows all stages, from the complete reproduction of the gourd form to the retention of only a few conventionalized features. Animal decorations on pottery cannot be accounted for in this way, but we know that in many cases the reproduction has religious or magical significance.

7. William Henry Holmes, "Textile Art in Its Relation to the Development of Form and Ornament," *Report of the Bureau of Ethnology*, ed. J. W. Powell, vol. 6 (Washington, DC: Government Printing Office, 1888) 189–252.

The palaces and sculptured reliefs of Assyria tell the story of the king's achievements in war and chase, and sprang from the desire to commemorate his glory and minister to his pride. The great achievements of Greek art, in temple, in sculpture of the gods and heroes, and in tragedy, were in source and purpose chiefly religious, although, no doubt, the keen aesthetic sense developed rapidly in appreciation of the qualities of line and measure due originally to constructive or other demands, and became a stimulus and reinforcement of the original purpose.

Self-decoration, whether in the form of dress, ornament, or tattooing, is due to a variety of motives. To show that the wearer belongs to a group or an order is one of the most common, which appears even today in military and other uniforms and insignia. Religious or other ceremonial or historic motives are prominent in the decorations with totemic emblems or for festal occasions. Protective or erotic purposes are served by special articles of dress.[8]

The marvelous development of realistic sculpture in Egypt was due, according to Perrot and Chipiez,[9] not to any aesthetic motive, but to the magical or religious belief that by providing a statue which should be the exact likeness of the deceased, the *ka* or 'double' would find in it a second body or dwelling, when the embalmed body should have perished. The beautiful painting on the walls of the Egyptian tombs owed its existence to the connected belief that the doubles of the slaves and of the food there portrayed would be at the service of the deceased in the other world.

In the arts of motion the influence of magical, military, erotic, and religious motives is also prominent. The dance before the chase or battle, the mimes at agricultural festivals, or at initiation ceremonies, which seem to the uninstructed onlooker crude forms of art, are to the mind of the actors entirely serious. They give success in the real activities which follow these symbolic acts. They bring the rain or sunshine or returning spring. The stimulating effect of music for the warrior, the influence of sex in dance or song, the influence of the desire to convey information upon pictorial art, the influence of the desire to commemorate the orator's deeds, or those of a patron, upon the development of epic and ballad, need no illustration.

8. Heinrich Schurtz, *Urgeschichte der Kultur* (Leipzig: Bibliographisches Institut, 1900) 330–411 is a convenient recent account.

9. George Perrot and Charles Chipiez, *A History of Art in Ancient Egypt* (London: Chapman and Hall, 1883) chapter 3.

No allusion has been made in the above to the play factor which, from Plato to Schiller, Spencer, Groos, has been found in art. But, as a result of the studies of Groos and other recent writers, it is now possible to place this play factor in closer relation to the serious activities than was formerly the case. It has been shown that the play of children as of animals is largely an experimentation with instinctive activities. It is as real to them as anything which they do. On the other hand, the interest felt is immediate, not remote, as in the case of most employments of adult civilized life. It is this which gives play its sense of freedom. And it is the sense of freedom and of power which finds added enhancement in the make-believe activities of certain of the arts, and hence gives to drama and music a part of the fascination which makes them enjoyed for their own sakes, though originated for other ends. Moreover, just as many of the games of childhood, and as the hunting, races, and sports of men represent former serious activities of the hunting stage, when the elements of hazard and tension and immediate interest were present, which have now disappeared from the commercial and agricultural life, so the arts of civilization, many of them, reproduce, in elaborated and refined form, the emotions of stress and contest and victory, which belonged to the earlier life. In any case, for the purpose of this paper, it is sufficient to note that art, as giving expression and reinforcement to the sense of freedom, has been a powerful factor in the development of the appreciative feeling.

Granted, however, that, as regards its end and content, art has sprung into being, not for its own sake, but from the various motives noted, is not all this beside the mark as regards the essentially artistic element—the form? Granted that primitive man wished to propitiate the divinity, or gain the favor of the opposite sex, or heighten his courage, or relate the deeds of himself or his clan, why need he do it in dance or music, in epic or lyric, and not in less artistic form? The answer to this has already been given in part. In the case of magical representations and conventional reproductions from conservative tendencies the end determines the form. Secondly, it is freely admitted that the principles of ease of apperception and of heightening or stimulating the consciousness—principles of individual psychology— may be used successfully to explain part of the artistic development and aesthetic delight. But for still other factors we must seek an explanation in the third proposition stated at the outset, viz.: Art is essentially social in its origins and development. Before considering this, however, we may sum up the significance of the second proposition in the statement that the value of early art was not distinctively isolated and differentiated as aesthetic. Such distinct emergence was the outcome, not the origin, of artistic production.

III. The third proposition, concerning the social origin of art, needs no proof. Grosse, Bücher, Brown, Wallaschek, Hirn, Gummere, and others have brought together the evidence from a multitude or observers, as well as from historic examples. Dance, song, and mime have always been social expressions and implied attendant social satisfactions and pleasures. Decorations, ceremonials, temples, pictures, and stories have evoked social feeling, and have been created and developed with constant reference to social approval.

But, while it is unnecessary to repeat here the evidence for this, it is necessary to analyze what is denoted by the term 'social' in this connection. To say that art is social in origin means:

(a) First and least important, that it arises—whether as dance, song, drawing, decoration, recital, or mime—when several people are together. Hence, by the simplest law of contagiousness, or 'imitation of the emotions,' its effect is not only shared by all, but is strengthened and reinforced, both by the infection from the joy or grief of others, and also by the mere social or gregarious feeling itself. These effects are experienced even by such a merely numerical group as now assembles to hear a concert or see a play. Even the measure of sociability goes beyond a numerical multiplication of the feeling experienced by an individual. It transforms its quality as well as increases the quantity.

(b) More important than the sociability resulting from contiguity and imitation is the social consciousness of a group bound together by ties of a common blood or common interest. In the first place, the art expresses the joy or grief or pride or heroism, not of an individual, nor of an indifferent person, but of a member of a group. Before any of the group can enter into the art and experience the emotion, he must be a member of the group; i.e., he must know the ideas and imagery, must cherish the beliefs and ideals, must share the common interest, and hence be in a condition to feel as a social consciousness. In the second place, the member of a group of this sort has his feeling reinforced, not merely by imitation of the emotions of others, but by the constraining and compelling group authority. For the Hebrew not to join in the song of praise of Jehovah, or for the Australian at an initiation ceremony to decline to play his part, would mean, not merely aesthetic indifference, but disloyalty to the group. The quality of the aesthetic feeling is further heightened and transformed, not only by gregariousness, but by the joys of common glory, common victory, and common possession, or by the grief of common loss.

The second and higher kind of social consciousness is very commonly the condition under which primitive art is exercised. The festal observances celebrated at birth, marriage, and death, at initiation into manhood or in connection with change of seasons; the celebrations of victories in chase or war; the recitals and chorals; the work songs and war dances; the temples and emblems—all appeal to such a social consciousness.

The peculiarly striking example of this group-influence is seen in certain phases of the comic. It is not necessary to accept entirely Bergson's thesis that the comic is the equivalent of the strange or the odd, to recognize that at least this is often the case, and that the weapon of ridicule is one of the most potent in the armory of the group for enforcing the group standards upon the would-be individualist. The man who 'doesn't see anything to laugh at' is usually the subject of the joke, and therefore, temporarily at least, out of the group. The ingenuity which groups of children display in controlling the new scholar by ridicule is well known. Aristotle's definition of the comic as a species of the deformed is thus given a more social standard by which the deformity is estimated.

(c) Yet a third aspect of the social origin of art is the relation between the artist and the spectator or hearer. Even more palpably in primitive art, and in the child, than in the artist of maturity, is the expressive function of art and its appeal to social judgment apparent.[10] Any intercommunication presupposes certain social standards and may be held to lead to the categories of the "world of description."[11] Communication intended to kindle the emotions or voice the purposes of others, as in military, religious, erotic, or magical performances, must necessarily imply a more intimate identification of the parties, and an emotional, as well as ideational, community of attitude.

This aspect of the social character of art becomes identified with that under (b) above in many forms of primitive art. For in the dance, the corroborree, the Dionysus choral out of which grew the Greek drama, the religious or military chant, the funeral wailings, and the

10. Cf. James Mark Baldwin, *Social and Ethical Interpretations in Mental Development* (New York: Macmillan, 1897) 147–153 [cf. 1898:03].

11. Cf. Josiah Royce, *The Spirit of Modern Philosophy* (Boston: Houghton, 1892) 397ff.

labor songs, the artist was not the individual, but the communal group. Hence the influence of the social upon the whole aesthetic consciousness was the more direct.[12]

The influence of the social origin upon the form as well as upon the content is also apparent in at least one of the most important elements of art-form, viz., rhythm, which Plato regarded as a distinctive mark of human art in contrast with the play of animals. Allowing any physiological basis we please for rhythmic action and its enjoyment, we must in any case recognize that any act performed in common by a group takes on naturally, if not necessarily, a rhythmic form. The sculptured figures of Egyptian laborers, with the *praesul* clapping his hands to mark time for their efforts, the sailors on the ship, the section hands on the railway, the mourners expressing grief, college students in a college yell, the pack of children deriding some unfortunate with their chanted "cry ba-by, cry ba-by"—all testify that, if people would do an act together, whatever it may be, or whatever their grade of culture may be, they fall into rhythm.[13] The common rhythmic action the stimulus and reinforcement of sympathy and social accord are felt, and whatever of pleasure there may be in the physiological process is immensely strengthened by this action of social forces.

We come now to the inferences as to aesthetic feeling and the aesthetic judgment which may be drawn from the above considerations.

1. The universality and objectivity of the aesthetic judgment. Universality means as we have seen, the elimination of the personal, individual, subjective attitude. Now this is precisely what is required by a consciousness in the attitude analyzed under (b) and (c) above. My attitude, when I hesitate to say positively and impersonally, "This is beautiful," and venture only to assert, "I like it," may be due in part to a query as to how far I am really viewing the object as an expert; i.e., how far I am aware of its full purport, and also able to estimate the efficiency and appropriateness of the means to express the end; but, in addition to this, it is due to the query as to whether the object stirs a genuinely social feeling, and as such has normative and objective value. The conviction that the object is really appealing to a social standard finds expression in an objective judgment. In pro-

12. On this see especially Francis Barton Gummere, *The Beginnings of Poetry* (New York: Macmillan, 1901).

13. See especially Karl Bücher, *Arbeit und Rhythmus*, third ed. (Tübingen: Laupp, 1901).

nouncing the judgment I do not consciously appeal to the actual spectators, the "man without the breast," of Adam Smith. Universality of this merely numerical form may belong much more to a judgment respecting strawberries than to judgments respecting Wagner. The aesthetic universality is qualitative and internal, not quantitative and external. It means that I judge as from a standpoint that is *allgemein-menschlisches*, and that this *allgemein-menschlisches* has been created and developed within me largely by the social experience and expression. An illustration of the extent to which a social attitude may transform even the most nonaesthetic of senses is seen in the difference between eating alone and sitting at a banquet. The music, the decorations, and the conversation are not merely aesthetic additions, which comprise the whole aesthetic value of the occasion; even the attitude toward the viands is affected until it becomes as least *quasi*-aesthetic.

2. The second category of the aesthetic was stated as disinterestedness or detachment and freedom. There are several aspects of this category to be distinguished. The 'disinterestedness' or 'immediacy' of aesthetic value may refer to its quality as pleasure. This would be a matter of individual psychology. It may also, however, have reference to a certain absence of egoistic desire, and this quality stands in direct relation to the social origins of art. Whatever is to be enjoyed in common and without egoistic appropriation must, almost necessarily, be enjoyed in contemplation—$\dot{\varepsilon}\nu$ $\tau\hat{\eta}$ $\theta\varepsilon\omega\rho\dot{\iota}\alpha$. And while we may not convert this simply, and assert that all pleasure of contemplative quality is due to social antecedents, it is obvious that nothing could conduce more effectually to the creation and development of a taste for such pleasure than the social attitude involved in the festivals and other fostering occasions of primitive art.

There remains to be noted under this category the aspect of freedom, of detachment from reality, or 'make-believe.' It is evident that this, as an aspect of aesthetic appreciation, is fostered, if not wholly created, by the social aspect of artistic production. Whether the work of art owed its origin to economic, or religious, or magical, or military purposes, on the one hand, or grew more directly out of the instincts which at an earlier period show themselves in what adults call play— in either case the imagination of spectator as well as of artist must widen beyond the present reality. As the magical performance takes the actor and spectators into the unseen world, as the recited deed of prowess, or the carved or painted form revives the past, as the festival of victory enables all the tribe to live over the triumphs of the warriors, as the ceremonials of initiation, or marriage, or funeral, or of religion, project the imagination into the future, the range of conscious freedom is broadened, and the broadening process, although due to other forces, brings with it a thrill and satisfaction of its own. It is not, of course, claimed that the child does not find instinctive delight in the free play of imagination, with all its flight of make-believe. The claim is, that the various forms of art have been the most effective means of developing this free play and the attendant delight. Further, in certain of the arts, notably the drama, we find a form of tension and excitement which, like certain of the games of childhood, or certain of the sports of maturer life, suggests previous periods in the race-history when life itself, as maintained by fishing and hunting, in battle or strategy, was a process containing far more of emotional strain and stimulation that the life of civilization.[14] May not the tingle in the nerves of the romance reader or the theater goer, like that of the gambler or the hunter, be reminiscent of the time when capacity for such tension was bred into the race by the struggle for existence?

3. The third category of the aesthetic was given as a widening of sympathy and an appreciation for the broadly significant. The bearing of the social origin of art and of the aesthetic sense upon the genesis of this category is too obvious to require any detailed statement.

14. William Isaac Thomas, "The Gaming Instinct," *American Journal of Sociology* 6: (1901): 750–763.

5 The Social Standpoint

The social standpoint is not wholly a recent discovery. Not to refer to ancient thought, Leibniz constructed a universe on the analogy of a 'kingdom.' Kant, by his transfer of the categories from the sphere of pure ontology to that of validity (Royce), made an important step in the direction of a social standpoint, for although his 'universality' was not based on the number of observers and reasoners, he did, in the case of aesthetic universality at least, distinctly raise the question how an *allgemeine Sinn* could be formed, and sought an answer in the fact of social conversation. We should naturally think also of the British moralists and the German idealists. The 'herding instinct' of Shaftesbury, the 'pliability' assigned by Mandeville as the medium for social influence, the 'sympathy' of Hume and Smith, the 'imitation' of Hartley—all suggest present terminology as well as present problems, although the analytic method of mathematics and physics determined in some cases the mode of approach. The German idealists, starting from the problem of freedom, went on to consider the development of the individual mind and of human institutions as the logical moments in the unfolding of complete freedom—of absolute mind; but the social causes of the process were not studied; psychology had not freed itself sufficiently to be able to take up its own problems, nor had the utilitarian and later ethical movements added their content to the conception of social welfare.

The present prominence of social problems, social categories, and social standards is doubtless due, to a considerable extent, to an increasing appreciation of an even more rapidly increasing influence of the social medium, whether of the past through tradition, education and the other media of 'social heredity,' or of the present through the

From *The Journal of Philosophy, Psychology and Scientific Methods* 1.8 (1904): 197–200 [1904:09].

greater massing of humanity and through the increased facilities for interchange of persons, goods, and ideas. The pressure toward cities is economic as well as gregarious in its motives. But the economic wants themselves which urge toward city life are largely created by social suggestion, the means for satisfying them exist largely because of the presence of masses of people living together and because of a more democratic diffusion of opportunities for education and amusement, and finally the possibility of satisfying these wants is brought more vividly to general attention through present agencies. The economic, while it *may* be 'egoistic' in its aim, is social in cause and content. Economic standards of value are determined less and less by the organic wants for food, shelter, and clothing, more and more by social suggestion and demand. Economic value is given to land by the very residence of large numbers in its vicinity; it is given to certain commodities by the elevation in standard of living due to greater intelligence and other social causes; and the owner of the land or the producer of the other commodities may not have contributed in the slightest toward the value of which he receives the benefit.

The bearing of these facts upon economics and ethics is apparent, although it has by no means received full recognition as yet. The bearing upon the psychology of the self is no less obvious. The increasing social influence, both from past and from present agencies, is not only enlarging and strengthening what James calls the 'social self' (it would have saved us from ambiguities if James had used a different term for this, so that the term social might have been left free for application to certain aspects of all the 'selves'), it is also transforming the content of material and spiritual selves—of the material self along lines already indicated, of the spiritual self along lines to be suggested below. The mode of functioning as well as the content is also affected, as Baldwin and others have shown. Perhaps the present danger is that we take the processes of imitation and social influence too simply, as Locke took his processes of sensation. Is there not to be worked out in detail a theory of apperception in the relation of the individual to the social influences, just as we have gradually worked out such a theory in the case of visual perception?

An ambiguity in the use of the term social calls for notice. In the looser sense social may be applied to relations between individuals. Any interchange of ideas, any influence of one by another, implies some ultimate community of intelligence, interest, or sphere, and may, therefore, be loosely termed social, and studied by 'social psychology.' But in a more restricted sense the term may be limited to the activity of a group as such. The group may be a group of two, and but of momentary duration, but there is for the time some unity of interest or sentiment which makes the group as such a force in the life of each member. The psychology of this group influence is highly significant for ethics and the philosophy of law. For the individual, having developed as a member of a group—clan, family, state, village, or religious community—has constant experience of group standards and group authority, and feels the stress of group motives, simply because a large part of his activities are for common or group ends, and are performed in ways prescribed or suggested by the tradition or opinion of the group. From conflicting interests and under highly complex forces emerge the consciously selfish or altruistic purpose, the asserted or recognized rights, the reflective jealousy or sympathy, but in them all is the pressure of a more than individual authority or claim which asserts its power ultimately as moral control.

In applied ethics the influence of the social upon theory as well as upon practice is no less marked. The old virtues of thrift and charity are rudely challenged. Trades unions form groups which present ethical phases strikingly analogous to political groups at the tribal stage—or, indeed, to our present states in their international relations, which are confessedly only very partially moral. Within the union there is a 'loyalty,' a solidarity, and a genuine self-sacrifice on the part of the naturally capable members, which are entirely comparable to the patriotic devotion of clansman or citizen. The man who seeks to better himself by leaving the union, or who actively or passively interferes with union success, is regarded very much as were the 'tories' and 'copperheads.' The study of group ethics in economic as well as in political groups helps to a juster estimate of the values and limitations in each. The question, What virtue is of most worth? is brought forcibly to consciousness by present conditions.

The conception of justice is also in a state of flux. When thrift was regarded as an unquestionable if not a supreme virtue, any possible acquisition not involving violence or fraud was accepted as a just reward. By giving a portion in charity the acquirer could experience joyously how much better it is to give than to receive. Now that the social factor in the production of wealth is being dimly recognized, the masses feel the inequality as well as the discomfort; the conscientious man of privilege feels a scruple about accepting education, art, wealth, opportunity of every sort, in such superlative measure. It is not merely that he feels bound to devote them to public service as his own immediate way of paying his debt; he wonders whether, if justice prevailed, some of the others might not have the opportunity for serving the public in such wise, and of enjoying the experience of personal independence in greater degree.[1] I have noted in the *American Journal of Sociology* for January an interesting attempt to give the new conception of justice a form capable of legal use.[2] The suggestion is to give the concept 'social debt' a legal as well as an ethical standing.

The philosophy of religion has been similarly affected. If the distinguishing mark of religion as contrasted with magic is found in the social relation between gods and people, we are in a position to interpret ancestor worship and similar facts in a way to show their ethical significance. The religious sanction of morality is seen to be rooted in intrinsic relations. The distinctive religious attitudes and sentiments may be analyzed and interpreted in a manner which supplements the classic interpretations of Kant, Schleiermacher, and Hegel.

Of the social standpoint in aesthetics I have written elsewhere.[3] Metaphysics might seem at first blush an unpromising field, but since Kant we have learned that reality, if known at all, must be known through categories; and if certain of these categories which give us a 'world of description' are themselves due to social influence, as Royce has maintained, the theory of knowledge is affected by the social standpoint in a fundamental manner. Accepting as in some sense true Kant's principle that the unity of self-consciousness is the ultimate principle of logic, we have still to ask how that demand for unity has been developed to the height found in the scientific mind. Assuming also with Kant that an irreversible sequence is the cue on the basis of which the mind interprets a connection as objective, we may yet seek additional factors in the consciousness of objectivity. The elements of objectivity in logical, ethical, and aesthetical judgments have their sources, in part at least, in the pressure of a social environment or the necessity of social communication.

1. On the relation between social and individual ethics, Jane Addams, *Democracy and Social Ethics* (New York: Macmillan, 1902). Compare Andrew Campbell Armstrong, *Transitional Eras in Thought* (New York: Macmillan, 1904) chap. 5.

2. Ed. note: Cf. 1904:04.

3. "On the Genesis of the Aesthetic Categories" [above].

Some Contributions of Psychology to the Conception of Justice

6

The two general standpoints from which all attempts to define justice and rights proceed are that of the individual and that of the social whole. From the standpoint of the individual, we have such principles as 'To every man according to his deserts,' or 'To every man according to his needs,' as well as the stubbornly surviving principle of natural rights, which is embedded in our institutions even though discredited by philosophers. From the standpoint of society, we have the principle that justice means the determining of individual relations by the general order and the subordinating of individual to public interests. From the individualistic standpoint, rights come before justice. Rights are the positive factor; justice is merely a term for the sum of individual rights, or a negative restraint upon interference. From the other standpoint, right and justice come, logically, if not historically, before rights. Before I can say whether a claim is a right I must prove it to be just, to be right; but just and right are terms which historically spring from law and custom, and which logically imply a general standard or authority. The two standpoints are both employed by utilitarianism when it asserts, on the one hand, that every man is to count as one, and, on the other, that acts are right as they tend to the greatest happiness of the greatest number. They are curiously conjoined in the thinking of the man who claims for his own vested interests the utmost freedom and protection and at the same time condones child labor or the sweatshop or the extermination of a race, on the ground that "individuals must of course be sacrificed to the general progress."

It is unnecessary to prove to a philosophical audience that neither standpoint by itself is adequate. An individual, apart from his membership in a social rational order, has no rights, divine, natural, or any

From *The Philosophical Review* 15.4 (1906): 361–379 [1906:10].

other. Conversely, a society may not fix its concepts of justice in such a fashion as to deny the worth of personality to any of its members, or to treat them merely as means. The controlling conception from which all principles of rights and justice must arise is that which may be stated either as that of the social individual, or as that of the society which recognizes individuality. It is only the rational and social individual who has any rights; conversely, a society has a moral status only as it is the organized community of free moral persons who are willing, through it, a general good, and therefore setting up a general moral standard, the right. The unsocial individual may by cunning or wealth "have a capacity of influencing the acts of another," to use Holland's phrase, "by means of the opinion or the force of society." But this gives him morally no rights. Society may pass laws which treat individuals as though they were less important than things, but this is not justice. It may neglect to provide for those aspects of individual development which are possible only through the general activity; if so, this is at best a justice which is immature and defective. In order to get a basis for settling any of the questions as to rights and justice which are now pressing upon us, we must therefore first of all, if possible, clear up the meaning of the conceptions 'social individual' and 'a society which respects individuality.'

Just here, I take it, is the opportunity for psychology. I can imagine the reader of my title inquiring, What has psychology to do with justice? Does not psychology tell us what is, not what ought to be? Does it not illumine impartially the evil and the good? Does not its method fall with scientific impartiality upon the just and upon the unjust? My answer is: If justice deals with persons, then it is important first of all to know what a person is. If, in particular, justice needs to understand a social individual, then we must find out the nature and meaning of individuality. Psychology studies just these problems. When we appreciate our facts we shall be able to state more intelligently how to meet the situation which they constitute. What, then, has psychology to say which bears upon our problem? What is the nature of persons in general and of social persons in particular? The more important doctrines of psychology upon these problems seem to be the following:

First, the individual is complex, not simple. The soul as simple substance has been banished from metaphysics; the individual as viewed by law and common sense is still relatively simple. The complexity of the individual is a complexity of origin and of structure. Let us note each of these.

The individual is complex in origin. Physical heredity and variation, social heredity and more consciously directed education, and, finally, conscious volition, all contribute. While the share of each may be impossible of exact determination, it is none the less a reality. This excludes conceptions of purely materialistic determinism on the one hand, and of 'self-made' men on the other.

The individual is complex in structure. Instincts bred into the organism by the whole biological process, impulses which spring from a variable psychological and mental structure, other impulses due to suggestions from the complex environment, physical and social, come in time to be organized and controlled. We call this organized unit a person or an individual, but this is in many cases a fiction; in any case, complete control of all these urgent, conflicting, multiple interests and selves is an achievement, not a starting point. No one is definitively either bad or good in early years. Only the abnormal and pathological individual becomes so completely absorbed in one interest as to be incapable of responding to any other.

The second important doctrine of psychology for our purpose is that the individual is both habit and adjusting activity. On the one hand, there is continuity which forms the basis of responsibility; on the other, there is something new which means growth. On the one hand, there is a definite structure already built; on the other, there is the living process which refuses to be identified with the structure already organized, and points forward to the future. On the one hand is the seemingly solid reality; on the other, the power of expanding life which is destined to condemn the present as outgrown.

The third doctrine of psychology which I select has various aspects, but they may all be brought under the head 'Forms without contents are empty.' The mind, the self, the person, the individual, is selecting, controlling, organizing, purposing, and willing activity; but it cannot operate *in vacuo*. We know that it has come into being in the biological process only through selecting from a varied environment and through control of muscular movements. I cannot, merely by taking thought, will to be wise, to control passion, to enjoy the refinement of civilization, any more than I can will to add a cubit to my stature. It is not merely that mind, individuality, personality have been developed in response to an environment; they are still dependent for the 'stuff' of thought, for the ideas which make thought possible, both upon material furnished to sense and imagination and upon actual practice in motor control.

Fourth, and most directly important for the conception of justice, is psychology's doctrine of the individual as social. It had, indeed, long been a commonplace that the individual owes much to language, to parental care, to education, and to community life. But recent psychology has brought to clear recognition a much more fundamental relation. Conscious personal life gets its stuff, its technique of control, largely through suggestions from other persons. Language affords it the medium for enlarging its life to past and future, to abstract and general. Contagious sympathy broadens the capacity for feeling; home and all the later agencies of association both offer opportunity for impulses to find real development, and give steadying support to the gradually forming will.

But the social origin of the person is less important than the social nature. On the material side, it is obvious that the individual of today depends upon countless of his fellows for his daily food and clothing, for opportunities to work, and for peace and security. All this, however, is but an external symbol of the social nature of his mental and moral life. He thinks in 'general' concepts and of objects; but this means he thinks and interprets his experience, not as it feels to him privately, but as he can describe it to another, or as it would appear to anyone else. He exercises some rights; he owns a home or a coat. The legal right for this, of course, depends on society; but the very idea of 'my' and 'mine,' the very rudiments of personality, presuppose a 'your' and 'their' to give them meaning. It is needless to point out how the whole moral and religious life is a life in and through relations to others. Even the realm of feeling does not remain wholly private. For the moment we pass from a particular thrill of emotion to the objective valuing of beauty, we have taken a point of view which is not private but general. The world of science, art, commerce, law, morality, and religion is a social world. The individual may try to ignore certain aspects of these facts; but if he lives in any of these spheres, he can no more escape the social than he can escape his own person.

These considerations, however, would only exhibit the individual as involuntarily social. They say nothing explicitly as to the very essence of personality, the conscious will. In this respect the individual may or may not be social. He may take up into his purpose and will the whole social situation. If so, his will becomes a social will. Just to the extent to which he does this, will he become a completely social person. Just to this degree will his will not only accord with right, but itself determine the right. Just to this will his claims, his interests, coincide with law.

Right and rights will be as one. This does not mean that the individual will cease to have any private interests, or to recognize any in others. A society of persons is not a series of facsimiles. The very essence of progressive society, as of advancing life, is that it includes a multitude of different people with differing bent and talent. The very range and power of every individual in society is itself due to the fact that other and different individuals are breaking out new paths, opening new windows, pushing back the limitations from human experience, and building new interests. But, on the other hand, much of this originality and diversity which has in the past assumed unsocial or even antisocial forms will in the future find social channels for expression. Genius will not die with war; individuality is not dependent upon exclusive interests.

We turn now to the problems of justice and apply these psychological doctrines to a few typical situations: the problem of the just distribution of wealth, the just distribution of education and other mental goods, the administration of justice by the courts.

To begin with a brief note on the last. Corrective and criminal justice employs certain abstractions which are in part inheritances from a crude past, in part conceptions which have served a useful purpose and must in turn give way to a less abstract, more psychological point of view.

First, it makes that abstraction of all conditions except the bare act, of all circumstances of its litigants except the contract, the tort, or the crime, which we call equality before the law. Ancient law began with individual decisions passed by the old men or the chief. These were liable to be partial and arbitrary. It was a great gain when precedent and statute substituted uniformity and impartiality for caprice and favor. Equality before the law was in these respects a great advance from the inequality which it superseded. But when we consider how this actually works we may see that the abstract equality often gives real inequality. Forms without content are empty. "Is not the poor man at a hopeless disadvantage in court," I asked a lawyer, "in view of the resources which wealth may employ against him?" "No more so," said he, "than in every department of life!" The reply speaks for itself. The justice of the courts is no harder upon the poor man than are the other conditions of society! The purely formal equality, impersonal and abstract, must give way in turn to a more personal and concrete equality if we are to have full justice—full recognition of the individual.

Or again, consider the criminal as to his supposed freedom and responsibility. In the eye of the law he is a criminal or he is not;

in committing the act he was free and responsible or he was not. Abstraction is made from all heredity and environment. This is certainly a case where forms without content are empty. Metaphysics used to discuss the problem of freedom in this purely formal way. Is man free? You answered "yes" or "no." But the psychologist may see that freedom in any case is a matter of content as well as form. It is a matter of degrees, not of yes or no. Am I free to prefer Beethoven to 'rag time'? Certainly not, unless I have heard Beethoven. Is the boy of the slums free to think of things pure, noble, and of good report? Am I free to play a crack game of tennis? I must first learn the existence of a host of new muscular 'feels' before I can control and organize the movements. Is the boy coming to manhood free to control passions? Not unless he has ideas of genuine interest in something better to set over against passion; not unless he has had training in the actual resistance to passion and mastery of himself. Responsibility has gradually moved from the extremely abstract to the more concrete views. In early German law the person was held responsible with little if any regard to his intent or personal agency. The owner of a weapon left for repair might even be held liable for a crime committed with it. A cart might be brought to trial and adjudged 'deodand.' The history of law has been a gradual introduction of a more psychological standpoint. That is, it has dealt more with the real man, less with a fictitious self analogous to the old metaphysical substances and essences; but there is still room for progress.

Finally, our criminal law, until recently, has abstracted from all but the self of the past, the self of the habit. It has taken no account of the self as activity. To treat any human being as though what he deserves is measured only by his deed, by what he has been or done, is, as Professor Dewey has pointed out, to make a monstrous assumption. We may not ignore the past, but we must not ignore the future and its possibilities of reform and reshaping of life. The parole system is a step in this direction. The juvenile courts permit the judge to treat the boys and girls as real persons, not solely as abstract criminals. May we not hope, and shall we not, as philosophers and psychologists, labor for the wider recognition of individuality and full personality in all our criminal law—for the banishing of abstractions which wrong humanity?

We come now to the problems of distributive justice. I shall not discuss the question whether any private property is just. I for one want my own coat and my own shoes; and though I do not expect to own much else, this admits the principle. I must be able to control enough of my surroundings to do my work efficiently and live in decency, if not in comfort. But the just distribution of property—that is another story. Our present system of distribution is not, of course, the product of any intentional plan by society to secure a just distribution. It is a combination of the old theory of seisin or possession with the theory of free bargaining. It is subject to some slight restraints, but these have been, in the main, intended to favor competition. It results in such vast inequalities that we no longer count our millionaires, on the one hand, and, on the other, there are estimated to be in this most favored country ten millions of persons in poverty; that is, ten millions who cannot procure food and other necessaries sufficient to keep them in full efficiency. In England apparently over twenty-five percent are in this condition of want.

Few would say, if the total wealth of the country were placed in their hands for distribution, "We will give the bulk of the whole to a small fraction, we will divide a lesser portion among a great many, and will leave a minute fraction to be distributed among a quarter of the people." The situation certainly seems to demand some justification.

Such justification is frequently attempted from the standpoint of society as a whole. "It depends on what use is made of the great fortunes. It may be to the advantage of society to have certain large accumulations which can be devoted to financing great industrial undertakings, supporting educational and philanthropic institutions, and fostering the arts." But this answer no longer satisfies society. It seems to neglect the individuals of which society is composed. Society is asking now, not only whether wealth is justly used, but whether it is justly acquired—justly, that is, to the other individual members of society. The question, Is it justly acquired? may be proposed from two points of view.

1. The economic process may be considered as one in which individuals are to be treated by society on some supposedly moral principle. The theory here would be that, as society is made up of its members, it must have their real welfare at heart. Its justice will be so to distribute its goods as to recognize personality and promote it.

2. The other theory would be that the economic process is to be viewed solely as one of contracts between free and independent individuals. Society has no concern and takes no responsibility except to enforce these contracts. It cares not whether they mean weal or woe. It views economic life purely as a game which is certain to enrich some and ruin others. Its justice is only to enforce the rules.

We will consider each of these theories. The first, which seeks some moral basis for the distribution of wealth, will naturally use either a principle of equality—a fair field and no favors, free competition, free bargaining; or a principle of inequality—to each according to his merits, or his efforts, or his needs.

Let us examine these maxims.

Equality we certainly believe in. Fairness, justice, seems to be in essence, equality. Indeed, both parties who object to 'equality' as a maxim are opposing not real equality, but an apparent equality which means real inequality. The individualist objects to equality of distribution because this would be treating men as if they were all alike. But to treat the useful and the useless alike is not equality. True equality is to treat usefulness alike and to give to equal units of utility equal rewards. On the other hand, the Socialist—and indeed every one whose eyes are open—objects to so-called equality of competition on the ground that it is not real equality. It is treating the people as if they were all alike. But to treat the rich and poor, strong and weak, educated and uneducated, alike is not equality. Our psychological analysis shows the precise fallacies of both these supposed systems of equality. Either the bare equality of distribution or the bare equality of competition treats the person as an abstract unit—the simple substance of old metaphysics. No system of justice can be adequate which rests on such an unreality.

We turn, then, to another set of maxims which aim at least at a less abstract conception of personality: 'To every man according to his deserts,' 'To every man according to his efforts,' and 'To every man according to his needs.' Each of these recognizes the complexity of personality. The psychological principle which exhibits the strength and weakness of the first and third of these maxims is the second. The self is both habit and ideal; both a structure and a reconstructing activity.

Evidently the first and third of these principles, as usually interpreted, seize each one half of this fact and ignore the other. 'To every one according to his deserts' recognizes the continuity of mental life. But, as usually interpreted, it stops here. It treats men as if they were dead, as if their structure, their past, were the only things of importance. There is no quicker way to kill a man morally than to treat him as though he were already dead.

Moreover, as applied to the question of just distribution of wealth, the maxim of reward according to deserts usually involves other psychological absurdities.

1. The first abstraction which this principle of reward according to

merit usually makes is that it gives a man credit for all he achieves, or charges him with all his failures, without recognizing the threefold origin of these achievements or failures. Heredity, society, personal choice, have each had some share in the result. But, in considering the ethics of competition from this maxim, there is evidently no attempt to discriminate between these several sources. The man born with industrial genius, presented by society with the knowledge of all that has been done in the past, and equipped by society with all the methods and tools society can devise, certainly has an advantage over the man of moderate talents and no education. To claim that the first should be justly rewarded for his superiority would imply that the reception of one gift constitutes a just claim for another.

2. Secondly, the maxim as applied to our present system is guilty of a further abstraction in assuming that the chief if not the only way to deserve reward is by individualistic shrewdness and energy.

3. It measures desert by service rendered without taking any account of motive or even of intent. The captain of industry performs an important service to society; therefore, it is argued, he should be rewarded accordingly, quite irrespective of the question whether he was aiming at social welfare or at selfish gain. It may even be plausibly argued that to reward men financially for good motives would be bribing men to be honest. I grant freely that financial rewards will not make good citizens, but this is irrelevant. The point is that whatever other reasons—expediency, difficulty of estimating intent and motive—may be urged for abstracting from everything but the result; the one reason which cannot be urged is, such abstraction is just. A person has rights only because he is a social person. But to call a man a social person because he incidentally produces useful results is to say that purpose and will are negligible elements of personality.

The maxim 'To each according to his efforts' corrects this last abstraction just reviewed. It is true to one aspect of personality—voluntary purpose. But this again is to be narrow. It ignores the element of the future. It is too apt to forget, in the second place, that even 'efforts' are not solely a matter of free choice. As pointed out in our first part, the efforts which a man makes are really to a great extent dependent on his training and environment. It therefore needs to be supplemented by the third maxim, 'To each according to his needs.'

This recognizes individuality in its aspect of possibility. It would give unfolding personality the chance to develop. This has sometimes been regarded as benevolence rather than as strict justice. But such a view assumes that the person has no claim upon the social whole as a constituent member, whose welfare is indispensable to the welfare of the whole. It assumes that the only basis of claim is what the member *has* done. The maxim 'To each according to his needs' has a sound basis in the psychology of the living, growing person. But, if taken abstractly, if the continuity of the self is forgotten, the maxim cannot serve as a basis for distribution. It must be combined with the principle of continuity—the man's past is a part of his personality; it must be further modified by the conception of the social self—only those needs are rights which are in the interest of the social individual.

If, now, with this corrected conception of personality we ask whether our present distribution of property based on seisin and competition can be called just, we need not delay long. It evidently can make no pretense to be a distribution according to merit, effort, or needs. It can, therefore, make no pretense to be just in the sense that it recognizes full personality in determining rights.

We turn, then, to our second theory of society to see if it affords basis on which we may consider the present distribution as at least not unjust. If we regard a contract or exchange as fair, if both parties agree to it—irrespective of any other consideration—then we may say that any system of distribution to which the parties consent is fair and just. Society names its conditions in the form of laws. Hence any individual who acquires property legally may be regarded as justly entitled to it. Or, to put the same thing in another form: Everyone wants to receive for his labor or skill what it is worth, and conversely, when I want goods I should give what they are worth. Now, what better way of deciding the value of goods can be afforded me than by the test of what I am willing to pay? They are worth that *to me*. In other words, the law of supply and demand locates the measure of value, and therefore the whole control of property, in the free choice of individuals. What can be fairer than this? Both these statements of the theory make an abstraction in another form. Whether such law as obtains and such consent as exists have any value, depends on how the law was made, or whether the party to supposed contract had any real alternative. If supply and demand were perfectly fluid, that is, if space and time, habit and training, responsibilities and duties, to say nothing of monopolies and black lists, had no existence—then the theory would be more plausible, though it would still abstract from any larger view of the individual than his present want measures. But, under conditions as they are, we must admit that the abstraction is a gross one. It is possible to say of a game, the players know the rules, and consent to them. They cannot complain if they do not win, nor need they feel unjust if they are successful. But in the game of the industrial process there is no option. One must play or starve. And usually there is no chance to consent to the rules. They are already made; and, when they are changed from time to time, it is not usually the loser who has the chief voice in the change. The world applauds a good loser, but when the player must stake not only his own welfare but that of wife and children, he can no longer greet its issues with the 'frolic welcome' of independence. To base the justice of our distribution of property upon naked, abstract consent—whether we call it open shop, or freedom of labor, or free contract, or competition—and take no care as to whether there is real freedom, whether there is real respect for personality, is too abstract a procedure to deserve the name of justice. It is more abstract and metaphysical than metaphysics ever was. We must ask, Does the system or law recognize the full individuality of its members, or does it deal only with fictions and abstractions?

In this full sense of justice, I think no one can fail to see not merely that our system is not just, but that no distribution of property is likely to be just. We may remove some of the inequalities, we may require decent sanitation and honest food, we may heed 'the bitter cry of the children,' handicapped by premature toil and indecent surroundings, we may give to all the best of education, we may even, if we please, attempt to restore equality by taking over as a community the land, or the means of production; but even then I believe no system of distribution in property can be devised which will be true to all the complex life of its members—which will be fully just.

Indeed, we may go on to say that the American people does not care very strongly that this is so. This may be due in some cases to a religious conviction that the social order with all its inequalities is divinely ordained; in others, to an optimistic blinking of the facts: but I believe that there is a more widely operative reason. The American prefers an economic order in which there are prizes and blanks, to an order in which every man will draw out in proportion to what he puts in. He prefers an exciting game to a sure but tame return of his investment. He may call for 'a square deal,' but we must remember that 'a square deal' in the great American game from which the metaphor is taken is not designed to make the game less one of chance. It is designed to give full scope to luck and nerve. A game in which every player was sure to win, but also sure to win just what he had put in, would be equitable, but it would not be a game. The American suspects that the measures advocated as giving juster distribution may somehow rob life of its excitement and its passion. Possibly he may even think that the very strain of the process develops some elements of character which he fears to lose. But whatever the motive, in the hope of better luck next time, or of a better start for his children, or in the very stress and struggle, he thinks little of the justice or injustice of it all. Psychology seems thus to lead us to a hopeless conclusion.

If life were wholly made up of exclusive interest, the outlook for any satisfying degree of justice would be hopeless. But it is good psychology as well as good scripture that man's life consisteth not in the abundance of the things which he possesseth. Many of the ends and interests in the complex life of humanity are not exclusive but social. Satisfaction in knowledge, in art, in association, in freedom, in service to man, is not diminished but increased when it is shared. Impulses towards these ends began to appear early in the process of human development, but at first had little chance; organization of life, institutions, and the progress of civilization were necessary to give them opportunity and power. The older philosophy of property laid stress upon the importance of property as necessary to the full realization of personality. This corresponded to the fact that at one time private property was not merely an important aspect of the assertion of the self or personality, but also a necessary means to most of the other goods of life. Neither of these is true to the same extent as formerly, and the future is likely to see still further progress along the same direction.

Consider first the intrinsic value of possession, as a psychological activity. To seize, master, and possess is certainly an instinct inbred by the biological process. It is necessary for life; it is a form of the *Wille zum Leben* or *Wille zur Macht* which need not be despised. At the same time, it is relatively simple. It starts low down in the process of animal evolution. It cannot be compared in rational value with the instinct of workmanship. In itself, it neither beautifies nor ennobles. It is power, but power in brute nakedness and simplicity.

Consider next possession when it is no longer the mere animal instinct, but through expression in a social medium and by a social person it becomes a right of property. This is certainly a far higher capacity; for, like all rights, it involves the assertion of a super-individual personality. It means the controlling of others. In early society this was, if not the only, at all events the most general and important right. It was therefore of undoubted value in the formation of personality. But democracy has formed new ways for developing the social consciousness and the personality of its members. The responsibility and power for law and government which falls to every citizen directly is sufficient, even if he has little reminder of his capacity of ownership.

But, it may be said, few would place great importance upon bare ownership as such. It is because ownership is a necessary means to so many other goods, that it is itself a necessity for individuality. It is in just this respect that the situation seems to be changing.

Modern man has been in past times largely compelled to own the goods he would enjoy. To sit down on a piece of ground and enjoy a fine landscape, he must own it. If he would have a plot where his children might play, he must own it. If he would travel, he must carry his own lantern, and furnish his own protection from thieves. If he would have water, he must sink his own well. If he would send a letter, he must own or hire a messenger. If he would read a book, he must not merely own the book, but own or hire the author or copyist. If he would educate his children, he must own or hire the tutor. In the case of persons living in rural districts, this is still true to some extent. But in the case of urban communities, where the extremes of property distribution are greatest, and the feeling of injustice provoked by them is keenest, progressive democracy is finding and providing through public agencies satisfactions for both bodily and mental wants. Fewer and fewer city dwellers can own a yard or play ground, but the parks are providing for old and young agencies for health and enjoyment. Few can own books, but all may read them. May we not expect that all the arts—music and drama included—will be brought within the possibilities of all?

The intellectual life and the means for its gratification are also entering broad paths. The fraternal relation increasingly manifest in the republic of science and letters is but emblematic of a far deeper socialization of all knowledge. Medical science is finding new avenues of bringing itself to bear upon every member of the community. Campaigns against tuberculosis and diphtheria are allowed to go unhindered by even the fiercest of individualists. The knowledge that frees from superstition and fear is permeating widely. The positive knowledge which gives a sense of power over nature, and makes man free of his world will follow.

The average teacher or preacher has little if any more property than the average wage worker. Yet in spite of the fact that he has no property, he has less feeling of injustice—and less reason for it. His life is less meager, because he can enjoy more of the social goods which civilization brings. This is partly a matter of education. He has wider and more social interests because these were stimulated at the proper time in home or school. The basis for social justice in this sphere of mental goods is therefore an education which shall awaken mental and social interests; the superstructure of justice which we may hope will rise is a satisfaction of these interests by social means.

Three objections to our demand for broader education and fuller social satisfactions may be briefly noticed. The first comes from the optimistic and self-satisfied American who says, "Of course education is good, but we have it already—grades, high schools, universities; why speak of this?" I speak of it, because, as every one knows who has looked into it, a pitiably small number ever get into the high schools. The subjects and the methods of instruction, due partly to educational narrowness and partly to financial limitations, afford interest to only a part—and in the case of boys, to an apparently small part. As a Chicago judge is said to have remarked, "A boy has to commit a crime before the city will give him a chance for a broad education." With salaries so small that we have almost no men in our teaching force, with the number of pupils to each teacher so large, and with equipment so meager that proper methods of instruction are impossible, with a curriculum which emphasizes learning so much and doing things so little, with little or no provision for boys and girls of promise whose parents are too poor to keep them in school, we cannot claim to be more than at the beginning of our educational program. We are only crudely and partially just to the individuals of our society. Some human beings have small capacities for education, but that every boy and girl should be given the opportunity and the needed aid to a development of his capacities through at least the high school age—this seems a minimum of social justice.

The second objection may come from several sources. From the sincere aristocrat and from the sincere—though in my judgment narrow—student. It runs, "Most men and women must walk the common paths of life, must do its manual labor and have only the satisfactions of food, shelter, and warmth. To awaken desires for more is to bring misery instead of increasing happiness." The answer to this objection is that it comes too late and in the wrong part of the world. It would be a fatuous policy to attempt to limit men to the sphere of simplest material wants, in which there is least that is social, most that is exclusive; least justice and least hope of justice. But this cannot be publicly and avowedly attempted. The American people may be careless, may be unconscious how inadequate their justice is, but they will not tolerate a theory which bluntly and openly denies the essence of democracy. They may permit the practical inequality; they will not admit that this should be frankly erected as a principle of justice.

The third objection comes from the orthodox individualist. "Such a program of satisfying wants through social and public agencies, instead of through private property, is paternalism. It leads to demoralization and pauperization. It is better, it is juster, to stimulate the individual's activity and do less for his wants, than to satisfy all his wants at the expense of his activity."

But this assumes, first, that what is done through public agencies is done for the people and not by the people. A democracy can do for itself what an aristocracy may not do for a dependent class. The greatest demoralization which is threatened at the present time is not to those who stand outside, looking hungrily at the board spread by the productive power of associated human invention and industry. It is rather to those who sit overfed and complacent in the supposition that they themselves have alone created what they enjoy. The danger to democracy itself lies not so much in the effort to awaken and satisfy essentially social interests through the common resources as in the disposition to appropriate common resources to private property. And here again the American people, more interested as they are in most respects in the stir of the game than in the justice of its awards, have shown that they may resent the use of public agencies for private gain. We conclude this consideration of distributive justice therefore with the hope, springing from what we already glimpse, that the goods which are not private, the goods which are so largely the product of social cooperation, may increase in value and may be the share of every member of society.

It is in the expansion of life along these lines that Plato's suggestive foregleam of a juster, because more social, order is to find interpretation. The social content and power of science, the interchange of material goods not only in commerce but in aid to the suffering, the communication of ideas and sympathy, the cooperation of countless associations to promote common welfare—these are some of the ways in which "things which are by nature private, such as eyes and ears and hands," have become common, "and all men express praise and blame, and feel joy and sorrow, on the same occasions, and the laws unite the city to the utmost."

7 The Adjustment of the Church to the Psychological Conditions of the Present

The pulpit must present to men a 'religious' view of the world and life; it must inspire and aid men to enter into a 'religious' experience and to live a 'religious' life. But to say this means nothing until we discover and define what is meant by 'religious.' The essence of the religious might conceivably be sought in some special quality of feeling, emotion, impulse, or intuition. This would be analogous to finding the specific character of the moral in a moral sentiment, or of the aesthetic in an art impulse, or a 'sense of beauty.' But just as we now recognize in ethics that no single emotion or instinct apart from ideas is distinctively and adequately *the* moral sentiment, so we may recognize in the history of religion that ideas determine religious emotion and experience in its higher forms, just as truly as the emotions and aspirations help to shape in turn the ideas. Primitive fear and awe, thrill or ecstasy, become transmuted into a genuine reverence, or elevation of spirit, when the idea of an ethical God has emerged from the stress of prophetic struggle with grossness and immorality. And again in turn the conception of God is touched with tenderness when the deity is viewed no longer as chiefly the protector in war, but rather as the Father, the Husband, the Goël or Next-of-Kin (Redeemer).

In modern times, as in ancient Israel, two conceptions of God have been especially prominent: the conception of sovereignty and the conception of kinship. These have very largely determined the type of religious experience, and the dominant note of preaching. They have had a basis in the psychological conditions of the age as well as in the scriptural phraseology. It was natural for the medieval church, the successor of the Roman Empire, to conceive God as an almighty sovereign, governing his subjects, accepting satisfaction and penance for their sins. The Reformers continued the same imagery. The Old

From *The American Journal of Theology* 12.2 (1908): 177–188 [1908:06].

Testament out of which was built the very structure of Puritan religious experience was in its historical books a record of a religious polity in which sovereignty was the all-important interest. Sin took the form of rebellion against God. Conviction of sin from this standpoint meant acute emotional consciousness of a conflict of the human with the divine will. The ordinary man, brought up in religious surroundings, might not be conscious of active opposition to God. But there was a way to rouse the feeling. The preachers of Calvinism had not studied modern psychology but they had discovered that emotion is brought out by tension. The doctrine of sovereignty in its baldest form as including the principle of "reprobation" was an effective instrument in bringing about the consciousness of opposition between natural feelings and divine law. As Nathaniel Emmons puts it, "There is no divine truth which is more directly suited to discover the hearts of sinners to themselves than the doctrine of reprobation; it never fails to awaken their native enmity to the divine character." If strong emotion was not aroused by this or other means, then this coldness was itself the sin. Wesleyanism, which emphasized the 'grace,' rather than the decrees, of the divine sovereign, preserved the general imagery and expected the same general type of emotional experience.

The past century has shown a tendency to shift the emphasis in imagery from the conception of sovereignty to that of kinship. God is the Divine Father. Men are to be brothers. The type of religious experience has been affected by this shift. The family relation appeals more strongly to the young and probably more strongly to women than to men. Or perhaps it is more accurate to say that it appeals to men and women more in times of sorrow or discouragement than in times of war against the sins of passion, or of fierce battles for the right.

These two conceptions of sovereignty and kinship are permanent aspects in possible religious experience. We shall always find religious expression in the prayer, "Our Father who art in heaven, thy Kingdom come." But they are not the only terms in which the divine may be imaged, and they are not the terms which best interpret some of the life and interests of today. Men—to say nothing of women and children—do not think of life largely in terms of allegiance, or obedience to a sovereign. Democracy has made all such ideas seem remote. Nor does the family relation mean to the present mind such an all-inclusive system of human interests and activities as to make it the sole and adequate symbol for all religious experience. In early life the kinship group did include all human relations, and the religious could appropriately be conceived in its terms. Authority, wisdom, protection, justice, were all administered through the father. But progress has brought the development of new institutions, new organizations, corresponding to more complex experience and expanding mental and spiritual life. The political, the economic, the educational, the ecclesiastical, have been split off or extruded and given new significance by their independence. And of these the political has been made the center of a specific religious life. The economic and the educational or scientific developments of experience have never as yet entered so intimately into western religious conceptions, if we except the remarkable interpenetration of religion and philosophy in the Logos doctrine of the early church.

The two lines of activity and thought which are most characteristic of our time are, first, the organization of men for industry and business; and, second, the promotion and application of science and education. Instead of the political, the economic and scientific-educational interests are in the center. Family relations keep their place as a part of life, but they are certainly not all.

The economic relation of man to man under the present system of collective production, machine industry, world markets, and financial systems is one of vastly increased interdependence. It is also one in which the individual is relatively helpless, either to protect himself or to accomplish unaided any effective moral act. This has brought to the front two great moral issues. First, this great collective system with its connected machine process is immensely more productive than any method of industry the world has known before, and is therefore capable of freeing men from the exhaustion and drudgery of overwork and from the misery of want. At the same time it has a fearful possibility of submerging the individual in a collective, impersonal whole, and of making the machine master instead of servant. Secondly, the industrial and business system affords the opportunity for a genuine social service and interdependence distinct from that of kinship or political cooperation. The exchange of goods and services may be no less a moral interchange because it is paid for. It may be all the more moral; or rather it may bring out a new and valuable kind of personal relation, over and above the sympathetic bonds of kin. It may preserve the dignity and self-respect of each party. Its specific note is then that it evokes the consciousness of rights, and at its best demands respect for rights of others. But undeniably it presents also possibilities of sacrificing others' interests to one's own in freer fashion than family solidarity allowed. It may mean exploitation, even if there is no question of violence or fraud. It is sometimes said that the conception of brotherhood among men, growing out of the relation of divine fatherhood, would solve all our social and industrial problems. This is open to serious doubt. Brotherhood does not place the emphasis where the present man wants it placed, or where the economic process naturally requires. Brotherhood stands for sympathy, for give and take without any careful reckoning of debit and credit, for loyalty and standing by in time of trouble. No one can question the need of all this in human society. But brotherhood does not most appropriately symbolize perfect fairness toward all men in relations where it is not sympathy but justice that is wanted. It does not suggest the guidance by reason rather than by emotion. It does not suggest the recognition of rights—that bulwark of personal worth which the modern man feels so strongly. The demand for social justice is becoming a dominant note in the moral consciousness of today. It is forced to its position by the very nature of the business and industrial world.

The second aspect of the present mind is the power of science and the general spread of education. There has been culture since the Renaissance; there has been free thought; there have been schools built and sustained by the church. But the present scientific spirit is not that of culture, nor is it primarily that of free thought—of the opposition of reason to dogma or superstition. The schools of today are not in the service of the church or of any other interest. The scientific attitude of today is that of positive investigation, partly for the joy of knowing, but largely to enable man to master his environment and move forward more surely in the overcoming of disease, in the use of natural resources, and in the better organization of society. The schools are based on the democratic conviction that every child should have a share in the social heritage, and so far as the elements of education can give it, an equal opportunity to enjoy the benefits and contribute to the welfare of society. Joined to the institutions for scientific research the schools make it possible for the general results of investigation to be taken up by people generally. The high schools of today have better equipment and represent more genuinely the scientific point of view than did the colleges of a generation ago.

And why are these obvious facts recited? Is it to urge ministers to leave ethical religion for economic discussion, and to accept boldly the doctrine of evolution? The purpose is to suggest a much more fundamental change in attitude, although it does not demand of the preacher that he leave his own field and pose as an authority where he is not competent to speak. The central fact is that if the preacher is

to present religious truth as something vital he must make it mean
something for the two fields in relation to which it is now essentially
an onlooker. To make it mean something in these two fields it must
identify itself with principles and conceptions which represent in
these fields the life of the spirit. It must invest these principles and
conceptions with the same larger relation to the divine by which it
has given religious meaning to the ethical conceptions of duty and
sympathy. In doing this it must enlarge our conceptions of God and
of religious experience, just as they have before been enlarged when
other ethical conceptions have been taken up into religion. What then
are the conceptions and principles which have such ethical significance
and generality in the economic and scientific worlds that religion may
use them as centers of recrystallization or as characteristic notes in
genuine types of religious experience? They will not sound novel, nor
will it be necessary to search outside the Bible for texts on which to
preach them. The novelty will be rather *in using these as central conceptions for defining the religious rather than as corollaries from other supposedly
more fundamental conceptions of sovereignty and kinship.* They are simply
the conceptions of personal worth, of justice, and of inquiry. The
words are indeed familiar enough, but the actual ideas behind the
words are getting new emphasis and definition from present conditions. Consider them further, therefore, before concluding that no
new message can be framed from them.

1. And first, the conception of personal worth. We are told that
this has ever been one of the keynotes of Christianity. Puritanism
proclaimed the equality of all before the Almighty; Wesleyanism emphasized the worth given the soul by Christ's sacrifice. The last century, and perhaps especially Unitarianism and transcendentalism,
emphasized the worth given man by his divine sonship and his spiritual capacities. These made worth a corollary. The present danger to
personal life is not in organizations of church or monarchy; nor is it,
as it appeared to more recent generations, in the abasement of man
before God, or in the seeming triviality of man as part of the physical
universe. Personal worth is now threatened rather by the collective
economic organization, and by the machine process. These, like the
political organization, have been brought about as a necessary instrument toward human progress. But just as political organization has
often been a tyranny when first effected, and has threatened to crush
out freedom and religion, so our collective and machine process has
thus far had perhaps as much moral and religious loss as gain. We
need not repeat how corporate organization loosens individual re-

sponsibility, and submerges the individual in some group. We know, if our eyes are open, how the machine process may lend itself to using up men, women, and even children, in order that more goods may be produced. And the peculiar feature of this collectivism is that no individual can effect much alone. The individual merchant, employer, labor unionist, is forced to act about as others do, or go under. What is needed then is general and united effort. Just as political organization, once largely selfish, has been converted to be, on the whole, a democratic institution, serving the common man, and making possible a far freer, nobler life, so we may hope that the collective methods of industry and business will be controlled by man in the interest of the moral and spiritual life, instead of dominating him for material ends. And just as the political triumph of democracy was won largely under the religious conceptions of divine sovereignty, God-given rights, and human equality before God, so it is at least possible that the reassertion in a new setting of the worth of man in comparison with what he produces or possesses may be a powerful factor in the democratizing of our economic process. This is not a partisan or divisive principle—except so far as every moral or religious principle is divisive. It is a principle that the individualist and the Socialist both profess to honor. But it is a principle that needs to be made so central, to be so reinforced by the earnestness and emotion which respond to the religious appeal, that it will become a dominant note in our business and legislation.

President Tucker has said that the man of today would scarcely understand how to repent of the sin of his city. He does not understand any better how to repent of the sin of his corporation or his union—or of the unorganized but no less potent collective action of the body of consumers of which he is a member. And yet most of the sin of today is being committed, not by individuals as such, but by nations, states, cities, corporations, unions, associations. They—not any individuals as such—permit exploitation, child labor, wage scales which encourage vice, unprotected machinery, mine explosions. The homicides due to individual intent are insignificant in number compared with the deaths due to society's neglect, or to the alleged 'expense' of proper care.

When the individual of the eighteenth or nineteenth century came to realize that he had 'a soul to save,' he felt the emotional enlargement and uplift which naturally attend the awakening of higher aims and ideals. It is for the preacher of the twentieth century to show men just what their soul, their personal worth, their true life, is, or may be, under present conditions. It is his further task to show how we may cooperate in saving the souls of multitudes which are now being lost by society's acts or neglect. If the preacher finds any awakening to this new life, let him not hesitate to recognize it as a new birth, a birth into the spiritual world, needing no doubt further experience and nurture, but nevertheless a genuine beginning.

2. Justice is likewise an old word, but it is getting a new meaning and is coming to be far more deeply the expression of man's inmost self than it has ever been before. Hitherto it has usually been invoked to obtain protection for person or property against force or fraud. But this is not its present aim. Men who believe that we need a larger social justice do not necessarily hold that present inequities are due to either force or fraud. They may be, in particular cases. But generally speaking, the inequities are due to the system for which we are all in a measure responsible, and to practices which are simply the carrying-over of the methods—and even the virtues—of one age into the changed conditions of another. When individuals tilled their own soil, or produced articles by their own unaided labor—relatively speaking—it was possible to say who owned the products. Justice could then mean protection to person and property. But now our production is by a gigantic pool. Capitalist, laborer, farmer, statesman, physician, teacher, judge, minister, are all cooperating, and who can say how much of the product 'belongs' to anyone? 'Supply and demand' is theoretically our method of division. But practically we know that this is often interfered with by legislation for special interests, and by combinations for the benefit of certain groups. The ethical point is that we are coming to be no longer satisfied to adjust our conceptions of justice to fit the workings of a supposed economic law, or of an economic law manipulated for a class. We are determined rather *to take advantage of our knowledge of economic laws in order to secure greater justice*. Knowledge of gravitation does not mean that we must all fall down and stay there. The principle of justice is based on the worth of every person, of every member of society. We demand that our systems of industry, business, education, sanitation, shall recognize this as paramount. Our Supreme Court, in extending the police power to include whatever is for the 'welfare' of the public, however much this may conflict with 'freedom of contract' or 'vested rights,' has given recognition to this new and far more thoroughgoing meaning of justice. If religion is to align itself with the social conscience of today it must recognize this fuller meaning. It must stand as broadly and yet as wholeheartedly for this as it has stood for chastity and for charity.

But it may be said, is not this to take sides in the as yet unsettled conflict between individualism and socialism and therefore to risk the loss of all the spiritual values in a partisan wrangle? No, it is not to take sides between socialism and individualism so far as these are sincerely animated by the desire to secure justice. Bentham and Carlyle, Mill and Ruskin, Charles Kingsley and Henry George, were all animated by love of justice, however much they differed in method of securing it. And if the preacher can awaken in his people the desire to promote justice in the school and library facilities, the parks, the taxation, the control of corporations, the adjustment of wage scales, he may very well decline to pose as the universal expert in the details of all these difficult matters. To one kind of individualism, indeed, this conception is opposed—namely, to the individualism, which holds that so long as the few rise high it matters not how many they crush in climbing. From the standpoint of ruthless sacrifice of the 'too many' for the sake of the 'superman,' Nietzsche was right in believing himself opposed to Christianity. But for the democratic individualist, as for the enlightened Socialist, the exact program to be followed is subordinate to the great aim of justice; and because the issue between the democratic individualist and the intelligent Socialist is one of intricate analysis and careful experimentation there is the more need that to these principles of personal worth and social justice the minister should add that of 'inquiry' as a third determining element in his message.

3. Inquiry—the open mind joined to the resolute use of all the means for reaching truth—this too is a familiar name. But in the past it has meant frequently a polemic against dogma or a destructive criticism of the received, rather than a positive method of analysis and construction in the service of human development and social progress. Most men of science today are glimpsing the possibility of assisting man to take possession of his inheritance. Science has been applied to many processes of manufacture, but in matters of health and disease, of marriage, of education, of economic methods, of social organization, we pursue our course largely by the guide of habit, tradition, or blind impulse. The demand of the scientific spirit is that reason, inquiry, patient investigation, carefully planned experiment, shall take the place of unreasoned advocacy or hasty fervor in all these fields. The very complexity of our present social conditions, as briefly referred to above, makes it doubly important that the preacher inform his message with this scientific spirit. He must make it clear that the very disposition to learn, to see every situation in all its bearings, to weigh

conflicting hypotheses, not to dogmatize on insufficient data, but to set at work to get data for judgment, is itself a moral duty—no less a duty than under other conditions may be immediate action of some sort. Tennyson gave religious value to 'honest doubt' but the attitude of science today is characterized not so much by 'doubting' as by constructing working hypotheses and devising experiments to try these out and test them. The preacher must then encourage this attitude toward the whole problem of life. He must lead the young man or young woman to see in it a genuinely religious attitude. To be either indifferent or uncandid is sin, from the standpoint of science; it should be no less sin from the standpoint of religion. And if the sincere mind is led to believe that in the very process of inquiry it is following a divine leading, the result will be to give greater sacredness to science and greater sincerity to religion.

In a recent address on "The Social Settlement: Its Basis and Function," Professor Mead has called attention to the function of the settlement in enabling us "to form new moral judgments as to what is right and wrong" and contrasts the settlement with the pulpit which "is called upon to inspire to right conduct, not to find out what is the right—unless the right is so plain that he who runs may read." In the case of new social and industrial problems, he continues, "the pulpit is unable to solve them, because it has not the apparatus, and the scientific technique which the solution of such problems demands. In the meantime it holds its peace, for it must give no uncertain sound to the battle. The only overt social issues with which the pulpit in recent time has identified itself have been temperance and chastity."[1] It may be freely granted that the pulpit has not the apparatus and scientific technique to solve the details of many of our intricate social problems. Neither has it the apparatus and technique for psychological analysis. Nevertheless, it has been able to urge with unhampered power the transcendent value of the spiritual life, and the kinship of man to the realizing purpose he discerns in the universe. And what I should maintain now is that although the pulpit must rely on the settlement, the university, and the courts to supply technique, it is not therefore compelled to hold its peace on the most important issues of life. It may intrepidly proclaim inquiry, rather than complacent acquiescence or partisan dogmatizing, to be the religious duty. It may

1. George Herbert Mead, "The Social Settlement: Its Basis and Function," *The University* [of Chicago] *Record* 12 (1908): 110.

assert the superiority of persons to products, and the passion for justice as lying at the very heart of religion. The 'living' God, interpreted for other times as sovereign and father, must mean for the present generation the source and inspirer of that specific life which is now in the deepest sense the life of the spirit. The prophets were able to take up the conception of justice into their conception of Jehovah. The early church was able to give religious meaning to the philosophy of its day by its conceptions of God as Logos and as Teacher. If the pulpit of today proves itself equally constructive, it may interpret the scientific and social conscience and make these the foci of religion more powerful, because more inclusive and vital, than the present uncertain position allows. So long as there is sorrow, defeat, and loneliness, the pulpit will preach the Father and Comforter. So long as there are lusts and passions, the pulpit will present a divine law which is holy, and a salvation from the sins of the flesh. But if it hears what the spirit says to the churches, will it not also present God as manifest especially in those movements and aspirations of our time in which man is seeking to gain a new vision of what spirit means, new instruments by which to secure the larger life of the soul, new guarantees for the citizenship of all in the City of God?

Other conceptions will find reshaping if the standpoint is once taken that inquiry, respect for humanity, and social justice are not merely corollaries from some other divine attributes but are themselves of the essence of God. Faith, for example, would mean from the standpoint of the religious value of inquiry, not the acceptance of certain fixed content of truth or value, but the resolute venture of the soul into the search, undaunted by the possible reconstruction required. Unbelief would mean such fear that this is not really a spiritual universe, or such apathy as to whether it be or not, that there would be no effort to enter into the larger possibilities of the as yet untraveled world. And from the standpoint of the worth of man and of social justice, unbelief would be the acquiescence in the physical 'struggle for existence' as a supreme law of life. Faith would mean the bold assertion of belief in the possibility of victory over the conditions which would crush or submerge the life of the spirit. It would mean staking oneself upon the possibility of securing a larger justice than the world has ever seen, or than the slow of heart think to be within the powers of human nature. For the true religious faith believes in a divine event larger than can be demonstrated from what has been— or is now. Such faith is already on earth; it is for the pulpit to say whether it may not be given the help which the great historic symbols and organization of religion afford, and whether it may not in turn give to religion that enlargement which is essential for every institution or system if it is to be a mansion or a temple of the soul and not a prison or an outworn shell.

How Far Is Formal Systematic Instruction Desirable in Moral Training in the Schools?

8

To answer this question intelligently it is desirable to ask what part formal moral instruction has played in the moral development of the race, and what is the psychological basis for moral instruction.

Historically, three sets of agencies have been at work, and still play their part in the moral training of most, if not all, of us. We may call these for convenience (1) the indirect agencies; (2) the agencies of custom; (3) the direct agencies of reflective morality.

(1) By indirect agencies are meant the various agencies which produce a moral result although the moral end is not consciously intended. Work is undertaken and carried on in order to earn a living, but it is perhaps the most effective of all agencies in developing responsible conduct. Family life is entered into because of the mutual attraction between man and woman, but it becomes a school of kindness and sympathy. Knowledge is sought to give power or success, or to gratify a craving to know; it refines and enlarges the objects of desire. The company of our fellows may be sought for economic gain or from a herding instinct; interchange of goods, services, and ideas undermines distrust and hostility. Struggles for mastery or liberty, or for possession, are prompted by conflicting interests; they force men to closer unions, to establish order, and to think of rights and justice.

(2) Society has in various ways, sometimes on rational grounds, sometimes through chance, come to regard certain ways of acting as important. These are customs or mores. Society impresses its judgments upon all its members through its praise or ridicule or blame, through taboos, or even through force. It trains its members by drill of ritual and ceremonial to observe them. It invests them with sacredness by all the forms of art and music.

(3) Finally, moral leaders have arisen who have set forth clearly and

From *Religious Education* 3.4 (1908): 121–125 [1908:10].

directly moral standards, or persuaded to moral advance. These have found their greatest opportunity for effective work when old customs are becoming unsuited to new conditions, and hence have come to be and to seem formal. Moses, Isaiah, Jesus, Socrates, are familiar examples.

If we look at moral growth psychologically we see what these historical agencies appeal to.

(1) The indirect agencies appeal to the instincts established in the race, and to the various insistent cravings of human nature. These urge men on not only to preserve existence and reproduce the species, but to obtain in various ways a larger, fuller life. They are at work on each of us from the earliest years and never let go their hold. They form what may be called idealizing and socializing agencies. They are not speaking directly the language of morals; they are doing its work silently and effectively.

(2) Society makes its appeal likewise to instincts and emotional responses rooted deep in human nature. It offers to the child copy for imitation, it suggests to him ways of thinking, and feeling, and doing. It makes appeal to love of approval, to the dislike to seem 'different,' to the shame before contempt or ridicule. Besides, it utilizes through all the agencies of custom the power of habit. When it has made us act repeatedly according to its tradition or its will, it has made sure that it will not be easy for us to break the bonds. Society is thus exerting a constant pressure to make the individual conform to the established order.

(3) Where then is the place for reflective and conscious morality, for the use of reason and the direct consideration of what is good and right? This conscious consideration and direct choice is forced upon us when we find conflict in the various ends or goods we seek; when some impartial or temporary impulse is met by some larger, more imperious law of life; when some habit resists the light of intelligence; when some private interest collides with social order or the welfare of others. Here we must puzzle out our decision as to what is best, and we naturally seek for some principle or rule; or we become conscious that the natural impulse, or the established habit, or the private interest ought not to dominate a more rational ideal or a more social order— *provided* that what claims to be more rational and social is really so.

Here then is the place where moral instruction is needed; to give us some aid in broadening our standards of value, and in showing what the claims of the social and moral order really are.

To come now directly to the question of *formal moral instruction in the schools*, we may infer that there ought to be some general correspondence between school training and the training by which society has advanced. The school may wisely rely in the earlier years largely (1) upon the indirect agencies of work and cooperation, of social sympathy and social demands for responsible action; and (2) upon the social pressure of the present society of the school as an institution having an order of its own, and upon the ideals of society as communicated through the art, music, and literatures of the masters, and through the living personality of cultivated, generous, and high-minded men and women.

This view that during the earlier years we may well appeal primarily to the forces of instincts, emotion, and habit, is reinforced by the general doctrine as to the purpose and method of elementary education which Dr. John Dewey suggests in his classic, *The School and Society*.[1] He holds that elementary education should enable the child to develop his instincts and bring these to effective and rational expression, rather than that it should present information and material valuable for the adult, no doubt, but not meaning much to the child at this early stage of development. He would have the teacher take the child's instincts for knowledge, for construction, for communication, and for expression, as the basis for work, and give to these instincts the training and enlargement which shall secure to the child thorough command of these resources in place of the somewhat blind and futile efforts which would be the result if the child were left to himself. This of course does not mean no intellectual content in teaching. It does not mean leaving the child to do just as he pleases. It does mean that we may hope to get the best results by working with the forces actually existing in the child's life rather than by introducing prematurely standards and methods for which the child is not ready. In terms of moral training this would mean that although we should avoid presenting an order, or custom, or ideal to the child as a mere blind and arbitrary or conventional affair, we should after all not bring prominently before the child problems of moral conduct which have no place in his immediate life, and should not give reasons for moral conduct which require a more mature point of view.

Moral Instruction in Secondary Schools. With the change from elementary to secondary work, and with the changed attitude and the changed capacity which this implies, there naturally comes the opportunity for a more direct and definite influence. There are three reasons

1. John Dewey, *The School and Society* (Chicago: U of Chicago P, 1900).

for this: (a) All the studies of the secondary period may well look less toward developing the child's instincts and more definitely toward preparation for future work. The child himself is beginning to look forward. He is not living so directly in the present. It is therefore entirely fitting, psychologically, to introduce more and more of information, more and more that bears upon his future vocation. (b) His whole mental development indicates a more rational and scientific attitude toward all problems. He can appreciate reasons and grasp a science more thoroughly in its relations. (c) The adolescent period brings a greater sensitiveness to social relations, which gives the basis for a more direct interest in moral relations.

What we should seek therefore is first of all a subject matter for instruction which will command the intellectual respect of the boy or girl at this age, and which shall not only give rational and scientific reinforcement to the general moral principles which society insists upon, but may also present such information as to the meaning and progress of human society as shall give new incentive to the individual to become a loyal member of society and intelligent agent of human progress.

The subject matter which seems to me best to fulfill this requirement is not at present organized in a suitable manner for high school students. Its central theme would be the relation of the individual to society: on the one hand what society means and does for the individual, on the other hand what the individual's part should be in the support and progress of society. We have indeed various materials for such a social ethics which are now studied in the schools and which have values of their own. We have civics, which deals with the processes of government; we have economics, which deals with the processes of industry and business; we have history, which for the most part deals with political development. But these give only one side of the story, and the connection of these with the moral life is not always evident. We have on the other hand texts in ethics which for the most part are more subjective than seems wise for secondary education, or else present the child with a list of duties which he is expected to fulfill. The more desirable line of procedure would rather seem to be to present such a view of the interrelation between man and society as would make the necessity of moral action appear inevitable. At this period of education it is out of place to make direct appeal to the emotions in a course of study. The great artist or writer may make this appeal successfully. The ordinary teacher is liable to become sentimental, or to cheapen instead of elevating the subject. The chief stress should be upon the intellectual method, and if the dependence of man upon the various institutions and processes of society, its laws and other agencies of justice, its opportunities for acquiring the goods of life and the means of happiness, its stock of inventions and ideas, its systems of education, its provisions for family life—if all this is presented, it can hardly fail to make a powerful impression.

In presenting this material stress may properly be laid upon the method of intelligent study as the most hopeful method for meeting the difficult problems of social, industrial, and political life. Society is just beginning to grasp the conception that it may go forward intelligently, that it may utilize all the discoveries of medical science to prevent disease in a systematic way. It is premature to attempt to teach boys and girls just how they may avert social and political evils, but it is not absurd to teach them that there is a scientific way of working at these problems, and that this method is more promising than the older methods of emotional appeal. Some things are still unsettled. It is not desirable for the public school teacher to be a partisan in issues which are matters of political debate, but if the whole occupation of the teacher and if the whole scientific method is worth anything, its function ought to be not to decide these questions off-hand for the pupils, but to give them a method of study which shall prevent them from being carried away by emotionalism on the one hand, or from being fossilized by tradition on the other. I do not think we have at present a subject matter of this sort worked out. I do believe that we need a discipline of this sort, and that a study can be worked out which shall be no more difficult than physics or Latin syntax, and at least as valuable to the American citizen as the history of ancient Greece or the rudiments of a foreign language.

9 American College Education and Life

There is evidently a feeling in the minds of the public that there is something the matter with our colleges. The more sensitive and alert educational authorities are likewise aware of certain defects, although they may not agree upon the causes. The more or less definite feeling is that college work on the one hand lacks intellectual seriousness, and on the other fails, somehow, to connect vitally with the present needs of society. Questions as to the length of the course, or the threatened partition of the college between secondary school on the one hand, and the professional schools, including the graduate school, on the other, are really subordinate to this broader question of seriousness and connection. If the college is really worthwhile we shall doubtless manage the external organization of our system so as to secure its continuance. If the conviction becomes general that it is a survival from the past rather than a useful institution for the present, the really vigorous and ambitious young men will pass it by, and the public will not care to maintain it for the benefit of those who wish merely to spend four pleasant years.

The two chief questions, I conceive, are the value of its intellectual ideals and methods, and the value of its corporate or social life at a certain period in the development of young men and women. I shall confine myself chiefly to the former, in the belief that the intellectual problem needs to be attacked first. The present paper aims to show (1) that the work of the colleges up to about twenty-five or thirty years ago fitted the social situation in both ideal and method; (2) that in the past three decades there has come to be a gap between theory and practice to which the colleges are only in part adjusted; and (3) that the solution is likely to lie through a reconstruction of the college ideal of liberal education under the influence of new vocational methods

From *Science* ns 29 (1909): 407–414 [1909:06].

and ideals. In return we may hope for a gradual permeation of vocations and social institutions by the new spirit and method, which will complete the readjustment between college and life.

I. THE FORMER IDEAL AND METHOD OF COLLEGE
AND OF LIFE

The intellectual ideal of the college has been that of a 'liberal culture.' This formerly meant three things: As contrasted with studies pursued for utilitarian ends solely or chiefly, it meant genuine intellectual interest. As contrasted with studies determined by the external requirements of future vocation, it meant study directed by the inner, personal valuations, aptitudes, or desires of the scholar himself. In both these respects it meant 'liberation,' and freedom—freedom for the life of the spirit as over against external necessities or constraints. And in the third place, as predominantly classical, it gave a glimpse of another and different civilization. To the boy or girl brought up in the meager and isolated environment of New England hills or pioneer farm it opened a vista. It gave the aesthetic value of detachment. Some of finer temper caught the full inspiration of converse and companionship with the great minds they came to know. In this sense it was really humanizing. And for ordering one's life and measuring life's values, how could one better gain a point of view from which to see life steadily and whole than in the perspective of the best that had been thought and said?

Now this general scheme of freedom and individualistic literary culture fitted admirably the religious, political and social ideals. For Protestantism was religious individualism. Governments were supposed to exist to protect individuals in their natural rights. With practical economic equality, and in a rural, independent mode of life, freedom from external constraint seemed to be the chief social good. And as regards utilitarian demands, in spite of the hard conditions under which life was often led, it was a tradition from early colonial days which had not failed of reinforcement that man's life did not consist in his possessions.

The prevailing *method* of classical study, and of the mathematics and philosophy that went along with it, was also strikingly adapted to the professional training and general social order of the period. For the three professions for which the college prepared were occupied chiefly in deducing the consequences from fixed first principles. Systematic theology or grammatical exegesis was the minister's task in the seminary. The statutes, on the one hand, and past decisions on the other, with some fundamental conceptions of natural rights, were the fixed datum of the lawyer. The physician might be less certain of his ultimate principles, but whether 'regular' or 'homeopathic,' his method was about as dogmatic; and as for society, its social, political and moral standards and categories were all supposed to be established. Even the movement for the abolition of slavery needed only the familiar conceptions of rights and freedom. The moral standards could still be regarded as unchanged. The Scriptures and the Declaration of Independence could be appealed to and although some went so far as to denounce the Constitution, American society as a whole strove rather to make its attitude seem to accord with the Constitution than to admit frankly that social needs had outgrown the Constitution. 'Legal fiction,' through which the courts like to preserve the semblance of fixed principles, could probably never have been taken so seriously, even by the law itself, if it had not suited on the whole the conservative temper of American society. On the one hand, therefore, the learned professions, on the other, society as a whole, had a relatively fixed system.

How admirably the classical and mathematical method of the time prepared the student for such a scheme of fixed conceptions! Syntax and prosody presented a perfect system, a logical whole, which needed not to be investigated, but to be learned and applied. The future theologian learned respect for authority as he searched the scriptures of Hadley and Goodwin, or Liddell and Scott. In the statutes and decisions of Harkness the future disciple of Blackstone gained practice in tracing subjunctive or dative back to its constitutional rights and limitations. To watch for agreement in gender, number and case, remains, I am told by legal educators, an unmatched training for legal procedure. Finally, Euclid's axioms were the favorite symbol for the supposedly fixed rules of eternal right which every good citizen should learn to respect and obey. If there was any doubt as to this fixity the course in philosophy was calculated to remove it.

This exact adaptation of the method of college to the methods of the professions seems to account, in part at least, for the results achieved in the way of efficient training. It was maintained and the claim need not here be challenged, that the old college training gave power and effectiveness. Modern experimentation has tended to discredit the abstract conception of 'power,' gained once for all by some hard study, and then applied to any task that presents itself. But the old training was not isolated or in a vacuum. It was about as near the

whole habit of mind and technique of method which later life would
employ as anything that could be devised. It was thus essentially,
although unconsciously, vocational in method, while 'liberal' in ideal.

Both in its intellectual ideal of liberal or free culture, and in its
method of instruction the college was therefore well fitted for its
former place in American society. No wonder that the educational
creator pronounced it all very good. And so long as the Sabbath Day
lasted the system was beyond criticism.

II. THE PRESENT SITUATION

The variety of subjects now offered, and the elective system as the
method of determining the student's course, are in part due to the
activity of science in organizing new materials. With the wealth of
resources offered by the natural and social sciences and by modern
literatures it seemed impossible to restrict access to the city of the elect
to the single straight and narrow path formerly followed. There must
be gates on four sides instead of on one. But there has also been a
social factor in the change, even if it has not always been consciously
recognized.

Economic and social expansion has increased greatly the number
of occupations for which trained intelligence is needed. Technical
schools have arisen in partial answer to this demand, but the college
has made its responses also through its variety of subjects with its
freedom of individual selection. The progress of science, as represented especially in the graduate school, has no doubt in many cases
given to subjects a specialized mode of treatment which is as technical
in its way as the method which any professional school pursues. This
apparently suits well the needs of one of the new vocations for which
the college has come to be a preparation—that of the teacher. The
young women who have come to form so large a part of our college
constituency, and who for the most part have been looking forward to
teaching, have found their needs well met. But for other occupations,
especially for nonprofessional life, no such vocational connection has
been worked out. Studies have become individualistic and detached
in a far greater degree than was true of the old curriculum, which was
really, though unconsciously, vocational.

But economic and social expansion has had another consequence
for the college. It has increased greatly the number of persons financially able to enjoy the best opportunities available. And whatever the
attraction which literature or science may have for some of these

intrinsically, or whatever the value a college degree may assume as a mark of social distinction, the real standard of value generated by this whole process, as Professor Sumner has pointed out, is that of 'success.' The studies of the college course seem to bear little relation to this ideal.

And this leads us to a broader statement. The fixed ideals and standards of the older society, which kept men in their place and held them to their work, have broken down. The churches are feeling the same difficulty. Men are largely absent from the pews. They, or at least many of them, are not taking the churches seriously. Many in former days were kept in the church by the general ideals of the community, and so in college many who had no absorbing interest in the work for its own sake nevertheless yielded to the spirit of college and society, and worked under the general idea that the discipline of the college course was validated in a superior law. Such students no longer feel any external pressure. Serious-minded men are groping for new conceptions in religion, economics, politics and law. But these have not been thoroughly enough worked out as yet to replace the old fixed control. Not only the flippant, but the earnest are more or less at sea as to standards and values. As Mr. Crothers puts it, even "the way of the benefactor is hard."

Some, indeed, seem to feel fairly well satisfied with the situation. President Eliot in his recent work on university administration[1] has a good deal of faith in the present system if there is a proper intrinsic relation maintained between courses, supplemented by a judicious arrangement of the time schedule. Some colleges have changed their schedules so as to require residence at the weekend from those students who had fallen into the habit of spending their leisure half week in neighboring cities. But such considerations, as well as reports like that of the Harvard Committee, and the frank statements of students themselves, point to a real defect. Some would attribute the difficulty entirely to the presence of a frivolous class. But this is evasive. Many, if not most, even of this class, settle down to hard work the moment they enter business or a professional school. And even those who are not on principle averse to anything like strenuous effort feel a certain unreality in the whole situation. There seems to be not only the attitude of 'detachment' belonging to the older conception of 'liberal' education, but also an attitude which the aestheticians call 'make-believe.' Now detachment, or even make-believe, may be valuable as a

1. Charles William Eliot, *University Administration* (Boston: Houghton, 1908).

factor in developing a broader, deeper interest, and a more significant, richer purpose. But four years of make-believe seems to be overworking this factor. The young men themselves are coming to think so, and the public at large, while taught to respect the wisdom of its educational experts, is beginning to ask questions.

III. SUGGESTIONS TOWARD READJUSTMENT

The general line along which remedy is to be sought for the present lack of seriousness and lack of connection seems to be a *reconstruction of the college ideal of liberal culture*. This promises to be brought about by a greater introduction of the vocational element and spirit into college work. And this introduction of the vocational into the liberal is being made possible and desirable because *the vocational is being itself permeated and transformed by the liberal*.

The reason for the old-time sharp opposition of the liberal to the utilitarian and professional was, as we have noted, to protect the intellectual interest and keep the self free from alien constraint or narrow bounds prescribed by vocational conditions. But a new face has been put upon this situation by the development which is going on in the industries and occupations, and in some, at least, of the learned professions. For the various occupations are being organized more and more along scientific lines; they are becoming permeated with intellectual and aesthetic interest; they demand of themselves a wider reach and stimulate a broader survey. Insofar as they do this they break down the distinction between the liberal and the vocational. Not the way in which knowledge is to be used—much less the fact that it is not used at all—but the method and spirit in which it is pursued on the one hand, and its breadth of human interest on the other, make it liberal. Any study is liberal, if pursued in a scientific manner and given significance for human life. Such studies call out a widening self. In such studies the mind comes to its own. In such it gains power. In such it is no longer determined by needs or conditions foreign to itself. Rather it is using these needs and conditions as the most effective instruments for asserting itself.

Medicine is perhaps the farthest advanced of the professions in this respect. And the college studies pursued by the future teacher, which are professional so far as their future use makes studies professional, show the absurdity of the old distinction on the basis of utility, or nonutility. For Latin or mathematics as pursued by the future teacher of these subjects is probably more liberalizing than when pursued by those who do not expect to make use of them.

Nor has the process of permeating vocations with scientific interest stopped with the so-called professions. Modern commerce and industry involve the use of intelligence in ways that are properly scientific. And there is no reason why, if studied in their historic development and in their bearing on human welfare, they may not call out as broad and as human an interest as any other field of human activity.

This mutual permeation of the vocations by the scientific and of the liberal by the practical looks, indeed, toward a more effective and positive type of 'freedom' than the older conception of the more romantic and negative sort, which sharply opposed the interests of the self to the sphere of its action. The older freedom from constraint corresponded to the formal freedom which was so important an element in political and religious liberty, and which was so prominent an ideal in the last of the eighteenth and during most of the nineteenth centuries. The courts by their distinction between law and in fact, which tends to prevent the contamination of legal doctrine by recognition of actual conditions, maintain this theoretical freedom as a basis in many of their decisions. But social and economic facts emphasize that it is positive resources which give the only freedom that amounts to anything. Psychological analysis shows that only as the mind has both ideas and positive control of its instruments is it free in any considerable degree. The student is then free of his world, is fitted to lead a free life, is having a liberal education, in proportion as he is getting such control of the instruments of knowledge and such efficiency in dealing with his fellow men as makes him master not merely of his ideas, his emotions and his purposes, but of his world. The old individualism in education as in religion, was largely to lose or hold off from the world in order to save the soul by culture. The new scientific and social situation demands, and in increasing degree will make it possible, that the educated man shall control his world. And in so doing he will save himself. When this conception is embodied in the college there will be no lack of seriousness.

When the colleges have made their work once more a genuine and serious preparation for the new social situation they will be able to give society in turn the aid it needs in changing from the old fixed conceptions, and finding a new type of social order—an order that shall make larger provision for progress. This help, I believe, is to come through the influence of the newer experimental method which largely under the influence of our graduate study is coming to leaven the best work in all subjects. It has its fitness for our new conditions as conspicuously as the older method fitted the conditions of a relatively fixed status.

The laboratory method of studying the sciences began to gain ground in the colleges at about the same time as the introduction of the elective system. It has been strongly reinforced by historical or genetic conceptions given prominence by the doctrine of evolution. Although still very imperfectly carried out, it is replacing more and more the scheme of fixed conceptions and deduction from established rules which constituted the older syntactical, mathematical and moral systems. If this can be carried over into professional conceptions and social organization there will be once more a close connection between the college and society. Medicine and philanthropy have already made notable progress. Theology and religion are feeling the need of reconstruction. The courts are perhaps necessarily the most conservative elements—unless possibly we except schools and colleges—but when legal education has felt fully the force of genetic study we may expect that both criminal and civil justice will consider in greater degree actual human and social conditions in controlling human relations.

And if the established professions need a new method to enable them to fulfill their vocation in the society that is to be, business and industry need the aid of scientific method and standards to make them professional in the true sense. Considering these occupations as nonprofessional, we have left them no test for the success that every normal man wishes to secure, but that of economic gain. And since economic gain may result either from service or from exploitation, our educational theory and training have lent no such powerful support to the conception of public service through one's vocation as the scientific standards of law, medicine and teaching afford members of those professions. As President Eliot has pointed out, this purely financial standard has not proved a conspicuous success even from the standpoint of efficient management of business enterprise. Is it not desirable that education should try to introduce other and more scientific standards? And is it too high-flying an optimism to hope that the time may come when it will be considered as unprofessional to manage a country's industries or transportation or banking with an eye principally to financial gain as it now is to practice medicine with such a standard of success? The scientific and the ethical here go hand in hand.

The professional schools themselves are not likely to embody this method in its full significance in their work. The function of the college intellectually is to make this the dominant temper of the student.

And the second intellectual function of the college is to give material for the future citizen. First of all, he must know society. The social sciences ought to be strongly developed. But training for a democratic society is not limited to a peculiar subject. Nothing human is foreign to the purpose of the college. But it is a fair question whether literary study may not be for the college less an end in itself and more an avenue through which one comes to know and sympathize with all sorts and conditions of men. And even the natural sciences need not hesitate to let their bearing on human welfare appear.

An experimental method and a social standpoint are, I conceive, the two respects in which the college should perform its office of liberal training in a way suited to our new conditions.

In view of the fact that women now form so large an element in our colleges, it may be permitted to point out some special applications of these considerations to women's education on the one hand, and to the determination of woman's place in the social order on the other.

College education for women has thus far followed essentially the lines laid down by the general system already in vogue. 'Equal opportunity' was the watchword at first, and it is probable that any differentiation in kind might have been regarded as involving inferiority in standard or value. 'Woman's work' is still, it must be confessed, often treated by the world in general as implying a depreciatory estimate. As already noticed, a large number of women, looking forward to the occupation of teaching, have found the existing courses largely vocational. For this, or other reasons, the lack of intellectual seriousness has thus far not been so much in evidence as with the men. But as an increasingly larger proportion of the women students will not become teachers, the question of connection between college work and after life is likely to become more acute. The need for introducing into college more material of a vocational sort, and conversely of permeating woman's vocational work of all kinds with a scientific method and a broadly human interest, is likely to become increasingly evident. The work of the woman in the home has lagged far behind the occupations of men in point of organization and of the use of scientific method. An educated woman is apt to feel, vaguely, that the whole household life—once the center of all the industries, and the place where discovery and invention had their chief seat—has now been left behind in the progress of civilization and is no longer a field for the exercise of intellectual powers of the highest order. This inevitably tends to depreciation of such occupation, and to strain in the family life.

Some would find the remedy by purely sentimental and emotional exaltation of home life. They would in effect continue the separation between the scientific spirit and the home. Is it not more promising to work, rather, along the lines suggested in the case of men's vocations, and try to liberalize women's vocations by scientific methods and a more broadly human standpoint? It is not yet sufficiently recognized, for example, that in modern city life the home is virtually coterminous with the city. The sanitation, the food supply, the health of the home are now dependent on municipal conditions; the education of the children, the influences that surround them, the ideals that influence them are reached chiefly by forces that are civic and philanthropic in a broad sense, rather than domestic in the narrow sense. And further, while the organization of production, the conduct of litigation, and various other traditional vocations are likely to remain predominantly in the hands of men, it is increasingly apparent that as wealth increases beyond provision for bare necessities woman becomes the more important factor in determining the course of consumption. Vocational training for woman will then be conceived broadly enough to enable her to plan not only economically, but with taste and refinement for those satisfactions that are permanent and genuine, and also with intelligent judgment for those that make for the larger social welfare.

And the final application of the experimental method in this connection lies just in the determination of what women's vocations are ultimately to be. The older society had no doubts. The religious, economic, political and social status of woman could all be deduced with perfect exactness. It was as easy as the agreement of a verb with its subject.The present equilibrium is unstable. Is it not a scientific method to work out the problem with careful reference to the new conditions as they emerge, rather than to decide by past history or fixed conceptions?

In conclusion I may barely hint at a question which no doubt arises as to the bearing of this whole discussion on the college as a distinct organization. If professional education is to become liberalized, what need of the college? And if the spirit of investigation is the main factor, why again the college? Why not the university joined directly to the secondary school? In the long run I think this is likely to depend on the need of a factor which has been barely referred to above. Effective education depends in part on a scientific factor, but there is also a personal factor. One must know his fellows and how to cooperate with them. This is increasingly important with the growing complexity of society. And this efficiency in dealing with others is not easily secured in professional or graduate school where the emphasis is on subject and method, and the life is individualistic. If the college can maintain a corporate life in which knowledge is vitalized, in which there is actual give and take, actual sympathy and friction, active interchange not only between mind and mind but between will and will, then it will find its own place, and live secure.

10 | Darwin and Evolutionary Ethics

It is opportune that while we are honoring Darwin for his far-reaching influence in almost every field of modern thought we should consider his relation to ethics. The power of his name is being used in support of policies and doctrines which he certainly did not favor in his writings, and which there is no good reason to think he would approve today. Speaking of the general reaction against humanitarianism which shows itself in so many forms today Mr. Hobhouse says that "the doctrine that human progress depends upon the forces which condition biological evolution has in fact been the primary cause of the reaction. Darwin himself, indeed, was conscious of the limitations of his own hypothesis," but

> what has filtered through into the social and political thought of the time has been the belief that the time-honored doctrine "might is right" has a scientific foundation in the laws of biology. Progress comes about through a conflict in which the fittest survives. It must, therefore, be unwise in the long run . . . to interfere with the struggle. We must not sympathize with the beaten and the weak, lest we be tempted to preserve them. The best thing that can happen is that they should be utterly cut off, for they are the inferior stock and their blood must not mix with ours.

Darwin himself certainly held a very different doctrine.

As has often been pointed out there are two distinct aspects of the relation between ethical theory and evolution, which have been termed respectively the 'evolution of ethics' and the 'ethics of evolution.' But historically, origin and validity have been persistently and almost inseparably connected. To show that a law is not binding, prove that it is a recent, or 'artificial' construction. To give a strong force to custom, say that "it is not of yesterday or today but lives

From *The Psychological Review* 16.3 (1909): 195–206 [1909:07].

forever, and none knows whence it sprang." In both ancient and modern times the question as to the origin of law or justice or current moral valuations has been forced to the front in times of conflict over the authority of institutions and customs. Such a situation called out the varying theories of the Greek enlightenment and the serious efforts of Spinoza and Hobbes, Locke and Rousseau. But whereas interest in the ancient world confined itself for the most part to the more objective questions as to the origin of institutions which likewise formed the initial question for modern reflection, the growing importance of the individual has brought increasingly to the front the more subjective problem: How does the moral consciousness arise? Is it an 'intuition' or 'sense' implanted once for all in human nature and incapable of further analysis? Or is it a product of gradual formation which can either be analyzed into simpler elements bound together by association or traced back historically to social forces? These are questions quite analogous to the general alternative between special creation of separate species or that continuity which Darwin maintained as his first premise.

The early evolutionary theories of morals were on their face primarily designed to condemn or approve the existing standards and institutions, and only incidentally as scientific accounts. Polus in the well-known passage argues that might is right by nature's law, and that all existing judgments to the contrary are a *Sklavenmoral*, set up by the weak, and gradually accepted by members of other classes who are 'charmed' from early youth by the suggestions emanating from dominant influence. Or again, what is 'stronger, freer, and more masterful' is admired when it does not infringe too strongly on the interests of others; hence the interest of the stronger is really the basis of all law and 'justice.' Democrats and aristocrats make laws and shape institutions each for their own interest. Our Καλοκαγαθοί are 'honorable' and 'excellent' from the standpoint of their own class; but this is because "Nomos is lord of all."

On the other hand, if it is desired to strengthen respect for existing codes, reverence and a sense of justice are attributed to a primeval gift of the gods, designed to make associated life possible and thereby afford man protection against wild beasts—aid in the struggle for existence. Or by Aristotle with a pregnant reversal of standpoint, nature is to be sought not in the beginning, but in the perfected realization of powers. The process of social and moral evolution begins with impulse (ὁρμή) to the life in common, but the increasing organization of society gives increasing opportunity for human powers. For though in complete development man is the noblest, yet without the conceptions and the practice of justice and the excellence for which organized society is necessary "no animal is so unscrupulous or savage, none so sensual, none so gluttonous." This doctrine, then, equally with the opposing theories sought a standard in 'reality,' in evolution. But in its intent it looked forward, not backward, to a social intelligence and not to a physical force. Nevertheless, it is obvious that the conception of a law of nature as universal in human institutions and innate in the human soul could easily become in legal doctrine a ground for justifying institutions as they now are.

The reason why 'nature' appealed so strongly to the Greek was not biological. He did not trouble himself particularly as to the future of the race. Professor Dewey has recently stated forcibly why nature was such a word to conjure with:

> What, finally, is this Nature to which the philosophy of society and the individual so bound itself? It is the nature which figures in Greek custom and myth; the nature resplendent and adorned which confronts us in Greek poetry and art: the animism of savage man purged of grossness and generalized by unerring aesthetic taste into beauty and system. The myths had told of the loves and hates, the caprices and desertions of the gods, and, behind them all, inevitable Fate. Philosophy translated these tales into formulae of the brute fluctuation of rapacious change held in bounds by the final and supreme end: the rational good. The animism of the popular mind died to reappear as cosmology.[1]

We find the evolution of morality and the law of nature the center of discussion once more at the opening of modern thought. A Falstaff might flippantly appeal to biology to justify his predatory designs upon Justice Shallow: "If the young dace be a bait for the old pike, I see no reason in the law of nature but I may snap at him." But Hobbes wished to establish a firm basis for government by showing the brutishness of a 'state of nature'; Spinoza to point the way of escape from 'human bondage.' The striking thing about these attempts is the discredit which has now fallen upon the natural. One school of writers, indeed, maintains the rational and social nature of man, and the rational laws of cosmic nature, but the most striking evolutionary theories, those of Hobbes and Spinoza, conceive nature as the realm where force, and the instinct for self-preservation, hold sway. This was doubtless due largely to the theological dualism between the

---

1. John Dewey, *Ethics* (New York: Columbia UP, 1908).

'natural man,' born in sin, totally depraved, with no good instincts, and the spiritual man who must needs be 'born again,' regenerated by special divine grace, before he could be just or good.

In the case of such a writer as Hobbes, very likely a reinforcement to the dualistic attitude came from the horrors of war which seemed to disclose the primitive passions of man when unchecked by the barriers built by law and government against them. In Spinoza's case there was a metaphysical reinforcement. For although it is the very essence of substance (or God) that involves existence and persistence and becomes in man the 'endeavor' for self-preservation, yet as 'the force whereby a man persists in existing is limited,' and as he is thus necessarily 'a part of nature' and 'passive,' "it follows that man is necessarily always a prey to his passions."

The forces adduced by the writers who sought to bridge the chasm without appealing to supernatural agency were various. The view of the world and life *sub specie aeternitatis* in which Spinoza saw the only relief from human bondage made the saved as few as the elect of Calvinism. Nevertheless, the measure of reason which men in general have is sufficient to lead them to seek greater power and advantage through union in the civil order. Man perceives his need of his fellow men and in this sense may be called sociable. Hobbes dwelt upon the fear which drove men to political life and legal morality. Mandeville introduced pride and susceptibility to flattery as affording the agencies on which superior classes could work in fastening the 'slave morality' (to borrow Nietzsche's phrase) upon the inferior class—thus "savage man was broke." It was avowedly against the supposedly evil effects of such a nominalistic and selfish theory of morals as that of Hobbes that the evolutionary theories arose which claimed a continuity in moral development.

The 'herding instinct,' the 'seed of a boniform nature,' the instinctive disgust or recoil from what is 'nasty,' the 'moral sense' of Shaftesbury and his school all reflect this standpoint. The optimism of 'natural religion' (the term itself was an abomination from the previous standpoint as to the wickedness of the natural), the era of comparative peace, the increase of commerce and general intelligence, all favored the spread of the conception of historical and psychological continuity in the moral process. Hume was able to effect a synthesis of the claims of reason and instinct in the rise of society and justice. Sex instinct starts the process and brings pairs together. The advantage of society when once experienced is then consciously appreciated. A civil order which included justice is 'artificial.'

Emancipated from unquestioning acceptance of the authority of the Church and the Leviathan, the individual was moved to examine the nature and origin of the inward authority which was replacing external control. If conscience has the right to govern the world how is such a right derived? The rationalist account of the 'moral faculty' did not lend itself easily to evolutionary treatment. Reason tended to be conceived mathematically or logically. It was 'timeless,' 'universal and necessary.' Kant, indeed, in his essay on political evolution for once seems on the verge of a very different conception. Men's passions and conflicting impulses call out a civil order and evoke a reason to recognize its values. And the later German idealism foreshadowed, at least, if it did not clearly grasp, the conception of an evolution of reason. But it was the 'moral sentiment' which lent itself most easily to genetic treatment whether by the associationist analysis of Hartley or by the brilliant beginnings of social psychology in Adam Smith.

The 'validity' of a moral sentiment was not necessarily threatened by considering it genetically. But when the process was conceived hedonistically, as an association of pleasurable elements, it was difficult to ascribe to the product any greater authority than that of any other pleasurable feeling. If my moral sentiment gives me pleasure in a generous act, well; if I find more pleasure in an egoistic act, who can say me nay? If it is a matter of individual association, why is my liberty judged by another man's conscience? J. S. Mill, as he tells us, felt in his own experience the artificial character of the theory, and in the *Utilitarianism* took two important steps toward a more adequate conception. On the one hand, the 'social feelings' took on the form of an active 'natural want' rather than of an association of pleasures. On the other hand, he considered that first the social state, so natural, so necessary and habitual, and then the necessity of cooperation with others and of proposing "a collective, not an individual interest" were agencies in bringing about the social feelings. It wanted but an additional step to disclose the individual as a 'social outcome' rather than as a 'social unit,' but this was a revolution for which the time was not ripe.

The social explanation through Sympathy, begun by Hume in hedonistic terms and developed along broader lines by Adam Smith, cast no discredit upon the product for a generation which valued the social. Not until race collisions, class contrasts, and the clashing of ideals of a new era had set up as morally desirable a sharp antagonism between the 'higher' and 'lower' races, between the 'fit' and the 'masses,' between the 'solitary' and the 'herd,' did sympathy become a synonym for weakness, and come to be regarded as fatally infecting the moral sentiment it had aided in producing.

The great contribution of Spencer was the he placed moral evolution—both moral progress and the formation of moral sentiments—in the sweep of his universal process. We may easily criticize his hedonistic analysis of the 'moral sense,' or, from another point of view, his belief that he has reconciled the empirical and a priori schools of thought by his doctrine of the experiences of the race. We may smile at his derivation of the consciousness of duty, and from our present standpoint of social psychology detect the fallacies of his atomistic conception of the individual in group life. We may think that his appeal to evolution in the *Social Statics* is rather to confirm a doctrine of political ethics already established on other grounds. The fact remains that he had conceived a worldwide movement. Mental and moral and social evolution gained immensely in their significance and definiteness when placed under a law asserted also of all the inorganic and organic world. And as compared with the great evolutionary conceptions of German idealism, the great advance in the natural sciences and the relative simplicity and clarity of their concepts gave Spencer a great advantage in power of appeal, even if this very simplicity inevitably brought it its own limitations for the explanatory principles so derived. Applied to morality the principle of adaptation makes "moral progress not an accident but a necessity. Instead of civilization being artificial it is a part of nature, all of a piece with the development of an embryo or the unfolding of a flower." For "all evil results from the non-adaptation of constitution to conditions"; but it is an essential principle of life that non-adaptation is ever being rectified until the adaptation is complete. Man's primitive predatory life required sacrifice of the welfare of other beings to his own, and his unfitness for present society is due to a survival of these traits formerly necessary.

The wide-reaching influence of Darwin upon ethical theory was not so much by his own discussion of the moral sentiments in the *Descent of Man*, as by the general biological and logical principles of his *Origin of Species*.[2] The question was soon raised as to the operation of natural selection in the social and moral sphere. No evolutionary theories had

---

2. Charles Robert Darwin, *On the Origin of Species by Means of Natural Selection, or the Preservation of Favoured Races in the Struggle for Life* (1859); *The Descent of Man* (1871).

brought home so vividly the continuity of the whole organic world. None, therefore, had seemed to immerse man so deeply in nature, and make him merely one link in a chain all forged of one metal and in one fire. Before Darwin's own discussion of morality in the *Descent of Man* numerous important contributions appeared. Among those which Darwin cites as most directly in the line of his problem were those of Wallace, Galton, Bagehot, and Greg.

It remained for Darwin to approach the problem "exclusively from the side of natural history" and "as an attempt to see how far the study of the lower animals throws light on one of the highest psychical faculties of man." The general lines of Darwin's theory are indicated largely by this standpoint and by the fact that the dominating English tradition of his time sought the distinctive character of the moral in the emotional rather than in the rational factor. His proposition is "that any animal whatever, endowed with well-marked social instincts, the parental and filial affections being here included, would inevitably acquire a moral sense or conscience, as soon as its intellectual powers had become as well or nearly as well developed, as in man."

The four steps in the development are the following: (1) The social instincts lead to pleasure in society, to sympathy, to aid. (2) With the rise of memory, pains due to unsatisfied instinct would arise when the more enduring social instincts had been overcome by some temporarily stronger desire. (3) The common opinion of a group, expressed in language, and appealing to the love of approbation due to sympathy, would become paramount as a guide. (4) These factors would be reinforced by habit.

The weak points in the scheme as worked out are due largely, first, to conceiving the moral consciousness too exclusively in instinctive and emotional terms. There is no reference to the part of choice in building up a moral agent. Thought or reason appears in it chiefly in the guise of memory and there is but a hint at an intelligent forecasting of the future, and weighing of values with reference to a purpose or end. There is thus little thought of a self, and the crux of the problem takes the form of setting "the more *enduring* social instincts" over against the more transient gratifications of bodily appetite or selfish desire. To throw the whole burden of the consciousness of duty on the single precarious support of the greater 'persistency' in consciousness of the social *instincts* would scarcely be possible for one who had read in ethics as thoroughly as Darwin had studied in the organic field.

The second weakness is of a very different sort, and one which all psychology shared until recently. The individual is conceived to a large degree as the unit, endowed to be sure with social instincts and sympathy which make him responsive to public opinion, but not social in the deeper sense which present psychology is working out and which, it is fair to say, carries out with far more adequate analysis the line of thought which Darwin did much to promote.

For the strong point in Darwin's method of approach was first that it gave to the whole theory of moral evolution a concrete setting in a process which was both broadly conceived and definitely evidenced, and secondly that it gave a much broader basis for the social nature of man than had usually been given by those who had considered man apart from animal life. The examples of mutual aid as well as of instinctive craving for the company of other animals of the species gave a fuller content to the term social, while his long study of animal instincts doubtless kept Darwin from becoming entangled in the hedonistic psychology by which English writers had so often been led astray. It is indeed a striking illustration of Darwin's independence and sagacity that he escaped the common fallacy on this point although, as he says, all the authors whom he had consulted, with a few exceptions, held to the hedonistic theory.

A point of greater present interest because it lies much closer to the question of moral standard is the question how far natural selection is an important factor in the growth of morality and the moral sense. On this point Darwin regards his own discussion as "imperfect and fragmentary." As already noted many writers in the period which had elapsed between the *Origin of Species* and the *Descent of Man* had broached this question. Wallace had pointed out that although man would be little liable to bodily modifications through natural selection his intellectual and moral faculties would be both variable and highly important, hence there would be a field for natural selection. Bagehot's *Physics and Politics* originally published in 1867–1869 has as its secondary title, *Thoughts on the Application of the Principles of Natural Selection to Inheritance and to Political Society,* and is in many ways the most brilliant discussion of the subject which has appeared. This as is well known had emphasized the necessity of coherence, of obedience and law, of the 'cake of custom,' as fundamental elements of strength. "The frame of their morals" must be "set by long ages of transmitted discipline" before there can be individual liberty or general freedom of intercourse. There are also other virtues which are selected by conflict. The military virtues may be said to be the 'preliminary virtues.' On the other hand, Bagehot points out forcibly the defects of the selection which depends upon war. "Humanity, charity, a nice sense of the rights of others, it does not foster." Contempt for physical weakness and for women which mark early society are survivals. So too are the metaphors from law and war which make most of our current moral phrases and frequently vitiate what they illustrate. Military morals exaggerate action and discipline, and place too little value on meditation.

Darwin emphasizes the survival value in primitive life of sympathy, fidelity, and courage. He points out, however, that within a specific group natural selection would frequently work to preserve those less virtuous rather than the more faithful and courageous. The primitive instinct would be gradually reinforced by purposive aid performed at first from selfish motives. Habits of performing benevolent actions would strengthen a feeling of sympathy and "habits followed during many generations, probably tend to be inherited." A more powerful stimulus to social virtue, however, is the praise and blame of fellow men, and this also rests ultimately on sympathy. With "an increase in number of well endowed men and an advancement in the standard of morality," there will be an "immense advantage" to one tribe over another. "A tribe including many members who from possessing in a high degree the spirit of patriotism, fidelity, obedience, courage and sympathy, were always ready to aid one another, and to sacrifice themselves for the common good, would be victorious over most other tribes; and this would be natural selection." With civilized nations, on the other hand, "natural selection apparently effects but little." "The causes which lead to the advance of morality are rather the approbation of our fellow men—the strengthening of our sympathies by habit—example and imitation—reason—experience, and even self-interest—instruction during youth, and religious feelings."

Noteworthy because of its significance for the present 'reaction,' and especially in view of Nietzsche's denunciations, is the stress which Darwin lays upon sympathy:

> Nor could we check our sympathy, even at the urging of hard reason, without deterioration of the noblest part of our nature. The surgeon may harden himself whilst performing an operation, for he knows that he is acting for the good of his patient; but if we were intentionally to neglect the weak and helpless it could only be for a contingent benefit, with an overwhelming present evil. We must therefore bear the undoubtedly bad effects of the weak surviving and propagating their kind.

As we have said, Darwin's own interpretation of the moral standard is not that currently associated with 'Darwinism.' The conception of a purely mechanical process, excluding all 'norms,' is what some find in the evolutionary process as Darwin conceived it. The supreme value of force or might is the lesson which others read in the same process. This makes strength the only virtue and weakness, of which sympathy is a fellow, the only unpardonable sin. A third conception is derived from the process viewed as a series of advancing types. If each lower type finds its meaning in serving as a means for producing a higher type, then man is no longer to be viewed as 'end in himself.' His end is rather to produce the *Übermensch*.

We cannot, of course, discuss these theories within the limits of this paper. As to the first, it is sufficient to remark that values are, of course, not to be sought in a process conceived as 'natural' in a sense which excludes self-conscious valuation. To suppose, on the other hand, that the 'mechanism' which 'governs' in nature excludes the possibility of a consciousness that could be 'normative' would be to interpret the 'continuity' of nature in a way to exclude totally all variation. To appeal to a logical value in urging the truth of the doctrine of mechanical evolution, and to use this appeal to deny all ethical valuation is a thinly disguised contradiction. The fundamental points at issue in the other questions are: (1) Granted the evolution of ethical values, has the process been so uniform and continuous that in seeking guiding principles for life it makes no difference what part of the process we consult? To affirm that such must be the case would be again to give no place to variation. It was the merit of Huxley to point out epigrammatically the difference between the 'ethical,' consciously directed process, and the 'cosmic' process prior to conscious activity. (2) Is the valuation of every man as 'an end,' with the corresponding implication of sympathy, an inherently suicidal moral principle? Will it, if followed, inevitably destroy all moral values by destroying all the more valuable strains and races? That there may be developed a science of eugenics is certainly a consummation devoutly to be wished, but until our civilization corrects some of the gratuitous evils which it now opposes to progress, until it plans dwellings, education, and conditions of work so as to remove the obstacles it now opposes to health and strength, it would seem that the obvious lines of effort were close at hand. For Europe and America to remove the degeneration due to poverty and disease among their own peoples would seem a more hopeful agency of progress than the exploitation of weaker races, and if the 'superior' will not continue their own stock, what will it profit to forbid the inferior to continue theirs? It would indeed be contrary to the implications of the evolutionary method to deny the possibility of new variations, of different standards. But if there is to be any standard at all it must be based on a common good. And if this is abandoned, moral values will not be endangered; they will have already disappeared.

11 The Present Task of Ethical Theory

A university teacher of engineering, in a recent conversation on general questions of human interest, lamented what he styled the 'cold-storage ethics' taught in our colleges and universities. I do not propose to discuss the appropriateness of his characterization, but shall assume that whatever may be true of the elements presented to beginners, ethical theory itself ought to make advance. As compared with logic and metaphysics, ethics has received less than its share of attention in this country. Even the pragmatist movement, which professes to be concerned especially with what is vital and practical, has given more discussion to almost every other part of the field than to ethical theory. The aim of this paper is to point out some of the reconstructions and new constructions which are called for in our fundamental ethical conceptions, if they are to maintain their scientific standing, to interpret the moral life of today, and to furnish guidance to education, jurisprudence, and other agencies of social reform.

Doubtless any such reconstruction in the light of what is temporal and practical will stand self-condemned in the eyes of those who see in ethics only a pure science of eternal truths, which has nothing to learn from the changing conditions of experience. As against the separation of all empirical material from ethics, I am content to side with the great idealist when, in response to the inquiry whether it is enough to have understanding of the essence of justice, and to be acquainted only with the divine circle and sphere, knowing nothing of the human circle, he replies, "The knowledge which is only super-human is ridiculous in man," and adds that even the impure and uncertain art which uses the false rule and the false circle must be thrown into the cup of the good "if any of us is ever to find his way home."

From *The International Journal of Ethics* 20.2 (1910): 141–152 [1910:01].

It may not be the province of ethical theory to organize prophylaxis, or guide criminal and civil jurisprudence. But I submit that it is the business of ethical theory to make such statements of the elements of the self as can be used by eugenics and education, and so to define personality and the state that jurisprudence may find a more adequate standard for its conceptions, when it considers either individual rights or social welfare. Anyone who reads judicial decisions in which these conceptions are discussed will recognize how often the conceptions of individual and society are mutually exclusive. It is rare that an opinion shows such awareness of the import of its terms as the concise comment of Justice Holmes: "The Fourteenth Amendment does not enact Mr. Herbert Spencer's *Social Statics*." No more important task confronts ethical theory, in the United States at least, than to frame conceptions which may do for our conditions what the ethical masters of former days have done for their age.

But there is a further reason for the reconstruction in question, namely, that the conceptions of ethics, however pure they may appear to be, bear unmistakable proof of their construction under special conditions, and are determined in their content largely by the special theories to which they were opposed. None of the conceptions of ethical theory can be regarded as 'pure.' Thus it is easy to see that the method of rationalism with the goal of freedom, which is conspicuous in Kant and his followers, reflects the modern political development on the one side, the movement for religious and intellectual freedom on the other. In political life, the way to freedom lay through the control of arbitrary power by law. In the religious and intellectual spheres, freedom from dogma and superstition was achieved under the flag of reason. Again, in utilitarianism the method of analysis and the definition of the standard were subsidiary to the goal of democratic satisfaction, as over against privilege fortifying itself by mysterious sentiments and intuitions. And in evolutionary ethics, the biological influence is too obvious to require mention.

Two features of the present situation which are highly important for ethical theory are (1) the increasing development of general scientific method, and its successful application to the mental and social sciences and the problems of human welfare; (2) the increase in social organization of all kinds, and the corresponding reaction upon the life of the individual.

The science of the seventeenth and eighteenth centuries gave man a far more intelligible cosmos. As Galileo showed the heavens to be of one sort with the earth, as Newton reduced their manifold movements to the expression of a simple law, as Kant and Laplace deduced present complexity from simple origins, the *flammantia moenia mundi* were opened far wider than by the speculations of Democritus and Epicurus. And the psychology of the eighteenth century made a beginning in the work of understanding the inner springs of conduct. But science seems to be taking on, more and more, a positive and constructive attitude. As astronomy, its function was primarily to enlarge the mental horizon. As chemistry and biology and electrical physics, it doubtless enlarges our views of the universe, but it also brings into the fore the control of natural resources, of health, and possibly of heredity. Economics, which at one time seemed merely a 'dismal science' of observing 'iron laws,' is now aware that the discovery of a law is only the first step in intelligent progress. The law of gravitation does not prevent men from flying. Political science, in the highly suggestive recent book of Mr. Graham Wallas, is likewise directed to the more positive tasks of comprehending the working forces of political life, and the moral possibilities of such knowledge are pointed out.[1]

The second factor which both requires ethical reconstruction and offers suggestions for it, namely, increasing social organization, need not be dwelt upon. It has received recently a lucid statement in Professor Cooley's *Social Organization*.[2]

It is proposed, then, to outline briefly certain reconstructions in such conceptions as Reason, the Self, Freedom, Happiness, and the State.[3]

'Reason' has doubtless been one of the most fruitful conceptions under which the moral life has been interpreted. It has always stood for an organization of life by intelligence, as contrasted with control by impulse, passion, habit, dogma, or political constraint. But in Kant's system it got its definition, to a considerable extent, by its opposition, in the theoretical sense, (1) to particulars of sense, and (2) to the understanding, which stood for the world of physical science. The

1. Graham Wallace, *Human Nature in Politics* (Boston: Houghton, 1909).
2. Charles Horton Cooley, *Social Organization, A Study of the Larger Mind* (New York: Scribners, 1909) [cf. 1909:16].
3. As one of the tasks of ethics I should certainly include that of a study of the actual ethical standards recognized in various sections and classes. This, however, has been so well enforced by Frank Chapman Sharp, *A Study of the Influence of Custom on the Moral Judgment*, Bulletin of the University of Wisconsin no. 303 (Madison, 1908) that I do not need to dwell upon it [cf. 1908:18].

particulars of sense meant the sensationalism which reduced all experience to its abstract analytic elements. The world of the understanding meant such a mechanically determined universe as that of the *Système de la Nature*, which had no room for purpose.

The situation today is changed. In the first place, 'sense' itself has been brought within the psychical and the rational. That is to say, modern scientific method does not recognize the mutual exclusion of sense-perception and reflective thought. It insists rather on the constant reference of hypotheses to particulars and upon the constant interpretation of particulars by theory. And in the second place, we do not need to set the world of law over against the world of purpose. The first formulation of social, economic, historical, political, and biological laws like the first formulations of mathematical physics seemed to carry this implication. Now we are realizing that the formulation of laws is itself a work of selective purpose, and is but a first step to the realization of further purpose. So in the psychological sphere, it is no longer a sharp opposition of impulse or habit to reason, but rather a question of the greater or lesser intensity and scope of attention. From the standpoint of present science, the great antithesis which is most important is that between the method of trial and error and the method of definitely adapting means to consciously selected ends. If this were the conception of reason held up as an ethical authority or an ethical value, it would not only command more ready assent, but would be far more fruitful as a basis for definite responsibility and direction.

The two conceptions, the Self and Freedom, were likewise defined by Kant largely by their contraries. The self which asserts itself in the moral life is the intelligible self, opposed, on the one hand, to the phenomenal world and self of causally determined time experience, and, on the other, to the lawless and selfish desires. In the former of these aspects, its supremacy means transcendental freedom; in the latter, the freedom of autonomy. Green, again, in his conception of self-consciousness as reproducing an eternal self-consciousness, and by its relation of particulars to itself, as rising above the animal life to moral capacity, shows a similar influence.

The conceptions suggested by the present scientific method and by the present social organization, seem more significant for ethical theory than these more negative determinations. Science does indeed transcend time, and social organization may be said to transcend—if not space, at least the separation of human individuals. But they both do this in a positive way. Science transcends time, not merely in framing timeless concepts, but also—and this is much more to the point—by its actual ranging through time in its every selection and purposive act. Science indeed 'discriminates itself' from the particulars with which it deals, and relates these to its purpose, and thereby distinguishes itself from the animal procedure. But the conception of a unity of purpose, rather than of a unity versus plurality, gives the conception of a self which is more adequate for moral theory.

It is perhaps scarcely necessary to say that this conception of the self needs to be supplemented by social psychology. This has been done in part, but only in part. Psychology has thus far been following lines comparable to those of general biology. Ethical theory needs for an adequate conception of the self in relation to conduct, studies comparable to ecology, on the one hand, and to the study of special types, on the other. Neither jurisprudence nor education can work effectively without such more specific determination of the self.

The positive conception of constructive science affords also a valuable point of view for considering what theory has tried to embody in the term Freedom. I do not question that there have been psychological analyses which have pointed out with sufficient acuteness the fallacies of the past. But the conflict is settled only to be reopened. And the reason for this is not mere stupidity. It is because the kind of liberty or determinism at issue is largely a matter of what it is opposed to. When the conception of outside control versus inner spontaneity was shaped by political imagery of slavery versus liberty, or anarchy versus law, the adjustment was brought about by the conception of autonomy. Or, insofar as the issue was directed against mechanically caused action by the libertarians and against uncaused, unrelated action by the determinists, the higher point of view was found in the insight that causality was itself a category of the mind in its synthesis of experience, and that mechanism was an abstract aspect of experience. Now, however, the issue is more frequently presented in the biological and sociological terms. Is one completely determined by heredity and environment? When the question is so stated, light seems near from the analogy of the sciences which deal with these fields. Insofar as science is taking active steps to control heredity through eugenics, it is certainly answering the first part of the question. Insofar as the methods of publicity and social influence give each a chance to know and affect the public sentiment, social psychology is answering the second.

The libertarian, one might say, has been right in the insistence that there is a distinctive characteristic of human conduct, as compared

with mechanism or brute life. He has been right in his conviction
that conscious decision involves a new element not contained in the
antecedents. He has usually been wrong in the conceptions by which
he has tried to interpret these convictions. Science in its constructive
work affords in its contrast with trial and error, or mere natural selection, a conception for the first aspect of the demand. Kant indeed saw
in part this active character of the mind in science, as versus the old
conception of passive copying of reality, but the selective, purposive
character needed the general advance of science, on the one hand,
and the special studies of comparative psychology, on the other, to
bring it clearly to view.

In some respects the teaching of social organization is still more
suggestive on the psychology of choice, and with the increasing recognition of the social nature of consciousness, the bearing of the method
of social organization upon the question of determination by environment becomes increasingly pertinent. The corresponding question
stated in social terms is whether the action or decision of any group—
political party, club, or the like—is all 'framed up,' or fixed in advance,
or whether in conference or discussion there is really a factor present
not already existent in the particular wills. It is recognized that this
very fact of conflict and collision, of mutual stimulation and modification, marks off a genuinely free body. In like manner the decisions of
the individual contain a distinctive character which we may, if we
please, call freedom, when they give to each impulse or idea its part
in the adjustment, and so involve a genuinely new factor.

But the moment we conceive our question in terms either of scientific control or of social psychology, we recognize that freedom is not
a question of yes or no, but rather of how far and how much. To say
that there is no control of nature by science is palpably absurd; to say
that all progress is due to natural selection of accidental variations is
becoming less and less plausible with the conscious organization of
industrial, social, and political agencies. On the other hand, the limitations of our education, our economics, and our legislation are too
obvious to need mention, and from social organization the same lesson
follows. For the conclusion and actions of a group vary greatly in the
extent to which all voices are heard and all opinions weighed. To get
the whole question of freedom conceived as a question of degrees,
and to get the conditions clearly defined would, I believe, be great
service to the work of education and the conceptions of jurisprudence.

Another great conception which ethical theory inherits is Happiness. No adequate system of ethics will fail to give some place to

human interests and their objects. The relation of happiness to pleasure, as presented in Mill's *Utilitarianism*, has no doubt been argued
and analyzed more than sufficiently. But the much more fruitful definition in his *On Liberty*—"utility in the largest sense, grounded on the
permanent interests of man as a progressive being"—has received less
attention. To find out, if possible, what these interests are, is a worthy
task for ethical theory. To apply a scientific method to this end, was
a thought that might well come to such a mind as that of Spencer. It
appears in his attempt "to deduce from the laws of life and the conditions of existence what kinds of action necessarily tend to produce
happiness." But it is evident that, as he carries out this plan, he has
failed to take into account sufficiently that it is a progressive being
whose interests are to be discovered. He deduces his conception of
justice largely from the conditions of survival in animal life. He deduces his conceptions of the sphere of government from the conditions
of military life. He does not consider that the whole method of human
progress in a scientific age may relate itself to that of earlier times, as
the psychological process of conscious, purposive action relates to the
cruder method of trial and error. He does not see that the different
method of social interaction now at work makes possible, and indeed
necessary, a very different conception of happiness from that which
could be possible in an earlier time. It is not intended to imply that
taking science and social organization as guides will mean defining
happiness as a combination of university research with unlimited
newspapers and social clubs. But that it may mean a progressive
sharing by each more fully in the thought and life of the world,
and that collective agency, whether of government or of voluntary
cooperation, will accomplish much for the interest of a progressive
being which has been impossible in the past, I do believe to be the
indication of both science and social organization.

Finally, there is the field of the philosophy of law and of the state
in which, despite our extraordinary political activity, American philosophers have had little to say. Individualism has expressed in classic
form its conceptions. Idealism has set another philosophy of society
over against the standards of natural rights and individual utility.
Idealism from Plato down has meant, in social philosophy, the discovery and emphasis of those new values which emerge only in association and organization, for it is in organized society that the 'general,'
the 'universal' relations, and hence the 'ideal' self, are realized. Now
it naturally goes along with this looking for what is universal that we
see things *sub specie aeternitatis*—that the sharp angles are rounded off,

that fret and passion seem too small in comparison with the larger movement. Hobhouse has forcibly indicted idealism in England for swelling "the current of retrogression" against democracy. In contrast with the "plain, human, rationalistic way of looking at life and its problems," "every institution and every belief is for it alike a manifestation of a spiritual principle." Its main effect has been "to soften the edges" of all hard contrasts between right and wrong, truth and falsity, "to throw gloss over stupidity, and prejudice, and caste, and tradition, to weaken the bases of reason, and disinclinement to the searching analysis of their habitual ways of thinking"—a charge which might be set over against Fichte's indictment of the eighteenth century. But it would be easy to retort that just at present it is individualism and a "plain common-sense way of looking at things" which govern very largely the conceptions of political life, in the United States at any rate; and it is under a governmental theory based largely upon them that individuals and corporate persons have been able to acquire such portentous power as to place privilege on a firmer basis, in certain respects, than it has ever held in the old world. Finally, socialism, borrowing from both English radicalism and Hegelian idealism, proposes a third view of social order and progress which attracts increasing attention.

The fact is that all three philosophies got their shaping under special conditions. The philosophy of *On Liberty* and the whole radical movement was a middle-class movement against privilege embodied in institutions and government. The socialism of Marx gloried in representing the proletariat. But just as definitely, the idealism of Hegel, which has been the prevailing type in recent English philosophy, was a military and professional class reaction[4] against particularism. Monarchy is for him a necessary part of the state. War is an agency for preserving ethical health, and preventing "the corruption which would be occasioned by a continuous or eternal peace." Neither the individualism of English radicalism nor the idealism of Prussian militarism nor the socialism of the German proletariat affords an adequate statement for present political and social philosophy. Scientific method suggests new possibilities for democracy, which none of these older schemes could conceive. Social organization makes it increasingly evident that no class philosophy, whether it be the philosophy

4. The class standpoint of Hegel is forcibly brought out in a recent monograph: Ernest Lynn Talbert, *The Dualism of Fact and Idea in Its Social Implications* (Chicago: U of Chicago P, 1910).

that announces itself as that of a class, or that which unconsciously reflects the point of view of a single class, can accomplish what it seeks. Some may hold that the idealism of Hegel yields just recognition to all elements of society. But by Hegel, the state, which, as he says, expresses the universal most clearly, is treated almost entirely in categories of authority and government. Interests of industry and education are given their place in the bourgeois society which represents the sphere of individual interests regulated by the community.

But in the century that has gone, and particularly in American democracy, other aspects of the universal element in human life have come to the foreground. Science and education are not at present merely means for individual development which the community may regulate. They are agencies through which a finer type of universal, a higher conception of unity, is gradually becoming conscious. Agencies for general information which Hegel could not have foreseen have rendered this possible. Or, again, our industrial and commercial life, in spite of all its opportunities for individual greed and its demand for regulation, is, nevertheless, aiding powerfully in a conception of sympathy, of common welfare, of constructive morality, which is gradually transforming the function of government. The legislature and the administrative officer may still be, as for the earlier idealism, the formal agents for the expression of the universal moral will; but the fact that this must now be guided by scientific intelligence in the framing of the laws for commerce, for education, for industry, for public health—all this requires such a different type of administrator that it makes the older conception of a monarch seem singularly ridiculous when emphasized as an important feature.

Unless signs fail, the people of the United States are to make an increasing demand for the reform and expansion of law to suit the new social and economic conditions. It is the privilege and duty of ethical theory to contribute conceptions which will aid legislatures and courts in their task—to take the words of the federal Supreme Court—of "so dealing with the conditions which exist as to bring out of them the greatest welfare of its people."

12 The Ultimate Test of Religious Truth: Is It Historical or Philosophical?

Truth in any sphere implies two things: On the one hand we have some experience, some immediately sensed or felt reality, and on the other hand we bring some other experience to put with it, some meaning, some idea, some purpose or emotion. If we select for our meaning some other partial aspect of experience, then we have the various kinds of knowledge used in common life, or, if more highly defined, that of the sciences. If we try to look at our part in the light of the whole, we have philosophy.

It is by this process of enlarging our impulses that we rise from the life of an animal or infant, to the life of the man who looks before and after, to the life of the scientist who, by selecting the aspects of experience that he will consider, is able to describe and predict, to the enhanced thought values of beauty, and finally to the life of the moral person who shapes his conduct by the ideas and meanings he sets up.

No mental or moral life is possible except with both these factors—the immediate experience on the one hand, the meaning or purpose which interprets it for science or shapes it for conduct on the other.

It is evident that in the world of intelligence and morality it is impossible to divorce these two aspects of truth, but it is convenient to lay emphasis for special purposes on one or the other. If we leave out of account for the moment all conscious reference to meaning and interpretation, to purpose and self, we have an abstraction which we call facts. If we leave out all the immediate, the real, we have another abstraction which we call ideas. We then by another artificial separation which is useful for the division of labor say that we can study each of these abstractions by itself. We assume to study facts and call this history; we assume to study the meanings, the relations, the

From *The American Journal of Theology* 14.1 (1910): 16–24 [1910:02].

values of these facts, and call this study science or philosophy. Instead of appealing to one wise Daniel to supply both the dream and the interpretation, modern life finds it more expedient to divide these functions. Historical research or observation tells the dream; reflection or philosophy essays its interpretation. Evidently, however, what we usually call history is three-fourths philosophy. For it speaks of men's purposes and plans not merely as facts, but as though they effected something; it speaks of causes and results, and these are never, and can never be, observed; it approves or condemns; it constructs far more than it records.

Philosophy, it must be confessed, has been more successful in its abstractions. It has at one time seized upon the spatial aspect of things and, forgetting all else, built a world of materialism. Again, fascinated by the power of thought in ignoring the here and now, and framing laws of universal scope, it has built a world *sub specie aeternitatis,* of eternal ideas, of a timeless, changeless absolute, or of eternal and immutable morality.

Against this abstractness of a rationalistic philosophy there have, indeed, been protests. The empirical Locke and Hume, Mill and Adam Smith, have taken their stand upon what is present and immediate. But they for the most part have made the opposite abstraction. They have failed to read the part in the light of the whole, and so have served rather to brush aside the airy cobwebs spun by the metaphysicians than to build a house for the soul of man.

Religious truth starts with three or perhaps four aspects of immediate experience, perceptions, needs, impulses, emotions. It gives these an interpretation, just as do science and philosophy. In which aspect is that peculiar character which marks the truth off as religious? Is it in the immediate impulse, feeling, sensation, or act on the one hand, as was held by Schleiermacher, and by those who talk of a religious instinct, or is it in the interpretation, on the other, as Hegel thought? Does it belong to history, or to philosophy? Let us postpone this until we notice briefly what these experiences are and what is the interpretation. The facts are of three or four kinds. The interpretation, however it differs in detail, has one common character: It seeks to read the facts in social or personal terms.

1. Simplest and crudest of these experiences, no doubt, but nevertheless the most vital to primitive man, is the bodily life with its urgent needs pointing beyond with the organism. Food supply, involving in most cases attention to the animating and reproductive powers of nature, the avoidance of mysterious dangers, the cure of disease, plays

a large role. Cults with ritual, prayer, taboos, and magic rites, embody interpretations of these needs. Plenty and famine, rain and harvest, sickness and cure, are explained by divine agency on the one hand, and over against it is conceived a human breath, 'double,' *anima,* or ghost, which is only a more tenuous and subtle body. Is our religious element here to be sought in fact, or in interpretation? The facts do indeed signify that man and nature, organism and environment, grow up together, and that it is abstract to consider man by himself. But later religion is apt to turn its back upon these simpler experiences, or assign them to science or to poetry, and to find a more congenial center in other phases of life.

2. The life in groups—clan, family, tribe—is both cause and effect of impulses and needs for companionship, sympathy, and protection. These are idealized in terms of Protector, Father, Redeemer, or Next-of-Kin, while the self becomes the group-member, continuing perhaps in the company of ancestral spirits. Here again there is an experience which points beyond itself, but it is only in the interpretation that it gets what can be properly called religious truth.

3. The perceptions of change and movement, of life, of order, and of might in the world awaken wonder and awe. Myths of the growth of creation gradually merge into the declaration that "the heavens declare the glory of God," on the one hand, or into the design arguments of philosophy, on the other, while the soul begins now to be conceived in terms of thought or reason. Decidedly, again, we have an unfolding of consciousness which suggests interpretation in terms of God and self, but the dream without the interpretation is not religion.

4. The moral experiences. These are of two sorts: those of inner life, of conscience and inner struggle, and those of outer act, of making the purpose effective. They are both an overcoming of the world—the world of evil within and without. These experiences are not so primary as the others. They arise as man begins to choose and value, to read his acts as a member of a social order, of a clan or family, and of the mysterious whole of which he is a part. The twofold aspect of conscious experience which in the previously described cases man finds pointing beyond himself to a helper or companion or creator, now calls for a new interpretation: Man feels that this choosing and approving, this law and ideal, are not merely a private and individual matter. He views himself as a member of a larger, and ideal order. As a member of such an order he is now a person, and the order is likewise personal. The larger life into which he is thus born is at once his

accuser and his helper. Sin and redemption are the interpretations of this new life within; a kingdom of God is the response to the demand that moral salvation shall mean not merely inner feeling and purpose, but outer act and a world of other moral beings.

Every great religion illustrates these facts and interpretations with varying fullness. In the Hebrew and Christian religion we recognize the Protector and Provider in war and peace, the personal Companion and Fountain of life, the Father and Creator who has clothed the heavens with beauty, the divine Sovereign whose love assists, the Messiah who is to secure the triumph of right and justice. Conversely man knows himself first as a creature of bodily wants, then as capable of friendship, and intellectual vision; finally as a soul with capacity for both good and evil, for the prophet's ideal, and for the messianic hope. We often read the Scriptures as though we were reading facts. But a moment's reflection tells us that the whole life of a prophet and priest and psalmist, of Jesus and Paul, was lived in and through, not the immediate facts but the ideals and visions, the faith and the hopes, of Israel's religion. And conversely, these ideals and hopes, these poignant judgments of sin and punishment, were not framed in the world of pure thought or of separate detached values. They were forced into consciousness and brought into the heart of a David or an Isaiah or a Jeremiah as he confronted plenty or famine or pestilence, victory or defeat, murder or adultery, injustice or persecution, and refused to go down in surrender to evil within or without.

Can the test of religious truth be historical? If we mean, can it be found in facts divested of any interpretation, the answer is plain: The bare facts of sensation, feeling, doing, or of outer succession of events, are not religious truth. Taken merely as facts they neither are, nor can they disclose, God or soul, sin or redemption, guilt or forgiveness, divine love or divine justice. None of these can ever be proved by any historical test. For these simply are not facts. These are in every case interpretations which go beyond any immediate experience. But, I suppose, those who would stand for the historical test would have in mind not the bare particular, immediate facts, but the doctrines proclaimed by Jesus and Paul and John and other founders of Christianity. Jesus and Paul, it may be thought, were witnesses, not philosophers. They testified to God's love and forgiveness. The death on the cross was an event which itself made things different ever since. Here was not a mere philosophy; here was a fact.

But I need not say that two difficulties at once confront us in adopting this standpoint advocated so impressively by some: (1) Shall we accept unquestioningly everything which we find ascribed to Jesus and uttered by Paul as being not only their belief but as objective fact? If so, what can we do with their views as to demons and the Second Coming? If we hesitate on these matters we are employing some criterion other than that of bare authority. (2) And again, does anyone know exactly what Jesus and Paul meant? Whatever their experience, or their knowledge, they had to express it, if they expressed it at all, in language. And this language was the language of other men. Its symbols and conceptions are borrowed from the experiences and ideas which Jews and Greeks had had. If Jesus and Paul had a new revelation it could be made known only so far as it could gradually induce new experiences in others and thus give a new meaning. The new bottles must be provided for the new wine, and the bottles could not be made at once. It seems impossible to sever what in the consciousness of Jesus and Paul was temporal and of their age and time, from what was for all time and all men, unless we take some standpoint outside history by which to test what was the divine and what the human. The test of religious truth for any man who questions an infallible book, a wholly magical view of revelation, and an external authority, cannot be historical in the narrow sense.

Can the test of religious truth be philosophical? There are two conceptions of philosophy and philosophical truth: According to one of these conceptions philosophy is to start with certain definitions and conceptions, as does the mathematician. It is then to develop these and test any proposed idea or proposition by its conformity to these premises. Its logic is that of identity and contradiction. This method as we all know has been a favorite in theology. You start with God as Substance, or First Cause, or Perfect Being, or Infinite, or Absolute, and you deduce the consequences with logical consistency. This gives indeed a world of reason, but it evidently proves nothing as to the world in which we live. Consistency is a necessary element in a world of rational beings, but as the modern mathematicians show us we may have many a consistent world which is not real. The other conception of philosophy is that it is to view all its interpretations, its conceptions, as merely experimental, and partial, as ways of reading new meaning into the crude, bare facts of feeling and impulse, perception and emotion—as a means of transforming the natural into the spiritual. On this basis the test of philosophy is not, Does my conclusion square with my definitions? but, Does my conclusion enable me to forecast nature, to guide my life into larger achievement, to disclose new values, and bring about a better world?

Can religious truth be tested by either philosophic method? Evidently not by the first. Religion must come to men with more than a consistent series of deductions from definitions. And if we turn to the second method and ask, Has philosophy yet furnished an adequate interpretation of religious experience? I should answer unhesitatingly, No! Various philosophies have helped man to understand more fully his life and his world, but only the complacent metaphysician of bygone days could suppose he had illumined more than a small circle in the unexplored and boundless ocean whose tides wash the shores on which we stand.

The Hebrew philosophy gave a profound meaning to one aspect of the moral life, but its philosophy of nature does not satisfy our present science, while its doctrine of the triumph of good through the sudden presence of God or his Messiah is not our working plan of life.

The Greek and the modern rationalist have had their philosophy. Fixing on the timeless procedure of thought they have made the religious world a timeless, eternal realm of lifeless being. God has been essence and substance, being and cause, changeless, infinite, and absolute. Moral struggle and victory find no place in such a being. They, like all finiteness and imperfections, must belong to appearance, not to reality.

Now, however well this may express certain intellectual and mystic longings of the religious consciousness, I believe that it is utterly inadequate as an interpretation of the moral life. It does not offer the redemption, nor the companionship, nor the actual making of new moral reality which the religious experience of today demands. The God who works in us and in whom we trust must in some sense be with us in the fiery furnace, must know struggle and purpose as reality, unless we dismiss the whole moral side of life as a dream battle.

Philosophy indeed took one great step in advance a century ago when Kant attempted to shift the center of philosophy from intellect to will. But, in the first place, the will with Kant was still too much the reason under another form. It had no place for sympathy and love as motives. And in the next place it shared the defect of all philosophy, which has lasted even to this day; it was individualistic, not social. The philosophy which is to test religious truth must be social. If the very essence of religious truth is a social, a personal interpretation of the world and of the inner life, then only a philosophy which employs social categories can meet the religious demand halfway. This gap has long been recognized. It has frequently been assumed that the situation is met by saying that man creates his gods according to his needs or his desires. Or it is said that religion uses the language of imagination; philosophy, that of thought. But to take one's stand on the private, subjective, individual half of this world of conscious experience; to assume that this is real, independent, self-sustaining, and that the Other, the *Socius*, the Over-Soul, the God, the Not-ourselves, is only a fancy, a fiction, a creation—this is sheer abstraction. In our social psychology we are learning that the individual comes to intellectual and moral birth only in a social world of fellow-men. Must not philosophy carry this insight as it essays to read the depths of human life, of conscience, of beauty, and of science, of spiritual power and spiritual achievements?

It has been a true instinct therefore which has led religion to refuse to trust its truth to philosophy for decision. There are more things in heaven and earth than have been dreamed of in the philosophies of Judea or Greece, of Germany or England. Our systems are still "but broken lights."

The historical—the fact—means nothing except as it is viewed in the light of other experiences, of some larger while, but in turn these larger wholes need to return again and again to earth to renew their strength. A great soul like that of Jesus—who shall sound its depths? Who shall say whence he drew inspiration, and in what strength he overcame the world? Certainly no doctrine of associational psychology, no doctrine of the soul as a simple substance. Who shall explain what difference his life and death did make in the actual universe?—certainly no doctrine of an eternal essence, or of a legal expiation. And what shall guarantee the triumph of good? What shall assure the soul, as baffled and perplexed by mystery and evil it cries in the *Te Deum* of the ages, "O Lord, in thee have I trusted, let me never be confounded!" Certainly no past can demonstrate *this* future. It is—and must be so long as moral life demands resolution—a supreme venture of faith. But if anything can give not only emotional cheer and contagious hope, but also the rational basis for this venture, it is the experience, the struggles, the serene calm, the confidence, the actual achievement of the world's great spirits. "Be of good cheer, for I have overcome the world" is the historic note which tells of reality—not only the reality of actual deeds, but as well the reality of a kinship of spirit that promises similar victory.

The vital religious truth underlying the views presented is this: Our theologies are none of them more than working hypotheses. They are all certainly inadequate. Nevertheless, just as in science every hypothesis helps us on, so without ideas and interpretations there is no growing life of the mind or of the spirit. We gain new glimpses into religious truth only as we bring to the great souls the new interpretations which their lives and teachings beget in us. In this sense the full interpretation of religious experience can come only when the Kingdom of God has itself become a reality. Just because the philosophies of the past are thus inadequate I conceive it our duty to rethink God and the religious life in new categories. Neither sovereignty nor fatherhood seems an adequate interpretation of the social conscience of today any more than the first chapter of Genesis is an adequate theory of evolution. Neither legal theories of atonement, nor timeless being, nor an absolute which knows no struggle, is adequate to our conviction of the reality of evil and the duty of overcoming it.

If we leave the shore and launch out upon the deep, what shall guarantee that here we shall find truth? We certainly cannot demonstrate the new by history or by philosophy. But religion is after all a venture of the soul, a venture of faith. If God and eternity were immediately present there were then, as Kant has taught us, no room for high resolve—no room to make the great decision to leave all and follow Him. But in spite of failures and shipwrecks, humanity has moved upward as it has made such ventures of faith. We cannot test *our* truth by the 'experience' of the child or the savage. We have moved on, and found a new evidence in the larger life of the spirit. If the humanity of a later time is to have a larger vision, a larger and richer revelation, it must test this by its own higher life. It must find God and soul, redemption and the divine kingdom, in new ways. It must not fear to leave its outgrown shell: but it will never outgrow the need of studying those profound and priceless experiences and deeds through which the divine has been revealed.

13   The Characteristic of the American College

Fellow Alumni: When Mr. McKim had looked over the Amherst grounds and buildings from the vantage point of the chapel tower, he said to President Harris, "College Hall is your best building, because it is most characteristic." I propose to consider with you for a few moments the question, What is most characteristic of the American college?

The two great educational advances of our day are the development of the endowed universities of research—Johns Hopkins, Harvard, Columbia, Chicago—and the rise of the great state universities—Michigan, Wisconsin, Illinois, Minnesota, California. The one type trains teachers and professional men, but its most distinctive glory is advancement of learning, discovery of new truth. The other type has its investigators, but its most brilliant achievement is its wide-reaching service to the community. Because each of these types of institution has embodied a great and vital principle, it has had within the past twenty years an extraordinary growth in resources, in attendance, in influence upon the country.

I do not think it can be said that the colleges, once supreme, have in any such degree gained in strength or in influence. Some spokesmen for the college, in their jealousy for their own ideal have looked with suspicion upon research. Many a great investigator, they say, is a poor teacher. The college must not imitate the research university. Others are repelled by the various enterprises of the state institutions. Agriculture and pharmacy, engineering and forestry, extension classes and correspondence courses—these are not Newman's idea of a university; still less are they the quiet college. In this, they urge, the student shuts eye and ear to the chaos of present impression and clamorous needs, while he singles out the great principles of

From *Amherst Monthly* 26.9 (1912): 265–269 [1912:02].

living or dwells patiently with Homer and Sophocles until he has learned to see life steadily and see it whole. They fear that democratic service of the community means materialism and lowering of ideals.

I do not think that our colleges have suffered, or are likely to suffer, from too much of the spirit of research, nor from too much of the spirit of democratic service to the state. They may well strive for more, rather than less, of the enthusiasm for truth and discovery which is quickening our educational world and which is so well set forth in the first issue of *The Amherst Graduates' Quarterly* by Professor [F. J. E.] Woodbridge. They may well have more rather than less of the zeal for wide-spread influence which has made many state institutions stimulating to instructors and students alike. Yet in both research and breadth of influence, the college must be second. It cannot rival the universities in their own fields. Is there any respect in which the college can be first? It is for this that we seek to find what was, and is, most characteristic of the college.

There were three elements in the early college. The first is at once suggested by such a body as this. Few universities have bodies of alumni which so embody comradeship and enthusiasm as do those of Amherst or Dartmouth or Beloit. You are comrades now because you were comrades then. There was a give and take which made each of us after four years of association—in class, in gymnasium, in tramps, on Pratt Field—not his bare single self, but a self enriched by its borrowings, rubbed smoother by its contacts, caught up into larger reaches by loyalty to class or college. Some of our groups lifted us into larger horizons, some may have made us exclusive or self-satisfied. But for better or worse I believe the group influence was and is one of the distinctive assets of the American college which must be reckoned with in solving its problem.

In the second place the college had its curriculum of studies, largely the classics, mathematics, and philosophy. College faculties have given largely of their time and thought to this element in recent years. It is the most definite and tangible of the three factors. It is natural to give to it the credit for what the early college accomplished, and to blame it for failing to meet present needs.

But, I venture to think, the curriculum was not the primary factor. It was not the writing of Latin verses nor the study of Aristotle which made Rugby and Balliol the breeders of England's rulers. It was not mathematics or tactics which made the spirit of old West Point. Nor was it classics and metaphysics that created personalities like Tyler, Seelye, and Hopkins. College Hall had a classical portico, but the

Puritan builders never conceived the portico to be the most important part. The main structure was the common meeting-house, where in the presence of God and of each other, men sought to learn the divine will, and to bring the kingdom of righteousness. Over and above the studies and the associations of various sorts was the animating spirit of a great faith, using these agencies to make the seriousness and nobility of human destiny and human duty appear. This spirit was the distinctive, the characteristic factor in the college. It was in the presence of this that men felt somehow the greatness of character, and were urged on to large achievement.

A spirit, we have to think, is immortal. But so far as we have experience, whatever is to live must renew its structure. What changes must the characteristic spirit of the college make, if this is to retain a commanding influence in education?

In a address nine years ago, Professor Garman summed up the changes of the preceding twenty years as a shift from the religious to the secular. He attributed this shift to three agencies: the spread of Darwinism, the rise of higher criticism, the dazzling influence of commercialism. In the decade since this analysis, there have been equally potent changes in the temper of the age. Three characteristics of the present which correspond broadly to the three mentioned by Professor Garman are the more constructive attitude of science, the shift of higher criticism from theology to law, and the rising wave of democracy. I have no intention of inflicting on this body which has gathered for a good time, an address upon science, politics, or social philosophy, and yet I must explain in just a word what I believe are the conditions which college education of the coming decade must meet. Let me comment on these in reverse order.

Commercialism is undoubtedly still a dazzling influence, yet if we take the country at large it cannot be said to be at present the dominant influence. The college will always need to show its students the relation of wealth to other values, yet a more widespread agency than the college has been at work all over the world, to displace commercialism from its commanding place. This is the extraordinary growth of democracy. In Russia and Portugal and China it takes political form. In England it reduces the power of Lords; it seeks to do justice to the classes which are at the bottom. In America it is insisting that however great the value of wealth, it is still after all "the incident of a justly ordered society and not the chief object of government." The economic causes for this widespread movement of unrest have been so luminously stated by one of your own number, Mr. Noyes of the class of

'83 in a recent article in the *Atlantic Monthly*[1] that I need not dwell upon them here. The legal obstacles which an eager and often impatient democracy encounters in our written constitutions have likewise been given their most recent and authoritative treatment by one of your number, Professor Goodnow, in his notable work on *Social Reform and the Constitution*.[2] It is not necessary to discuss the merits of the various aspects of this movement. Enough that in any case we must reckon with it. The aristocracies of earlier days might reck little of the thoughts and feelings of the great majority of their fellows, but for better or for worse *we* are embarked on a venture of democracy. We have staked as a people "our lives, our fortunes, and our sacred honor" on this principle. We hold that every one so far as ability, and character, and the common weal allow, should share in the fuller life which human genius, through its conquests over nature, and human will, through cooperation in organized institutions, are making possible. There are inequalities in ability and in service. The American people wish to give large incentives to ability and large rewards to service; but it asks if it may not be possible to encourage ability more effectively in every rank, and to reward service more justly.

If then, the dominant temper of the age is no longer commercialism, but democracy, the task of education is primarily not that of resistance, but that of providing sympathetic and intelligent guidance. In particular, the college, if it be true to its characteristic spirit, must ask how it can use all its unique resources—intellectual, social, athletic—to make its contribution toward the juster and nobler social order, how it can unify college life for the furtherance of the great end.

If we wish a single name for this purpose, I don't know that we can find a better than that which has kindled men's hearts through many centuries—the 'Kingdom of God.' But our day is making certain very important changes in the way in which this is conceived. Our fathers thought of this, I will not say exclusively, but largely, as a fixed and eternal pattern, and for its coming they relied largely upon proclaiming this pattern to the world. Partly as a result of our general acceptance of evolution as the method of progress, we have come to think of this order as not fixed but unfolding. More important still is another change—the taking over into the moral realm of the modern scientific,

1. Alexander Dana Noyes, "Politics and Prosperity," *Atlantic Monthly* 109 (1912): 183–195.

2. Frank Johnson Goodnow, *Social Reform and the Constitution* (New York: Macmillan, 1911).

experimental spirit. This means that we do not merely watch ideals unfold; we have to construct them. And we have to construct them not as dogmatic standards, but as working hypotheses. It is as hard to define what right is in our complex conditions, as to do it. We have to test, bit by bit, our proposed conceptions of justice. The seer of the New Testament saw a heavenly city descending, all perfect in its walls and streets. Our fathers thought it necessary only that men should be prepared to enter. Today we believe that we must quarry its stones and plan the architecture.

This involves also a wider range of agents. Under the older conception the chief agents of the better Kingdom were the heralds. No age ever needed more than ours the man of vision in the pulpit, but the newer order will not come by the methods of the preacher alone. The investigator and the engineer, the scientific physician, the fair-minded and humane judge, the organizer of industry and commerce, the labor union which attempts to see that products do not cost us too dear in the exhaustion of the workman himself—all these are needed for the order that is to be.

If this shall be the characteristic spirit of the college, it will in ways that have not yet been worked out, find increasing aid in the studies of the curriculum and the social organizations. The studies of the curriculum—these must certainly prepare the student to know human life from its biological basis, to its highest institutions. They must train in the scientific method which is so fundamental for the new morality. As literature and art, in Sophocles or Job, or Shakespeare or Beethoven, they must help the boy to feel as well as know the greatness and worth of the human spirit.

The associations of college life—athletic, fraternal, class—may these not become broader and more effective agencies for democratic fellowship? May not the loyalty which swells so fervently for the victories of college days over friendly rivals, kindle also the larger loyalty for the higher causes? May not the practice, team work, and leadership be connected more closely with producing men who are men of leading as well as of light?

The great difficulty for working out such a conception of a college, and for maintaining such a spirit, is no doubt the difficulty of obtaining and of holding great men. The universities, during the past decades, have continually attracted many of the brightest and most ardent minds. It has not been solely a larger equipment or a higher salary. It has been perhaps in even greater measure the stimulating atmosphere and the chance for cooperation from expert colleagues. To have the opportunity at lunch time to get from half a dozen specialists the very suggestions you need to help out your own deficiencies, to be stirred by the new work which your friend in a widely different field is doing—all this is not to be despised. And yet, the college even more than the university must depend for its success upon great men; for the spirit and the power which are its hope reside even less in books and laboratories than do the spirit and power of the university. To secure and keep such great men is indeed a most serious problem, and yet I cannot believe it to be hopeless. Two great rewards lure the scholar and teacher. One is the delight in discovery or expression of what is true or fine and worthy. The other is the possibility of personal influence—the immortality, as Plato calls it, of living on in other lives. The university career may appeal more successfully to the first. The college at its best ought to appeal more successfully to the second. The firmament of stars is a magnificent spectacle, but it is not so well adapted for taking photographs as the rays from the single source of light. The student in a great university, often, I think, gets a blurred impression, but in the mind and heart of the student of the college there was usually a clear impression of some one with whom he had lived and worked. How many an Amherst man of older days can find the clear imprint of Tyler or Seelye; how many of later years, to speak only of those not living, would find the portrait of Garman, and the tender memory of the Doctor. One need not feel himself a sun of the first magnitude to hope justly amid the intimate associations of the college for some measure at least of such influence.

   At the last Harvard commencement, Justice Oliver Wendell Holmes of our federal Supreme Court is reported to have said, "The root of joy in duty is to put out all one's strength to a great end." The studies of the college, its associations and activities of many sorts—these should train a man to use his strength more effectively. But besides all these, there should be a spirit; in the presence of this the more responsive and generous, at least, will find a great end.

14 The Study of Public Morality in High Schools

As an aid toward making clearer and more definite the aims and methods of moral education, and particularly of moral instruction, in high schools we may make certain distinctions:

The first is the distinction between public and private morality. Public morality would include (1) the conduct of public officials; (2) the attitude of others toward such public interests as government, taxation, education, provisions of health, recreation, safety; (3) in part, at least, the general conceptions under which business and industry are carried on. Private morals would have to do with personal conformity to established codes rather than with general standards, with attitudes and feeling rather than with overt acts, or with acts that concern a small group of family or friends. If a boy is disobedient to his parents, or lies to his employer, or throws dice with his companions, if a girl through ignorance or from choice is irregular sexually, these are first of all cases of private morals. Of course many aspects of conduct fall in both fields, and the transition is often easy. If the question is one of the permission of commercialized vice the private problems become public. If it is a question whether I shall follow the prevailing codes of morals as to the public welfare or the rules of business, then public problems become private.

Another distinction which to some extent gives cross divisions is that between evils and offenses due to special or sudden strain and those due to more permanent factors. The sudden strains may be in turn brought about chiefly by outside conditions, e.g., the drudgery of work combined with the glitter of city amusements, or by the development of inner desires and passions, such as the love of adventure, or the impulses of sex. In *The Spirit of Youth and the City Streets*,

From *Religious Education* 7.6 (1913): 631–636 [1913:03].

Miss Addams has brought these vividly before us.[1] More permanent factors are either negative, such as ignorance, or the lack of purpose, or the absence of the motives found in family, business ambition, public sentiment; or they may be positive, such as eagerness for private gain.

Those liabilities to fall which are due especially to sudden strain demand several kinds of remedies. Vocational education which enables boys and girls to find suitable occupations is one of the most needed features of city schools. Proper provision for recreation and better housing are other needs. In the schools, personal influence of teachers, athletics, group activities, studies which bring inspiring examples from history and offer employment for clean and noble use of the imagination are all valuable.

But for public morality and for certain of the more permanent factors in private morality there is an especially promising field for instruction for three reasons:

(1) As regards need, the problem here is not that of training a boy to follow already established traditions, or of forming good habits. The problem is rather of discovering and setting up better standards, of framing ideals which will meet our present changed conditions. Habits alone will not accomplish the desired results. A large part of the evil in our public morality is due to the persistence of methods and ideals which worked very well under former conditions. The maxim 'Mind your own business' has its value in country life; in the city it would give occasion for pestilence. The changes from country to city life, from home to factory industry, from individual to corporation business, from homogeneous race and religious traditions to the varied standards of our many races and religions, and finally from a society of independent farmers and tradesmen to a society with more sharply marked classes of rich and poor, capitalists and laborers—all these must be met not by any simple appeal to 'old-fashioned virtues' and not by emotion and sentiment, important as these latter are in their place. They must be met by study of the new conditions and by a comprehension of the fact that the order is changing.

(2) As regards the method of instruction the field of public morality is especially available. The difficulty which is felt by many to be serious in the field of instruction in private morals is twofold: There is danger

1. Jane Addams, *The Spirit of Youth and the City Streets* (New York: Macmillan, 1909) [cf. 1910:06].

of overdoing or else of underdoing. There is overdoing—of a sort—if the pupil becomes introspective and priggish. There is underdoing if what should be vital and deep-going is treated indifferently or unintelligently by a teacher not well fitted for that most difficult of tasks, the direction of personal morality. Many hesitate about urging general moral instruction because of the belief that this is a peculiarly difficult task and requires not only high personal character, but a training in psychology and ethics which many teachers at present lack. Public morality may be studied with less difficulty. It is not subjective but objective. It lies close to the fields of economics, civics, and history, for which we already have in our high schools well-trained teachers.

(3) There is the additional reason that there is greater need. As President Hadley has pointed out, the standards of private morals in the United States are much higher than those of public morality. The former are relatively good; the latter are bad.

The study of public life, of business and government, of social classes, and the moral standards involved in all these, does not mean any ignoring of the worth of personal character and integrity, of right springs to action, of reflection upon life's great goods and of choice instead of impulse or passion. It simply implies first that to know what to do the boy must know the world of action in which his life is set, and further that even for the important side of attitude or conscientiousness much may be gained by a flank movement, by the objective way of approach.

The study of public life aims to kindle purpose and direct action by showing what there is to be done in the world and how one may go about to make at least a beginning toward the doing of it. It recognizes that the boy must first find a job and get a living; but it believes that every job which has any excuse for being has some human value other than merely paying a wage. It holds that our great machinery of business, industry, and government ought to make possible not only a living, but a noble life. It realizes that too often the boy on entering the great whirl finds it disheartening drudgery, brutal competition, undisguised self-seeking, with sharply defined class interests. If he belongs to the so-called working classes he will find a business organization and a legal system which will very likely seem to be expressly devised for his exploitation; it will not be surprising if he grows bitter as well as hopeless. The public morality—or lack of it—breaks down his good intentions and his nobility of purpose. How can instruction help in this situation?

I suggest that a study of our industry, business, government, social structure, and general moral judgments, so far at least as these are embodied in laws and customs, may contribute toward three objects:

(1) Consider what ought to come from a study of business and industry as a whole. To see all the relations of the detached kinds of work which most men must do is at once to give the work greater intellectual value and greater human value. A considerable part of what appears to us as the naked selfishness and brutality of modern trade and industry is simply its impersonal and mechanical character. In neighborhood life and industry a man hesitated to sell his neighbor bad eggs, nor would he work his help seven days in the week with a twenty-four hour shift at the end while he himself attended divine service. If there were long hours and dangerous tasks, the employer shared them. But in our present organization the workmen see little but their machines; the clerks little but their accounts; the employer has a plant on the one hand and a market on the other.

Now obviously no course of study will humanize this process. But it ought to be of some use to point out in advance clearly and strongly the social side. For after all the whole organization is here to supply human needs and wants. It is a tremendously efficient tool for this. It is making possible an enormous surplus for the few who are getting the margin. It ought to provide decency and comfort for many more. To get before boys and girls at the outset the idea that all our business and industry has as its great end to serve men would be a great gain. It is so easy to think of it all as like the ocean—a great fishing place, where each may cast in his hook with no thought beyond that of good or bad luck in the catch—or else a bottomless gulf eager to swallow all but the strongest craft. Apparently much of our commercial morality is based on the fishpond view. The post office inspectors tell of the millions extracted from the public each year by schemes which come under the head of fraudulent use of the mails. But these schemes are probably only a drop in the bucket. The fascination of getting something for nothing is present in a large proportion of our methods of capitalization, in our opposition to pure food laws, and in our evasion of the tax assessor. The first step, even if it be a very short one, toward changing the general attitude is to show the whole process for what it is—a method of serving men and not a fishing pond, or a mere murderous abyss.

(2) The study of our institutions of government should serve to show both their values and their defects, and to show these in just proportion. One complaint commonly made against our American

morality is that there is lack of respect for law. This is evidenced in
the violence often shown in strikes; in the contemptuous disregard of
the intent of the law by great corporations whose attorneys advise
them how to keep within the technical phrases; and finally in the
outbreaks by individuals which fill the columns of our newspapers
and the dockets of our police courts. This third sort is due to individual
passions and cannot be much remedied by any process of instruction
as such. But the more public forms of the evil are part of a more general
attitude which may be called lack of a public or social consciousness.
This has perhaps been more conspicuous in our city life than elsewhere. The actual necessities of mutual defense forced early communities to consider common interests and common needs. But in time of
peace the value of the national government is not so obvious, while
the city is too easily viewed merely as the place where one gets his
living. Nation and city have done much of their work so well that we
are apt to overlook the great services they render. To point out the
actual gains for humanity in the establishment of order, in the guarantees of liberty, in the provisions for communication and education is
a way, and probably the most effective way, to cultivate respect for
society, and respect for its laws. It is difficult if not a hopeless task to
endeavor by any appeals to authority to secure regard for law. The
best way is to show what law has really accomplished for man.

(3) A study of the growth of our institutions will no less disclose
their defects. But it will show not merely that laws are often partial,
in the interests of a class, ill-adapted for our present society; it will
show why they are so. The injustice which is so often apparent will
appear usually as the result not of deliberate purpose but of changed
conditions. The clumsiness of present methods will be seen to be due
not to sheer stupidity, but to the carrying over into present civilization
of methods that worked well under simpler conditions. This knowledge of course does not in itself improve anything, but it makes two
important contributions: In the first place, it removes some of the
bitterness. You may think a hand-plow a poor tool, but you may
respect its maker for doing a good work for his time. Further, it shows
that bad social conditions are not due to necessities of nature. What
is due to human contrivance can be changed. What is due merely to
lack of control can be remedied by substituting control for neglect—
or at least it will be worthier of rational beings to make an attempt
even if they fail than to acquiesce in wrong.

It was a great advance in private morals when here and there a
conscientious soul took the stand that he must see his own duty and

follow it. Occasionally a prophet has challenged public morality. But to study this public morality calmly and coolly, to get young people to make some intelligent appraisal of what society does for them, and what it ought to do that it fails to do, to get definitely before them the vision of the public interests and public welfare as having claims paramount to private gain—this is a task for the future. Existing materials are not adequate; new materials must be provided.

15 The University and the Advance of Justice

Five thousand years ago, we are informed by our colleague who is learned in all the wisdom of the Egyptians, the word for truth, right, justice emerged. It was the earliest abstract term discernible in the ancient world. Its earlier occurrence is largely in claims for merit before the gods. But a thousand years later, the same shift in emphasis had taken place which marks our century as compared with the Middle Ages. The demand was then to reform conditions rather than to justify the soul. The appeal of the wronged peasant comes down to us as the first of many rising through the ages, invoking a higher power when, in the corrupted currents of this world, offense's gilded hand has shoved by justice. "Do justice," cries the wronged peasant, "for the sake of the lord of justice. For justice is for eternity."

It may be doubted whether any of the words since framed to express human values takes so strong a hold as 'justice.' It embodies the claim of personality, of the aspirations and expanding life of the human spirit. In disclosing the rights of each as the concern of all it bears constant testimony to the essentially social nature of man's higher development. Denial of justice stings because it is virtually a denial of humanity. He who has no rights is not a person but a thing. The history of justice is then the history of the emerging one by one of higher and more social powers—life, property, liberty of thought and speech, education—and of the recognition and protection of these by society. It is the history of various standards or balances for measuring these claims—custom, the decrees of rulers and assemblies, the will of God, the rule of reason. It is the history of various agencies for holding the balances—religion, philosophy, government, and, I venture to add, the university.

From *The University of Chicago Magazine* 5.6 (1913): 186–198 [1913:04].

Did time permit, it would be instructive to trace in outline the successive types which have stood out in the more direct lines of our own spiritual ancestry. We should see the justice of the kinship group insuring every member his share of food, allotting him his wife and his place by the hearth, protecting him against violence by its law of blood-revenge, measuring its dooms by ancient custom, enforcing its most sacred interests by taboos. In transfigured form this tribal justice pleads the cause of the poor through Israel's prophets; through the symbol of the Next-of-Kin or Redeemer it appears in the divine judge who is also the protector, and thus passes over into the conceptions of Christendom.

We should see again the justice of the city, based not on unity of kin but on the class groups of citizens, traders or artisans, and slaves. Justice will first of all mean giving each class its place. Industry and commerce have made possible greater wealth; private property gains larger recognition and protection. Household and family are more firmly organized; they likewise gain new powers and obligations. The measure of justice changes from custom and taboo to the will of the ruler or the decision of the assembly, and although this latter may condemn a Socrates it means, on the whole, discussion and advance. When indeed the clash of private interests and the tyranny of the one or the few or the many become too great for easy endurance, the search for a deeper basis leads to two conceptions which have proved a possession forever of our civilization. On the one hand rises Plato's vision of a city where classes shall at least be based on merit, where intelligence shall rule, and the larger public good dominate all private interests in a harmonious order. On the other rises the conception of claims so deeply rooted in human nature, yes even in the order of the universe itself, as to deserve the claim of laws of nature. These are found not in the urge of passion or desire, nor yet in blind habit or tradition, but rather in the reflective search of reason for principles of order and right living, for what is equitable and good. If the vision of Plato has taken its place with that of the prophets of Israel as the inspiration of those who have repeatedly challenged the existing order, the standard of Aristotle and the Stoics has proved its mastery in successive legal systems, from that of Rome to that of the United States. Especially when the city-state of Rome expanded to an empire did this conception of a law of nature evince its fitness to widen the law of a city to the law of a world. The idea of a justice universal in its principles and its sway came to clearer consciousness. If slavery was justified by the law of reason, it was nonetheless true that the same law would one day be invoked to resist the monarch and defend the liberties of the subject.

Our first glimpses of justice in the land where our institutions were built are once more of a world of customs and blood-revenge. The sword of justice is raised above its scales. Our forefathers, British, English, or Norse, had their virtues, but a modern observer of one of their courts, says the learned historian of English law, might "think that for a long time before and some time after the Norman conquest our ancestors occupied such leisure as they had in cattle-stealing by night and manslaughter and perjury by day." Piracy, tempered by the slave trade, was a common pursuit. In heaven, likewise, the divine sovereign sat to rule a world of largely hostile subjects, and conducted a vast assize in which the great mass were to be found guilty and condemned. The first business of justice was then to put down violence and maintain order.

But when order had been established and the modern world gradually found itself, it saw a new unfolding of individual powers and a higher worth given to individual claims than the ancient world allowed. Commerce, invention, and discovery gave new opportunity. Art and letters reflected the new spirit and in turn gave it imagery and power. A more inward and personal religion demanded liberty in what had of old been fixed by birth or state. The subject who had been given protection for life and property against all but the government gradually won the guarantees of civil liberty. The common law established by a Henry proved a defense against a Stuart. As a witty historian has recently said, its valiant champion, Sir Edward Coke, even invented Magna Carta in this cause. And finally the right of men, not merely to protection against the government, but themselves to choose and depose their rulers and even to make their laws, was achieved.

It was not strange that, as the result of these centuries of development and struggle, liberty and equality were the notes that sounded deepest in the chord of justice. To these, men were ready to pledge their lives, their fortunes, and their sacred honor. These rights they believed to be 'natural' and God-given, based deeper and sanctioned by higher authority than any human powers or statutes. Due process of law was the agency for their defense.

Even so hasty a glance has at least shown that justice takes many forms, ranging from the emphasis upon social classes to the insistence upon equality, from the conception of a harmonious city life as paramount, to the doctrine that governments exist to protect private liberty and private property. It has shown custom give place to decrees of rulers and these to acts of popular assemblies as standards. Even the rule of reason, which, to philosophers at least, has often seemed changeless and eternal, we should find, could we examine it in detail, varying with the habits of thought, the philosophies, and the prejudices of the times, and beset by the idols of the tribe, the den, the market, and the theater.

We are prepared, then, to find the conditions of the present disclosing to us new human values and calling for new agencies to aid in their measuring and protection. The external conditions are familiar—the machine in industry, the collective and impersonal organization of capital and labor, the change to city life. Under all these, only half realized as yet, is the closer interweaving of all our interests, the deepening interdependence of all our lives.

As we become more and more aware of this, as our means for communication increase, as public opinion and public sentiment become greater powers, we are forming a social consciousness. We are seeking, even if somewhat blindly and uncertainly, a 'social' justice. No one can pretend to state as yet just what the standards and demands of this new justice are. One characteristic is that it is open, experimental. Like the old justice, it must protect all members of society—even the least—from violence and fraud, but it seeks to distribute more fairly the burdens and gains; it would keep open the way of opportunity. But above all perhaps is its conviction that society by taking thought can move on to a new level; that no longer living from hand to mouth, no longer groping, or blundering by trial and error, men may through the new science and the new spirit achieve what has been impractical before. All these demands of the time indicate, I believe, the need of the university as an agency of justice—a need to which it is already beginning in numerous ways to respond.

Let us begin with our attitude toward the old dangers which threaten the old familiar values—that is, the crimes against person and property. I do not intend to repeat indictments against the criminal procedure of the courts, or against our penal institutions. These criticisms usually assume the necessity and adequacy of these institutions if efficiently carried on. A more fundamental question is persistently forcing itself upon us: Is our whole machinery of criminal justice anything more than a superficial effort to deal with certain symptoms? Even if it does not—as some believe—make more criminals than it reforms, so much at least is evident: it does not stop the supply; crime continues with little if any decrease. This certainly compels the query whether something more adequate cannot be provided. Our ideas and agencies of criminal procedure derive mainly from the primitive days. Reliance was long almost wholly upon terror. More than two hundred varieties of crime, we are told, came to bear the death penalty. So helpless was the professional mind of a century ago to conceive any better form of security that when it was proposed to abolish the death penalty for thefts of articles exceeding in value forty shillings, Chief Justice Ellenborough declared: "The learned judges are unanimous in their opinion that justice and the public safety require that the death penalty should not be remitted. . . . If we suffer this bill to pass we shall not know where we are, and whether we are standing on our heads or our heels." Nor has the humaner treatment which the last century demanded gone far beneath the surface. The present demand is that we find out causes. Of course older thought had its theory of causes. On the one hand, general depravity made us all evil-disposed; on the other, free will made us all responsible. These theories fitted excellently into a scheme of divine justice which consistently condemned all alike. But human justice never has meted out such equal sentence. It has dealt with specific offenses, and now we seek to know likewise specific causes. We recognize that freedom is a matter of degrees, not of yes or no. And even if we are all sinners we don't all take the same forms for our offending. We want to know specifically just why this boy steals and that girl goes wrong. If it is heredity, we want to know it; if it is home conditions, if it is city life, if it is our method of dealing with first offenders, we want to know it. The old justice began too late when it waited until the evil had been done. It must be supplemented by a new justice which begins earlier.

This is a task which calls for all the agencies and methods of the university. It means study of heredity and growth. It calls for new developments of physiology and psychology. It means knowledge of economic and social conditions. It means justice as much more adequate than that of the present as ours is above that of the savage in the kinship group.

But in our day the great dangers, even to person and property, are not from criminals or from foreign invader. The great dangers to life are from the machine. The dangers to security of goods are from the industrial or commercial process. Murders occupy large space in the press but they are trivial as sources of sorrow and misery compared with the fatalities from mine, and mill, and railroad; thirty-five thousand killed and half a million injured annually is a record which it is difficult for an academic audience to appreciate. If we add the occupational diseases, the lead poisoning, the tuberculosis in dust-producing industries, and the numerous byproducts of our factory system, we have perils which as yet are not accurately known, but which dwarf into insignificance the dangers from violence. Here, then, is a new demand upon the justice of the state. It must in some manner protect its members, or confess impotence and injustice.

Closely connected with the problem of protecting life is that of carrying the heavy burden of economic loss which follows industrial accidents. This was at first piled almost entirely upon those least able to bear it, the wives and children of men earning small wages. The courts sought a partial remedy by developing the doctrine of individual responsibility. The employer was held liable for death or injury if he was unquestionably and solely to blame. The attempt was doubtless well intentioned but it has proved so futile either to protect life or to distribute the burden, and in general so much more like a lottery than a just process, that at last we are giving up in such cases the method of litigation. We are seeing the folly of trying to deal with a machine as though it were a person. It is better to control it than to sue it at law. Hence on the one hand the public requires safeguards for the machines, and on the other hand the public requires compensation for the families, ceasing in some degree to visit the misfortunes of the fathers upon the children.

This specific case is but one illustration of a general tendency to meet our new and complex life by public instead of private law. We might take similar illustrations from commercial life. In dealing with railroads, or other public service corporations, individual effort to prevent unfair rates or secure redress has proved futile. As against the twentieth-century devices for disguising nature's defects the individual food buyer is helpless. In the commercial world the individual is as helpless to avert the loss of all his goods in the event of a panic. Society steps in and substitutes its own action to protect life and health, to make fair rates and fair burdens. Administrative law gains over litigation. Expert commissions are employed. And as this method must not merely decide particular cases but rather formulate standards for state- and nation-wide application, the necessity for scientific procedure is increasingly felt. The important commissions have made large use of university men, and their methods are essentially university methods. We might indeed almost say that while the courts represent the deductive aspect of logic, and legislatures find their task in framing major premises, often on very hasty induction, the commission at its best represents the scientific union of the two in the working hypothesis. Commissions make a large use of the familiar standard of 'reason.' Rates must be reasonable. Machinery must be made reasonably safe. But instead of the judgment of the common man on the one hand, or the 'artificial reason' of the law on the other, a scientific conception based on thorough and expert investigation is gradually being worked out.

But the service of the university to the older agencies of justice is no less important. Those of us whose memory reaches back a quarter of a century may recall that the public mind was then deeply stirred upon a question of justice. An important religious body was nearly torn apart upon the question of divine justice to the heathen, but decisions of state and federal courts attracted little attention. When this university opened, he would have been a bold man who said that these decisions would ever rouse so earnest a controversy as the higher criticism of the Scriptures. Today, however, no aspect of justice stirs feelings so strongly as the instances of opposition between the law as interpreted by the courts and the law as made by the people in legislatures. Besides the strain between a written constitution and the voice of a majority, is the deeper issue which our former colleague, Professor Pound, pointed out in an address in this place—the unsettled question as to which is the supreme authority, on the one hand reason as interpreted by the courts, on the other the will of the people. It is easy to say that reason ought to mean not merely consistency, but a consideration of all relevant facts, and a scientific method of dealing with them; that it should mean not merely the principles recognized in the seventeenth and eighteenth centuries, but the emerging principles of the twentieth. The question is *how* it shall come to mean these new things. It is easy to say, on the other hand, that the will of the people ought to be reasonable and its legislation intelligent and deliberate. The question is how it can become so. In solving each of these problems the university is able to render aid.

The shortcomings of the courts have been set forth so diligently of late that it may be well to notice, first, some of the defects of legislative methods, even when no special interest has secured public favor for private ends. These methods, Professor Freund has pointed out, "are perhaps the natural result of leaving the entire work of legislation to a large body constituted primarily for purposes of policy and not of justice." They show such inherited faults as "no definite responsibility for the introduction of bills; no thorough preliminary investigation of the conditions to be remedied; no adequate public discussion of the terms of a proposed measure, and involved if not faulty phraseology of statutes," often, no previous hearing of interests affected.[1] In order to get action, public interest must be aroused, but this necessity often works against due consideration of means and measures. We lack statistics in many fields. We need a history of legislation and a history of the operation of statutes. Our legislation as compared with the common law is comparable to experiments in justice. But experiments without records and without comparison are not calculated to make sure progress. They resemble more the trial-and-error method of the squirrel in the psychologist's maze. They explain in part the indifferent if not hostile attitude of the courts, noticed by legal writers.

These defects are evidently of just the sort which the university might be expected to remedy, and the legislative reference bureau, founded under university influence in Wisconsin, is the pioneer in what promises soon to be a general movement. It places information and expert aid at the service of the lawmaker. Its fitness is so evident that we wonder why it has not come before. It brings into the service of the public resources which in the past have too often been available for special interests only. And it is distinctly a university contribution to the advance of justice.

If we turn now to the difficulties of the common law and the courts, we are told that the first of them is that we no longer have a common law. Instead, we have fifty more or less divergent systems, and this is not merely an inconvenience for the lawyer but a serious burden upon the process of justice. Under present conditions of short tenure and crowded dockets, judges, we are told, are no longer able to do the work of organizing the law. The task is passing to the law teacher and the law writer[2]—that is, is becoming essentially a university duty.

The task of bringing the new economic and social science into legal doctrines is quite as evidently laid in large measure upon the university, which will thus follow in the line of the church, the customs of merchants, and the legislation of the last century as liberalizing agencies for the common law. And another influence may be expected to flow from university contacts. One source of strain in the accommodation of law to present needs, we are told, is that lawyers on the whole still appear to hold, consciously or subconsciously, that "the

1. Ernst Freund, "Jurisprudence and Legislation," *Congress of Arts and Science*, ed. H. J. Rogers vol. 7 (Boston: Houghton, 1905–1907) 628ff.

2. Roscoe Pound, "Taught Law," *American Law School Review* 3.4 (1911–1915) 164–173.

principles of law are absolute, eternal, and of universal validity."
Philosophers have frequently held the same thing about morals. But
the spirit of a modern university, quick with inquiry, seeking the
origins of suns and atoms and organic life, of language, customs,
government, morals, and religions—this spirit must prepare the future lawyer and jurist to say with Kohler, "There is no eternal law.
Law must adapt itself to constantly advancing civilization. This civilization it must aid, not hinder or repress."[3]

In venturing to bring before you these features of the university's
service to justice I have transgressed, I fear, the first principle of
university life. For I speak with only the layman's claim of an interest
in the subject. But there is one aspect of justice which we cannot, if
we would, leave entirely to courts and legislatures. Great as are other
agencies of justice, public sentiment is ultimately the most powerful.
From it springs legislation. By it judicial opinion is insensibly but
inevitably affected. Many questions do not require coercion by law if
public sentiment is clear and positive. Now, however, more than ever
before, public sentiment is confronted with tasks for which it needs
expert guidance if it is to meet its responsibilities and do justice.
Among the numerous problems of this sort I select one.

In our present process wealth is produced by the most intricate
subdivision and cooperation. What share ought each contributor to
have? Put in this general form the question is doubtless futile and
negligible. But in one of its aspects it is more and more taking a specific
form. What is a fair wage? Under older conditions this was largely an
individual matter. At present, wages are settled for large groups and
the public tacitly if not openly appealed to for its opinion as to what
is just. Two recent cases bring out alike the public interest and the
magnitude of the problem. A year ago two strikes were threatened,
one in the anthracite coal mines, the other by the locomotive engineers. In the one case, an increase of four millions of wages was
granted; in the other, thirty thousand men asked for an increase of
seven millions of dollars, which in the judgment of the railroad officials
would suggest proportionate increases among other employees,
amounting to sixty millions more. The interest of the public in the first
case is indicated by the recent government report that to pay the four
millions increase in wages the public contributed thirteen millions
through the higher prices of coal. The interest of the public in preventing a strike in the latter case is forcibly presented by the commis-

3. Josef Kohler, *Lehrbuch der Rechtsphilosophie* (Berlin: Rothschild, 1909) 6.

sion constituted to arbitrate the issues. A strike by the locomotive engineers of all the eastern roads, the commission declares, would largely shut off food supplies from the great cities of the East and practically paralyze industry in that region. "If a strike . . . lasted only a single week the suffering would have been beyond our power of description, and if it had continued a month the loss not only in property but in life would have been enormous." For the public simply to form a ring and let the parties fight it out is obviously to abandon justice and revert to barbarism. Both sides wish to conciliate public opinion. The arbiters, of whom the president of the University of Wisconsin was chairman, seek to discover "the basis of a fair wage." The eminent commission finds this task highly difficult with the inadequate data available. How impossible for the general public to frame a just opinion! It is only by continuous investigations and expert judgment that a more adequate basis can be laid. It is only by university methods that public opinion can find guidance.

It may appear to some that it is exaggeration to treat this just-settled controversy of the engineers, or the pending controversy of the firemen, as typical. Unskilled labor is the larger factor and this is unorganized. Society, it may be said, need fear no concerted strikes from this labor, and hence is not compelled to form judgments, or intervene. But society is not so interpreting its duty. Quite apart from such possibilities of sudden fusion as the Lawrence strike revealed is the feeling that the ignorant and less successful who fill the ranks of the unskilled need the protection and aid of society if they cannot act collectively. A minimum-wage law for women, enacted in one state and proposed in others, whether economically sound or not, is evidence of the conviction that the wage of women is as vitally "affected with a public interest" as the charges of warehouses or the fares on railways. There is no question but that society will take a position on the question of fair wage for men likewise, though it may not attempt to put this into law. The only question is, how can this position be made as intelligent as possible?

In seeking some principle on which to form a judgment it is noteworthy that the tendency is to abandon the older tests of merit, "How much does the man earn?," or of market price, "How much does unskilled labor command?" The first test is too difficult for public opinion unless one can use the market price as a measure, and in proportion as we approach monopoly conditions the market price seems to be more than dubious as a moral standard. Instead, the conception of a 'living wage,' 'a standard of living,' is advanced as the test. At some future time this may be so defined as to take its place, along with property, as a value which law will protect. It stands for many of the same ends which property has served—food, shelter, security, permanence, decency, education of children, and some degree of comfort. But it seems to suggest also a share in the ideals of the time, as well as in its material resources. Its claim doubtless rests upon the belief that if one of the members of society sinks or degenerates, all are sooner or later bound to suffer with it. But just because it is really far more complex than older 'natural rights' it needs and is beginning to receive increasingly the most careful scientific study. Surveys and investigations—one of the most thorough made by our own University Settlement—are preparing the way for translating the figure of wages into terms of actual living and making possible a use of the scales of justice.

In recounting the service of the university to this task of forming an intelligent public sentiment it would be impossible to leave out the work of the social settlements. Founded and largely developed under university influence and by university men and women, they have been seeking underlying social causes, as well as the more external facts which can be enumerated for the census. But they have contributed especially to the common understanding which is the first requisite for justice. If I am to be fair to the other man I must first of all be able to see things from his point of view, even if it is not my point of view. For the justice of today, which must reside so largely in public sentiment, common understanding is as essential as was for earlier justice the common law.

But I should be willing to waive all that has gone before if I might yet justly claim for the university a share in this which follows. To one who compares the attitude of society today toward the problems of justice with that of even a quarter-century ago, one general character stands out which is more significant than any detail. This may be called the creative and constructive attitude. The American has never lacked courage and constructiveness in business enterprise. The spirit of the founders and of the frontier was creative along the lines of political and educational institutions. But a quarter of a century ago we were not creative in problems of political and social life. We accepted many evils as inevitable. To say that a proposed measure involved some change in human nature was to condemn it. Economic laws appeared to many to be sentences of fate, rather than instrumentalities by which man could intelligently master conditions. Poverty, crime, vice, disease, ignorance, were facts to be accepted. Religion, philanthropy, law, sought to save individual souls or to remedy individual ills or wrongs. But there was no large constructive policy. The day of conservation, of city planning, of municipal efficiency, of such sanitation as that on Panama, of expert aid to agriculture, had not dawned. Now we are facing world-old evils as well as new dangers, with a new spirit. We are taking a larger view. No longer frightened by the plea, "Such is human nature," we are beginning to realize that human nature itself, as we know it, is mainly an artificial product. We are looking farther back, and taking courage as we see how much has been done. We are beginning to conceive faintly how much may be done in the future if we plan largely for our cities, our resources, our citizens, instead of dealing one at a time with results of failure to plan. Is not this creative, confident spirit due in large measure to the work of the university? For by its discoveries and its organization of methods there has come for the first time a confidence based on knowledge as well as on faith.

Visions of a juster order have come to seers and philosophers many times since the Egyptian of four thousand years ago described his ideal kingdom. Oftenest perhaps religion has embodied this ideal in its future. But with all its power to lift the imagination and stir the longing for a reign of right, religion has lacked ability to organize our present society. Philosophers since Plato's paradox have more than once been kings, and yet have failed to give his royal city to the light of day. The university spirit of today is not visionary, but it has a right to believe that many things impossible for prophet or individual philosopher are possible by the patient and courageous work of the great force of university men working with scientific methods.

If the university is to do the work which society is asking from it, and is certain to ask increasingly as need increases and scientific methods develop, it is evident that large additions will be necessary to its resources in certain lines. The natural sciences developed earlier, and properly received at first the larger equipment. The task of the social sciences needs, and we may believe will find, larger equipment than heretofore, not in laboratories—these are in the cities and the shops, the legislatures, courts, and schools—but in the men to observe, to interpret, and to plan constructively in the cause of justice.

It may have occurred to someone to ask, "Why do you speak of the *university* and the advance of justice?" Is it not rather the scientific spirit and method which have been shown to be our need and hope? In part these are the same. Investigation is mainly carried on in universities. And on the other hand, nothing is so characteristic of the modern university as the zeal for original inquiry. But great as is the scientific spirit, for purposes of justice the university is more than science. Its task is not only to professionalize a part of society but to socialize the professions. It stands for the spirit to use science for human advancement, rather than for private ends. It stands for the enrichment and socializing of human life by interpretation and appreciation of art and letters as well as of institutions, religion, and philosophy. It stands for the kindling of generous impulses, for the enthusiasms and challenge of youth not yet so accustomed to unjust usages as to accept them, or so cautious as to be overtimid. It stands not only for the forces of ideas but also for the interaction of men in democratic association.

In the thought of the ancient Egyptian, truth and justice were not distinguished. As civilization advanced society found for them different words and intrusted these two great values to different institutions. Universities have been founded to seek for truth; governments and courts to do justice. But with all the gain of specialization, has there not also been somewhat of loss? Some truth pursued by universities has been so abstract as to lose even the value of being true. Some justice exercised by rulers and courts has failed to be just. Society today is finding that justice needs truth for its method and that truth needs justice to make it vital. The universities are increasingly conceiving the business which is in hand not as "an opinion to be held, but as a work to be done"; and an increasing share of this work not only lays "the foundation of human utility and power" but contributes to the deeper, finer values which emerge as utility is justly measured, and power is justly used. Those who are today passing here from the smaller division of our university to the larger, and are to be enrolled among the alumni, are to be welcomed to fuller cooperation in this task.

You may find many ways of making your contribution. So young a university as ours cherishes examples which range from the devotion of a Ricketts to the sympathy of a "Gloucester Moors"; it includes among its living members in Chicago and wherever its alumni are found those who are serving human weal in ways more numerous than I could recount. To have some part however small in the advancement of justice is the privilege of all members of the modern university—of this university.

16 Ethics in High Schools and Colleges: Teaching Ethics for Purposes of Social Training

In certain respects the teaching of ethics in high schools is a different problem from the teaching of ethics in the colleges. The college student comes to the study of ethics with greater intellectual maturity, and usually with some previous work in psychology and the social sciences. The high school student cannot be presumed to have much of this background, except some work in history, which often is not so treated as to be directly very helpful for the specific purpose we are considering.

A difference which is at least as important is in the instructor. A college instructor in ethics is presumed to be specially trained for the purpose. In Japan the high school teacher of morals, as I understand it, must have taken his doctorate in ethics, but with us this is not likely to be the case for some time to come. The teaching of ethics, or of what corresponds to it, must be by the particular layman on the staff who is best fitted for it. This is in itself an almost decisive reason for a minimum of theory or of ethics in the technical sense in high school teaching. One might apply to such teaching the remark made to a judge, "Your decisions are likely to be right; your reasons are more than likely to be wrong."

In a period of ethical reconstruction like ours there is also a further danger. The layman, however admirable in his personal code, is more liable than the trained student to insist upon fixed standards which lead to pharisaism or abstractness, or else to fall into the opposite error of pure relativism and make morality a matter of temperament or sentiment. This means that in the high school I should make the teaching of ethics as objective as possible and should seek its material in the world of action rather than in the more subjective world of motives and reflection.

From *Religious Education* 9.5 (1914): 454–459 [1914:05].

In college the three or four years additional experience makes it possible to analyze conduct more reflectively and seek its principles by negative criticism, as well as by positive construction. Yet there are certain elements of common purpose. First, the central object of teaching in both high school and college I believe to be not so much to influence the private morals of the individual student, as to affect the standards of public morality. Second, the chief agency available in the ordinary school or college for this purpose is that of training the intelligence, rather than that of habit formation, or appeal to sentiment.

This position may be made clear by contrasting it with two views which deny it in different ways. The first contrasted view is found in various complaints. It is alleged that there is lawlessness and a breaking down of family life. But 'lawlessness' is too broad a term to satisfy anyone who cares more for accuracy than for rhetoric. So far as the old well-established laws of person and property are concerned I can find no evidence whatever that boys and girls who come to us are less well-intentioned than formerly, or that high school and college graduates fall more than of old into vicious practices. Recent figures, so far as they go, indicate that of women offenders against sex morality, and of male inmates of an Indiana penal institution, only about three percent ever saw a high school. The kind of lawlessness most in evidence is in the two special fields of labor troubles on the one hand and business methods on the other. The conspicuous symptom of evil in family life is the increasing frequency of divorce. In these three spheres there is no escape from President Hadley's logic: "If here and there some individual misuses his money or his office, we are justified in putting the blame upon him individually. But if a large number of people are misusing their money or their offices, the fault cannot be theirs alone. The community is a partaker in that fault. The chief trouble lies in the public standard of morals."[1]

The simple fact is that the public conscience is not at all clear. Congress, presumably in good faith, passes a law in the interests of greater freedom. The Supreme Court declares that such a law is an arbitrary interference with the liberty of contract, which no government can justify in a free country. A prominent man of affairs says he is prosecuted for acts which in other countries would be rewarded

1. Arthur Twining Hadley, *Standards of Public Morality* (New York: Macmillan, 1912) 5.

by marked public recognition as distinguished service. So long as conditions are confused doubtless many may make this state of affairs an excuse for ignoring their own better judgment. But many are honestly in doubt. And the lack of certainty operates to dull the scruples of the citizen of average intentions. Our inheritance of puritan individualism may lead us to forget that only a small part of any one's moral action is sustained by his private conscience; in the greater part of our acts we are guided, controlled, and kept in the straight path by public opinion—the *Sittlichkeit*, as Chancellor Haldane has recently reminded us. This *Sittlichkeit* used to be clear and definite for the tasks of the average citizen. It is now uncertain. And failing of its guidance and steadying power many a man goes to pieces when confronted by critical situations.

The second view with which the position may be contrasted is that the work to be done is that of habit formation, or of developing moral sentiment—in other words, that people go wrong not because of lack of knowledge but because of lack of heart and will.

I do not question that the school should do a work of habit formation. It has in its school discipline, its athletic teams, its organization of study, it various groups for social purposes, its studies of literature and biography, valuable resources for this work. But so far as the especial task of teaching ethics is concerned we have a different problem, and need to appeal not to emotion but to intelligence. Moreover we must bear in mind that the school is not the only agency in moral education. Certain work can best be done by the agencies of family, church, law, and public opinion.

If the work were primarily that of establishing right sentiments with reference to matters of private morals, the family would be the more hopeful agency. If it were primarily a matter of reverence for the finer and more spiritual values of life or of inspiration for the great heroisms of devotion to struggling causes, the church would have resources not found elsewhere. Were it a matter of bringing into line this and that individual, or group of individuals who are not in accord with public standards, then public opinion and law, as Plato's *Protagoras* long ago pointed out, are constantly bringing their pressure to bear on him. But the family cannot give advice about modern perplexed conditions. The church is not usually equipped with the tools for the patient and detailed study of specific problems. Public opinion will enforce what is already established, but is likely either to favor blind acceptance or else in a sudden wave of radicalism to substitute emotion for intelligent purpose. School and college are precisely the agencies which in cooperation with the press and public discussion must serve democracy in working out better standards.

Assuming then that the school and college are to aim primarily at public morality and address primarily the intelligence, just what is it that needs to be emphasized? First of all it must be remembered in all our teaching of morality that this is a democratic country. If we are training citizens to take their place in a monarchical system or in a system of fixed classes with subordination of lower to higher, established by all the traditions and institutions whose influence makes our very atmosphere, we might proceed to inculcate certain authoritative and fixed standards. But the very spirit of our institutions forbids this method. The logic of our institutions suggests rather frank insistence upon the fact that we are making our own laws and standards and must take the responsibility of it.

In the second place, we are training our students for a dynamic and not for a static society. America is a very confusing place just now to some people, because various traditions of the fathers are being upset. But it is futile to be upset over this. President [Woodrow] Wilson has remarked that our political thinking of a century ago was in the concepts of statics, of balance and equilibrium, the concepts of the Newtonian physics. We are living today, however, not in the century of Newton, but in the century of Darwin. The important attitude to foster is that of a constant attention to the demands made upon us by present conditions. If we can encourage the process of definitely attacking and working out one problem after another, there need be no fear for our idealism. No people is likely to disintegrate morally, to become either materialistic or lawless if it is seeking constantly to work out better standards and better methods.

In the third place, the present situation requires greater recognition of a public and common welfare as distinct from individual rights and private good. In the early part of our national history public welfare and private good largely coincided. The need now in many lines is for concerted action in both national and city life. Conservation, the Panama Canal, the development of the police power, are objective responses by collective action to great public needs. Public morality implies getting clearly before us the fact that we are a nation, that we are communities, and that we have common interests which can be met only by loyalty to the public weal.

Fourth, one of our most serious problems at present is class separation and the subordination of public to class standards of morals and loyalty. The chief remedy for this which school and college can offer is not denunciation, but an attitude of knowing all facts and understanding all sides—rather of understanding all our fellow men. We have no basis for asking any group to lower its class consciousness until we have come to understand that consciousness and to recognize all its values as well as its defects.

How shall these problems be met? Most fundamental of all is doubtless such a shift in our appraisal of educational values as to make the meaning and value rather than the technique of our industry, business, society and government the great thing of our curriculum. At present we have reached a high degree of success on the statement of the technique—the arithmetic, the language, the governmental machinery. We have scarcely yet asked in our high school instruction, What are all these for? On the other hand, in ethics we have too often studied meaning and value apart from the actual ongo of public life. An ethics which is to help public standards must first know the conditions.

The teaching of ethics must aim to produce an attitude which is at once critical and constructive. Critical, because one who is satisfied with things as they are is of no use in helping to make things better. Constructive, because the man who merely finds fault gets his cause hated as well as himself. The emphasis should be differently placed in high school and in college. In the high school emphasis may well be placed upon the great constructive forces of civilization. The process of political development may be traced in fascinating perspective as analogous to the discovery and control of great natural forces. Power of association first used for plunder and wielded by irresponsible leaders has become increasingly beneficent and increasingly democratic. In like manner the extraordinary powers of modern wealth built upon association and the machine we may hope are to be converted increasingly toward the common good and are increasingly to come under control of moral motives.

In particular, we may wisely point out the great progress in the recognition of good faith and responsibility which is implied in such departments of business as banking, insurance, and in all such contracts. On this great positive basis we can see how much of the strife and unrest in our industrial situation is due to the fact that between capital and labor for the most part there are no permanent contracts, no assurance of the future.

Or again we may appropriately point out that while the desire for gain or some form of personal advancement is no doubt the active motive in business enterprise, society has always recognized the necessity of controlling this for public welfare. Our common law is full of illustrations. Our recent conceptions of police power and property affected with a public interest are but extensions of such a social control resting upon the necessities of free and well-ordered common life.

In both high school and college the genetic method rightly interpreted is of great value. In a volume called *Moral Training in the Public Schools*, Dr. Stevenson maintained that the law of the land was the proper vehicle for teaching morals.[2] This is what the public enforces; this is what the public should teach its children as its standards of morals. Objection was at once raised that to teach the law just as it stands would give a false basis, for much of our law is confessedly imperfect and even worse. If, however, we take the more fundamental principles embodied in the law and treat them genetically; if we ask how they have come to be asserted, what their purpose is, and how far they meet the needs of our time we have a use of the law which is highly valuable. On the one hand, it affords at once a presumption of reality, a reality as firm as any of the facts which the boy will meet when he enters business life; on the other hand, it reminds him that there is no real which does not rest upon the ideal.

In college teaching we need not forget the constructive side, but we may well bear more heavily upon critical analysis than is possible with younger students.

Some form of the case method or of inductive study and analysis is undoubtedly important. Law affords one source of excellent material, literature another. I have found another source in the individual experiences of a class. A student describes the groups to which he has belonged, singles out the group which has most influenced his standards, describes as far as he can the code of this group. While this does not involve priggish introspection it does set before a student in a somewhat objective way the actual moral standards which he has. By considering them primarily as the standards of some group he is led naturally to question their infallibility and completeness while at the same time he respects their positive value. Sometimes also actual moral crises which have been met are stated and made available for class study. A series of decisions mimeographed for the class use forms a very interesting method of testing such theories as those

2. T. P. Stevenson, "The Necessity for Moral Training in the Public Schools," *Moral Training in the Public Schools*, ed. C. R. Brown, et al. (Boston: Ginn, 1907) 53–88.

of hedonism, eudaimonism, loyalty, social welfare, the categorical imperative, self-realization. While they need not be taken as ultimate authority they form a very good beginning for testing hypotheses.

The great thing whether in school or college is to convince the pupil that the business in hand is not that of an opinion to be held but that of a work to be done. If we set this before us we shall seek contact with reality, but we shall also remember that what ought to be rests on a deeper reality than what is.

17   The Present Significance of Scholarship

The scholar is not as old as humanity. Even if we include the scribe of ancient Egypt within the rank the scholar is still modern. He is not directly productive of the means of sustaining life and hence must always be obliged to justify his calling. In the old world, when leisure was regarded the privilege of every Athenian citizen, the leisure of the scholar did not call for especial defense. As Socrates sat in the gymnasium or theater, or talked with citizens upon the street, he found others as free as himself. The question was not why should one be excused from the world's work; the few accepted their leisure as a boon of citizenship, and regarded a large share of mankind as by nature incapable of free and rational life.

Nor did the question arise to the medieval scholar. For he was dedicated to the service of God. His learning was of things divine. His vows made his life professedly one of renunciation rather than of privilege. The gifts by which his simple wants were met he believed to be a blessing to the souls of the givers.

But in our modern world neither the Greek nor the medieval conception applies. No one can justify a freedom purchased at others' expense unless he is somehow making a contribution to the common weal. And today scholarship is not limited to divine themes, nor to those who have taken vows of separation. Its range is infinite; and though it calls for devotion and sometimes for poverty, it yet beckons to a life of enrichment rather than of limitation; when the president of the United States is a member of the Phi Beta Kappa society, and when the chancellor of Washington University sits in the cabinet we may say that scholarship has at least ceased to be a bar to service in the highest offices of the nation.

Education and scholarship in the country have drawn from two

From *Washington University Record* 10.2 (1914): 1–12 [1914:08].

streams and have had two chief functions. The Greek and Renaissance spirit on the one hand, the Medieval and Puritan spirit on the other, have supplied the inspiration. Freedom and individual development have been the note of the one; responsibility to a higher law than that of individual liberty has been the underlying conception of the other. Their fusion has been so intimate that it is often difficult to discern the separate motives. But it will be instructive to consider each of them for a moment before passing to the present significance of scholarship.

The spirit which prompted the founding of our earlier institutions of scholarship was no doubt that of religious duty. The belief of the fathers was that only through an educated ministry could the church be maintained in its purity. For this purpose contributions were solicited from those whose meager circumstances would preclude them from the thought of present day college officers, and while attendance at college was never limited to candidates for the ministry, few of the colleges would have been founded had not the necessity of a knowledge of divine things for the ministry been a matter of general conviction.

And yet in the colleges, shaped as they were for the vocational training of ministers, there was nonetheless present also the spirit of the Renaissance, the spirit of liberal study. The curriculum of our colleges, even down to twenty-five years ago, consisted largely of Latin, Greek, mathematics, a little science, a bare taste of modern literature, and a senior year of philosophy. I am not sure just how much of the preeminence of Greek was due to its being the language of the New Testament and how much was due to the supposed origin of political freedom in the republics of Greece and Rome, or how much may have been due to the influence of university tradition. But apart from all these, Homer's stories of the youth of the world, Plato's high thought upon the soul and the universe, or the great tragedians' portrayal of the lot of mortals overshadowed and controlled by destiny, could not fail to find response in the more ardent minds.

If Latin offered no such splendid vistas it was at least congenial to the spirit of American life and to liberation of powers in one important respect. Through all our early history the spoken word was potent. Debates in colonial assembly or later in Congress and legislature were great agencies in the arousal and direction of public thought. The pulpit and the lecture platform attracted the ablest men of the day. There was little competition with the printed page. It is significant that in his *On Liberty*, John Stuart Mill relies upon free discussion as the great agency of intellectual progress. Men through all the country waited eagerly for the pronouncement of a Calhoun or a Hayne and for the reply of a Webster. A Beecher was more powerful to conciliate the good will of England than the forces of official diplomacy. With this demand for oratory it is not surprising that Cicero and Quintilian as well as Demosthenes should be studied. Rufus Choate describes his practice of careful translation in order to perfect his style.

The philosophy of our earlier period was also both vocational and liberal. It was taught by the president of the college who had not usually read more in the subject than could be expected from his preoccupation with pastoral duties and the responsibilities for the finances of the college. When a great mind like that of [Jonathan] Edwards turned to this field it was usually to the more definitely theological problems. And yet even here the student was at least given great themes. He might hear conclusions as to God, Freedom, and Immortality which were based on insufficient evidence, but he did, at least, like Augustine and Spinoza, seek to consider the world from the point of view of eternity. Or if, as was customary, he turned to what would seem today a very crude science of the mind, he was at least learning to look within.

Of the scholarship found in our colleges, we may say, therefore, that it served to open a wider horizon of life for the individual and to prepare him for such vocations as the ministry and law. It was in this respect like the earlier views of salvation. It opened opportunity for the individual spirit. It was a privilege. It made lives more useful and gave them greater freedom and scope. Yet after all it was an individual salvation which religion taught and individual opportunity which scholarship presented.

Outside the colleges there was comparatively little scholarly activity, if we except the field of history. There were almost no organized academies or foundations. The government scientific work had few resources at its disposal as compared with those which it at present enjoys.

But whether the scholarship of earlier days be considered as vocational or as liberalizing in its end, it had one preeminent characteristic. The scholar was the man of learning and culture. He knew many things and knew them exactly. He made no blunders in accent or quantity. He never confused gerund and gerundive, or the subjunctive of purpose with that of result. He did not mix John Scotus with Duns Scotus, or attribute Ben Jonson's poems to Boswell's idol. He was never uncertain as to whether Stephen and Matilda came before or after the Henrys or as to the precise basis of the respective claims of

York and Lancaster. He knew the species and genus of plant and animal and never was at fault in stating the distance of earth from sun or the velocity of light.

These more external notes were, however, the signs of an inner spirit. What lent vitality to learning as an ideal was the conception of the scholar's world which was shaped in Hellas and found its rebirth in the Renaissance.

The Greeks thought of their world as preeminently a world of light and order as contrasted with the dark confusion of barbarism. In religion, the Olympian deities, in architecture the severe Doric lines, in sculpture the perfect matching of form to idea, in mathematics the definition of abstract relations in number and geometry, all manifested the love of clarity and order. The formulation of the method of science by Socrates, Plato, and Aristotle, as that of discovering the concept, the class, the essential character, was the supreme illustration of this vision of Hellenic genius. It appeals to emotion as well as to intellect, for if it lacks passion it possesses universality, dignity, and repose that make perpetual appeal. Entrance to this world, moreover, was for the scholar gained not so much by the lonely path of the pioneer as by sympathetic companionship with those who had already traversed the way. Homer and Virgil, Thucydides and Cicero, Sophocles and Plato not only pointed out the glories but lent the charm of imagination and the grace of human society to the quest. This personal element justly entitled such studies to be called the humanities.

In other words, the older conception of scholarship as learning and culture stood for one of the two great means by which the civilized man is superior to the savage. It is not, say the anthropologists, that civilized man has better brains; we have no evidence that the modern European is superior in gray matter to the men who left the wall paintings in Santander's caves. But the man of today inherits through tools and institutions, through language and techniques, through art and letters, the painfully accumulated treasures which give him at once material resources and spiritual freedom.

There was, however, an implication under this conception of scholarship. It suggested a world complete rather than world in the making. It suited admirably a theology of eternal and changeless decrees; it suited a morality of immutable laws discovered by innate ideas or intuitive reason; it suited an economic man moved by a single motive along unvarying lines of action. In law it grasped the great value of general rules and established precedents as over against confusion and vacillation. It tended to view a fixed constitution with its certainty and its invitation for deductive reasoning as the ideal of legal science. If the world of religion, of morality, of commerce, of government stood still, scholarship as learning would be a sufficient ideal.

But the world does not stand still, and scholarship is not standing still. There is more than analogy between the movements going on in society and the movement in scholarship. Instead of the ideal of learning has been set the ideal of investigation and reconstruction. It is easy to distinguish in this as in the ideal of learning a less significant and a more significant aspect. It has no doubt led to some researches which are profitless. It has added at times to the sum of useless knowledge. Of some of its contributions it may doubtless be said it is more blessed to give than to receive. But if, as with the other ideal of scholarship, we look deeper, we find implied a certain theory which is gradually reconstructing not only science, but religion, law, and society itself.

Notice then that in investigation the scholar is more selective. He cannot merely investigate in general; he must choose. He focuses all his resources upon his problem. Instead of a broad survey with accurate classification, his purpose is now a definite answer to a specific question. This leads almost inevitably to a greater specialization. Scholarship loses something of the breadth of learning; it loses some of its lure and charm.

Investigation is also more critical of received laws and conceptions. Instead of living himself into a structure already built and appreciating its beauty, the scholar begins to doubt its security, to tear down here and to rebuild there. He uses the method of a working hypothesis, and regards this hypothesis as by no means an exact pattern of God's plan in creation. It is a point of view, but not the only one. In psychology, for example, the older scholarship described powers and operations of mind or consciousness; the newer psychology asks whether mind and consciousness are terms that really help us to any valuable knowledge and one school proposes to omit them for a time and try other points of view. In chemistry we of an older generation learned much of the atom; we pictured a world built up of these changeless elements. In a recent text the atom is not mentioned until the 193rd page, and is referred to as a fiction convenient for explaining certain behavior but less convenient for other purposes than the conception of energy. In history investigative scholarship does not, perhaps, question the existence of certain men, or the occurrence of certain events. But it does question whether the men or the events were at all what we supposed, or more fundamental still, it questions whether many of the personages and recorded events, which in the past have bulked large, are of any scientific value.

The classical studies have undergone change likewise. When language and literature, art, and institutions are seen in their relations they become not less, but more significant. For they illumine one of the rare moments of human progress. In ethics we accept neither the infallible intuitions, nor the equally infallible pleasures and pains of the former rival schools. We are coming to see that good and right stand for nothing which can be exactly defined and envisaged once for all. They symbolize rather the progressive ideals and standards of a growing moral life, and are constantly taking on new meaning as man knows more fully his powers and kindles more deeply in sympathetic response to his fellows.

It is in our great institutions of religion and law that the work of investigation promises to be of the highest significance. For centuries theology had in one respect seen little change. Many viewed with apprehension the application of investigative scholarship to sacred origins and experiences. But the present interest in the psychology of religion is bringing a new sense of the reality of a great experience. We may have given it wrong interpretation and we may in the future sit more loosely to our readings of experience. But we are less likely than of old to confuse our interpretation with the experience.

In law and politics the investigative method is likely to have results as far-reaching and beneficent. No field has better illustrated the value of that order and exactness for which the conception of learning has stood. Beginning in customs guarded and administered by elders of the tribe, law in both Rome and England passed, we are told by legal historians, to a period of strict law whose watchwords were certainty and uniformity. Justice by rule was better than justice by arbitrary dictum of monarch or assembly, or local squire. Certainty enabled men to know upon what they could count. The common law thus built up a series of precedents which served not only as a rule for settlement of the multitude of private controversies, but as a bulwark of liberties against royal power. Liberalizing and enlarging its scope by including principles of equity and customs of merchants, the common law continued to guard jealously its esteem for rule and precedent. In England this has been to some extent supplemented and modified by the supreme authority of Parliament. In this country a written constitution has added a further factor making for fixity. Under such conditions the man learned in the law has been the preeminent type of legal scholar. And the great mass of people have come to look upon law as a body of rules too complex for comprehension by the laymen, although this has not prevented them from adding freely to their number at every session of every legislature. Between a legal attitude which has tended to an exclusive emphasis upon learning, and a legislative procedure which has often been painfully lacking in scholarship our law has found increasing difficulty in meeting its persistent problems. The application of the investigative and critical method to legal doctrines and procedure has been looked upon by some with apprehension precisely as was the case a generation ago in religion. But abler jurists and publicists recognize that nothing will conduce more to the advance of justice and good order. The only security for law in a democratic society is that it shall be true to the fundamental sense of what is right and fair. It is the task of investigative scholarship to reinterpret this sense, and to direct its expression with the light of intelligence and with the resources which the newer scientific methods afford.

For the point of view of present scholarship is not only investigative, it is constructive. Certain aspects of this are too familiar to need mention. We know how chemistry has revolutionized modern industry and promises to cooperate with biology in revolutionizing agriculture. We have seen our children protected by the researches of Pasteur and Behrens. We look almost daily for tidings of new triumphs over disease, now that methods of investigation have been worked out. We look as eagerly for the discovery of possible utilization of nature's forces which may have profound social results, which may perchance counteract congestion in cities and make for saner living.

But in the social sciences and institutions the reconstructive tendencies of modern scholarship are no less apparent. Mankind has long looked upon the social and economic process as something to be understood but scarcely as a power to be controlled. We have indeed gone much farther in the management of steam and electricity than in the management of business or of politics. We have depended for moral advance chiefly upon exhortation; we have not planned for a genuine social life. We have followed in human affairs too nearly the trial-and-error method of the squirrel in the maze.

It would be easy to take illustrations from many fields. The recent troubles in the Calumet mining region and in Colorado are present to us all. Without attempting any judgment as to the exact apportionment of blame, one thing seems clear from even such meager knowledge as has reached the general public. No adequate and broad-minded knowledge has been employed in dealing with the conditions. I do not refer to the present conditions. I mean the preconditions. If anything like the skilled intelligence and broad study and careful foresight had been applied to the human side of the mining situation which has been applied to the mechanical and commercial sides of it, can anyone suppose that we should have had the bloodshed which stamps us as still crude in our civilization?

Or if we take politics, our cities have many of them passed through periodic seasons of reform, to return later to only moderate standards of honesty and efficiency. It is only recently that we have come to deal with efficiency not in terms of vague demands but in the light of actual standards of what government should cost. It is only recently that we have been able to translate the meaning of good city government into terms of health, of recreation, of better ideals for growing boys and girls.

Perhaps the most conspicuous opportunity for constructive scholarship at present lies in the problems of our modern cities. In this country we have planned but one of our large cities. In most cases we have allowed congestion to steal upon us while we slept. But even more fundamental than the striking evils of congestion is the fact that our cities have grown up about factory, office, and store with no apparent anticipation that homes might be necessary or that children might need especial provision. In early days, of course, the child needed apparently no play space except the vacant lot, and the school needed no playground since each child could play at home. But with the filling up of all vacant lots the result has been practically to abolish the possibility of play except for the very few who are fortunate enough to be near a park. Is it surprising that under such conditions we find young people in our cities a constant source of anxiety if not of actual crime?

Fortunately the constructive spirit has set to work upon this great social problem. In the old world where the evil has been of longer growth, far-sighted measures have been taken to develop cities as nurseries of a free, joyous, and orderly life. Our own cities are beginning to plan along similar or even bolder lines.

The meaning of the conception of learning for the individual we saw was that of liberation. It delivered him from the limitations of his age by making him acquainted with all ages; it delivered him from the limitations of place by enabling him to range through all the universe; it delivered him from the limitations of birth by making him free of the republic of letters. As the freedom of the medieval city not seldom replaced the old class distinction between gentle and simple with a new class privilege of its own, so freedom of scholarship sometimes, no doubt, brought with it a certain pride of citizenship in the class of learned scholars. In this respect it but repeated the course of human emancipation. For man has seldom achieved liberty alone or as a member of humanity at large. He has needed the support of a limited group and he has usually achieved for this limited group a privilege which later could be more widely shared and beneficently used. The spirit of the Renaissance, like its prototype of Greece, doubtless had within it this element of aristocracy. Yet when we compare the aristocracy of learning with that of political power we must at least recognize that there is within it no necessity of exclusiveness. Its freedom is not lessened because it is widely shared. Its power to give elevation is not diminished because of the increasing number who find it.

The meaning of the investigative and constructive ideal of scholarship for the individual is found, I believe, in the conception of power rather than of liberation. It marks a somewhat higher level in the progress of the human spirit. It has passed the *flamantia moenia mundi* which limited man's part in nature to a comprehension of her forces and an acceptance of her laws of destiny. Limited as we are and shall always remain, so far as we can see, in our bodily existence; determined as we are by forces that limit our individual life, we are nevertheless far less limited than the individual whom Aeschylus and Sophocles presented as helpless against fate, or than he whom the stern theology of our fathers presented as the object of a no less inflexible decree, or than the creature whom our first reading of evolution conceived as determined absolutely by heredity and environment.

For if we look back over the world of civilization and culture we see that it has been built up by thought and struggle in which man has gradually transformed his environment. And if we look within we see that in the world of art which imagination has constructed, in the world of conduct where ideals and values give laws, in the world of friendship and love where nothing external has power to rule, 'Man is the captain of his soul, the master of his fate.'

So much might have been seen by scholarship as learning, or if not clearly seen at least felt. But scholarship as investigative and constructive may add a yet more positive note, for it is beginning at least to suggest that the individual may be not merely master of his own values but may also help bring those values into other lives far more effectively than the more individualistic idealism supposed. We find that response to environment may mean hope as well as resignation, for if we can give to the child—to every child—the atmosphere of sympathy and of intelligence, we can insofar make for him his world. And if we may not as yet forecast with assurance a positive control of heredity equal to our control of environment, we can at least prevent a large part of the pathetic and sometimes positively evil consequences of our previous ignoring of nature's laws. We are in the mere beginnings of possible control over human association, of politics, and of economic life. But if there is any maxim that we may cast to the rubbish heap it is the dictum 'You cannot change human nature.' Human nature is in certain respects at least the most changeable thing, the most flexible and adaptive thing in the universe, so far as we know. It apparently would not survive at all were it not flexible and adaptive. Why should we not assume that science can do more intelligently and directly what has thus far taken place so largely by the method of trial and error?

The investigative and constructive ideal of scholarship has thus its implied theory of the world. The ideal of learning seemed to suggest a world of fixed classes and types. Investigation would not necessarily change the picture if the investigator's task ceased with his discoveries. But if he sets an experiment he is to this extent varying the conditions. And if as the result of his experiment he tries upon a larger scale another experiment he is to this larger degree changing the conditions. This may not be creation in the metaphysical sense of summoning worlds from a void, but it is nonetheless creative intelligence. It is certainly shaping the world in which our children are to live.

In Goethe's great poem of modern culture the master of learning is surfeited of his possessions. His spirit tires of the past. It seeks through magic some control over unseen forces which has not been vouchsafed through all accumulated wisdom. Life is poor and mean without this past and yet no heaped-up treasures can satisfy it. In the spirit of romanticism Faust turns from books and seeks in the adventures of youth the satisfaction for his expending, eager powers. And when in its later symbolism the poem gives suggestions of emancipation, of achievement, these speak still the language of imperfect union of scholarship with life. There is the union of the Greek spirit of order and beauty with modern passion; there is promise of salvation through public activity rather than through private adventure. Faust will found a society in which his citizens must purchase security and freedom by perpetual effort:

> Wer immer strebend sich bemüht
> Den können wir erlösen.[1]

But there is no recognition of the possibilities of the completer satisfaction of all human capacity through the constructive power of thought which is rising vaguely before the prophetic minds of today. If Goethe were writing the vision of the twentieth century as he wrote that of the Renaissance and of his own time, would he not show us a solution of life which lies not merely in the splendor of the quest, which finds the redemption of humanity not merely in its incessant activity, its romantic adventure, its pursuit of the eternally fascinating and attractive, but in the yet more positive consciousness of enlarging powers, of directive control? Scholarship, indeed, is not all of life. If we have to make our choice, we shall continue with Kant to say that the primacy lies with conduct. It is a more distinctively creative act to guide life by the practical reason than to understand it by the speculative reason. Yet the scholar of today may well feel that no such absolute alternative is called for. The interpretation of the world and of life through both learning and investigation is necessary for the creation of ideals that can really work; the struggle with the conditions of life evokes interpretation. Not in any aristocratic conception of superior privilege, and not by any factitious aids of circumstances, but by the simple strength of his knowledge of past resources and his forecast of future powers, the scholar will more and more enter into the promise by becoming servant of all.

---

1. "We can save all who ceaselessly strive to save themselves." Johann Wolfgang von Goethe, *Faust* (11936–11937).

18 The Test of Religion

Unto thee, O Lord, do I lift up my soul,
O, my God, in thee I have trusted,
Let me not be put to shame. (Psalm 25:1–2)

Ever since man's intelligence has lifted him to a life of imagination and thought, as well as of sense and feeling, the struggle for existence has taken on for him a larger significance than it has for the brute. He does not adapt himself so passively to nature; he is in a sense 'nature's insurgent son.' He fashions his actions in some degree by ideas of past or future. He summons to his aid not only the cooperation of his kin, but the protection of the very forces that oppose him. With magic and ritual, with sacrifice and prayer, he compels or entreats. He enters into sympathy and cooperation with the unseen. He lifts up his soul. He trusts in a Helper. He seeks salvation. He would in some sense overcome the world. But while the persistent effort remains, the sort of salvation he needs and the sort of cooperation he would gain vary with the man's ideal. The test he applies will vary likewise. To appreciate what may be called the modern test we may contrast it with some of the earlier tests man has proposed.

I

1. The earlier need man felt was naturally that for food and shelter, for protection against foes of famine and pestilence, darkness and storm, or the often more pressing enemies of hostile tribes.

What, under these conditions, was the test of religion? The religion

Reprinted by permission of the publisher from James Hayden Tufts, "The Test of Religion," *University of Chicago Sermons*, ed. T. G. Soares (Chicago: University of Chicago Press, 1915), 89–104 [1915:01].

that brought victory over enemies, that brought health, that gave good luck in the hunt or sent the rains that made the land yield her increase, that guarded from the pestilence in darkness or the destruction at noonday—this was the religion man craved in early time. Greek or Semite, American Indian or Australian black tested his religion by its ability to give such help. The god that answereth by fire, he is the god; the Lord of Hosts is the helper. And the test works both ways: The man who prospers in all these ways is sure that the Lord is with him. Success is the test of piety and faith; calamity or defeat is evidence of sin, or of failure to unite forces with God.

But in time man came to feel new needs. The old tests no longer satisfied. New kinds of conflict arose which the older religion could not put to rest. Out of the stress and anguish of these crises came a vision of a higher world than man had known before. To enter this new world a new religion was needed. A far subtler conception of salvation made its way into human consciousness. A new kind of aid was required. New tests replaced the old. The older and simpler religion broke down at two points.

It broke down as a means of getting nature's aid or as a protection against the dangers from nature and man. It did not give the worshiper sure harvests or safe voyages. The flight of birds or the freshly opened bodies of victims failed to inspire confidence as revelation of God's will. Asshur did not protect Nineveh, nor Bel Babylon, nor Jehovah Jerusalem, nor Athena Athens. And finally the Eternal City of Mars, of Jove, and of all the pantheon was sacked.

And on the other hand, the man who sought to follow the guidance of right in his relations to his fellows—he likewise might fail to gain the blessing of God. Though he gave his bread to the fatherless and upheld justice in the gate he might perish.Which, then, should he trust, conscience or religion? In such a crisis many would stand by the older view of religion and go after any who promised prosperity. But a Job would hold fast to his integrity and an Amos and a Hosea would find a new religion which put justice and mercy before sacrifice.

Out of the collisions and wreckage of these older forms and the breakdown of the earlier tests came gradually higher types of religion in Europe and in Asia.

2. Corresponding to that aspect of religion which sought to control nature through magic or mystic union, there emerged the methods of scientific thought. Astronomy began to guide the sailor, medicine to understand and sometimes to heal disease. Mathematics was for Plato

a surer path to the divine than the religious myth of the poets. The life of plants and animals, the practice of the creative artisan or creative poet gave Aristotle his clue to the nature of God; and, above all, the splendor of the new world rose into man's vision. The universe lay open to him who had the key of logical method. It was a universe of order, of law, of consistent reason.

For more than a thousand years, though submerged from time to time by waves of ignorance, this seemed to many of the choicest minds the true realm of reason. Reason is man's divine life, say Plato and Aristotle, St. Thomas and Spinoza. In comparison with this, the life of sense belongs to our animal and mortal part. Let man put off his mortality and find God in the immortal and changeless realm of thought. Let him find the beautiful vision in the contemplative life. Let him view all things under the aspect of eternity. Nor can we forget the eloquent words of the modern expounder of this view: "In religion we withdraw from what is temporal—religion is for our consciousness that region in which all the enigmas of the world are solved, all the contradictions of deeper-reaching thought have their meaning unveiled, and where the voice of the heart's pain is silenced—the region of eternal truth, of eternal rest, of eternal peace." Religion of this sort finds in God a cause, a substance, an absolute. It seeks to view all things from the standpoint of eternity. Its test is that of logical consistency.

3. While the thinker seeks to rise above the world of sense on wings of thought, another pilgrim climbs step by step a stony path to the divine. Not the illusions and perplexities of the universe, but the passions and lusts within the soul, vex and baffle him. 'Satan' symbolizes an adversary more active and dangerous that 'Chaos.' Persian, Indian, Greek, and Christian seek helper and companion in these conflicts. The way upward is steep, but it too, no less that the soaring flight of reason, yields visions. The higher world of God lies beyond, and a Paul or a St. Bernard catches glimpses of its splendor. For such a religion desires and passions, the lust of the flesh and the pride of life, are the deadly foes. They blind the vision; they fetter the aspiring soul; they shut him away from God. Only by freeing himself as far as may be from these can he enter the presence of the pure and holy. Fast and vigil, poverty, chastity, renunciation, mortification of the body—these form the *via crucis*, which is the *via lucis*. And for the saint of this type of religion the test will be, Have I completely escaped the vanities and deceptions of this sham world? Have I ceased to lust

and to will? Have I merged and hid my life in God, and does his spirit in turn give me victory over the world of the flesh and of desire? This is the ascetic's test.

4. But beside the thinker and the saint, another type of man sought another and a different salvation. Man early learned the necessity of government and law if he were to rise above quarreling and enjoy life and peace. But power is often ruthless. Greed and ambition trample on laws. The just perish; the wicked prosper. The seeker for truth is condemned in Athens; the prophets in Judea are stoned. Superhuman help is needed. Unless there is some divine rule, some guiding Providence, some just judge and final appeal, wrong triumphs over right, and all the moral conviction is put to confusion. The political and legal conceptions of religion were the response to this demand: God is the true sovereign of the world. He is the righteous judge. Religion is to do him homage and obey his rule. And in place of the earlier cities and empires the religion of John and of Augustine builds a City of God, a Kingdom of Grace.

Greek, Roman, and Jewish elements found their place in these legal and political conceptions of religion. The Greek projected an ideal city with little hope that it would rise on earth. The Roman thought that in the universal principles of justice implanted in all men is found a revelation of the divine reason. The Jew saw in God not merely the ruler of Israel but the sovereign of all worlds. But in the actual fusion of these elements in the time of savage and barbarous men it was criminal justice which became the determining factor. God was the almighty judge; man was a rebel. Religion was repentance and submission. Salvation was escape from wrath to come. The test of religion was, Can it take from me the fear of punishment, and give me instead the assurance of a forgiving grace? This was the test for the ages of Dante and of Calvin.

But there was another form of the political and social ideal. National hopes gave rise in the heroic souls of Israel's seers to a grander vision of a kingdom of righteousness not limited to the sons of Abraham. Yet it needed the complete destruction of the earthly Jerusalem and the opposition of the little group of Christian disciples alike to their old countrymen and to Roman power to prepare the way for a union and cooperation of man and his fellows for a purely spiritual end. The older faiths had been national. The essentially new in the idea of the church was that it represented unity of man with man in God. And when Augustine saw the Roman imperial power disintegrate he hailed the coming City of God as the destined end of creation. The church became the earthly way of entrance to this city. Its universal catholic sway embraced the faithful. The test of religion for the individual became obedience to its rule. The test the anxious soul propounded was, Have I been blessed through its sacraments, absolved through its divine commission, included in its saving fold?

5. When the modern world came in, religion, like other forms of human experience, took a more individual and personal attitude. Personal accountability to God, personal faith, personal salvation, personal regeneration and penitence, an inner light within the soul— these became notes of true religion. With most men there was no intellectual question as to the existence and sovereignty of God. The question was rather as to man's own conscious attitude toward his creator, lawgiver, judge, and redeemer. The cry of the Psalmist, "Let me not be put to shame," as it was repeated by our fathers, sprang from fear that they might be put to shame because of their own deceitful hearts.

As we read the writings of Edwards and his followers or of Wesley and his school we can but appreciate the fervor and intensity of feeling which dwelt within them. It offers a parallel to the emphasis laid upon the affections by the 'moral sense' school of contemporary ethical writers. It was perhaps favored by special external conditions which turned the spirit within upon itself. Although the Calvinist conceived God primarily as governor of the universe—of a universe, moreover, in which the great majority of men were through another's act in hopeless enmity, and under certain condemnation to endless misery— they nonetheless looked for a type of affection appropriate to personal relations. If the object of affection was the divine-human Savior there might be an even more vivid imagery and emotion. In their fear of an external religion of works, or a selfish religion of gain, men of spiritual temper sought in the 'exercises,' or 'taste,' or 'experience' of the individual soul the supreme test of the work of God within.

But in the effort to make religion inward there was often a tendency to read inner experience in terms of emotion. Love of God—love disinherited, self-forgetting, and utter—was demanded, and was often tested by 'warmth' or 'coldness' of heart. Repentance was evidenced by the depth of depression under conviction of sin. Regeneration was known by the joy with which the heart responded to a new hope.

6. But the emotional was not the only test offered by the individual movement. The type we have just considered centered its experience about the conceptions of a sovereign God, a broken law, a divine

redeemer, and found in man's own heart no element of good save as almighty grace overcame all natural depravity. A deeper insight into the very essence of moral experience disclosed a factor overlooked. "The world that I bring thee this day," we may read Kant's message, "is not far off. It is not in heaven, nor beyond the sea. It is very nigh thee. The voice of duty is in the heart. Its authority is first of all *there*, or it is nowhere." And if the very essence of 'I ought' is that I command myself, this lifts man above himself. It shows him, in spite of all his selfishness, as belonging to another world. He himself is sovereign as well as subject. He has found a surer sign than hitherto for the confidence that he need not be ashamed in his trust. Kant himself did not give to his interpretation of religion the full breadth of the horizon which he had thus disclosed. But in the principle which he established lay the promise of religious faith.

II

What now shall we say is the modern test of religion?

I confess that when I began to write I had in mind to point out chiefly why these older tests had failed—to show that for us of the modern world, religion is not tested without by miracle nor within by emotion, nor even by the intellectual method of logical consistency. But as I reflected upon what each of the successive tests had meant to the men of faith who framed them, I thought I saw in each a truth as well as a defect. And I believe it is possible for us to shape our test, not so much by setting aside these others, as by recognizing what each aimed at and in what respect it failed. Then perhaps we can add what our day may make as its contribution to the common work of those who have walked by faith.

The evident trend of all man's religion has been to come into a larger world; to find in the Great Companion sympathy and support for aspirations and hopes; to overcome evil; to make good and justice prevail. Let us then see how each of the tests we have noticed records some effort.

And first in miracle. This seems to us an impossible way to test the spiritual. That sun should stand still or dead should rise, or lightning flash on the right, would be but physical fact to be explained as such. It would tell nothing of moral character. But to early man it did mean at least that nature was in some sense his friend. It responded somehow to his prayer. It behaved as he would himself behave. But it was a crude and limited conception of the spiritual world which was thus suggested. And the Great Teacher sighed deeply in his spirit when men sought of him a sign from heaven. "An evil and adulterous generation seeketh after a sign." "If they hear not Moses and the prophets, neither will they be persuaded if one rise from the dead."

We turn then from the test of miracle to its farthest extreme, the test of knowledge. And it is not hard for us moderns to appreciate its profound significance. To search for causes, to organize all nature's variety into classes and finally into one comprehensive system, to bring all scattered events under universal law and banish contradictions—all this was indeed to open a new vision of the universe. The faculty which so manifests its power may well seem man's most divine prerogative. To think God's thoughts after him is to enter into union with the divine. In knowledge man finds the control over nature and the support he needs. The fatal defect in the test as it was applied by scholasticism was the method of knowledge it pursued. It mistook the scaffolding for the temple, the telescope for the heavens. The principles of causation, of unity, of consistency, or, in modern days, of evolution, are the clues with which we explore; but no analysis of definitions of First Cause, of Pure Being, of Absolute, of Evolution, will take the place of exploration. It is in observation, experiment, and reflection combined that we of today believe we enter into the kingdom of knowledge, and therefore of cooperation with the world of nature and of man. Religion cannot afford to drop this test. Rather it needs to carry it farther, and by more careful penetration into just the religious life of man to give due weight to the most important facts of human life. It is not hard to explain why religion at first sought God in the heavens, and watched with jealous eye the progress of astronomy or geology or biology; the time has now come when we are searching also the mind of man.

I need not dwell long upon the ascetic and mystical tests. We do not enter the hermit's cell nor seek the beatific vision through cutting off all desire and will. And yet the lusts and passions war against the soul and he that would live the life of the spirit must make them its subjects, not its masters. This test persists until the ape and tiger die.

Is then the test of religion to be found in the legal conceptions of atonement, forgiveness, and salvation from punishment? No one who ponders human life will deny the consciousness of guilt, or fail to see how this consciousness has itself helped man to find in a world of justice a higher development, a spiritual life. But the older conceptions of criminal law, born as they were in blood-revenge and sovereignty of force, are not the justice or religion for today. "The very notion," says William James, "that this glorious universe, with planets and winds, and laughing sky and ocean, should have been conceived and had its beams and rafters laid in technicalities of criminality is incredible to our modern imagination. It weakens a religion to hear it argued upon such a basis."

If it be true of law that her seat is the bosom of God, it is religion to seek justice. But we have sometimes forgotten that, like other institutions, law is a mixture of higher and lower. Our justice is in part the divine principles, but it is also in part the work of barbarous times and selfish men. It embodies class interests and vested wrongs, as well as fairness and hard-won rights. The sacredness that belongs only to the one is sometimes invoked for the other. Nor has the other separation been less fatal. Because human government is imperfect and human politics corrupt, the religious man in the past has too often kept aloof. The most hopeful signs of our day to my mind are on the one hand the efforts to make law and government more responsive to all the ideal ends of man, to give him education and sympathetic care as well as to guard his life and property, and on the other, that good men and women are finding place for their religion in political life. Perhaps never before in the twenty-five centuries since the words were spoken has Micah's first test for religion seemed so vital, "What doth the Lord require of thee but to do justly?"

And lastly we may consider together the two remaining tests we have mentioned, since they seem to represent opposing views. One was membership in a universal corporate body, the other was an inner and personal experience. The latter we certainly shall not give up. The whole scientific spirit of our day urges us to seek what is real and vital in concrete facts of some experience, rather than in general concepts. But it is inadequate to seek this in emotion. Emotion may well be the moment when higher life begins—when the older, narrow self gives way, and one enters into larger reaches of life. But it is only a partial or occasional experience.

Deeper than this is the experience of conscience and duty as the ever-present witness within the soul of its sublimity, as the constant symbol of the actual existence of moral values, as the evidence of horizons yet unreached. The profoundest and most truly religious faith is the faith that 'right makes might.' It is through this witness of the moral conviction that we get the best interpretation of the test spoken to a generation not yet ready to receive it: He that wills to do God's will shall know.

But how shall one be sure of duty? How shall one know God's will?

And is the knowledge—the test—a purely subjective one? In contrast with this there was a great principle beneath the conception of the church. My feelings, your struggles for righteousness, are very likely to go wrong if you and I keep separate from our kind. Above all, in the life of the spirit, recent science emphasizes that social cooperation is necessary. Religion expresses the fact that the deepest spiritual nature is social. Where two or three are met the divine presence is with them. The test of membership in this cooperative union was indeed misapplied when it was taken as a substitute for the others, or when the special ecclesiastical organization, built as it was from Roman empire and oriental magic and Gothic rites, was identified with the spiritual temple. I am not here to argue for any specific form of ecclesiasticism, nor as to whether the church of the future shall even be called by that name. But the test of cooperation, of union in spiritual sympathy and purpose, of loyalty to the cause of the Kingdom of God, of active participation in the efforts to make this kingdom come—this is a modern test.

> See! In the rocks of the world
> Marches the host of mankind,
> A feeble wavering line.
>
> Factions divide them, their host
> Threatens to break, to dissolve.
> Ah, keep, keep them combined!
> Else, of the myriads who fill
> That army, not one shall arrive.

Only under the inspiration of great religious leaders do we feel our need, and quicken into unity and strength. Only thus united shall our march lead

> On, to the bound of the waste.
> On, to the City of God.

19   Ethics of States

The lover of paradox can find no richer field than that of the ethics of states. On the one hand no institution has commanded nobler devotion or inspired loftier art; on the other, none has lent itself so ruthlessly to the destruction of every human interest and value, or has practiced so consistently what in common life we would call crime. On the one hand it has been presented by philosopher and publicist as the institution in which man may live nobly and well, as the institution in which freedom may be secured, or as the institution in which the organic unity of mankind is realized and the individual is raised to higher consciousness and larger horizons. On the other it has been convicted by history of organizing hatred more effectively than love; of organizing oppression more resolutely than safeguards of liberty; and of bending its energies and using its resources more unsparingly to destroy life than to save it. We should not expect to find in it the family affections, the charm of friendship, the ideals of religion. But we might look for respect for elementary rights. What are the facts? The state hales private persons before its bar if they violate person or property, break contracts, or enslave their fellows, but itself commits homicide, trespass, breaks treaties, and takes possession against their will of the persons and property of multitudes who have done it no harm.

And if we seek a final paradox, more striking than the others, we find it in the real or assumed solemnity with which nations at war on the one hand suppress discussion, claim that political considerations take precedence over morality, and regard victory as a mark of divine approval, while on the other they appeal to the justice of their cause and recognize the importance of giving it the color of self-defense.

Reprinted from *The Philosophical Review* 24.2 (1915) by permission of the publisher [1915:05].

"Even victorious wars," said Bismarck, "cannot be justified unless they are forced upon one. . . . Success," he explained to Moltke when revising the Ems telegram, "however, essentially depends upon the impression which the origination of the war makes upon us and others; it is important that we should be the ones attacked."[1] The present war has exemplified these various paradoxes in more striking form, but we do not need to look beyond the seas for illustrations of practically all of them. The story of Naboth's vineyard has been often repeated in the dealings of the United States with Indian lands. Our dealings with Colombia excited alarm in South America and have been condemned by many of our own citizens. Our first proposal as to the Panama tolls was at least a violation of what the other party to the treaty understood to be its meaning. The neglect of Congress to pass laws giving the federal courts the power to enforce treaty rights if these are violated by local communities like Louisiana or California seems almost an equally flagrant sin of omission—it involves making promises which we do not take measures to carry out. If a private individual were similarly neglectful the law would certainly know how to deal with him. We know our own countrymen. We know English and German and French and Slav. We find their private morals not so very different from ours. How can we explain the contrast between private and public conduct?

The simplest answer is that all the paradoxes come from confusing politics and morals. Politics is politics, as Machiavelli well knew. To apply morals to politics is like appraising electricity in terms of virtue instead of in volts and kilowatts. This is, however, too simple to answer, for it does not explain the anxiety of states for moral approval. Another simple answer is the old one that might is right. This may take either the cruder form that might makes right, or the more pious and plausible shape that strength of nations, though not of individuals, is the divine evidence of right and therefore any objections to the ethics of successful powers are to be condemned as puerile.

On either of these theories it is pedantic and futile to apply to great elementary forces or to the cosmos and its laws the petty measures set by human conventions of philosophic systems. It is like finding fault with the firmament because its stars are not arranged in kindergarten patterns, or complaining that gravity is inconsiderate to the man walking on an icy sidewalk. Another easy solution is, "My nation

1. Otto von Bismarck, *The Man and the Statesman* vol. 2 (New York: Harper and Bros., 1899) 101.

is sincere; others are hypocrites." But I venture to think this is too simple for the impartial scholar. I shall not essay the task of an appraiser of just what is right and wrong by an absolute standard. I attempt the more modest task of noting some of the historical and logical grounds for the paradoxes in political ethics. Such an explanation may not yield the virtuous thrill of superior morality which we feel when we hew Agag in pieces before the Lord, but it is perhaps more fitting for the consideration of a group of scholars in a neutral nation.

We should probably agree that the actual morality of men of European stock is a conglomerate of several codes. Five of these are (1) the code of self-interest, based on the instincts for self-preservation, self-assertion, mastery, and possession, taking the rational forms of prudence, insistence upon rights, or ambition for expression and power. This is insofar praiseworthy as compared with inertness, sloth, or general weakness. (2) Closely related to this is the code of honor, which governs our behavior as members of certain types of special groups with some dominant interest or temper. (3) A third code, of legal standards, less emotional than that of honor, safeguards person, property, and contracts. It is important not between intimates but between dwellers in a country or parties to a bargain. (4) Fourth comes the code of family behavior, taught by the natural responses of parent to child, child to parent, or brother to sister. (5) Fifth, some more ideal code inspired by some cause, some personality, some imaginative vision, some response to personal relations of friendship, or of a wider human group than that of honor.

Nations have the first two of these codes, self-interest and honor, strongly developed; they have rudiments of the third in international law. Some beginnings of the fifth we thought we had in science, art, literature, religion. But the balance of power between these different sets of controlling principles in the national state is very different from that which obtains in at least the more intelligent and orderly private citizen. In the individual the web of social relations of a positive sort has increased until it is unusual for even the selfish to assert nakedly his belief in the rightful preeminence of relatively exclusive self-assertion and self-regard. The reverse is true of nations. Preservation and even national expansion comes first, says Rümelin in his classic address—*salus publica suprema lex*. In the absence of any authority to secure mutual confidence a condition of mutual distrust prevails which enables a government to justify to itself almost any act on the ground of self-defense, and a proper manipulation of the press will go far toward convincing the people of the justification of the government. In the case of the individual's morals, laws brings codes of honor before the bar of more rational and larger groups. With nations honor is given precedence over right. The statement of Sir Edward Grey that Great Britain would act in view of British interests, the national honor, and the nation's obligations, was perhaps not designed to place these three grounds of action in order of importance, but it would probably be generally accepted as representing such a scale in national ethics. In this series the order is: first, the direct, nonsocial, if not antisocial interests; second, the emotional interest bound up with some relatively exclusive group; third, recognition of relations to others, whether of free contract or of status. In individual morality the order is either reversed or else the terms interest, honor, and obligations, are given such ideal meanings as to make the exclusive aspect no longer relevant.

The important differences between the ethics of individuals and those of states are due in part to historical, in part to intrinsic conditions. Historically we have in states a longer survival of the traits of morals between hostile or unfriendly groups. Intrinsically, organized states, like other corporations, are both more and less than individuals. They are more because they are trustees and protectors of certain interests and values for many members. They are less because in representing certain interests and purposes they take no account of many other interests and purposes. They are thus impersonal and subject to the limited morality which present society finds in all impersonal corporations.

Historically, two great forces have been active in the building of nations and empires, lust for conquest and desire of gain. The state has not ordinarily arisen as a further grouping of families and tribes. Practically all modern European states have arisen through conquest. The king and his band of warriors, gathered frequently from various tribes and countries, united only by lust of conquest and plunder, formed the political body which triumphed over clans or neighborhood communities. Here was a new method of organization which was more powerful than the old. After the first battle William the Norman with his handful of experts could hold in subjection the whole realm of England. Usually the political body included only the king and his warriors; the great mass of conquered natives remained in their kinship or communities, or as slaves outside the organization. They must obey it; they were not within it.

When once the conquest had been made, the king would defend

the land against outside attacks, the enforce order within. He would impose his own peace and permit none but himself to seize person and property. Defense and sovereignty came first; protection to rights of subjects was not in the original intention but was wrested from the ruler by bargaining or by battle or by gradual enlargement of privileged groups. Law, which at first recognized few rights to any except the military masters, gradually gave protection to subjects, but it was only after centuries of struggle that the great mass of the people found freedom and a sense of participation in the power which previously they had been compelled to obey, or had followed with doglike devotion at the risk of property and life. Only in still more recent times has the state undertaken the care of health, the education of its children, the encouragement of science, the bringing of opportunity which makes the common resources available for the common man. The tradition of the national state is thus one of force, of hostility toward other nations, and of corresponding morals.

Within the last three hundred years another process has been operative in the formation and enlargement of states, which has also had an important influence upon public morality. The great colonizing movement, which began with the discovery of America, was more definitely and consciously economic in aim than the earlier types of state formation. North and South America, and later India and Africa, transformed England, Portugal, Spain, and France from nations to empires. The new possessions were at first managed largely for profit rather than for the benefits of the colonists or of the natives. The chartered companies, such as the East India Company, empowered to "make peace and war with the heathen nations" had little scruple as to the means by which they defeated rival companies or gained control over the lives and resources of millions. And when the home government began to look into the purposes and methods of these governments organized for profits, and to control the more flagrant abuses of power, there remained in the case of most of them a factor of differences of color, race, and religion between ruler and ruled. Imperial power under such conditions has been doubly dangerous to moral standards. "Impunity," says Bryce, "corrupts the ordinary man."[2] It was generally understood that the American soldiers in the Philippines did things which they would have considered quite unworthy of military standards at home. It was publicly stated by

2. James Bryce, *The Relations of the Advanced and Backward Races of Mankind* (Oxford: Clarendon, 1903) 40.

members of the war department that the United States in its conduct of the war was not bound by international laws of war because the Philippinos had never been parties to international agreements. The famous order of General Smith in the Philippines to kill and burn and spare no boy over ten, or the address to the German troops departing for China at the time of the Boxer outbreak, could scarcely have been issued for warfare in the United States or Europe. Water torture or dumdum bullets may be used against men of lower civilization. The insidious and corrupting influence of almost irresponsible government exercised by people of one race over those of another has been impartially set forth by Hobson. No doubt the administrator of high purpose and broad sympathy finds in such a situation opportunity for the finest loyalty to duty and the most sensitive regard for those who cannot help themselves; but not to look beyond our own borders, we know how shameful has been much of the history of our own administrative officials in dealings with the American Indians. If we are correctly informed, the zeal for the exploitation of this race has not lessened to this day and is still engaged in manipulating government for selfish ends.

The intrinsic character of the state and the nature of its organization are well adapted to maintain and reinforce the historical precedence of self-preservation and honor over justice, not to mention benevolence. On the positive side, as already noted, the state is more than the individual. It is in its idea the organization of men through which they achieve what is impossible for them singly. By its restraint of violence, by its enforcing of contracts, but its protection of rights, it makes possible in the individual just those moral virtues founded on peace, confidence, truth, and freedom from fear whose absence we deplore in the conduct of the states themselves. It may be fairly said that the evils of present international politics are due not to too much but to too little political organization. And, in defense of the national state, it may be urged that it represents about as large a group as in the present stage of civilization can act harmoniously and feel its order to be autonomy and its culture its own free creation. We cannot do justice to the men now yielding up their lives, we cannot be fair to the honored and respected men, our own friends and colleagues on both sides of this present war, except as we recognize the full worth of that which enlists their devotion. We may freely acknowledge the high purpose of the state; we may even agree with Rümelin that the state is bound to maintain itself, and that under existing conditions this may involve means that are abhorrent to our standards of morality.

But at the same time let us not fall into the fallacy of saying that evil is good. Going about armed, spending a large part of one's days and wealth in revolver practice, and of one's nights in listening at the neighbor's door to discover plots, devising means to catch him napping and studying the precise moment at which one may shoot first and still call it self-defense, lynching suspects, burning houses, and incidentally shooting the children of bystanders, all this may be 'necessary' in certain stages of savagery or frontier life. But no man can call it good. And insofar as nations conduct themselves in this fashion, we must challenge the situation. We must maintain that if our end requires such means we are in a stupid and pitiable condition. It is scarce worth applying terms of right and wrong except that the whole situation is wrong. Instead of glorifying national or imperial states, we should say, If this is the best they can do, we had better look for another principle of organization and reserve for that our enthusiasm and moral applause.

We are forced then to look to the aspect in which the state is not more but less than the individual, its abstractness of purpose, its methods of organization.

We are familiar with corporations organized for various specific ends and with the limits which these ends impose. Banks and manufacturing concerns are organized for profit. If a bank is asked for charity we feel it an appropriate answer that, while its stockholders or directors as individuals may respond, the bank's purpose does not authorize such use of funds. The manufacturing concern as such may serve the public, but its primary duty is to pay dividends upon capital invested. Our law and morality both recognize that bodies organized purely for acquisition need public control. Incorporate acquisitiveness is felt to be dangerous. The political corporation is more complex. It may include in its professed aims not merely the common defense, the establishment of justice, the blessings of liberty, but also the promotion of the general welfare. But even our federal government, organized with so broad a purpose, has been very chary of the general welfare in comparison with the common defense. Millions for defense, thousands for health or education, has been our national policy.

It may go without saying that the country has spent largely for education through state and local bodies. But the fact remains that the national government has not been concerned with the social and human needs of the people, and has probably suffered by its abstractness. European national states have concerned themselves more largely with human interests, but other conditions have kept the balance from inclining far in that direction. The central object of the national state has been on the whole power. The evils from which it suffers are, in part at least, due to the unregulated and only very partially responsible organization for power. Such an impersonal corporation has no room for feelings either humanitarian or resentful. It spares no one who opposes it; it turns not aside to indulge triumph or hatred. If I appeal again to Bismarck it is because he embodied more abstractly than any other this political principle and described more frankly its nature.

The consolidation and organization of Germany was for Bismarck a supreme consideration which sometimes called for war, sometimes for peace; sometimes for urging conquest upon a reluctant king, sometimes for a checking of that king's desire for triumphal entry or for seizure of territory; sometimes for exciting public opinion through a revised telegram, again for bold resistance of a military party that would defend by striking first in order to catch the adversary unprepared. In all these the political as such is brought clearly into relief. For example, in speaking of the situation during the siege of Paris, when operations were delayed because of influences of a professedly humanitarian nature, Bismarck wrote:

> A decision, memorable in the world's history, of the old struggle for
> centuries between the two adjoining peoples was at stake, and in dan-
> ger of being ruined, through personal and preponderating female in-
> fluences without historical justification, through influences which
> owed their activity, not to political considerations but to feelings
> which the terms humanity and civilization, imported to us from En-
> gland, still rouse in German natures.

On the other hand, of the needs in 1866, he said:

> Moved by this consideration [i.e., whether the feelings we left behind
> in our opponents were implacable] I had a political motive for
> avoiding, rather than bringing about, a triumphal entry into Vienna in
> the Napoleonic style. In positions such as ours were then, it is a politi-
> cal maxim after a victory not to enquire how much you can squeeze
> out of you opponent, but only to consider what is politically nec-
> essary.

If power and prestige, or repute of power, are thus the primary purpose of national organization, it is natural that governments should have agencies in army and navy to maintain this power, and conversely that these agencies should react strongly to strengthen the national bent. It is against all human nature that a man of ability should be content to devote his life to practicing for a game of golf without ever playing it. And here again we have the competent testimony of Bismarck. The man who deliberately planned to achieve by blood and iron the unity of Germany was not a mollycoddle or even a pacifist. Of Moltke he says, "[H]is love of combat and delight in battles were a great support to me in carrying out the policy I regarded as necessary in opposition to the intelligible and justifiable aversion in a most influential quarter." And then referring to various occasions on which this professional zeal proved inconvenient he makes the following highly significant reflection:

> It is natural that in the staff of the army not only younger active officers, but likewise experienced strategists, should feel the need of turning to account the efficiency of the troops led by them, and their own capacity to lead, and of making them prominent in history. It would be a matter of regret if this effect of the military spirit did not exist in the army; the task of keeping its results within such limits as the nation's need of peace can justify is the duty of the political, not the military, heads of the state. That at the time of the Luxemburg question, during the crisis of 1875, invented by Gortchakoff and France, and even down to the more present times, the staff and its leaders have allowed themselves to be led astray and to endanger peace, lies in the very spirit of the institution, which I would not forego. It only becomes dangerous under a monarch whose policy lacks sense of proportion and power of resistance to one-sided and constitutionally unjustifiable influences.[3]

The other organ of the state which shows the abstractness of corporate morals is the diplomatic service. The traditions of this service call for cunning, as those of the military arm for force. Its personnel is drawn largely from a special class. Its environment is specialized. Like the agents or attorneys of corporations it is urged to press claims which it knows are dubious or worse; it is supposed to have little discretion or conscience of its own, but to be governed by the needs of the government it represents. As is pointed out forcibly by [Arthur A.] Ponsonby in a recent article, it is in many ways a very inadequate medium for the great interests of the people concerned. Like the corporation attorney it is trained to be astute; it is not always likely you think greatly or to consider all the human issues at stake.

At this point the objection rises from many impatient of academic criticism, "You speak as though self-preservation needed apology or

3. Bismarck 121, 42–43, 102–103.

could be subjected to some assumed higher standard, whereas it is either itself the supreme value which tests all others or else is at least the most conclusive evidence of worth." In great part this is the familiar doctrine of survival of the fittest which it would be impossible to discuss within the limits of this address if such discussion was necessary. But in part it has some new features. It professes to find that in modern conditions of struggle and survival it is really moral qualities which count. For Jack Horner the inference from plums to virtue may have been premature, for there was too much luck. Or to put it in religious terms, it is not capable of absolute demonstration that God was rewarding virtue. But now when plums are extracted not by rule of thumb but by organized research and systematic industry, when survival depends upon efficiency and efficiency depends upon science, organizing power, temperance, chastity, self-sacrifice, and all the virtues, the case is changed.

Professor Münsterberg draws a parallel between success in war and success in business competition:

> [O]n the whole our economic system is backed by the belief that free competition brings gain to the worthy and keeps down the less efficient. In this sense certainly no unfailing justice lies in the decision of the weapons, but, in the great average, history has proved that those nations will rise which are worthy of it and those will fall which deserve punishment from the higher point of view of civilization.

If it be objected that an army is no better test of a nation's character than a football team of a university, the reply is, "The intellectual and moral qualities of a nation do come to expression in a modern war. It is not mere strength and not mere pluck, and least of all mere possession of guns which decides today in warfare. It is the total makeup of a nation with its thoroughness and its energy and the mentality and its readiness to bring sacrifices." The superiority of the German army "does not result from a merely outer professional war technique, but comes because the German army is the embodiment of the national soul with all its intellectual and moral energies." To be sure, the result of this present war may not afford an accurate test of moral superiority because there are more nations on one side than on the other. "The allied nations cannot prove any higher qualities . . . as their final victory would mean only a quantitative superiority."[4] If one stood

---

4. Hugo Münsterberg, *The War and America* (New York: Appleton, 1914) 199–202.

James Hayden Tufts

against one the proof would be conclusive. No one is concerned to deny the consummate scientific ability, the intellectual energies, the discipline, the loyalty, the heroism which are shown in a successful army. Yet when it is proposed to test moral superiority by a one to one contest, irrespective of the size of nations, it is difficult to see how we are eliminating quantity. Great Britain against the Boers, the United States against Spain, Germany against the Belgians—these were one to one, but it would be a bold inference that these contests established such superiority as would justify the extinction of the lesser power.

The doctrine of efficiency as a moral criterion is also given a religious turn.

> Victory in war is the method by which, in the economy of God's providence, the sound nation supersedes the unsound, because in our time such victory is the direct offspring of a higher efficiency, and the higher efficiency is the logical outcome of the higher morale. . . . The Lord of Hosts has made righteousness the path to victory. In the crash of conflict, in the horrors of battlefields piled with the dead, the dying, and the wounded, a vast ethical intention has still prevailed.[5]

Or finally war is given the moral function of serving as the instrument of a redistribution of territory from time to time according to the strength and therefore, it is assumed by those who would in this associate strength with merit, according to the desert or need of nations.

On this I offer two comments. (1) If any one thing stands out clearly before the judgment and conscience of the American people as the result of the recent decades of economic struggle it is this: While success may be secured by public service it may also be secured by strangling competitors, and for this latter purpose the moral virtues are not the qualities chiefly necessary. There is both fair and unfair competition, and the unfair has resources which will often win the day. Is there any less reason to hold that the political power which is most astute in forming alliances, shrewdest in calculating a favorable moment to strike, subtlest in provoking its rival into taking the offensive, most unscrupulous in bribery, will often find these means effective? And there is a deeper consideration for the sensitive conscience. Looking at business competition from a purely economic point of view, we might regard it as fair that the weaker should go to the wall,

5. Harold Frazer Wyatt, "God's Test by War: A Forecast and Its Fulfillment," *The Nineteenth Century and After* 76.3 (1914): 493, 496.

and the great corporation absorb all the smaller producers. Looking at political competition merely as a means of securing efficient organization, we might be indifferent to the disappearance of small states as political entities. But if economic replacement means at the same time reduction of the great body of citizens of a community to the status of employees; if it means control of legislatures, courts, schools, and churches by the great and efficient corporations, we pause. We have seen this tried more or less successfully in various cities and states and we don't like the taste of it. We have decided that unregulated business, even if more successful, is not to be trusted. An organization existing abstractly for profit needs to be controlled, we believe, by the conception of personal worth. Similarly, if we should look at political competition merely as a meaning of testing efficiency of government we might be indifferent to the disappearance of smaller states or to the tendency to monopoly. But despite all our own inefficiency in national, state, and city government, we of America still believe there is a value in self-government. We are young compared with many of the lesser states of Europe or Asia. But to extinguish our national life would be we think a loss of something inseparable from our personality. The national tradition, with all its sins, does make a genuine factor in the higher spiritual life. To destroy any of the peoples which have come to a sense of national life violates the same sense of justice which holds sacred the life of the individual. To reduce by force the variety and richness found in the many peoples and races to one or a half dozen patterns might make for political efficiency, but it would be a hideous wrong. Lord Cromer well observes that democratic imperialists have two ideals which are apt to be mutually destructive, the ideal of good government, and the ideal of self-government. Every dweller in a democratic nation feels the conflict, but we of America at least are not ready to abandon the principle of self-government. Only by this is the kingdom of ends possible.

(2) The second remark is that the doctrine of survival as value, or as evidence of value, persists because it is half true. All value does presuppose some living, willing agent to appreciate and maintain the good. And while ideals transcend the immediate present life, it is also true that life transcends all present ideals and is constantly giving birth to new ones. Moreover, even as self-consciousness involves a world of objects, moral valuation implies shaping out a moral world, and this means real achievement. Moral energies mean not thwarting and extinction but fuller life.

Yet it is certain that the doctrine in question in either form is only half true and is, in my judgment, the great materialism—the only one likely to do serious harm. Unless we are ready to go the whole way and deny that anything that exists is evil, we must use some other standard of value than existence, not to mention the fallacy of ruling out of values the sympathy which may interfere with self-assertion, the love of art and letters which does not necessarily make for existence. If we admit—and I suspect that if the advocates of the doctrine should find themselves in the defeated party, they would be first to make the admission—that sometimes the worse conquers the better, if we grant that God ever permits truth on the scaffold, wrong on the throne, then, we abandon the principle of survival as a reliable criterion. *Die Weltgeschichte* may be indeed *das Weltgericht*, but it is itself judged by a still higher court. All that we prize most has come from the spirit which has not accepted the cosmic process or the historical process as a final valuation. Small as the world of the free creative spirit appears, its values are for its members supreme. The still small voice is more significant than the earthquake and the fire. It alone decides whether we shall acquiesce or fight on for what we hold to be right and truth.

Let us look also at honor which is often ranked highest in the ethical codes of states. There is no doubt that the appeal to honor touches deep chords in the natures of all of us. It lies near to splendid virtues. It seems to strike a higher note than self-interest. The latter can be stigmatized by opponents as greed or jealousy. But honor is so noble in its associations that if a nation goes to war to maintain its honor apparently there is nothing more to be said. To question the morality of such an act is to write oneself down as a coward or poltroon, and who of us wishes to be so regarded? It often asserts supremacy over any rational interests and brings nations to rash and destructive enterprise of war. It is relied upon by masterful directors of states to achieve results for which calm reflection upon future advantage would be inadequate.

To be sure, honor in the individual, though it vibrates with the finest emotion, is very curious in its workings. The honor of a soldier has almost to the present moment required him to fight duels, quite irrespective of the law of the land. It is only a decade since an incident in one of the European armies showed the military code. Two boys grew up as playmates; one later entered the army and became a petty officer, the other entered the navy. On shore leave the sailor met his old comrade and extended his hand in friendly greeting instead of giving the due salute. The army officer in return ran him through and

killed him. When asked why he did not arrest the sailor if he thought
him wanting in respect, he replied that he remembered X, from whom
a civilian had escaped, and who in consequence had been so taunted
by his fellows that he was driven to suicide. A nominal penalty was
imposed, but the man felt proud of his action and was no doubt
honored by his fellow officers. The honor of the gentleman has also
been highly technical. To cheat at cards has always been dishonorable,
to cheat a woman of lower station not always. Gambling debts are
characteristically debts of honor; the tradesman may wait. If any
doubted a gentleman's word honor must be kept bright by proof of
sword, but where a lady was concerned honor required one to lie like
a gentleman. With the rise of the middle class to dignity and power we
begin to hear of business honor, which likewise has its peculiarities. It
is scrupulous in the payment of debts, but men of high standing have
done some queer things in corporation finance without regarding
them as dishonorable; and, on the other side of business relations,
honor would hardly be tarnished by any sort of exploitation of employees. With the rise of the laborer to class consciousness he too has
framed a code of honor, a *Herrenmoral*—paradoxically as such an idea
would have seemed to the gentleman of older days. He looks upon
the scab as the older gentleman looked upon the villein. The unionist's
sense of honor will not permit him to take another union man's job;
it would not be offended by soldiering on his own.

In certain respects the conception of what honor requires of the
individual has been modified, largely by the leveling forces of law,
and the rise of new classes with new standards. In America it is not
considered necessary to maintain honor by the duel, nor is manual
labor so dishonorable as entirely to unclass the worker. A man may
be willing to have a cause, even a murder, submitted to a court without
losing honor. He may make it a part of his honor to be reasonable, to
keep his word, to protect the weak, in a word to incorporate into his
code of honor the elements of justice and sympathy, as well as of
strength.

National codes of honor resist this reconstruction. The essence of
national honor to be guarded at all hazards is repute for strength. The
way to maintain honor is to show strength, preferably by war, or, in
the case of a backward or smaller peoples, by punitive expeditions.
Former President Taft has pointed out several instances in the diplomatic history of his country, as in the Canadian boundary question,
or the Trent affair, when it has been loudly asserted that to recede
from a claim or even to arbitrate would be to lose honor. "To lay

a finger on the honor of a State is to contest its existence," says
Treitschke.

> That State which will not be untrue to itself must possess an acute
> sense of honor. It is no violet to flower unseen. Its strength should be
> shown signally in the light of day, and it dare not allow that strength
> to be questioned, even indirectly. If its flag be insulted, it must ask
> satisfaction; if that satisfaction be not forthcoming, it must declare
> war, however trifling the occasion may seem.

By this conception of honor a democratic nation like our own is
seemingly as likely to be swept off its feet as the more military nations
of Europe. The fact is we are hypnotized by the words 'honor' and
'the flag' without asking whether honor may not have other standards
than repute for strength, other supports than the sword. A press
urged on to war by private interests of invested capital, no less than
a press manipulated by governmental agencies, may make effective
appeal to popular passions if it strikes this note.

It was such a conception of honor that inspired the demand in the
United States for war with Spain when the *Maine* was supposed to
have been sunk by external force. It was this which nearly involved us
in war with Mexico. It was apparently a belief that Austria-Hungary's
honor had been infringed upon and could only be satisfied by blood
which lay back of Germany's declaration, "It is impossible for us to
bring our ally before a European court in its difference with Serbia."
It has since been shown that all ends not covered by the military
conception of honor would have been secured by peaceful negotiation
with Spain.

The legal code depends for its origin in the individual upon the
presence of organized society, and in particular upon an authority
which defends and enforces standards. The good citizen makes this
legal code a moral law as well. Under this he is no longer compelled to
defend himself by arms or to live in continual fear of lawless neighbors.
Nations, unfortunately, have no such protection by a commonly recognized superior authority which is able to enforce the standards of
right. Hence they live under more or less constant mutual fear. They
act as judges in their own causes. They are not daily reminded of the
presence of a law higher than the will of the individual. The process
of building up a moral consciousness without any actual organization
of international society is necessarily slow. We may sometimes affect
to estimate lightly the standards of law in comparison with those of
morality, but no student of history can doubt the influence of law

upon the formation of a moral consciousness. Law has been the school-master to develop the consciousness of duty, and we need not be too cynical in our judgment upon the morals of nations which have lacked this education.

For no one who looks at the world process as a whole can fail to note that in the situation which has driven us almost to despair of civilization there are, on the one hand, elements of crisis and special strain, and, on the other, indications of an enlarging public conscious-ness which promises better conditions for the future. The elements of crisis and strain are familiar: the rapid growth of European civilization due to science, invention, improved health, enlarging intercommuni-cation and trade; the nearing completion of a process of conquest, settlement and establishment of markets, "by which all the races of the world have been affected, and all the backward ones placed in more or less complete dependence upon the more advanced";[6] the disintegration of states whose civilization has no unity of spirit and no genuine liberty or progress; the intensifying of race pride and national feeling due in part to the awakening consciousness of back-ward or hitherto suppressed or isolated groups.

The indications of an enlarging public consciousness out of which a higher public conscience may be built are also evident. For economic purposes the whole world is becoming one, and each people is com-pelled to know and judge the foreign conditions which causes strin-gency and distress in its own land. As the enormous business corpora-tions have brought out into the open the naked forces of competition, divested of all personal checks, society has been forced to a deeper view of the relations of economic forces to human welfare. It has adopted measures for control on the basis of fairness, not merely of efficiency. Politically are we not at a similar stage? The smaller states formerly carried on their petty intrigues, their petty wars; they re-sented with fierce irrational duels real or fancied insults to their mili-tary standards of honor; they pursued the ethics of self-preservation and expansion without serious check. But now we see the full meaning of it all. We see not only the survival of past jealousies and the rankling of past injustices, but also the results of making strength and power and selfish exploitation the determining forces in politics. The appeals which both sides make for moral approval mark a new stage in the development of a world conscience. Scientific studies are showing the artificiality of most of the differences between races and nations,

6. Bryce 7–8.

sometimes regarded as so radical, and now in the heat of passion magnified into fixed grades of moral worth or infamy. May we not see also some promise of hope that, when the consequences of past political ideals and methods have been brought home in all their horror to all peoples, there will be felt the need of adding to political codes of self-preservation and honor the further codes of justice toward others, of friendly intercourse, and even, remote as it may seem, of devotion to the uniting ideals of mutual understanding, mutual aid, common sympathy, and common humanity?

20 The Services of Present-Day Philosophy to Theological Reconstruction

The philosopher is engaged in a task which in many ways is similar to that of the theologian. He is trying to see life and the world as a whole, to interpret the experiences of the here and now in terms of the ideas which represent meanings, purposes, and values. Hence two tendencies have always disputed the field: Some, the empiricists, prize more the here and now—for this is sure and vivid; others, the idealists and rationalists, prize more the generalizations which offer to transcend time and show us the eternal.

In the past it has usually been idealism and rationalism that have appeared to be the friends of theology. It was with Plato's conception of genera and species that doctrines of the Trinity, one in essence, three in person, and of original sin were shaped; it was by Aristotle's conceptions of form and matter that the relation of God and nature, of soul and body, were framed; it was by Descartes's doctrine that the soul was conceived as a simple substance, and therefore as immortal. Later it was by the transcendentalism of Coleridge and his American followers that a new life was breathed into the theology of the last century. And at present Bosanquet in England and Royce in this country are able representatives of the idealism which would solve all troubling doubts, all clashing contradictions in the Absolute.

Another type of idealism is that of Eucken, who through all his many volumes insists upon the importance of the inner life, of the activity of the spirit. His present vogue would indicate that to his countrymen at least his message has a value. He feared the world's attention was so occupied with material interests as to cause forgetfulness of the activity of the spirit. But he tells us little of what he means

Reprinted by permission of the publisher from James Hayden Tufts, "The Services of Present-Day Philosophy to Theological Reconstruction," *Biblical World* 46.1 (1915), 9–14 [1915:10].

by spiritual activity. If, as his most recent book seems to indicate, he finds in the present German activity—fine as patriotic devotion and loyalty may be—his conception of the life of the spirit, many Americans will refuse to follow. They will say that activity may be as completely 'inner' as we please and yet be lacking in certain other important qualities; they will say that idealism is not by its name protected against defects as serious as any that opposing theories have disclosed.

It is to the opposing schools that I wish at this time to call attention. Five notes in their writings are suggestive for theology.

First is the new empiricism. Empiricism has a bad name with theology because it has usually meant that we have no knowledge except of experience and no experience except through sense or feeling. This last half of the doctrine is not real empiricism; it is dogmatism. The empiricism that James advocated in his theories of religious experience as well as in his lectures on pragmatism and the pluralistic universe is an empiricism which bids us to search human nature through and through, to go with open mind into every path where the spirit of man has led, and to include in our view of the world and of life all human activities, feelings, thoughts, whether they are respectably introduced to us or not.[1] This is a note which I believe the minister might well follow in the religious field. The old-time preacher dwelt much upon the religious experience of biblical writers. He dwelt upon the religious experience of a very few types of conversion, but he left unexplored and uninterpreted great regions of religious experience because they were not always so labeled. Professor James in his own book, *The Varieties of Religious Experience*,[2] selected chiefly emotional types. He left out the experiences of thought and will. What is still more remarkable, he omitted the great field of social experience, of cooperation, of sympathy, of common purpose. We are so near to what is passing that it is not easy to see it with the eye of an Isaiah. We are likely to use old terms and conceptions rather than to form new ones. There are suggestions in the poetry, the fiction, the drama, and the essay, but there is need of deep and intimate appreciation of all the stirrings and questions of our day in order that one may see what its religion is.

The second note of a present philosophy which is closely related to

1. William James, *Pragmatism: A New Name for Some Old Ways of Thinking* (New York: Longmans, Green, 1907); *A Pluralistic Universe* (New York: Longmans, Green, 1909).

2. William James, *The Varieties of Religious Experience: A Study in Human Nature* (New York: Longmans, Green, 1902).

the new empiricism is the emphasis of Bergson upon the creative aspect of evolution. In the fifty years since Darwin's writings we have passed from the more obvious doctrines of natural selection and the continuity of plant and animal and human life and now are raising the deeper question as to the agencies in the process and the meaning of it all. The earlier theological attitude of challenge gave place to the too easy solution of its difficulties. The fear that evolution banished God from the world was too easily met by the answer that evolution was simply one method of divine creation. We today do not feel that this latter answer is more than a hopeful anticipation of what may one day be the result of long study and analysis. We feel that we must not for purposes of philosophy assume too hastily what faith may offer. We must stand in the river and study the currents that come within our reach. We must grant that they come from an unknown and that the horizon which binds our vision is not a limit of things but rather a limit of our own vision. Nevertheless for us it marks the range within which we can experiment.

Now the great method of science in examining the world, as we know, is to discover causes and effects, to link together the successive moments of the stream, to find identities. We predict the future only as we find in it elements of identity with past and present. We even make equations and see that the quantity of motion is the same, that the quantity of matter is not diminished. It is easy from this to make the further and quite unwarranted assumption that, because our yard-stick of matter and force remains unchanged as we measure and count the atoms and mass, therefore the stream of life itself flows on the same in quantity and quality, and that what shall be is not more nor less than what has been.

It is of this false inference that Bergson's doctrine offers a corrective. Life, human or cosmic, may be conveniently measured for many purposes in terms of atoms, of electrons, of energy; but these measurements, so necessary for estimating the future, for observing its continuity, are yet not adequate to tell the full story. Especially they are not adequate to measure mind itself, which uses them to measure the world. Life as we experience it in the immediate ongo of the feeling and thought is not chopped up into pieces; it is a whole. Nor is it a repetition of past units. Every moment is a new. Evolution is through and through creative. Variation is a fact as important as continuity, and variation means a something new.

This may not seem to the theologian a great step in constructive thought. It may appear a far cry from creative evolution to the Creator to whom religion has looked as the Father of spirits as well as the Author of the world. There may seem to be no passageway between this very limited and timid groping for the meaning of change over to a divine providence ordering all things with full intelligence, and I should agree that as yet there is no easy transition. But the deeper recognition of the process of life to which such reflection is bound to lead is far more stimulating to genuine constructive work than either the closed system of the scientist or the closed system of the systematic theologian.

A third element in modern thinking is voluntarism. Voluntarism has often played an important part in theology. Jesus said, "If any man willeth to do his will he shall know of the doctrine." The Middle Ages debated long and strenuously which is prior, will or intellect? Descartes found the source of error in our haste to decide before evidence was sufficient. Kant removed knowledge to make room for faith, and Fichte proclaimed that either necessity or freedom is a logically consistent system. One must *choose* between them. But it has been the effort of the modern pragmatist to analyze more thoroughly this old relation of faith and reason, will and intellect. He points out first that our conclusion depends, not only upon thinking straight, but upon what premises we begin with, and it is partly a matter of choice which facts and premises we use. The opposing opinions on the present war make it more obvious than ever that thinking is no dry light. Conclusions here seem to depend largely on how far back we choose to begin and which facts we play up. But further, the pragmatist claims that the factors or elements in truth—the demands for consistency and continuity, the conceptions of cause, the interpretations of 'things'—are constructions of the creative intelligence seeking first to live and act, and that they are all processes through which the mind comes to itself. In the field of comparative religion the tendency is more and more to explain myth by ritual rather than ritual by myth. This would suggest the inquiry, how far our Christian doctrine has been shaped by the needs of the soul as these have been felt from generation to generation rather than from more purely intellectual sources, and then the further inquiry, how far the present needs justify a reshaping of truth.

This does not mean that we have a right to believe anything we like, anything that makes us more comfortable. It may be pertinently said that the need for truth is itself the supreme need. But it is nonetheless in point to note that truth implies both putting questions and finding answers. Natural science puts one kind of questions, chiefly those of cause and effect. Ethics puts at least two: It asks how it is that we behave as we do and judge as we do; it asks also what we ought to do and to judge. Before it can answer this second question completely it must inquire what the consequences will be: Will they be good or bad? But the 'good' or 'bad' must in the last analysis contain a factor of choice, of voluntary attitude.

If we seek religious truth we must recognize that it too means first of all asking a particular kind of question. If we frame this question in the familiar form, Does God exist?, we must recognize that it implies at least two prior questions: What do we mean by 'God'? and, What do we mean by 'exist'? Successive ages and varying schools of thought have meant by God, now an invisible helper in war, now a sender of rain, now a defender of right, now a savior from passion, now an eternal being including all reality, now a sovereign, now a father. Evidently the truth of God's existence would have different meanings and differing tests depending on which sort of God we seek. We are not now confident that success in war or a prosperous crop is an infallible test of righteous sovereignty, or that an all-inclusive being is to be identified easily with personal attributes. Ultimately the religious question is not one solely of fact. It implies both fact and values and may be put, Is the world in which we live a world that bears any relation to our moral ends? Is it a world of mechanism or of purpose, of necessity or of freedom?

On this world-old question philosophy is beginning to take a view which is not precisely either of the older views. On the one hand science is step by step finding uniformity and law. It is reducing the processes of earth and heavens to order—so far it seems to exclude freedom. But on the other hand it is constantly speaking of all this scientific knowledge as a method of control, of utilizing natural forces for human ends. This is freedom. Another angle of the problem is the twofold question, Is God's will to be done certainly, inevitably, or is it dependent upon human cooperation? What does it mean to be workers together with God? It was the merit of James in all his various writings to sound one note clearly: The universe is not complete, but is in the making. You and I are sometimes called upon for decisions which may contribute to turn the scale for good or evil. Decision is not an empty form; it is real and serious. In such cases truth is made and not merely discovered. It may be then that the triumph of right is not a matter of yes or no, but, as in all past history, a relative process. I suspect that for generations to come this will continue to be the case. The practical religious question from this point of view would be, Can we give to this view of God, of the progress of righteousness, the same power over the more intelligent minds of today which the God of absolute decrees, and with cruder heaven and hell, had for earlier generations and still has for many in our own?

Fourthly, the thought of the time along lines of social psychology is a needed corrective to whatever of the personal and subjective lies in the teaching of voluntarism. To struggle for what I believe is my duty, but it is nonetheless my duty to make as sure as I may that my view of right is a right view. My own feeling, my own judgment, is likely to be mistaken, or still more likely to be partial. Social psychology is calling attention to the intimate dependence of our mental life, not only upon the physical organs, but upon the give and take, the interaction of person with person. The value of the church, of the religious community, has always been one of the factors in theology. But I venture to think that the value of cooperation in thought as well as in organization has never received full appreciation. The Catholic church has realized the tremendous power of organization, but its principle has been that of authority. The Protestant church has been democratic, but has suffered from lack of unity. The problem is how to get the great values of common thought and common purpose while yet remaining true to the principle of democracy.

The fifth element which has value for theology in the thinking of the time is the ethical trend. Theology at its best has been more ethical than metaphysical. It has thought more of guiding men to better living than of experiencing the mysteries of creation and calculating the future of the cosmos. But the ethics of religion, like its metaphysics, has necessarily borrowed largely from the philosophy of the age. The ethics of Christianity has been very largely legal. It has seen the world from the throne of the ruler or the bar of the judge rather than from the ethical point of view of a community of spirits. This newer ethics is itself as yet uncertain of its categories. It does not know exactly what justice is. It would like to find out, but it does not expect to find out by any process of intuition or of deduction from definitions of equality, or of giving every man his own, or of respecting the rights of others—definitions and methods which were so easy to our fathers, who thought it possible to know what belonged to a man or what his rights were. In theology we might assume that we thought that the laws of God were just and righteous and that the Scriptures gave us a knowledge of these laws. But in ethics we are in doubt what the rights of man are because we do not yet know man. We are not satisfied with formal phrases of equality because we see so many abstract uses of the term, wherein the old equality straightway turns into inequality. Equality before the law, for example, may mean inequality, because of inability to provide a good lawyer. It sends the poor man to prison when he cannot pay his fine and takes from the rich the price of a box of cigars for the same offense. We shall not know what is right, what is just, in any full sense until we know more of the powers of human life and the means by which these may be freed and enlarged. This points a task for theology. Its older conceptions of sin and evil, of justice and atonement, we well know have been largely shaped by legal minds. It is the task of constructive thought to find new interpretations which are more adequate than the legal for the undoubted facts of human, moral experience.

21 The Ethics of Cooperation

I

According to Plato's famous myth, two gifts of the gods equipped man for living: the one, arts and inventions to supply him with the means of livelihood; the other, reverence and justice to be the ordering principles of societies and the bonds of friendship and conciliation. Agencies for mastery over nature and agencies for cooperation among men remain the two great sources of human power. But after two thousand years, it is possible to note an interesting fact as to their relative order of development in civilization. Nearly all the great skills and inventions that had been acquired up to the eighteenth century were brought into man's service at a very early date. The use of fire, the arts of weaver, potter, and metal worker, of sailor, hunter, fisher, and sower, early fed man and clothed him. These were carried to higher perfection by Egyptian and Greek, by Tyrian and Florentine, but it would be difficult to point to any great new unlocking of material resources until the days of the chemist and electrician. Domestic animals and crude water mills were for centuries in man's service, and until steam was harnessed, no additions were made of new powers.

During this long period, however, the progress of human association made great and varied development. The gap between the men of Santander's caves, or early Egypt, and the civilization of a century ago is bridged rather by union of human powers, by the needs and stimulating contacts of society, than by conquest in the field of nature. It was in military, political, and religious organization that the power of associated effort was first shown. Army, state, and hierarchy were its visible representatives. Then, a little over a century ago, began what we call the Industrial Revolution, still incomplete, which com-

From *The Ethics of Cooperation* (Boston: Houghton, 1918) [1918:02].

bined new natural forces with new forms of human association. Steam, electricity, machines, the factory system, railroads: These suggest the natural forces at man's disposal. Capital, credit, corporations, labor unions: These suggest the bringing together of men and their resources into units for exploiting or controlling the new natural forces. Sometimes resisting the political, military, or ecclesiastical forces which were earlier in the lead, sometimes mastering them, sometimes combining with them, economic organization has now taken its place in the world as a fourth great structure, or rather as a fourth great agency through which man achieves his greater tasks, and in so doing becomes conscious of hitherto unrealized powers.

Early in this great process of social organization three divergent types emerged, which still contend for supremacy in the worlds of actions and of valuation: dominance, competition, and cooperation. All mean a meeting of human forces. They rest respectively on power, rivalry, and sympathetic interchange. Each may contribute to human welfare. On the other hand, each may be taken so abstractly as to threaten human values. I hope to point out that the greatest of these is cooperation, and that it is largely the touchstone for the others.

Cooperation and dominance both mean organization. Dominance implies inequality, direction and obedience, superior and subordinate. Cooperation implies some sort of equality, some mutual relation. It does not exclude difference in ability or in function. It does not exclude leadership, for leadership is usually necessary to make cooperation effective. But in dominance the special excellence is kept isolated; ideas are transmitted from above downward. In cooperation there is interchange, currents flowing in both directions, contacts of mutual sympathy, rather than of pride-humility, condescension-servility. The purpose of the joint pursuit in organization characterized by dominance may be either the exclusive good of the master or the joint good of the whole organized group, but in any case it is a purpose formed and kept by those few who know. The group may share in its execution and its benefits, but not in its construction or in the estimating and forecasting of its values. The purpose in cooperation is joint. Whether originally suggested by some leader of thought or action, or whether a composite of many suggestions in the give and take of discussion or in experiences of common need, it is weighed and adopted as a common end. It is not the work or possession of leaders alone, but embodies in varying degrees the work and active interest of all.

Cooperation and competition at first glance may seem more radically opposed. For while dominance and cooperation both mean union of forces, competition appears to mean antagonism. *They* stand for combination; *it* for exclusion of one by another. Yet a deeper look shows that this is not true of competition in what we may call its social, as contrasted with its unsocial, aspect. The best illustration of what I venture to call social competition is sport. Here is rivalry, and here in any given contest one wins, the other loses, or few win and many lose. But the great thing in sport is not to win; the great thing is the game, the contest; and the contest is no contest unless the contestants are so nearly equal as to forbid any certainty in advance as to which will win. The best sport is found when no one contestant wins too often. There is in reality a common purpose—the zest of contest. Players combine and compete to carry out this purpose; and the rules are designed so to restrict the competition as to rule out certain kinds of action and preserve friendly relations. The contending rivals are in reality uniting to stimulate each other. Without the cooperation there would be no competition, and the competition is so conducted as to continue the relation. Competition in the world of thought is similarly social. In efforts to reach a solution of a scientific problem or to discuss a policy, the spur of rivalry or the matching of wits aids the common purpose of arriving at the truth. Similar competition exists in business. Many a firm owes its success to the competition of its rivals which has forced it to be efficient, progressive. As a manufacturing friend once remarked to me, "When the other man sells cheaper, you generally find he has found out something you don't know."

But we also apply the term 'competition' to rivalry in which there is no common purpose; to contests in which there is no intention to continue or repeat the match, and in which no rules control. Weeds compete with flowers and crowd them out. The factory competes with the hand loom and banishes it. The trust competes with the small firm and puts it out of business. The result is monopoly. When plants or inventions are thus said to compete for a place, there is frequently no room for both competitors, and no social gain by keeping both in the field. Competition serves here sometimes as a method of selection, although no one would decide to grow weeds rather than flowers because weeds are more efficient. In the case of what are called natural monopolies, there is duplication of effort instead of cooperation. Competition is here wasteful. But when we have to do, not with a specific product, or with a fixed field such as that of street railways or city lighting, but with the open field of invention and service, we need to provide for continuous cooperation, and competition seems at least one useful agency. To retain this, we frame rules against 'unfair competition.' As the rules of sport are designed to place a premium upon certain kinds of strength and skill which make a good game, so the rules of fair competition are designed to secure efficiency for public service, and to exclude efficiency in choking or fouling. In unfair competition there is no common purpose of public service or of advancing skill or invention; hence, no cooperation. The cooperative purpose or result is thus the test of useful, as contrasted with wasteful or harmful, competition.

There is also an abstract conception of cooperation, which, in its one-sided emphasis upon equality, excludes any form of leadership, or direction, and in fear of inequality allows no place for competition. Selection of rulers by lot in a large and complex group is one illustration; jealous suspicion of ability, which becomes a cult of incompetence, is another. Refusals to accept inventions which require any modification of industry, or to recognize any inequalities of service, are others. But these do not affect the value of the principle as we can now define it in preliminary fashion: union tending to secure common ends, by a method which promotes equality, and with an outcome of increased power shared by all.

II

What are we to understand by the ethics of cooperation? Can we find some external standard of unquestioned value or absolute duty by which to measure the three processes of society which we have named, dominance, competition, cooperation? Masters of the past have offered many such, making appeal to the logic of reason or the response of sentiment, to the will for mastery or the claim of benevolence. To make a selection without giving reasons would seem arbitrary; to attempt a reasoned discussion would take us quite beyond the bounds appropriate to this lecture. But aside from the formulations of philosophers, humanity has been struggling—often rather haltingly and blindly—for certain goods and setting certain sign-posts which, if they do not point to a highway, at least mark certain paths as blind alleys. Such goods I take to be the great words, liberty, power, justice; such signs of blind paths I take to be rigidity, passive acceptance of what is.

But those great words, just because they are so great, are given various meanings by those who would claim them for their own. Nor is there complete agreement as to just what paths deserve to be posted as leading nowhere. Groups characterized by dominance, cutthroat competition, or cooperation tend to work out each its own interpretations of liberty, power, justice; its own code for the conduct of its members. Without assuming to decide your choice, I can indicate briefly what the main elements in these values and codes are.

The group of masters and servants will develop what we have learned to call a morality of masters and a morality of slaves. This was essentially the code of the feudal system. We have survivals of such a group morality in our code of the gentleman, which in England still depreciates manual labor, although it has been refined and softened and enlarged to include respect for other than military and sportsman virtues. The code of masters exalts liberty—for the ruling class—and resents any restraint by inferiors or civilians, or by public opinion of any group but its own. It has a justice which takes for its premise a graded social order, and seeks to put and keep every man in his place. But its supreme value is power, likewise for the few, or for the state as consisting of society organized and directed by the ruling class. Such a group, according to Treitschke, will also need war, in order to test and exhibit its power to the utmost in fierce struggle with other powers. It will logically honor war as good.

A group practicing cutthroat competition will simply reverse the order: First, struggle to put rivals out of the field; then, monopoly with unlimited power to control the market or possess the soil. It appeals to nature's struggle for existence as its standard for human life. It too sets a high value upon liberty in the sense of freedom from control, but originating as it did in resistance to control by privilege and other aspects of dominance, it has never learned the defects of a liberty which takes no account of ignorance, poverty, and ill health. It knows the liberty of nature, the liberty of the strong and the swift, but not the liberty achieved by the common effort for all. It knows justice, but a justice which is likely to be defined as securing to each his natural liberty, and which therefore means noninterference with the struggle for existence except to prevent violence and fraud. It takes no account as to whether the struggle kills few or many, or distributes goods widely or sparingly, or whether indeed there is any room at the table which civilization spreads, though it does not begrudge charity if administered under that name.

A cooperating group has two working principles: first, common purpose and common good; second, that men can achieve by common effort what they cannot accomplish singly. The first, reinforced by the actual interchange of ideas and services, tends to favor equality. It implies mutual respect, confidence, and goodwill. The second favors a constructive and progressive attitude, which will find standards neither in nature nor in humanity's past, since it conceives man able to change conditions to a considerable extent and thus to realize new goods.

These principles tend toward a type of liberty different from those just mentioned. As contrasted with the liberty of a dominant group, cooperation favors a liberty for all, a liberty of live and let live, a tolerance and welcome for variation in type, provided only this is willing to make its contribution to the common weal. Instead of imitation or passive acceptance of patterns on the part of the majority, it stimulates active construction. As contrasted with the liberty favored in competing groups, cooperation would emphasize positive control over natural forces, over health conditions, over poverty and fear. It would make each person share as fully as possible in the knowledge and strength due to combined effort, and thus liberate him from many of the limitations which have hitherto hampered him.

Similarly with justice. Cooperation's ethics of distribution is not rigidly set by the actual interest and rights of the past on the one hand, nor by hitherto available resources on the other. Neither natural rights nor present ability and present service form a complete measure. Since cooperation evokes new interests and new capacities, it is hospitable to new claims and new rights; since it makes new sources of supply available, it has in view the possibility at least of doing better for all than can an abstract insistence upon old claims. It may often avoid the deadlock of a rigid system. It is better to grow two blades of grass than to dispute who shall have the larger fraction of the one which has previously been the yield. It is better, not merely because there is more grass, but also because men's attitude becomes forward-looking and constructive, not pugnacious and rigid.

Power is likewise a value in a cooperating group, but it must be power not merely used for the good of all, but to some extent controlled by all and thus actually shared. Only as so controlled and so shared is power attended by the responsibility which makes it safe for its possessors. Only on this basis does power over other men permit the free choices on their part which are essential to full moral life.

As regards the actual efficiency of a cooperating group, it may be granted that its powers are not so rapidly mobilized. In small, homogeneous groups, the loss of time is small; in large groups the formation of public opinion and the conversion of this into action is still largely a problem rather than an achievement. New techniques have to be developed, and it may be that for certain military tasks the military technique will always be more efficient. To the cooperative group, however, this test will not be the ultimate ethical test. It will rather consider the possibilities of substituting for war other activities in which cooperation is superior. And if the advocate of war insists that war as such is the most glorious and desirable type of life, cooperation may perhaps fail to convert him. But it may hope to create a new order whose excellence shall be justified of her children.

III

A glance at the past roles of dominance, competition, and cooperation in the institutions of government, religion, and commerce and industry will aid us to consider cooperation in relation to present international problems.

Primitive tribal life had elements of each of the three principles we have named. But with discovery by some genius of the power of organization for war the principle of dominance won, seemingly at a flash, a decisive position. No power of steam or lightning has been so spectacular and wide-reaching as the power which Egyptian, Assyrian, Macedonian, Roman, and their modern successors introduced and controlled. Political states owing their rise to military means naturally followed the military pattern. The sharp separation between ruler or ruling group and subject people, based on conquest, was perpetuated in class distinction. Gentry and simple, lord and villein, were indeed combined in exploitation of earth's resources, but cooperation was in the background, mastery in the fore. And when empires included peoples of various races and cultural advance the separation between higher and lower became intensified. Yet though submerged for long periods, the principle of cooperation has asserted itself, step by step, and it seldom loses ground. Beginning usually in some group which at first combined to resist dominance, it has made its way through such stages as equality before the law, abolition of special privileges, extension of suffrage, influence of public sentiment, interchange of ideas, toward genuine participation by all in the dignity and responsibility of political power. It builds a Panama Canal; it maintains a great system of education; and has, we may easily believe, yet greater tasks in prospect. It may be premature to predict its complete displacement of dominance in our own day as a method of government, yet who in America doubts its ultimate prevalence?

Religion presents a fascinating mixture of cooperation with dominance on the one hand and exclusiveness on the other. The central fact is the community, which seeks some common end in ritual, or in beneficent activity. But at an early period leaders became invested, or invested themselves, with a sanctity which led to dominance. Not the power of force, but that of mystery and the invisible raised the priest above the level of the many. And, on another side, competition between rival national religions, like that between states, excluded friendly contacts. Jews and Samaritan had no dealings; between the followers of Baal and Jehovah there was no peace but by extermination. Yet it was religion which confronted the *Herrenmoral* with the first reversal of values and declared, "So shall it not be among you. But whosoever will be great among you let him be your minister." And it was religion which cut across national boundaries in its vision of what Professor Royce so happily calls the Great Community.[1] Protest against dominance resulted, however, in divisions, and although cooperation in practical activities has done much to prepare the way for national understanding, the hostile forces of the world today lack the restraint which might have come from a united moral sentiment and moral will.

In the economic field the story of dominance, cooperation, and competition is more complex than in government and religion. It followed somewhat different courses in trade and in industry. The simplest way to supply needs with goods is to go and take them; the simplest way to obtain services is to seize them. Dominance in the first case gives piracy and plunder, when directed against those without; fines and taxes, when exercised upon those within. In the second case, it gives slavery or forced levies. But trade, as a voluntary exchange of presents, or as a bargaining for mutual advantage, had likewise its early beginnings. Carried on at first with timidity and distrust, because the parties belonged to different groups, it has developed a high degree of mutual confidence between merchant and customer, banker and client, insurer and insured. By its system of contracts and fiduciary relations, which bind men of the most varying localities, races, occupations, social classes, and national allegiance, it has woven a new net of human relations far more intricate and wide-reaching than the natural ties of blood kinship. It rests upon mutual responsibility and good faith; it is a constant force for their extension.

The industrial side of the process has had similar influence toward

1. Josiah Royce, *The Hope of the Great Community* (New York: Macmillan, 1916).

union. Free craftsmen in the towns found mutual support in guilds, when as yet the farm laborer or villein had to get on as best he could unaided. The factory system itself has been largely organized from above down. It has very largely assumed that the higher command needs no advice or ideas from below. Hours of labor, shop conditions, wages, have largely been fixed by 'orders,' just as governments once ruled by decrees. But as dominance in government has led men to unite against the new power and then has yielded to the more complete cooperation of participation, so in industry the factory system has given rise to the labor movement. As for the prospects of fuller cooperation, this may be said already to have displaced the older autocratic system within the managing group, and the war is giving an increased impetus to extension of the process.

Exchange of goods and services is indeed a threefold cooperation: It meets wants which the parties cannot themselves satisfy or cannot well satisfy; it awakens new wants; it calls new inventions and new forces into play. It thus not only satisfies man's existing nature, but enlarges his capacity for enjoyment and his active powers. It makes not only for comfort, but for progress.

IV

If trade and industry, however, embody so fully the principle of cooperation, how does it come about that they have on the whole had a rather low reputation, not only among the class groups founded on militarism, but among philosophers and moralists? Why do we find the present calamities of war charged to economic causes? Perhaps the answer to these questions will point the path along which better cooperation may be expected.

There is, from the outset, one defect in the cooperation between buyer and seller, employer and laborer. The cooperation is largely unintended. Each is primarily thinking of his own advantage, rather than that of the other, or of the social whole; he is seeking it in terms of money, which as a material object must be in the pocket of one party or of the other, and is not, like friendship or beauty, sharable. Mutual benefit is the result of exchange—it need not be the motive. This benefit comes about as if it were arranged by an invisible hand, said Adam Smith. Indeed, it was long held that if one of the bargainers gained, the other must lose. And when under modern conditions labor is considered as a commodity to be bought and sold in the cheapest market by an impersonal corporate employer, there is a strong presumption against the cooperative attitude on either side.

The great problem here is, therefore, How can men be brought to seek consciously what now they unintentionally produce? How can the man whose ends are both self-centered and ignoble be changed into the man whose ends are wide and high? Something may doubtless be done by showing that a narrow selfishness is stupid. If we rule out monopoly the best way to gain great success is likely to lie through meeting needs of a great multitude; and to meet these effectively implies entering by imagination and sympathy into their situation. The business maxim of 'service,' the practices of refunding money if goods are unsatisfactory, of one price to all, of providing sanitary and even attractive factories and homes, and of paying a minimum wage far in excess of the market price have often proved highly remunerative. Yet, I should not place exclusive, and perhaps not chief, reliance on these methods of appeal. They are analogous to the old maxim 'Honesty is the best policy'; and we know too well that while this holds under certain conditions—that is, among intelligent people, or in the long run—it is often possible to acquire great gains by exploiting the weak, deceiving the ignorant, or perpetrating a fraud of such proportions that men forget its dishonesty in admiration at its audacity. In the end it is likely to prove that the level of economic life is to be raised not by proving that cooperation will better satisfy selfish and ignoble interests, but rather by creating new standards for measuring success, new interests in social and worthy ends, and by strengthening the appeal of duty where this conflicts with present interests. The one method stakes all on human nature as it is; the other challenges man's capacity to listen to new appeals and respond to better motives. It is, if you please, idealism; but before it is dismissed as worthless, consider what has been achieved in substituting social motives in the field of political actions. There was a time when the aim in political life was undisguisedly selfish. The state, in distinction from the kinship group or the village community, was organized for power and profit. It was nearly a gigantic piratical enterprise, highly profitable to its managers. The shepherd, says Thrasymachus in Plato's dialogue, does not feed his sheep for their benefit, but for his own. Yet now, what president or minister, legislator or judge, would announce as his aim to acquire the greatest financial profit from his position? Even in autocratically governed countries, it is at least the assumption that the good of the state does not mean solely the prestige and wealth of the ruler.

A great social and political order has been built up, and we all hold that it must not be exploited for private gain. It has not been created or maintained by chance. Nor could it survive if every man sought primarily his own advantage and left the commonwealth to care for itself. Nor in a democracy would it be maintained, provided the governing class alone were disinterested, deprived of private property, and given education, as Plato suggested. The only safety is in the general and intelligent desire for the public interest and common welfare. At this moment almost unanimous acceptance of responsibility for what we believe to be the public good and the maintenance of American ideals—though it brings to each of us sacrifice and to many the full measure of devotion—bears witness to the ability of human nature to adopt as its compelling motives a high end which opposes private advantage.

Is the economic process too desperate a field for larger motives? To me it seems less desperate than the field of government in the days of autocratic kings. One great need is to substitute a different standard of success for the financial gains which have seemed the only test. Our schools of commerce are aiming to perform this service by introducing professional standards. A physician is measured by his ability to cure the sick, an engineer by the soundness of his bridge and ship; why not measure a railroad president by his ability to supply coal in winter, to run trains on time, and decrease the cost of freight, rather than by his private accumulations? Why not measure a merchant or banker by similar tests?

Mankind has built up a great economic system. Pioneer, adventurer, inventor, scientist, laborer, organizer, all have contributed. It is as essential to human welfare as the political system, and like that system it comes to us as an inheritance. I can see no reason why it should be thought unworthy of a statesman or a judge to use the political structure for his own profit, but perfectly justifiable for a man to exploit the economic structure for private gain. This does not necessarily exclude profit as a method of paying for services, and of increasing capital needed for development, but it would seek to adjust profits to services, and treat capital, just as it regards political power, as a public trust in need of cooperative regulation and to be used for the general welfare.

But the war is teaching with dramatic swiftness what it might have needed decades of peace to bring home to us. We *are* thinking of the common welfare. High prices may still be a rough guide to show men's needs, but we are learning to raise wheat because others need it—not merely because the price is high. Prices may also be a rough guide to consumption, but we are learning that eating wheat or sugar is not merely a matter of what I can afford. It is a question of whether I take wheat or sugar away from someone else who needs it—the soldier in France, the child in Belgium, the family of my less fortunate neighbor. The great argument for not interfering with private exchange in all such matters has been that if prices should by some authority be kept low in time of scarcity, men would consume the supply too rapidly; whereas if prices rise in response to scarcity, men at once begin to economize and so prevent the total exhaustion of the supply. We now reflect that if prices of milk rise it does not mean uniform economy—it means cutting off to a large degree the children of the poor and leaving relatively untouched the consumption of the well-to-do. Merely raising the *price* of meat or wheat means taking these articles from the table of one class to leave them upon the table of another. War, requiring, as it does, the united strength and purpose of the whole people, has found this method antiquated. In Europe governments have said to their peoples, "We *must* all think of the common weal; we *must* all share alike." In this country, the appeal of the food administrator, though largely without force of law, has been loyally answered by the great majority. It is doubtless rash to predict how much peace will retain of what war has taught, but who of us will again say so easily, "My work or leisure, my economy or my luxury, is my own affair, if I can afford it"? Who can fail to see that common welfare comes not without common intention?

The second great defect in our economic order, from the point of view of cooperation, has been the inequality of its distribution. This has been due largely to competition when parties were unequal, not merely in their ability, but in their opportunity. And the most serious, though not the most apparent, aspect of this inequality has not been that some have more comfort or luxuries to enjoy; it is the fact that wealth means power. Insofar as it can set prices on all that we eat, wear, and enjoy, it is controlling the intimate affairs of life more thoroughly than any government ever attempted. Insofar as it controls natural resources, means of transportation, organization of credit, and the capital necessary for large-scale manufacturing and marketing, it can set prices. The great questions then are, as with political power, How can this great power be cooperatively used? Is it serving all or a few?

Two notable doctrines of the courts point ways for ethics. The first is that of property affected with public interest. Applied thus far by the courts to warehouses, transportation, and similar public services, what limits can we set ethically to the doctrine that power of one man over his fellows, whether through his office or though his property, is affected with public interest?

The police power, which sets the welfare of all above private property when these conflict, is a second doctrine whose ethical import far outruns its legal applications.

Yet it is by neither of these that the most significant progress has been made toward removing that handicap of inequality which is the chief injustice of our economic system. It is by our great educational system, liberal in its provisions, generously supported by all classes, unselfishly served, opening to all doors of opportunity which once were closed to the many, the most successful department of our democratic institutions in helping and gaining confidence of all—a system of which this University of California is one of the most notable leaders and the most useful members—that fair conditions for competition and intelligent cooperation in the economic world are increasingly possible.

V

What bearing has this sketch of the significance and progress of cooperation upon the international questions which now overshadow all else? Certainly the world cannot remain as before: great powers struggling for empire; lesser powers struggling for their separate existence; great areas of backward peoples viewed as subjects for exploitation; we ourselves aloof. It must then choose between a future world order based on dominance, which means world empire; a world order based on nationalism joined with the nonsocial type of competition, which means every nation the judge of its own interests, continuance of jealousies, and from time to time the recurrence of war; and a world order based on nationalism plus international cooperation, "to establish justice, to provide for common defense, to promote the general welfare, and to secure the blessings of liberty to ourselves and our posterity."

It is not necessary to discuss in this country the principle of dominance and world empire. It contradicts our whole philosophy. Safety for dominance lies only in a civilization of discipline from above down, in ruthless repression of all thinking on the part of the subject class or race.

Nor can I see any genuine alternative in what some advocate—

reliance by each nation on its own military strength as the sole effective guarantee for its interests. After the military lessons of this war, the concentration of scientific, economic, and even educational attention upon military purposes would almost inevitably be vastly in excess of anything previously conceived. What limits can be set to the armies of France and Great Britain if these are to protect those countries from a German empire already double its previous extent, and taking steps to control the resources of eastern Europe and the Near East? What navy could guarantee German commerce against the combined forces of Great Britain and the United States? What limits to the frightfulness yet to be discovered by chemist and bacteriologist? What guarantee against the insidious growth of a militarist attitude even in democratically minded peoples if the constant terror of war exalts military preparations to the supreme place? Something has changed the Germany of other days which many of us loved even while we shrank from its militarist masters. Is it absolutely certain that nothing can change the spirit of democratic peoples? At any rate, America, which has experimented on a larger scale with cooperation—political, economic, and religious—than any other continent, may well assert steadily and insistently that this is the more hopeful path. It may urge this upon distrustful Europe.

The obstacles to cooperation are (1) the survival of the principle of dominance, showing itself in desire for political power and prestige, and in certain conceptions of national honor. (2) The principle of nonsocial competition, exhibited in part in the political policy of eliminating weaker peoples, and conspicuously in foreign trade when the use of unfair methods relies upon national power to back up its exploitation or monopoly. (3) The principle of nationalistic sentiment, itself based on cooperation, on social tradition and common ideals, but bound up so closely with political sovereignty and antagonisms as to become exclusive instead of cooperative in its attitude toward other cultures.

The principle of dominance deters from cooperation not only the people that seeks to dominate, but peoples that fear to be dominated or to become involved in entangling alliances. Doubtless a policy of aloofness was long the safe policy for us. We could not trust political liberty to an alliance with monarchies, even as with equal right some European peoples might distrust the policies of a republic seemingly controlled by the slavery interest. At the present time one great power professes itself incredulous of the fairness of any world tribunal; smaller powers fear the commanding influence of the great; new national groups just struggling to expression fear that a league of nations would be based on present status and therefore give them no recognition, or else a measure of recognition conditioned by past injustices rather than by future aspirations and real desert. All these fears are justified insofar as the principle of dominance is still potent. The only league that can be trusted by peoples willing to live and let live is one that is controlled by a cooperative spirit. And yet who can doubt that this spirit is spreading? Few governments are now organized on the avowed basis that military power, which embodies the spirit of dominance, should be superior to civil control, and even with them the principle of irresponsible rule, despite its reinforcement by military success, is likely to yield to the spirit of the age when once the pressure of war is removed which now holds former protesters against militarism solid in its support. For all powers that are genuine in their desire for cooperation there is overwhelming reason to try it; for only by the combined strength of those who accept this principle can liberty and justice be maintained against the aggression of powers capable of concentrating all their resources with a suddenness and ruthlessness in which dominance is probably superior.

Yet cooperation for protection of liberty and justice is liable to fall short of humanity's hopes unless liberty and justice be themselves defined in a cooperative sense. The great liberties which man has gained, as step by step he has risen from savagery, have not been chiefly the assertion of already existing powers or the striking off of fetters forged by his fellows. They have been *additions* to previous powers. Science, art, invention, associated life in all its forms, have opened the windows of his dwelling, have given possibilities to his choice, have given the dream and the interpretation which have set him free from his prison. The liberty to which international cooperation points is not merely self-direction or self-determination, but a larger freedom from fear, a larger freedom from suspicion, a fuller control over nature and society, a new set of ideas, which will make men free in a far larger degree than ever before.

Similarly, justice needs to be cooperatively defined. A justice that looks merely to existing status will not give lasting peace. Peoples change in needs as truly as they differ in needs. But no people can be trusted to judge its own needs any more than to judge its own right. A justice which adheres rigidly to vested interests, and a justice which is based on expanding interests, are likely to be deadlocked unless a constructive spirit is brought to bear. Abstract rights to the soil, to trade, to expansion, must be subordinate to the supreme question,

How can peoples live together and help instead of destroy? This can be approached only from an international point of view.

The second obstacle, unsocial competition, is for trade what dominance is in politics. It prevents that solution for many of the delicate problems of international life which cooperation through trade might otherwise afford. Exchange of goods and services by voluntary trade accomplishes what once seemed attainable only by conquest or slavery. If Germany or Japan or Italy needs iron or coal; if England needs wheat, or if the United States sugar, it is possible, or should be possible, to obtain these without owning the country in which are the mines, grain, and sugar cane. The United States needs Canada's products; it has no desire to own Canada. But in recent years the exchange of products has been subjected to a new influence. National self-interest has been added to private self-interest. This has intensified and called out many of the worst features of antagonism and inequality.

Few in this country have realized the extent to which other countries have organized their foreign commerce on national lines. We are now becoming informed as to the carefully worked-out programs of commercial education, merchant marines, trade agreements, consular service, financial and moral support from the home government, and mutual aid among various salesmen of the same nationality living in a foreign country. We are preparing to undertake similar enterprises. We are reminded that "eighty per cent of the world's people live in the countries bordering on the Pacific Ocean, and that as a result of the rearrangement of trade routes, San Francisco's chance of becoming the greatest distributing port of the Pacific for goods en route to the markets of the Orient, are now more promising than ever before." Can the United States take part in this commerce in such a way as to help, not hinder, international progress in harmony? Not unless we remember that commerce may be as predatory as armies, and that we must provide international guarantees against the exclusive types of competition which we have had to control by law in our own domestic affairs. An Indian or an African may be deprived of his possessions quite as effectively by trade as by violence. We need at least as high standards of social welfare as in domestic commerce. I cannot better present the situation than by quoting from a recent article by Mr. William Notz:

> During the past twenty-five years competition in the world markets
> became enormously keen. In the wild scramble for trade the standards

of honest business were disregarded more and more by all the various rival nations. In the absence of any special regulation or legislation, it appeared as though a silent understanding prevailed in wide circles that foreign trade was subject to a code of business ethics widely at variance with the rules observed in domestic trade. What was frowned upon as unethical and poor business policy, if not illegal at home, was condoned and winked at or openly espoused when foreign markets formed the basis of operations and foreigners were the competitors. High-minded men of all nations have long observed with concern the growing tendency of modern international trade toward selfish exploitation, concession-hunting, cutthroat competition, and commercialistic practices of the most sordid type. Time and again complaints have been voiced, retaliatory measures threatened, and more than once serious friction has ensued.[2]

Mr. Notz brings to our attention various efforts by official and commercial bodies looking toward remedies for such conditions and toward official recognition by all countries of unfair competition as a penal offense.

What more do we need than fair competition to constitute the cooperative international life which we dreamed yesterday and now must consider, not merely as a dream, but as the only alternative to a future of horror?

Free trade has been not unnaturally urged as at least one condition. Tariffs certainly isolate. To say to a country, "You shall manufacture nothing unless you own the raw material; you shall sell nothing unless at prices which I fix," is likely to provoke the reply, "Then I must acquire lands in which raw materials are found; I must acquire colonies which will buy my products." Trade agreements mean cooperation for those within, unless they are one-sided and made under duress; in any case they are exclusive of those without. Free trade, the open door, seems to offer a better way. But free trade in name is not free trade unless the parties are really free—free from ignorance, from pressure of want. If one party is weak and the other unscrupulous; if one competitor has a lower standard of living than the other, freedom of trade will not mean genuine cooperation. Such cooperation as means good for all requires either an equality of conditions between traders and laborers of competing nations and of nations which exchange goods, or else an international control to prevent unfair competition, exploitation of weaker peoples, and lowering of standards of

2. William Notz, "Export Trade Problems and an American Foreign Trade Policy," *Journal of Political Economy* 26.2 (1918): 117–118.

living. Medical science is giving an object lesson which may well have a wide application. It is seeking to combat disease in its centers of diffusion. Instead of attempting to quarantine against the Orient, it is aiding the Orient to overcome those conditions which do harm alike to Orient and Occident. Plague, anthrax, yellow fever, cannot exist in one country without harm to all. Nor in the long run can men reach true cooperation so long as China and Africa are a prize for the exploiter rather than equals in the market. Not merely in the political sense, but in its larger meanings democracy here is not safe without democracy there. Education, and the lifting of all to a higher level, is the ultimate goal. And until education, invention, and intercommunication have done their work of elevation, international control must protect and regulate.

In many respects the obstacle to international cooperation which is most difficult to remove is the strong and still growing sentiment of nationality. This is not, like dominance, a waning survival of a cruder method of social order; it is a genuine type of cooperation. Rooted as it is in a historic past, in community of ideals and traditions, and usually of language and art, it wakens the emotional response to a degree once true only of religion. Born of such a social tradition, the modern may be said in truth mentally and spiritually, as well as physically, to be born a Frenchman or a German, a Scotchman or Irishman or Englishman. He may be content to merge this inheritance in an empire if he can be senior partner, but the struggles of Irish, Poles, Czechs, and South Slavs, the Zionist movement, the nationalistic stirrings in India, with their literary revivals, their fierce self-assertions, seem to point away from internationalism rather than toward it. The Balkans, in which Serb, Bulgar, Romanian, and Greek have been developing this national consciousness, have been the despair of peacemakers.

The strongest point in the nationalist program is, however, not in any wise opposed to cooperation, but rather to dominance or nonsocial competition. The strongest point is the importance of diversity combined with group unity for the fullest enrichment of life and the widest development of human capacity. A world all of one sort would not only be less interesting, but less progressive. We are stimulated by different customs, temperaments, arts, and ideals. But all this is the strongest argument for genuine cooperation, since by this only can diversity be helpful, even as it is only through diversity in its members that a community can develop fullest life. A world organization based on the principle that any single group is best and therefore ought to rule, or to displace all others, would be a calamity. A world organization which encourages every member to be itself would be a blessing.

Why do nationalism and internationalism clash? Because this national spirit has rightly or wrongly been bound up so intimately with political independence. Tara's harp long hangs mute when Erin is conquered. Poland's children must not use a language in which they might learn to plot against their masters. A French-speaking Alsatian is suspected of disloyalty. Professor Dewey has recently pointed out that in the United States we have gone far toward separating culture from the state, and suggests that this may be the path of peace for Europe.[3] We allow groups to keep their religion, their language, their song festivals. It may perhaps be claimed that this maintenance of distinct languages and separate cultures is a source of weakness in such a crisis as we now face. Yet it may well be urged, on the other hand, that a policy less liberal would have increased rather than diminished disunion and disloyalty.

VI

The student of human progress is likely to be increasingly impressed with the interaction between ideas and institutions. How far does man build and shape institutions to give body to his ideas? How far is it the organized life with its social contacts, its give and take, its enlargement of its membership to see life *sub specie communitatis*, which itself brings ideas to birth? Desire may bring the sexes together, but it is the association and organized relationships of the family which transform casual to permanent affection and shape our conceptions of its values. A herding instinct or a common need of defense or of food supplies may bring together early groups, and will to power may begin the state, but it is the living together which generates laws and wakens the craving for liberty and the struggle for justice. Seer and poet doubtless contribute to progress by their kindling appeals to the imagination and sympathy; the philosopher may, as Plato claimed for him, live as citizen of a perfect state which has no earthly being, and shape his life according to its laws; but mankind in general has learned law and right, as well as the arts of use and beauty, in the school of life in common.

So it is likely to be with international cooperation. Fears and hopes now urge it upon a reluctant, incredulous world. But the beginnings—

3. John Dewey, "America and the World," *The Nation* 106 (1918): 287.

scientific, legal, commercial, political—timid and imperfect though they be, like our own early confederation, will work to reshape those who take part. Mutual understanding will increase with common action. When men work consistently to create new resources instead of treating their world as a fixed system, when they see it as a fountain, not as a cistern, they will gradually gain a new spirit. The Great Community must create as well as prove the ethics of cooperation.

22 Ethics and International Relations

Is there, can there be, any ethics of international relations? Or must we recognize that as regards actual conditions, ethical theories are as hopelessly in conflict as warring nations, and that as regards the future, the best that ethics can offer is a choice between radically different views of human responsibilities, standards, and values?

Such conflict seems to deny the basal presuppositions of ethics. If there can be no genuine moral principle that does not hold good for all rational beings, if consequences of happiness or well-being for all rationals must be reckoned with, if good and bad are properties of things independent of opinion, or if good is the transcendent and eternal—on any of these ethical theories right and good should not be determined by national frontiers. Yet apart from recriminations as to specific acts which seem to one antagonist either intrinsically good or else entirely justifiable as means, whereas to the other they appear so utterly abhorrent as to condemn any end which incorporates them, there are no doubt fundamental differences in moral attitude. As in the historic battles between national religions, or as with such issues as split Loyalist and Puritan in England, North and South in our Civil War, great causes are more or less masked under particular occasions; the names under which men fight do not by any means always show what are the real principles which contend for victory.

I propose to outline certain of the more typical of the issues, combining to some extent the two methods of approach: psychological explanation of what is, and consideration of what ought to be. The questions may be conveniently grouped under the heads of responsibility, justice, and ultimate values.

Reprinted by permission of the publisher from James Hayden Tufts, "Ethics and International Relations," *International Journal of Ethics* 28.3 (1918), 299–313 [1918:05].

I. CAN NATIONS BE REGARDED AS MORAL AGENTS?

International conflicts are not so much moral events as they are the clashing of social forces.[1]

The author seems to be quite unaware that he is being guilty of an unpardonable confusion of thought. All ethical considerations are completely alien to the state, and the state must therefore resolutely keep them at arm's length.[2]

The first of these quotations would suspend ethical prosecutions in war time in view of the disagreements of juries, and substitute the activity of sociology which raises no question of responsibility, but merely traces forces at work.

The second would demur absolutely to any ethical judgments upon states. The private citizen cannot try the government. The state knows neither right nor wrong, justice nor mercy. Whether one views the state as above morality, as *ex lex*, like the God of certain scholastics, or places it in a distinct compartment—'politics is politics,' just as 'business is business'—the practical outcome is the same. All ethicists are hereby solemnly suspended from their occupations so far as states are concerned. Let them consider private morals, or the absolute good. But when the state kills or makes alive, covenants or breaks covenants, seizes or defends, the proper attitude for philosophy is *'nicht sich ärgen, nur bewundern.'*[3]

Professor Warren's attention was challenged by the disagreement of moral judgments pronounced not only by the warring nations of Europe, but also by psychologists and philosophers of this country before we entered the war. One of Professor Warren's inferences may be provisionally accepted: "The nations which are brought into conflict by clashing ideals are not governed by the same ethical standards." But are we thereby forced to conclude that there is "no alternative open but to judge it from a wholly non-ethical standpoint"?[4] True enough that most, if not all, civilized nations in the past, and even in

1. Howard C. Warren, "Social Forces and International Ethics," *International Journal of Ethics* 27.3 (1917): 355.

2. Franz Eulenberg's discussion of Wilhelm Jerusalem's *Der Krieg im Licht der Gesellschaftslehre*, in his "Literatur über Krieg und Volkwirtschaft," *Archiv für Socialwissenschaft und Socialpolitik* 43.1 (1916): 317.

3. Ed. note: Philosophy "should just observe the situation, rather than getting worked up over it."

4. Warren 352.

the not very remote past, have broken agreements and invaded smaller states, and in this country we know how radically sincere men in North and South differed on the ethics of slavery. All this is in point against certain ethical attitudes which presuppose universal intuitions or inevitable logic, or an absolutely unquestionable scale of values with its possibility for conclusive weighing the consequences. But the important question is, Will the world gain, or shall we as thinkers gain, by abdicating all moral jurisdiction?

The half truth in the contention is that as yet social forces are imperfectly understood and imperfectly controlled. As Professor Dewey said in substance at the twenty-fifth anniversary exercise of the American Psychological Association, one great reason for the ills under which politics and society suffer is that our social sciences have not kept pace with our physical sciences. We have tools of production and weapons of destruction, but not the means for their control in the interest of human welfare.[5]

But two things ought to be said further: First, the forces which issue in individual action are likewise imperfectly understood, and with some men and women, very imperfectly controlled. Yet we pursue a steady policy of holding the individual responsible for acts which cause injury to his fellows. To 'shoot up' a continent is an act for which the plea of 'social forces' cannot be accepted as a bar to ethical judgments. If the philosophers hold their peace, the dead must cry out. The jury may stay out long for the evidence; it may find various degrees of murder; but the old verdict of death by the act of God will not satisfy. And in the second place, control over social forces is not entirely lacking. Bismarck did not think so. He informed Crispi as to the methods of guiding public opinion. He himself gave a brilliant example of ability to make public opinion in two countries demand war. Is it to be presumed that both instruction and example have been forgotten or neglected? There is much to indicate that no such logical inconsistency or practical non sequitur as praise of his methods and failure to follow them has been committed.

What can we say to the more absolute demurrer of Eulenberg? In its extreme form it refutes itself. For if there is anything essential to the existence of a modern state, it is the loyalty of its citizens; and loyalty in its highest, most enduring form demands ethical approval. When the state consisted of an absolute monarch, or an

5. John Dewey, "The Need for Social Psychology," *Psychological Review* 24 (1917): 266–277.

absolute few, governed solely by greed for power and gain, secure by its resources of armor, or cavalry, or castles, as against the great mass of subject peoples or individuals, no ethical pretense was needed for conquest or plunder. But now the state finds that even for such wars, moral justification is necessary strategy. It must make its wars appear wars of self-defense, as Bismarck taught. It still uses the political maxims cited by Kant in his *Essay on Perpetual Peace*, "fac et excusa," "si fecisti, nega"; but it does make excuses; it does make denials; it may even prepare the way for outrages by fictitious reports of similar outrages on the part of the enemy; it finds it wise to disguise annexation under the camouflage of 'self-determination.' Now the militarist or Machiavellian may for a time succeed in playing the shrewd game of gaining ethical support for a nonethical state; but the philosopher, at least, ought not to be privy to such a logical sleight of hand, and the common people are likely to be increasingly suspicious.

It is in a modifiable form that the theory of no jurisdiction is more plausible. Ethics has a relation to international relations, the theory asserts, but the ethics which applies is not the ethics of individual life; the clash in ethical judgments is due to confusion between standards for the individual and standards for nation or state.[6] If the state is a supreme and transcendent entity; if in it all individual good culminates and all obligation is fulfilled; if it is the embodiment of reason, God on earth, then obviously the safety of the state *is* the supreme law. How shall mortal man be more just than his maker? So runs the thought of Hegel and essentially of Rümelin. Supplemented by the doctrines that history is the march of God and that the superiority of a given state proves it the representative of reason, the incarnation of the *Idee*, it sufficiently explains why those who hold such a doctrine must clash in judgments with those who do not. The infallible state denies the right of private judgment. Morally, as legally, the state can do no wrong. Englishmen and Americans, Münsterberg explains, are too hedonistic and egoistic in their ethics to apprehend such a superindividual object of loyalty.

It would doubtless be futile for the American to discuss this view if he is incapable of understanding it, but the query must be raised, whether at any rate any concrete particular state as yet fills the specifications of absolute reason. Granted that mankind—when mankind

6. Edward Robert Lytton, *National and Individual Morality Compared* (Paris: Symonds, 1888).

shall have progressed in wisdom, sympathy, and goodwill—organized for living nobly and well, may claim the loyalty of all men, does this give any particular state the right to trample on human life, pervert truth, poison good faith, and practice ruthless frightfulness under the plea of necessity? I may pass over further discussion of the dangers of human values in an abstract idealistic deification of the state, as they have been so admirably set forth in Professor Dewey's *German Philosophy and Politics.*[7]

But a more downright and plausible form of removing nations from moral control while seeming to maintain an ethical standard is that of Treitschke. Starting plausibly with a maxim of Kant, it ends with complete justification for *Machtpolitik*—the politics of power. The state is a collective personality. Every personality must be treated as an end, not as a means only. Man and every personality

> attains the highest perfection possible when he has recognized and developed the most essential part of himself. When we apply this standard . . . to the State, and remember that its very personality is power, we see its highest moral duty is to uphold that power. . . .
> The injunction to assert itself remains always absolute. Weakness must always be condemned as the most disastrous and despicable of crimes, the unforgivable sin of politics.[8]

If we admit this absolute right of self-assertion, no other justification for any act by the state is pertinent. The measure of ruthlessness is solely its success in increasing or maintaining power. The only refutation it can admit is failure. If other persons are not in sympathy with this idea, then their resentment may turn strength into weakness and thus prove the immorality of a specific act of ruthlessness. Likewise for a state to conquer what it cannot assimilate is immoral, for it displays weakness.

International law faces the doctrine in the following form: Aside from those provisions based upon treaties, there are other provisions which are in the nature of usages initiated or practiced by certain states, and accepted or at least tolerated by others. Such was the doctrine of 'continuous voyage' put forth by the United States government during the Civil War. The German government desires to introduce a doctrine of 'war zones.' If we say that international law is

7. John Dewey, *German Philosophy and Politics* (New York: Holt, 1915) [cf. 1915:11].

8. Heinrich von Treitschke, *Politics*, vol. 1 (New York: Macmillan, 1916) 94–95.

anything that a power can carry through with the acquiescence of other powers, the question recurs: Shall other powers allow the power in question to 'get away with it' or shall they resist? If it is an absolute duty of power A to assert itself, and an equally absolute duty of power B to assert itself, are we not confronted with a contradiction which must at least awaken a doubt as to the absolute morality of power?

On this basis we might have an internal limit of power set by the ability to assimilate diverse elements into one national whole. Just as there is a point at which the superior efficiency of great corporations becomes doubtful, so a world-capturing policy in an empire may develop weakness.

If now proceeding from this absolute duty of self-assertion we should attempt to forecast the ethics of international relations, we might at first sight suppose world domination the logical expression of any power strong enough to carry through such an aim. But too complete dominance would mean peace and this would be fatal to another militarist value—war. For Treitschke the logical outcome is, first, pluralism: "The state is power, precisely in order to assert itself against other equally independent powers"—and then war: "The grandeur of history lies in the perpetual conflict of nations." The same view of war as the "best and noblest form of the struggle for existence," in the words of Schmidt; "the main factor in true, genuine *Kultur*" according to Nippold; "A holy thing," "The holiest thing on earth" according to Sombart; is apparently shared by many besides Bernhardi.

It cannot be said that this scheme of power and conflict is absolutely nonethical. Its scale of values places the heroic at the head, or it considers struggle as nature's and therefore as man's, highest law.[9] As to the first point of view, I do not see how anyone can demonstrate by argument the values of other virtues to be superior to those of war. I can only wonder whether those who have actually been close enough to the trenches and the empty homes to take in the full experience of such a war as this will still regard it as the best life. If so, I fear no arguments from pure reason will have consideration. I can only say in the words of Lincoln, "I should think that any one who likes this sort of thing would be very much pleased with it."

As for the second point, that since conflict is nature's law, it should also be man's, I reply that the very essence of ethical life according to

9. Compare Prof. Vernon Kellogg's account of his conversations with the biologist in "Headquarters Nights," *Atlantic Monthly* 120 (1917): 145–155.

pragmatist, idealist, and at least one realist is the possibility of at least partial control by intelligence instead of by trial and error, partial freedom from blind necessity, partial massing of forces against a reluctant cosmos.

One great task of ethics in relation to international relations is to discover and point out how far intelligent methods of cooperation may supersede conflict as an international process. Münsterberg draws the analogy between war and prevalent methods of industrial competition, and uses it to justify war. But we have learned in the economic world to discriminate between a competition directed toward the conquest of nature which stimulates invention and thereby improves the conditions of all, and a competition toward conquest of competitors, which substitutes brutality for ideas and profits only the winner.

Power is indeed by tradition the essence of the state. It was in military operations that the enormous power of human association and organization on a large scale first emerged. Political organizations followed military lines. The cruder processes of violence were at first largely met and controlled by blood and iron. And as a whole, Europe has never been able to cooperate. The colonies in this country nearly fell into the same slough of despond. Fortunately, they decided to cooperate, by trade, canals, railways, migrations, postal service, instead of competing by tariffs and maintaining armies. Economic power, only in the last century exercised on a scale comparable to political power, has been likewise proceeding wastefully, but we are now facing the elemental problem of economic supply of human needs more directly. Shall we go back to the older wasteful process?

I conclude that the doctrine of the state as naked power issues in an ethics of power which doubtless has claimed admiration, but which when universalized, so to speak, becomes too horrible a thing for most men to tolerate, and which even in its own test of power ignores the greater power of cooperation and goodwill as compared with conflict. For cooperation and goodwill never are evoked by power as power.

True it is that state and nation have peculiar tasks, peculiar responsibilities. They have been defenders of liberty and order, arbiters of justice, bonds of unity, preservers of culture, and agencies for common welfare of large groupings of men, though also agencies for strife and tyranny. True likewise that it is difficult for the individual, especially if he be of a different nation, to judge these adequately and fairly. Yet if the world is to remain tolerable for man no single group or organization, whether it call itself 'state' or by less pretentious name, can claim exemption from moral responsibility. It is by international responsibility, ecumenical conscience, and international guarantees that the great interests, of which nations have in the past been necessary trustees and defenders, must be increasingly maintained.

II. CONFLICTING STANDARDS OF JUSTICE

A second issue, more or less clearly emerging between the warring groups, is, What is the standard for justice? Stationary nations, or those which have already obtained what they want, are naturally insistent of the rights of the existing status. Those which are in process of rapid growth, or which have not reached territory adequate for their wants, would use for their measure of justice their need of expansion.

Several aspects of this issue have emerged in the present war: (a) treaties versus needs of the situation when conditions change; (b) the right to areas of the earth, based on occupancy, or past conquest, as versus claims based on the need of a growing population, or the merits of superior civilization; (c) established rules for land and sea warfare, designed to mitigate injury to noncombatants, as versus the changes necessary if a new invention such as the submarine is to be used with a maximum of result.

The question of treaties was well discussed by Mill, who took the ground that no government had the right to bind a people indefinitely. Treaties, he urged, should be for limited periods. It is noteworthy that the principle of the Dartmouth College case has been more and more strictly construed and limited by our courts in the interest of preserving freedom of action on the part of the public. Ethics must, however, distinguish between needs that commend themselves internationally, and needs that are egoistic. If the purpose is aggression, a nation can hardly command international sanction until this aggression is able to prove its claim.

The question of the right to occupy or control areas now sparsely occupied, or unimproved, is one that Americans decided in their own case on one basis when dealing with Indians, and on another when dealing with individual land ownership. Broadly speaking, the right of the whites to the territory controlled by the United States rests less on any treaties with the Indians than on the fact that under the civilization of the whites the land supports a hundred millions and may support many more, whereas under the Indian, and even Spanish control, it was far less fruitful. On the one hand, individual Indians ought to have been treated with consideration and humanity; on the other, it can not be said that the collective units, the tribes, ought to be preserved forever in their original status of exclusive occupancy of the whole continent. The case is analogous in part to the introduction of machinery. Individual workers ought not to bear the burden of readjustment, but society cannot refuse to accept inventions on the ground that some men will lose their employment in tasks for which they have acquired special skill.

Applying this principle to international affairs, and beginning with an extreme case, no small group of men can equitably possess or control indefinitely a great area, if it is thereby kept from contributing to human well-being. But as civilization advances attachment to the soil increases, and the web of human relations grows stronger and more intricate. The case of actual occupants becomes stronger before the test of satisfying human needs, as well as in sentiment and legal title. Just here exchange of goods without surrender of soil has provided a solution. Just as it is no longer necessary to own an Epictetus in order to read his book, or to be lord over a villein in order to get the aid of the tiller of the soil, so it is increasingly unnecessary for a nation to own mines or forests or soil in order to obtain heat and metal, wool and wheat. This principle, however, must be carried farther. We have heard chiefly of an international court. My colleague, Dean Hall, urges that it is equally important and probably more important to set up an international legislature which shall have power to provide on the one hand for access to raw materials or such exchange as may secure them, and on the other, for suitable markets. Serbia ought to have had more than one market. Germany makes splendid uses of iron; she ought to have iron without going about to get it by conquest. It is easy to see difficulties. Shall France be required by an international legislature to furnish iron wherewith Essen may forge weapons for the conquest of France? On the other hand, can such an international legislature prevent Germany from using the iron as it pleases when once it is in possession of it? Yet who can doubt that the path of progress must lie along the direction of providing for all legitimate needs by other than the crude method of ownership of men or dominion over the earth?

The most difficult obstacle in the way of a nonpolitical method of providing for needs is the seeming diminution of political prestige. Will it answer to let England govern a district while Germany has the trade, or vice versa? Such was often the situation before the war. We get on harmoniously with Canada on this basis, yet the appeal to political interests when the reciprocity treaty was under consideration and the overturn of the Canadian government on this issue shows how easily such a question becomes delicate.

III. ULTIMATE VALUES—ARISTOCRACY VERSUS DEMOCRACY

The third great issue which divides the contending groups is that of aristocracy versus democracy as a political and social order. Not that all the inhabitants of the Central Powers are Junkers, not that all British, French, and Americans are democratic in ideals and sympathies. But the dominating agencies in the first group, from the Hohenzollerns who have refused power offered by popular voice in order to hold it more securely when achieved by blood and iron, to their ecclesiastical and academic supporters, believe in direction by the few, discipline for the many. They maintain or accept the militarist scheme of subordination of civil to military power. The dominating forces in the opposing group are increasingly democratic and have no disposition to allow military forces the decisive word in national policy.

The psychology of Germany has been acutely analyzed by Veblen in his *Nature of Peace* as that of a feudal state.[10] The religious ideas which come to us in such phrases as 'the German God,' or in the recent language of the emperor, "The year 1917 with its great battles has proved that the German people has in the Lord of Creation above an unconditioned and avowed ally on whom it can absolutely rely," belong naturally with the feudal stage of society. A feudal morality finds in loyalty to a superior complete satisfaction and sufficient ethical sanction for any act. Bismarck's morals seem to have been of this sort, although sometimes in Prussia's interest he might resist the monarch. And on its other side, feudal morality is the *Herrenmoral* of the ruling class. It is not necessary to charge Nietzsche with bringing on the war, but he certainly thought he was advocating (1) a *Herrenmoral*, and (2) a morality the reverse of the general morality of Christendom. A class which believes in its divine right to govern will naturally find such a morality of masters convenient. And if a people believes its own culture so superior to that of other peoples as to make international law impossible,[11] it will easily accept so much of superior class morality as to make explicable collisions with codes of inferior cultures.

10. Thorstein Veblen, *An Inquiry into the Nature of Peace and the Terms of Its Perpetuation* (New York: Macmillan, 1917).

11. Josef Kohler declares English, French, Russians, Italians, and Americans as impossible members of any international law association. They have no "living conscience."

But let us look away from historic reasons why men are so, and consider in barest outline some of the values claimed for aristocracy and democracy respectively. If we are to have increasing unity, increasing organization, shall it be along the line of superior-inferior class rule, that is, of empire, or along the line of self-direction and equality? When I call this a question of ultimate values, I do not mean that none of the values have any common denominator, but that although some have, others apparently have not. Let us notice some of the issues which are arguable. They turn largely on whether we stake our case on what is, or on what may be, on nature or on intelligence, on mechanism or on consciousness.

(1) There is first the question of efficiency. This is based in part on specialization of function. If men are in fact different in both kind and degree of ability, is it not obvious that some should rule and others be ruled? From Plato and Aristotle to the present day, this has seemed to many axiomatic. A second closely related argument is that democracy will refuse to use experts. It is a "cult of incompetence," as Faguet put it. A representative of a group is chosen by the group, and therefore is below the level of the group who choose him; he sits in a group and therefore when in parliament sinks below his own level— such is the social psychology of Christensen.

The democrat replies, Admitting there are differences between men, the great question is, do we propose to *crystalize* these or to encourage the emergence of new powers? A class system takes the first course. Its machinery, social, political, educational, is all based on the theory that nature has said the last word. Democracy believes in experimenting with human nature, in taking chances, that new power may unfold. While it relies mainly on bringing on the whole mass, it sometimes finds genius coming out of Nazareth. It admits a good deal of lost motion, but it is willing to pay the price.

And as to the cult of incompetence, democracy urges that this is a relic of the time when office meant dominance. No one objects to the expert surgeon or the competent musician. Undoubtedly the legislator or judge or executive must have authority as well as expertness, but with a genuinely democratic conception of government it is at least plausible that suspicion of the expert as official may decrease. Early democracy in America, fresh from the recollection of old world governments, was actuated by fear of governmental usurpation of power. Its system of checks and balances was intended, as Professor McLaughlin has put it, to provide a government that could not "do things." Now that we demand increasingly for our complex conditions a government that *can* do things, the need of the expert is increasingly apparent. There is likely to be less suspicion of his ability.

(2) Aristocracy claims that specialization of function not only means efficiency, but also individual liberty and culture. It asserts that liberty and democracy are inherently contradictory. It will have naught of the herd, of the mishmash and its control. There is undoubtedly an individuality of the aristocratic type. It seeks intellectual, aesthetic, or economic distinction. And in past ages with inadequate production very likely culture could flourish only by building upon the submerged foundations of slaves, villeins, artisans, or some other exploited class. In the language of Nietzsche, "[W]e children of the future . . . ponder over the need of a new order of things, even of a new slavery—for every strengthening and elevation of the type 'man' also involves a new form of slavery."

But is not this merely another illustration of the disposition of the aristocratic theory to fall back upon what has been, upon nature as versus creative intelligence? It is by no means certain that individuality requires class aristocracy. There is certainly in intellectual development as such no necessary dependence upon comparative superiority. If there is an aristocratic art which expresses rare and unique experiences of a few gifted souls, there is certainly also a democratic art which sounds chords of common emotion. If there is a type of individuality which increases its values by being different from others, there is another which seeks them through contacts, and defines its own ideals by comparison with those of equals, as Professor [Warner] Fite has well pointed out.[12]

(3) We come finally to a comparison in which there is no apparent common denominator. The final issue between aristocracy and democracy is the relative value of power over another, as compared with free association among equals. I do not see that the partisan of aristocracy can demonstrate his case to the advocate of democracy, or vice versa. There can be no question of the reality and urge of the will to power. There is little doubt that to many natures the consciousness of power over other human beings is more satisfying even than that of power over nature. This consciousness of power is enormously increased by membership in a military or other ruling class. A *Herrenmoral* will seem to such a class the expression of the eternal fitness of things. "To demand of strength that it should *not* manifest itself as strength—that it should *not* be a will for overcoming, for overthrow-

12. Ed. note: Cf. 1917:02.

ing, for mastery, a thirst for enemies, for struggles and triumphs, is as absurd as to demand of weakness that it should manifest itself as strength."

The democrat, however, on his side urges that equality is satisfying to those who live it. Friendship is good, and friendship rests on equality. The religious ideal of equality before God, the implication of equality before the law, the give and take of scholarship in pursuit of truth bespeak a democratic value that is real. It is the appeal of the finer institutions which man is building; it is more and more gaining ground.

23 Judicial Law-Making Exemplified in Industrial Arbitration

Of the various experiments in collective bargaining, industrial democracy, and the quasi-judicial arbitrament of industrial issues, the agreements in the men's clothing industry have certain features of peculiar interest to the legal profession. It has been pointed out by Professor [John Henry] Wigmore that the procedure is broadly analogous to that by which standards were developed in the Law Merchant which later found their place in the law of the land. It is not impossible that the courts may later find aid for standards of industrial justice in the cumulative work of the industrial boards which are patiently building up precedents. Indeed the issues presented to the arbitrator involve the same ultimate problems which confront the judicial lawmaker in any new field where standards are still to be worked out for dealing with opposing interests.

While my experience as chairman of the Board of Arbitration, under the Hart, Schaffner and Marx agreement, and later in a similar capacity for the Chicago Men's Clothing Industry, was not a long one, it nevertheless presented certain problems that may be of interest from a legal as well as from a social and philosophical point of view.

The essential features of the plan have been stated in print but may be briefly summarized for the convenience of those not familiar with them. The fundamental idea is that of securing a peaceful and mutually advantageous method of carrying on industry. The method provides (1) for collective bargaining between firm and union both in making the original contract and subsequently to some extent in dealing with new matters; (2) for a permanent body (a board, or boards) to act judicially in interpreting and applying the agreement and, what is

244 *James Hayden Tufts*

fully as important, to maintain as a living process the central idea of a joint interest in the ongo and conditions of the industry. To a degree as yet undetermined this 'impartial machinery' also takes account of 'public' interest, as distinct from the interests of the contracting parties.

The firm and the union, accordingly, negotiate an agreement which (a) declares the general end sought through the agreement by the respective parties; (b) lays down a very few specific terms, e.g., the number of hours that constitute a week's work, the provision for equal division of work in slack periods, the general schedule of wages with the methods for making readjustments where needed during the period covered by the agreement, the rights of the two parties as to hiring, discharge, and discipline; (c) sets up one or more boards to act both in a judicial procedure by hearing cases and rendering decisions, and in an investigative, mediating and quasi-legislative capacity in dealing with situations not clearly covered by any rules. In this latter capacity the general end or purpose of the agreement is regarded as supplying a principle to which recourse can be had when specific rules are lacking. In the Chicago agreements distinct functions are assigned to two separate boards called the Trade Board and the Board of Arbitration. The first is the primary board for adjusting grievances, and changes in piece rates due to changes in style, and for determining questions of fact and testimony. The second hears appeals, but concerns itself mainly with questions of principle and the application of the agreement to new issues as they arise, which may either be referred to it by the Trade Board or brought directly before it by petition from either party. In cities other than Chicago the dual system of boards has either not been set up by agreement, or not used in practice. But in a market as large as Chicago where some forty thousand workers are employed there have seemed to be sufficient issues to keep two Trade Boards and a Board of Arbitration occupied pretty continuously. The period observed included parts of an unusually active and an unusually slack season and hence offered many special problems as well as the ordinary cases.

The outstanding procedural features that have legal interest are (1) the more permanent character of the institutions thus set up and the consequent continuity of 'legal tradition'—if such it may be called; (2) the semiprofessional status of the representatives of the parties—the 'counsel.' The substantive problems are numerous, but I select (1) the relation of law to power in such arbitration based on voluntary contracts; (2) the mutual obligations arising out of the status of the parties and the general purpose of the agreement as over and above those expressly written into the text of the agreement; (3) the weight to be attached to usages or customs of the trade: Are they a sort of property right, and what if they conflict with the general public interest in improved methods of production?; (4) elements which enter into setting standards for a 'just' or 'fair' wage.

I

(1) The agreement is for a term of years (three in Chicago) and the chairmen of the boards are chosen for the same periods. All decisions are made in writing and are preserved and cited. The boards ordinarily follow precedents unless circumstances are seen to be clearly different. This tends to make the boards take account of the long run as well as of the immediate consequences. It makes the Board of Arbitration cautious about sweeping statements and inclined to follow in new situations the example of the federal Supreme Court in its pragmatic method of gradually determining the bounds of police power and individual rights. The continuity of tradition has been substantially aided by the relative permanence of the personnel of Hart, Schaffner and Marx boards. It is creditable alike to the parties and the two chairmen that Mr. [John E.] Williams served as chairman of the Board of Arbitration from his first election in December 1912 to his death seven years later, and Mr. [James] Mullenbach, chairman of the Trade Board, originally chosen in 1912, is still in office. The tendency is decidedly toward that certainty and generality which are among the marks of law.

(2) The parties immediately concerned do not ordinarily present their own cases. The firms, or the foremen and superintendents, are represented by 'labor managers,' who are, on the one hand, supposed to be expert in dealing with labor, and, on the other, to be informed as to the past decisions of the boards and to take an interest in making arbitration succeed. The men and women whose wages or working conditions or tenures are concerned are represented by deputies, who are usually continued in office year after year, and come to consider it their concern to maintain the dignity and authority of the boards, as well as to look out for the interest of their clients. In short the same influences of group psychology which tend to make lawyers not only attorneys for their clients but also members of the court are at work in the sittings of a permanent board, if the spirit and temper of the board manifest respect for a principle higher than any private interest.

One fact tends to emphasize this aspect of responsibility. A court of law has its own agents for enforcing its decisions. The boards have to rely upon the parties to carry them out in good faith. Requirements upon employers are likely to be of more definite character—an increase of wage, a reinstatement of a suspended employee. Requirements upon the union frequently involve specific performance where an element of goodwill is involved—e.g., a fair day's work in occupations not capable of exact standardization. Hence it was not uncommon to hear from union representatives the request, "In making a decision please remember that we have the job of getting it carried out by our people. It is one thing for us around this table to say what we think is right; it is another thing to convince ten thousand people of various languages, degrees of education, and attitudes toward the organization." The boards have felt their task to be partly one of education, and not merely one of pronouncing decisions without taking account of the psychology of the parties.

II

(1) As clearly stated in Professor Hale's article any such plan of arbitration based on voluntary contracts involves a balance of power as well as a supposedly impartial justice.[1] The relative bargaining powers of the respective parties find expression in the wage scales adopted, except insofar as certain minimum wages for beginners may be based on cost of living. This is in its way analogous to the adoption of any constitution or the enactment of any legislature not due to unanimous vote. The federal Constitution, if in one sense the will of the people, was just as clearly a series of bargains between opposing groups. Every tariff law is a similar coercion of a minority—by the method of counting ballots instead of breaking heads. The check upon the extent to which the stronger power will go in formulating its terms, i.e., its legislation, is partly the fear of a political defeat through a shift of voters if too extreme action is forced, partly the economic consequences of too exclusively selfish a class measure, and partly perhaps the more creditable motive of not wishing to crowd the weaker too closely to the wall. The courts do not ordinarily go behind the legislation to ask whether the fundamental forces which gave it existence were in their opinion beneficent. A Democratic judge

1. Robert L. Hale, "Law Making by Unofficial Minorities," *Columbia Law Review* 20.4 (1920): 451–456.

administers a Republican tariff, and a Republican judge administers a Democratic income tax. So the voluntary contract in the labor agreements reflects the limits of concessions which each is willing to make and the limits of the demands which each is prepared to insist upon in the existing circumstances.

Nor does the question of power disappear in the issues raised before the boards—any more than it disappears in injunction proceedings against labor unions in the courts, or in questions of constitutional law under the Fourteenth Amendment.

The immediate issue presented for adjudication does not always disclose the root of the matter. Shall there be any limit to the number of apprentices, or shall a firm engage as many as it desires? At first it seems a simple matter of recruiting and training necessary craftsmen, or, to a teacher, a matter of affording a vocational opportunity to a boy. But it soon appears as a question of balance of power: the more apprentices, the greater the supply of skilled cutters; the fewer apprentices, the better control of the situation by the union. Who shall select the candidates? It appears at first the obvious province of employment management. But it soon emerges that the foreman who has it in his power to appoint may strengthen his hold upon a given worker by promising to appoint the worker's son, whereas if the union has the right to nominate, the prestige of the union organization is correspondingly increased. Shall a more effective process or method of production be installed? The obvious fact is that apparently the public as well as the firm will gain, and the worker will not suffer any direct reduction in rate of pay. But if the improved process means that fewer men are needed, if the more efficient subdivision of the process means that the all-around craftsman is no longer essential, the union sees power slipping away and reappearing in the employer's scale of the balance. At the expiration of an existing agreement the parties negotiate a new one and the terms of the new agreement represent the bargaining power of employer and workman. Is it fair for the arbitrator to render a decision which shall not merely affect wages and working conditions during the life of the agreement but shall to some extent affect the bargaining power of the parties in making another agreement?

The problem is analogous to the distinction between legal and political functions. What is the province of courts, and what the province of legislatures and elections? How far should society be shaped by the 'rule of reason' and how far by the will of the people? When

John Marshall and Thomas Jefferson took office in 1801, no reader of Beveridge's *Life of John Marshall*[2] can fail to recognize that Federalism, with its supporting nationalistic, commercial, and creditor interests, was to continue on the bench the contest it had lost in the Congress and the presidency against the local, agricultural, and debtor interests. And I suppose that no one attributes the decisions of John Marshall to the fact that his logic was superior to that of Thomas Jefferson. The syllogisms had their major premise in a political philosophy, not in a written document. I suppose that the same is true of the decisions which deprived the Fourteenth Amendment of most of its significance, so far as protecting the Negro was concerned, and more recently of *Coppage v. Kansas,* and *Hitchman Coal and Coke Co. v. Mitchell.*[3]

How far should an arbitrator essay in a humble fashion the role of a statesman and endeavor to advance a philosophy of social order, and how far should he follow the policy of "hands off, let the contending interests settle for themselves the issues involving balance of power!" just as the courts often refuse to pass on matters which, they say, belong to the legislature? If the arbitrator sways the balance strongly he is likely to make the losing party so dissatisfied that it will refuse to renew the agreement. If his decision is merely a reflection of the actual balance of power, he seems not fully to justify the confidence reposed in him by the parties. For they seem to ask him to see farther from his position above the battle. And if he does rely on some philosophy of society in making his decision, shall it be the prevalent philosophy of present American life, or shall it be that of some supposedly better order? During my own experience the decisions of the board on which I sat aimed in general to avoid any permanent displacement of the balance of power toward either end of the beam. They sought to effect this by giving increased power to the impartial machinery pending negotiations and revisions of the agreement by the parties at the proper time, i.e., when the existing agreement should expire and the question of renewal should arise. For example, temporary increases in apprentices were allowed as an emergency matter to firms which should satisfy the board of their need for them, the percentage to revert automatically to the previous ratio as fast as apprentices should complete their term. In its general attitude I presume the board

2. Albert Jeremiah Beveridge, *The Life of John Marshall* (Boston: Houghton, 1916–1919), 4 vols.
3. Coppage v. State of Kansas, 236 US 1 (1914); Hitchman Coal and Coke Company v. Mitchell, Individually, et al., 245 US 229 (1917).

was, unconsciously perhaps, acting in accord with the views of Mr.
Justice Holmes as expressed in his address on law and the Court,
although this address had not then come under the eye of the board:

> [W]hile there still is doubt, while opposite convictions still keep a bat-
> tle front against each other, the time for law has not come; the notion
> destined to prevail is not yet entitled to the field. It is a misfortune if a
> judge reads his conscious or unconscious sympathy with one side or
> the other prematurely into the law, and forgets that what seem to him
> to be first principles are believed by half his fellow men to be wrong.[4]

Central decisions which involve a social philosophy will be noted
under subsequent heads.

(2) A frequent question was that of broad versus strict interpretation
of the agreement and of the rights and duties of the parties under it.
One party would claim it had a right to a certain course of action
because nothing in the agreement forbade; or again a party would
deny that anything in the agreement authorized an assertion of authority demanded by the other party in the interest of 'justice.' A typical
case which brought up the issue of possible mutual obligations not
specified in the contract was as follows: A certain firm in addition to
its main factory had opened and carried on for some weeks another
factory, in which a different quality of clothing was made. This proved
unprofitable and the firm decided to close this branch. The agreement
had no clause explicitly covering such a situation. A clause which was
framed for a somewhat analogous situation reads, "When sections are
abolished, the company and its agents shall use every effort to give
the displaced workers employment as much as possible like the work
from which they were displaced, within a reasonable time." There
was some dispute as to whether the firm had given any previous
notice to the workers of its intention to close the factory. But when
the case was originally heard the evidence did not show any such
notice: In fact the men first discharged professed not to know why
they had been discharged and it was only after questioning by the
chairman that the manager stated that these men were not discharged
for any fault but because the factory was to be closed. It appeared on
inquiry that men from this branch shop could not well be provided
for in the main shop on account of limitations of space and because
of conditions in quality of the work. The board ruled that some notice

4. Oliver Wendell Holmes, Jr., *Collected Legal Papers* (New York: Harcourt,
1920) 294–295 [cf. 1921:10].

of the intention to close the factory should have been given to the workers and that as this had not been done a week's wages should be allowed to all workers in the factory to support them while looking for other positions.

The firm appealed from this decision to the Board of Arbitration and claimed that nothing in the agreement applied to the closing of an unprofitable factory or justified the requirement that wages should be paid for services not rendered. The Board of Administration upheld in principle the ruling of the Trade Board which had first passed upon the case. It took the position that, so far as the parties to these agreements were concerned, labor is not merely a commodity. It held that the fundamental understanding which underlies the agreement is that the parties treat each other with mutual consideration, and that this would require either notice of sudden closing of a shop, or some provision to enable workers to find positions, or such other method of meeting a situation as might appear proper to the board. In other words it held that here was an obligation arising out of the status of the parties. In reply to the objection that men not infrequently left employment without notice, the board declared that if the whole body of workmen or such a large number of them as to cripple business were to leave suddenly without notice and go to another shop or for any other purpose, the board would consider that this firm had a just grievance and would hold the union responsible to prevent such mass movement without proper notice. This decision implied of course a theory diametrically opposed to that of the *Adair* case[5] and to the usual theory as I understand it of the courts where there is no explicit time contract. It is generally held that one or all workmen may be dismissed at any moment or may leave at any moment. The basis of this 'right' may be supposed to be, as by Mr. Justice Harlan, 'freedom,' but the actual working of it is to render industry insecure. It is finding frequent illustration in the wholesale discharges and generally ill-distributed readjustments of the present business deflation. It is in small an expression of our general irresponsible method of carrying on business enterprise which often distributes rapidly to stockholders the huge profits of an advancing market and makes no provision for steadying the shocks and distributing the burdens of a declining market. It was of interest to the board to note that in a decision of the Kansas Industrial Court shortly following the above case the principle of a mutual obligation was recognized.

5. Adair v. United States, 208 US 161 (1907).

(3) A highly difficult problem which has its interesting legal analogies made its appearance in several cases: the problem of rights connected with certain usages of the trades or crafts employed. The firm claimed a general right to introduce improvements in machines, or in operation, or in organization and division of labor, with the provision that if any workman should be thereby affected injuriously in wages or in the difficulty of his work he should have redress through the impartial machinery. The particular cases which brought up the issue were seemingly of slight importance. Should the linings to be cut by machine be piled one hundred high or only ninety as had previously been the case? The operator was working by the week and consequently his wages would not be affected. Should fabrics of different weave or color be piled together and cut in one operation or must each style of fabric be cut separately? At the time when this latter question arose there was a greater demand for cutters than could be supplied by the union and hence there was no question of displacement involved. The union considered the methods in vogue as standards sanctioned by usage. It maintained that the industry had formerly been in a deplorable condition not only in the matter of wages but also in relation to the health and general comfort of the workers; that these conditions had been step by step improved and standards made by agreement or otherwise; and that if these standards or usages could be broken down at will by the employer or even questioned by the board their whole position was rendered precarious. They felt not only that change in these standards by the employer would be like depriving them of their property without due process of law; they felt that here were certain absolute rights, which were not subject to law, but which on the contrary were to be supported by law. In other words they felt as judges have frequently felt about rights of private property. In certain cases where an improvement in process could evidently be secured, the union was quite willing that this should be effected, but just as the private landholder whose property is taken for public use expects to receive some compensation, so they would expect if they granted to the employer or to the public a waiver of valuable customary rights to receive a quid pro quo. Of course the issue is an old one. It arose when machines were introduced. If one compares it broadly to the issue raised by certain legal titles to property he will probably find the equities and morals of the situation not wholly dissimilar. Much landed and personal property undoubtedly represents little or no service rendered to society, and at present may be at least as great an obstacle to public welfare as an inefficient method of cutting up cloth.

Suppose my ancestor bought the island of Manhattan for a hundred dollars, or stumbled upon a coal or iron mine or an oil deposit in his pasture, or secured valuable franchises for a song, is it just that on this account I, myself, should be exempted from the necessity of any useful work and should be supported by the hands of society? Suppose my trade ancestor or predecessor bargained for a certain conception of a valuable service called 'a cut,' does this entitle me, his industrial or trade-union heir, to a continued advantage therefrom as though it were a specie dollar of specified weight and fineness? The prescriptive factor, undisturbed possession, is similar. From the standpoint of individualistic natural rights, I see no radical difference. If a trade unionist instead of a farmer or a merchant were writing a bill of rights he might easily understand his craft-customs to belong to what Locke called property and Blackstone liberty. From the standpoint of social welfare the justice of recognizing the right of property inheritance, even when the property title was originally due to no useful service and now involves a burden of supporting an idle owner, depends on how much society can afford to pay, first, for the general permanence of conditions in the social order, and second, for the unity and continuity of the family group in particular. The justice of recognizing a title to an inherited craft-usage may be conceived to depend on how far it is worthwhile to maintain a stable industrial order, and to encourage unity and continuity in a worker's group.

The board found itself in several decisions coming to a view which suggests certain tendencies in the public attitude toward property. It held that usage, whether in craft-practice or in interpretation of the agreement, does establish a sort of *prima facie* claim, but that until this claim has been presented, discussed, and considered before the impartial machinery, it cannot be considered as settled. In particular it held that a worker's group, like the family group, should be encouraged, since under our system it is the only institution for protecting the interests of a class which is not upon an equality with the employer in bargaining power. Hence the board was unwilling to assert unqualifiedly that the employer might change a usage without the approval of the impartial machinery. But when a usage conflicts with public welfare as involving restriction of output and where no matter of health is concerned, it has seemed that usage should give way, provided some measure at least of compensation be awarded the worker for the loss of an asset or bargaining point. I incline to think the temper of the American people is moving in this direction as regards certain forms of property. The growing uneasiness over such a coal situation as would have resulted in serious hardship this season had it not been for an exceptionally late and mild winter, and numerous less conspicuous instances make it likely that if the public sees clearly that property rights are restricting production, it will insist on a more efficient method. During the war we had brought to our attention very forcibly that to conduct a business in such a way as to produce the most is not necessarily the same as to conduct a business in such a way as to yield the greatest profit. The present theory of conducting business is that profit is the primary consideration. If it should become clear that this method of conducting business is contrary to public interest in certain fundamental industries, would not the public attitude be the same as toward definite adherence to customary standards which restrict production on the part of laborers? If the courts are ever called upon to face one of these problems, will they not be obliged to consider the other also?

(4) Wages are agreed upon by negotiation when agreements are entered into, but a safety valve for market fluctuations is provided by a section in the agreement which reads as follows:

> If there shall be a general change in wages or hours in the clothing industry, which shall be sufficiently permanent to warrant the belief that the change is not temporary, then the Board shall have power to determine whether such change is of so extraordinary a nature as to justify a consideration of the question of making a change in the present agreement, and, if so, then the Board shall have power to make such changes in wages or hours as in its judgment shall be proper.

Cases under this section have arisen from time to time, especially under the rapidly rising markets and costs of living since 1917, and this has compelled the board to consider what changes are 'proper.' In other words, are there yet any standards for the 'fair wage' which all statesmen at election time assure the workman he ought to receive? During the war the rapidly increasing costs of living was generally recognized to be a ground for increase of wages. The extraordinary demand for labor in many occupations brought with it an offer of wages often in excess of the increased cost of living. In the most important case which came before the board during my tenure, the union asked for an increase of wages which should not only correspond to the increased cost of living but should make possible an improvement in the standard of living if the industry could afford it. It appeared from figures submitted that previous increases had in the main been sufficient to maintain the previous standards of living. In some cases previous increases had exceeded the increased cost of living. The question then was, should a further increase be granted which would permit an improved standard of living? It was shown that such increases had already been made in other competitive markets. Should those who wear clothing pay a higher wage to those who make clothing? According to views of older days when people were divided into successive strata of worth and every occupation had its rank, one might consider seriously the question as to where the maker of clothing ought to rank in the social and economic scale. Our method of individualism and the competitive social order is either less or more rational as one pleases to look upon it. A short time ago it located makers of clothing nearly at the foot of the ladder in sweatshop conditions. Today they are in the upper group of skilled crafts and, if the industry were not still to a considerable extent seasonal, would be as well paid as clerical work and as public school teacher or post office employee. Should it, then, be said that in the public interest further improvement in standard of living for this group was not justified?

The board held that there is as yet no clear standard in our social order for assigning a relative position to any group of workers and that so far as the public interest is concerned, it would not be justified in singling out the clothing workers for an accounting unless data were also available for every stage in the process of production and marketing, and unless the test of fair profits as well as fair wages were to be made. In the absence of such data the board held therefore that the workmen in this industry were entitled to take advantage of the increased demand for their product and their labor and to receive an increased wage.

The broader interest of the problem is that it compels a frank acknowledgment of our present basis and the ambiguity in all such phrases as 'fair wage' and 'fair profits.' If we mean by 'fair' anything which is agreed to by the parties under the laws of supply and demand, that is one thing. If we have lurking in our minds the conception of some moral standard not for election purposes only, that is another. The standard of 'what the parties agreed to' under laws of supply and demand is commonly said to be fair only if the parties are equal. Under modern conditions this is so complicated a question as to yield little hope of any satisfactory standard. We are then actually forced to the conclusion that in a democratic society governed by supply and demand the actual standard is bound to be what the public is willing to pay. The best hope for making public opinion approach a reasonable standard lies in educating the public taste and the public judgment of different goods and services, and for this education the indispensable conditions are (1) greater publicity as to rewards which various members of society are now obtaining for their services, (2) more scientific methods of judging the quality of goods and the efficiency of production, and (3) a broader cultivation that we may all know and prize the goods which enrich and ennoble life.

24 Religion's Place in Securing a Better World-Order

The hour calls clearly for the statesman, the engineer, and the economist. Is it a time for priest or prophet? The demand for science and skill gains in assurance as the war crisis recedes, and questions of trade, industry, finance, and lowered vitality of peoples press upon us. The need of religion in the task of securing a better world-order is not proclaimed with the same assurance, at least among the intellectual classes. There is, indeed, a serious question which sometimes finds expression: Has religion met its responsibilities? Has it done what, in view of its claims upon human allegiance, it might reasonably have been expected to do toward preventing the catastrophe which has come upon the world?

For religion is no newcomer; it was perhaps here in some degree in the Old Stone Age. Dolmens and pyramids testify to the power of ancient beliefs. For more than two thousand years the visions and warnings of the prophets of Israel have summoned man to a better social order, and the teachings of Gautama have called to ways of righteousness and peace. For sixteen centuries Christianity has been at least the nominally accepted creed of Europe. Why then have these faiths, and in particular why has Christianity, as the prevalent creed of Europe, no better credentials to present before the world's bar of public opinion today?

Some answer, "Christianity has not yet been tried, or if Christianity has been tried, it is not the original, simple religion of love to God and man which the carpenter of Nazareth taught and lived; it is not the religion of mystic faith and of membership in a community of true believers which the tentmaker of Tarsus brought from Asia into Eu-

Reprinted by permission of the publisher from James Hayden Tufts, "Religion's Place in Securing a Better World-Order," *Journal of Religion* 2.2 (1922), 113–128 [1922:03].

rope when he announced the advent of a social order in which there should be "neither Greek nor Jew, barbarian, Scythian, bond or free, but all members of one another." The Christianity that has dominated Europe, these defenders of religion would say, has been rather the heir of imperial Rome than of that Kingdom of God which Isaiah saw and Jesus proclaimed. Its dogmas have spoken the language of Greek metaphysics more often than that of the humble and contrite heart.

Another defender of religion points out that it would be poor psychology to expect from religion a complete control over human life, even though the religion were itself ever so pure in the breasts of its sincere followers. For religion is not the only power at work in human life. It is fundamentally contrary to certain other strong and ever active tendencies and interests of mankind. Religion bids man reverence a law and power above him, but the gods have given to man not only the sense of justice and reverence, as Plato tells us, but also self-assertion and the lust for power. The forces developed and selected in the struggle for existence have indeed touched man's heart with sympathy, but they have also made him keen to grasp and to hold. The extraordinary range of communication, of credit, of resources in earth, ocean, and sky, which modern science and invention have brought into man's ken have but intensified the zeal as they have enlarged the field of these primeval passions. The voice of religion, even when it has sounded clear and true, has fallen on ears in which the voices of this world are calling in ever louder tones and richer harmonies. Small wonder that, whatever the nominal adherence of men to outward forms, few listen to the voice of a Master who bids the faithful leave all and follow him. And especially today, when the cathedral no longer dominates the city, when in fact office buildings, banks, shops, and factories have practically banished the church spire from the centers of power, when the church feels itself fortunate if, instead of the two days or one day in the week which it once controlled, it can now claim an hour from golf or business interests or studies, when the wheels of many industries and of transportation stay not even for this one hour, it is surely asking much of religion to expect it to prevent a war. If it can scarcely interfere with a golf game, can it be expected to halt a battleship or an army?

Without attempting to estimate how much of truth there may be in these two answers, I shall assume for the present purpose that there is still in the world such a thing as religion, and shall ask whether there is work for it to do. I do not propose to consider at all its truth or error; I simply assume it as one of the present facts and forces in the world, along with certain other facts and forces of human nature. As such, we may consider what it fundamentally signifies, and what part it has to play in securing a better world-order.

In view of certain types of religious appeal, it seems necessary to notice two or three aspects or types of religion—widespread, significant for certain purposes or at certain times—which do not appear to offer great promise for the matter in hand.

First, ritual. Ritual is perhaps the oldest aspect of religion; certainly it is very early. It was a force in the New Stone Age. It is no less effective in Buddhism, Judaism, Mohammedanism, and Christianity. It impresses upon the young the traditions of the past; it brings a sense of mystery and solemnity; it enhances and elevates emotion. But ritual as such, and the piety which finds chief expression in ritual, has little to say when the great need is of reconstructing society. Of ritual, certainly there was no lack in 1914. The orthodox Greek of Russia and the Balkan states was unsurpassed in his devotion to ritual. The Mohammedan's call to prayer sounded daily. Catholic and Lutheran showed no intermission of mass, sacrament, or prayer. These might then symbolize, as they have symbolized through the ages, the deeper significance of certain great experiences of human life. They console the dying and the sorrowful. They do not seem to meet the particular need which we now contemplate.

Nor is it the mystical type of personal religion which offers promise. The essence of this mystical type is its withdrawal from the clashing antagonisms and fierce passions of this world to find calm and peace in the eternal. To individuals it may bring relief. But society cannot withdraw into the mystic experience.

Nor is what is frequently called the 'old-fashioned gospel' the kind of religion to which the world may look for any important contribution toward society's present need. Some persons who are perhaps fearful lest religion should interfere with their methods of conducting business and industry and take an uncomfortably active part in the world of affairs are frequently heard to clamor for a return to this type of religion. It does not meddle; it takes no stand on social, political, or economic questions; its concern is with saving the soul. The old-fashioned gospel is usually assumed to emphasize three things: first, a story of certain historic events of nineteen centuries ago; second, certain dogmas interpreting these events in terms of metaphysical conceptions; third, certain emotional experiences undergone by the individual under the influence of these events and dogmas. I do not wish to speak slightingly of what this type of religion may have done for individuals. It has, no doubt, played its part in the making of individual character. My grandfather preached it. I have read numbers of his sermons. I do not think anyone could discover from them whether they were prepared and preached in Vermont or Judea, in the seventeenth century or the nineteenth. They dealt with the timeless and placeless themes of sin, atonement, conversion, and the future life, with no reference to any social, political, or economic fact. The personal religion which interpreted its experience in those terms had little direct bearing on behavior in public life. In the days before and during our Civil War, men of equal piety and of equally sincere and devout personal religion were on opposite sides of the question of slavery. In this last Great War, the same was doubtless true. The man who was very generally charged with being more than any other one man responsible for the final decision was rather notably faithful in his religious observance. It is then something more than the so-called old-fashioned religion, or personal religion, that is needed.

But religion has had another side. It has not only appealed to the individual soul; it has sought to transform society. It was nothing less than a new social, political, and economic order which the prophets of Israel heralded; it was a social revolution which Jesus proclaimed in his Sermon on the Mount. It is this social aspect of religion which must assert itself at the present time if it is to contribute to a better world-order.

There is, however, one great attitude of individual and social religion alike which has a fundamental place. That is the bold assertion of faith. The equilibrium between faith and knowledge is difficult to preserve. The Middle Ages, we say, were ages of faith. There was then too little of knowledge, too little regard for science. At present we have a vast increase in scientific knowledge. We know more of human nature through our psychology and biology, we know more of history, more of economic, political, and social facts; and no one can say that we know too much. But there is such a thing as being so overwhelmed by the multitude of facts as to be blind to their profounder implications and timid in our dealings with them. We are assured, for example, that man has always been pugnacious and violent in the assertion of his interests; therefore wars can never cease. We are told that races are different and therefore that there can be no common ground except on the assumption of fixed superiority and inferiority. We are told that the economic tendency of capitalism is to produce in far greater measure than civilized countries can consume, and therefore that the irresistible and inevitable result is and must be the exploitation of backward peoples and the oppression of the weak. We are told that the will to power is so fundamental a part of human nature that when it is organized into political states or economic corporations nothing can successfully restrain or oppose it. The race for power is bound to go on, even though it crush civilization and all that humanity holds dear in its progress. We are told that the struggle for existence is so fundamental a process that we neither can nor ought to interfere with its course.

These conclusions would indeed tend to paralyze action if unrelieved by any other considerations. They remind us of the logic by which slavery was proved essential to civilization, aristocracy essential to secure government, child labor necessary in order to make industry profitable. But aside from the question as to whether the logic is rigorous, there is a fundamental challenge to the premises which religion has always dared. Over against facts which can be demonstrated and measured, it has asserted possibilities in man and in the universe which cannot be completely demonstrated. It has believed in soul and God. Granted that science as such can recognize no soul and find no God—consider even, if you please, that soul and God are audacious fictions, or at least that they are unprovable postulates—religion maintains, nevertheless, that there is such a reality as moral freedom, moral responsibility, moral courage, and moral worth in man, and that the universe is not merely and exclusively mechanism. In other words, religion maintains that there is, in the moral meaning of that word, a soul in man, and that the universe is in some sense kin to spirit. Staking itself upon this belief, religion has moved forward to great enterprises. It has attempted to lift individuals, races, and peoples from degradation and barbarism, in the faith that they have souls. It has joined hands with democracy in bold defiance to plain hard 'fact.' It has asserted that before the bar of God, that is to say in their claims to fair treatment and fair opportunity, all souls are equal. There, says Plato, men are stripped of all distinctions of wealth and rank, and stand face to face, naked soul with naked soul. More audacious still, in its doctrine of immortality, religion has ascribed to the soul a worth transcending the bounds of time.

At the present time, is anything more needed than faith in the moral possibilities and worth of human nature? Not that we are to shut our eyes to what biology, psychology, and social science have taught and are still to teach. But all these teachings are simply tools with which we build our house. For themselves they build no houses;

they found no families; they save no souls; neither do they save societies. Granted that no fundamental and permanent reform in our economic conditions or our international relations can take place in neglect or defiance of the forces of human nature, nevertheless we shall woefully fail to meet the crucial situation of the present moment, if we ignore the power of spirit to achieve, to create, to build more stately mansions, to take wider and more generous interests.

Religion has also asserted faith in God. What does this mean in moral terms? Is it not essentially the same thing as applied to the universe which belief in the soul means as applied to man? Certain it is that it is very difficult, if not impossible, to *demonstrate* any power not ourselves that makes for righteousness. Some minds are indeed so repelled by what they find in the universe about them that they can see in it no encouragement to look for more than a transient day for man and all his values. Man is the outcome, says Russell, of "an alien and inhuman world," alone amid hostile forces,

> powerless before the blind hurry of the universe from vanity to vanity. . . . That man is the product of causes which have no prevision of the end they were achieving; that his origin, his growth, his hopes and fears, his loves and his beliefs, are but the outcome of accidental collocations of atoms; that no fire, no heroism, no intensity of thought and feeling, can preserve an individual life beyond the grave; that all the labors of the ages, all the devotion, all the inspiration, all the noonday brightness of human genius, are destined to extinction in the vast death of the solar system, and that the whole temple of man's achievement must inevitably be buried beneath the debris of a universe in ruins—all these things if not quite beyond dispute, are yet so nearly certain, that no philosophy which rejects them can hope to stand. Only within the scaffolding of these truths, only on the firm foundation of unyielding despair, can the soul's habitation henceforth be safely built.[1]

Like Job, who holds fast to his integrity in the face of a seemingly immoral, or at least unmoral, power; like Prometheus, who defies the Zeus that has fastened him to the rock for bringing the divine fire to mortals, Mr. Russell finds the object of the free man's worship not in the cosmos without, but in the ideal of goodness which man may set up from within.

Now, whether rightly or wrongly, religion has never acquiesced in the doctrine that the universe is absolutely unmoral, naked power.

1. Bertrand Russell, "A Free Man's Worship," *Independent Review* December 1903.

The protest to the Everlasting No has not limited its range to man's own soul. It has asserted a confidence that somehow there are moral forces in the universe. If we distinguish as Huxley has done so keenly between cosmic process and ethical process, religion has nevertheless believed that man's moral nature, his soul if you please, no less than his body with its passions and appetites, is rooted in the nature of things. Sometimes in its story of beginnings, according to which God created man in his own image; sometimes by carrying over into the Unseen the attributes of fatherhood, of love, of justice; sometimes in the subtler interpretations of nature with which an Emerson surveys the laws of compensation or a Wordsworth finds duty in the most ancient heavens—in all these the fundamental religious aspiration and faith are uttered that there are possibilities not yet completely observed and demonstrated, which are, did we but know them, on the side of good; that there are resources not yet exploited upon which we may count for the completion of the house we have begun to build.

A faith of this sort may have a very vital and important part in a better world-order. We are told that one of the greatest obstacles to the resumption of normal production and trade in many regions of Europe is despair of the future. There is indeed enough to justify despair if we consider, not merely what has been, but the resources which we are told science can bring to bear in the next war. What use in accumulating treasures to be destroyed? What use in bearing and rearing children to be food for cannon, to be drowned under the sea, to be dashed headlong from the clouds, to be choked and poisoned by gases? There is ground enough for suspicions and jealousies, for fear and discouragement. If the world is not to yield to these suspicions and fears two things seem to be equally necessary. One is the determination to take all practical means to avoid these threatening evils; the other is a willingness to take some risks in the great adventure of a better world-order. The good faith of France and Germany or Russia or Japan is not a matter of demonstration any more than Heaven or a better moral order has ever been a matter of demonstration. It has always been largely an adventure of faith.

In the third place, religion has meant a faith in the possibility of change, of regeneration, of new birth, for men and society. In the past, this has often, although not always, been conceived as a miraculous event. By some of philosophic temper it has been conceived as due to a larger perspective, a vision of the great values which quenches the fiercer divisive passions. No one has expressed this latter conception more profoundly than Spinoza. Men are jealous and envious and hostile because they have such limited and partial views of what is good. Each sees but a little way, and conceives that his own gain is his neighbor's loss, and that his neighbor's gain is his loss. A larger vision would enlighten us. If we but looked at the world and at life, not from the narrow vision of the present moment, but from the point of view of eternity, we should see these divisions between us fall away. All are but parts of a larger whole. In the presence of this vision of ourselves as parts of a moral universe that we call God, our passions grow calm.

What Spinoza attributed to knowledge, others have assigned to love. Lusts of the flesh master us, and the law proves weak to deliver us. But the love of God has the power to subdue human passions. In the presence of this supreme reality, this supreme worth of pure, unselfish love, the harder, fiercer appetites and interests soften. Various works of kindness and helpfulness which practically all religions have made a part of their program have been an expression of this conception. No doubt charity has often been mixed with feelings of class or with conceptions of merit. No doubt it has sometimes been used as a veil to cover up the deeper-seated diseases of society which call for justice. Nonetheless, he was a great philosopher of values, as well as apostle of religion, who set love above knowledge, above visions, above all else in its enduring worth—"but the greatest of these is love."

Faith in the possibility of regenerating society, not by miracle, but by the great and profound agencies of larger vision of life's true values and of love to mankind, has a place in a better world-order. Without this our inventions, our statistics, our economic science, and even our world conferences for limitations of armaments will fall short of their objectives. When the nations have calmed their passions, General Diaz told us in a public address, arms will drop from their hands. I do not think we need to wait until they drop entirely of themselves; by mutual consent we may agree to lay aside at least a percentage of our guns and warships, and this very act will in itself help to calm the passions. Nevertheless, it will make a great difference whether we believe that as things have been, so they must always continue to be, or whether we have faith that human nature can improve, that nations as well as individuals may have a change of heart.

We have frequently been reminded of the great step taken by our fathers when they made the agreement of 1817 for the limitation of ships of war on the Great Lakes. The men who made this agreement were, in one sense of the word, not visionaries; they were sagacious and in the best sense practical. Nonetheless, they were making a bold experiment. If they had believed that human nature could not change for the better, they might well have distrusted the safety of such a step. They had in many ways more grounds than we for fear; but they took counsel of hope, and not of fear; they staked something on the possibilities of regenerating human society and building a better house than that in which the world till then had lived. It was a profoundly religious attitude—religious in its vision, religious in its faith, religious in its purpose. If the world today could combine with its science and sagacity a larger measure of faith like theirs, who can deny that it would at least be a magnificent venture. In such a cause, it is better to venture much than to lose all by too great distrust.

Coming at last to the more definitely social aspect of religion, we find this expressed in some sort of community. In early days this religious community was limited to the kinship group. Family or tribe or nation had its god; other families or tribes or nations had theirs. The bond which united the 'we-group' was at the same time the means of dividing the 'we-group' all the more sharply from the 'others-group.' Between followers of Jehovah and followers of Baal there must be war to extermination. "Accept Allah and Mohammed his Prophet, or perish by the sword." And when Europe portioned out its religious boundaries on the basis of *cuius regio eius religio*, the religious community was subservient to political power. Wars of religion, as well as wars for glory and wars for gain, have vexed the world.

But despite all these separatist and nationalistic limitations of religion, a deeper and more unifying tendency has emerged. It has found expression in religious communities not identical with political, racial, or economic groups. Communities of believers united by devotion to some cause, by sympathy under some oppression, by loyalty to some leader, have embodied a larger unity. Such was the little community of believers in Jerusalem. And underneath all divisions of today, the sympathy that is felt with the suffering of all lands, the deep desire to realize in some degree that brotherhood of man, of which religion has so often spoken, are the basis of a genuine, if as yet unorganized, spiritual kinship.

Religion in its social aspect has stood not only for a community, but for a just society. More than four thousand years ago, in ancient Egypt, justice found its place in the divine attributes and in the conception of a social order. The prophets of Israel, in their indignation at the wrongs they saw about them, found assurance for their moral consciousness in the justice of the coming king of the new age. In

Greece the just society was for Plato the city whose pattern is laid up in heaven. *Justitia* had her place in the Roman Pantheon. Two root ideas seem to have combined in religious conceptions of justice: One, springing from ancient blood and religious kinship, and reinforced by conceptions of the worth of all souls, has insisted upon protection to the orphan and the widow, to the poor and him that hath no helper. The idea appears in what today we call social justice. The other root springs from the soil of a supposed divine order. As the stars keep their appointed courses, as every part of this universe which the Greeks fittingly called the cosmos has its place in a system, so should order obtain in human affairs. "Nothing too much" was the motto of the Delphic temple. Arrogant pride and anarchy were alike abhorrent to the gods of Greece and of Israel. Rather, says religion, let all recognize the majesty of law, whose "seat is the bosom of God, whose voice is the harmony of the world, to whom all things do homage, the very least as feeling her care, the greatest as not exempted from her power."

These noble conceptions were indeed twisted and perverted by influences derived from certain vindictive elements of human justice. It is, perhaps, significant that Israel's God, when he proclaims himself as "visiting the iniquities of the father upon the children unto the third and fourth generation," styles himself the "jealous God," not the just God. Vengeance upon enemies was a natural attitude in early days. But Rhadamanthus, though inexorable and stern, would show no partiality, and it is notable that Christianity in its conception of redemption and atonement tried to mitigate the more rigorous conception of imperial authority and impersonal order by the old personal and humane conception of the next-of-kin who would represent and protect his brethren. Justice and love were somehow to unite.

In the task that lies before the builders of the better world, only large and generous conceptions of justice will serve the day. No adjustments of boundaries or balances that will not in the long run commend themselves to the conscience of the future, which is perhaps the nearest we can come to a criterion of religious justice, will accomplish the largest results. To establish a world-order—call it a league if you like one word, call it an association if you like another—in which law, not power, shall rule, in which each people shall be enabled to contribute as members to the welfare of all, in which weaker classes and backward peoples shall be protected from greed and aggression—this is a task in which the religious conception of justice should be the spirit within the wheels.

As we look upon the actual situation in the organized religions of today, it is undoubtedly with mixed feelings of hope and depression. Churches, synagogues, mosques, and temples seem helpless in many things; they do not exercise the influence upon statesmen, or men of affairs, or upon the ranks of labor which we might expect if they were less divided. Their hold upon the intellect of the day seems tenuous. Their very beliefs, as embodied in the symbols now in use, seem no longer charged with the fullness of fervor and conviction that once led men gladly to die in their behalf. The great realities of present experience do not seem to find their most vital expression in the language of the pulpit, the altar, or the hymn. And it is not completely satisfactory to charge religious indifference to the superior attractions of golf, or the automobile, or the movies, or to the native unresponsiveness of men of higher and finer things. I fear that religious teachers must bear their share of the blame, if blame there be. It is no doubt an era of transition between the imagery, doctrines, and conceptions which served to interpret man's deeper life in days past, and those as yet unframed symbols and conceptions which shall both interpret and inform the deeper life of the future:

> But now the old is out of date;
> The new is not yet born.

Yet, while we await the new, we may, if we are sensitive to the deeper life of our time, find religion in many a type of expression which is not tagged with an ecclesiastical label. The beloved community has other language than that of creeds, and other organs than church or synagogue.

One of these institutions of religious spirit and influence should be the institution of education. In a notable address, the late President Harper spoke of the university as representing in present-day democracy of threefold function of the religious organization of ancient Israel. The university, he suggested, is today serving democracy as prophet, priest, and king. Similarly, are not college and university called to serve a genuine religious function both in our domestic economic and industrial order, and in the international world-order toward which we are being irresistibly driven? In wartime colleges and universities in all lands contributed to the resources of their governments. But all college and university men, I am confident, would feel it a far greater privilege to contribute to the constructing and unifying forces of a better day. In ways somewhat inarticulate, they are indeed so contributing. The world of ideas is not, like the world of material interests, in its nature exclusive. Our sick are healed through the researches of a Pasteur and a Behrens, a Lister, an Ehrlich, a Noguchi. Generous rivalry in the promotion of truth unites. The presence of students from all parts of the world sitting side by side as they now sit in all our larger universities is a significant and hopeful sign of the unifying function of education.

And besides the organized agencies there is a third agency, in some respects the broadest channel of unifying feeling—the world of arts and letters. Art has many functions—to give joy, to make us forget grim reality, or to enable us to apprehend it more profoundly and so to appreciate its pathos, its tragedy, and its humor. But, as Tolstoy so forcefully insisted, it has for one of its functions the task of uniting men through common sympathies. The opportunities of the present day for sharing the great creations of literature which stir in us the common and uniting emotions are greater than ever before. It may not be in the near future that we shall experience

> One common wave of thought and joy,
> Lifting mankind again,

but as we are learning, through their art and literature, to understand the peoples of the earth better, and to sympathize more fully with all sorts and conditions of men everywhere through realistic portrayal of their daily life, or through imaginative symbols of their aspirations, we surely have the media for a broader community of feeling, the materials for what may ultimately be a wider religious community than has yet been organized under any creed or found its unity in any ecclesiastical assembly.

The Kingdom of God, we have to remind ourselves, cometh not with observation. The filaments that bind together men and peoples into a freer, juster, more harmonious and helpful order, are subtle and often invisible. They are spun from many materials. Many were torn apart in the Great War. But the needs of men are at work in bringing divided peoples together. From exchanges of goods and services, from intercommunication of knowledge and ideas, from aid to suffering children or famine-stricken provinces, from the world of art and letters, new filaments are being spun. The conference at Washington, so far as it brings men together and attempts a method of reason rather than of force, is one such uniting bond. If the conference had taken place in Judea, it would belong to sacred history. It is a test of our own religious insight that we recognize the significance of all these many expressions of the religious motive. It is a test of our own religious faith if we find opportunities for its expression, not only in the recognized channels of older language and older activities, but also in the language and activities of our own day. And despite cynicism, if we are genuinely religious, we shall make our own the faith of Lincoln—the faith that right makes might.

25   A University Chapel

We lay today the cornerstone of the University Chapel. In accord with the desire of the founder, its tower and vault will rise as the "central and dominant feature of the University group." It is to symbolize the place of the "spirit of religion." It is to stand for a "feeling" that inspires all its departments. It is to tell in its own language that all the work of the university "is directed to the highest ends."

Such has been declared to be the aim of this building. Such a declaration would have raised no question when Oxford's towers were rising, when the schools of Paris clustered about Notre Dame, or when Harvard was founded, *Pro Christo et Ecclesia*. But the passerby and even the university member today may, I doubt not, have in his mind a question, "Why a chapel?" The university stands for science; science and religion are at least different in their aims. How then can religious feeling inspire all departments of the university, and how, in turn, can a scientific spirit find itself completed in religion?

Great questions, these; too great for adequate discussion at this hour, or in this day, when science is only in its beginnings, and new reconstruction in religion is yet to come. Still we may not wholly ignore them, for they present the problem to be worked out if this university chapel is to fulfill the purposes and hopes which prompt its building.

The university is in truth not a church, nor is this structure a church or a cathedral. The direct and immediate purposes of the university are the enlargement of knowledge, the education of successive generations, and the training of men and women for their professions to meet society's needs. Its lecture halls, laboratories, libraries—from Harper and Ryerson to Theology and Billings—speak broadly one

Reprinted by permission of the publisher from James Hayden Tufts, "A University Chapel," *Journal of Religion* 6.5 (1926), 449–456 [1926:01].

language and are animated by one spirit. What is the spirit and feeling which it is hoped will find its awakening and larger consummation in this building which seems to bespeak a different purpose?

Before we attempt to answer directly, let us be clear that it is the spirit of religion, and religious feeling that we are to foster; we do not commit ourselves to any formulations through which men in past ages have attempted to symbolize this spirit and feeling. The symbols which men have hitherto framed to convey what they have deeply felt, or ardently aspired to, or in great moments envisaged, were all for the most part conceived in imagery of long ago. They differ in different religions. They gather associations of long familiarity and deeply rooted sentiment, and tend to be identified with the very essence of religion itself. They inevitably come into conflict with advancing thought. But the symbols are not the spirit. We remember also that science too has its symbols and that some of these are from time to time outgrown. Even now it speaks of mechanisms, atoms, and forces without taking these terms too seriously, for such terms of the childhood of science seem scarcely adequate to interpret the universe as it appears today.

What we have to consider in both science and religion is not the symbols, but the spirit and feeling. We know well the spirit of science. It is, in a word, the search for truth. What is the spirit of religion? In its deepest root, although not always in its visible form, religion springs from a certain divine discontent. Man is, on the one hand, limited; he is a very tiny part of the world he sees; his powers are puny; his glimpses of meanings are fragmentary; the good he would, he does not; he encounters pain and death. Yet, just as truly, he refuses to recognize or accept limits to his enterprise of knowledge, his control of nature, his achievement of good. He is not content to view himself with all his conscious life as a being separate and different from this world of movement. He tends to respond in feeling, and also in action, as if to a kindred and living universe. He may not prove that what is good within him will find support and fulfillment in this universe, but he believes; and even thought it threaten to slay him, he strives to maintain his trust, and to help make good prevail. He does not rest in any partial version of the total meaning of things; he seeks somehow, if not to know, at least to feel life and the universe in all their wholeness.

This underlying root has put forth many forms of stem and leaf. It has borne many kinds of fruit. The desire to gain the aid of unseen powers, the response to what seemed personal behavior in the move-

ment of natural forms, the wonder at the season's changes or the cycle
of birth and death, the thrill of kindred feeling and ancestral reverence,
the aspiration toward some distant good, the struggle against defeat
and evil—all these were different gropings of a mind that is limited
yet not content. But crude as were the beginnings in simple rituals or
in efforts to interpret them, nonetheless the half-felt, half-imagined
companionship with nature kept alive the consciousness in man that
his reach ever exceeds his grasp. They were a constant reminder that
man and nature are somehow one. If many of those earlier imagined
possibilities of identification with the universe or of control over its
forces by ritual seem now a dream, it is nonetheless true that this
dream, in the words of America's foremost living philosopher, "implies a unity with the universe that is to be preserved."[1]

As intelligence grew and new powers and objects of desire and
aspiration came into view, products of many kinds appeared. Kinship
to a common deity knit tribal members in closer ties. Trust in this
tribal protector led men to beware of offending him by trespass or
disobedience. His holiness called for purity, and purity was gradually
transformed from purity of hands to purity of heart. Sabbaths became
symbols of peace. The second birth, the craving for a union with
the Deity which would guarantee escape from death, helped man in
deeper sense to put off his mortality and find release from the evil
which dogged his steps. To resist death, he reared pyramids; to find
fitting home for sublimity, beauty, or tender grace, he built the Par-
thenon, the Gothic vaults and windows. When he found himself
helpless under calamity, a Job, an Aeschylus, presented evil and
destiny as poignant and tragic facts which may not be denied. Yet, on
the other hand, faith that somehow good must triumph embodied its
hopes of peace and justice in a vision of a Kingdom of God. Love was
set as a supreme value in place of power. National bounds and class
distinctions were crossed. Many a restless soul rose above conflicts
within and clash of arms without to affirm, "His will is our peace." In
our own country the doctrine that all souls are equal before God has
been a reinforcement of fundamental democracy. Our colleges and
universities have, many of them, been founded from religious motives. Our philanthropy has had in these a principal source. Other
values than power, wealth, pleasure have been set before men for
their choice.

Despite such contributions of religion in the past, we stand today

1. John Dewey, *Experience and Nature* (Chicago: Open Court, 1925) 420.

at a turn in religion and society which seems to repeat with greater emphasis the question we have already asked as to the place of religion in the university. For in the extraordinary change taking place in symbols of religion, many find it difficult to believe that religion abides while symbols are changed. The whole system of ideas and imagery which has formed the framework and pattern of Christian doctrine for the Western world since Augustine's *City of God* is now in flux. The thoughtful seek new interpretations of this unity of man and his world of ideals, but no new ways of thought have as yet met at once the demands of the scholar and the claims of the heart which clings to the wonted and familiar and fears to lose all if it loses the form. The religion of a university chapel may at least avoid this snare. For those who have gained in a university even occasional glimpses of the long, slow road of man's progress in religious as well as in scientific ideas and have had their look turned also to the rich and quenchless life which has been constantly seeking to fulfill its visions will not easily confuse symbol with inner reality.

And a university chapel will not be disturbed by a second perplexity in which religion and society find themselves as to social responsibilities which in the past have been carried by religion. At present society finds its situations so complex that it calls increasingly upon professional and expert aid, or it appeals to the authority and resources of the state. Or it even hopes to abolish poverty and prevent wars by financial and economic agencies which have in time past been under suspicion as antisocial. Now the university itself is taking a leading part in just these functions. It is investigating the causes of evils which religion has confronted for centuries. It is trying to understand the forces of the modern city which destroy the older bonds and restraints and tend to leave the dwellers detached, homeless, religionless, and too often lawless, units. Its laboratories aim to make nature the friend of man. Its schools of medicine will carry on the ancient task of healing and add the newer task of prevention of disease. Its school of social service administration fits for the personal guidance and relief which belonged formerly under the cure of souls. It is thus directing work to highest ends.

And yet society dares not trust any of its deepest interests completely and unreservedly to a profession. Perhaps it fears that head and heart may somehow become separate. At any rate, it has refused to entrust justice to the sole guardianship of the law, or health to the physician, or education to the teacher. It is only through the deeper unities, through sympathies and contacts of many types, that we supplement the abstractness of our special and partial pursuits. It is, then, our hope that in our chapel the spirit of service to mankind in its special forms will find reinforcement in common purpose and feeling; that our partial interests and sympathies will be broadened and deepened by contacts with those of like minds and hearts; and that the common purpose will find renewed vitality and ampler range as the ties which bind mankind are felt to be but manifestations of the larger life in which we share.

Yet the central fact as to this building and all the service it may render remains to be stated. This chapel is primarily for the young. And certainly the young of today have not merely the needs of youth in all ages which religion has aimed especially to meet; they have peculiar conflicts, some thrust upon them by the war, some due to changes in civilization itself. They are confronting one of the most fundamental reconstructions of morals which the world has known. Inventions which multiply our powers beyond previous dreams, un-exampled wealth and luxury, city life, violent experiments of radical-ism in Russia, extreme reactions of political conservatism and religious conservatism in this and other countries, the divided attitude of re-spected citizens toward observance of law—all this may well bewilder mind and conscience. Youth, we say, should learn from age, but what wisdom has age now to offer? Can we wonder if the youth who finds such confusion in the present world should, like Descartes, resolve to doubt?

What has the religion of this chapel to offer him?

First, a religion for the young will emphasize open-mindedness to truth of every kind. It will be infused by the same experimental spirit which animates the best work of a university in all fields. It will be slow to close any door. It will be sure of but one maxim, that there is more in heaven and earth than is dreamed of in our philosophies. It will be sensitive to meanings and values which are not always capable of scientific formulation. It will remember that the individual and the personal, and therefore perhaps the universe itself, can never be exhausted by any of our concepts, for these are only ways of looking, which give different facets, not the whole—or, if you will, they are cross sections of the stream whose beginnings and future are alike beyond our horizon. It will cherish the religious vision in the phrase of Whitehead as "an adventure of the spirit."[2]

2. Alfred North Whitehead, *Science and the Modern World* (New York: Macmillan, 1925) 269.

In the second place, the religion of a chapel for the young should present great problems and high tasks. Those who know best the character and questionings of students are not likely to make the mistake of supposing that religion for the young means a religion that is superficial or a call to a life that is easy. The danger is rather that we elders conceive life too readily in terms of accepted ways, and under the specious maxim of being 'practical' fall short of offering worthy objects of loyalty and devotion. We who saw the young college men and women of 1917 cannot listen patiently to doubts of skeptics or aspersions of cynics. The young of today are as ready to be loyal to a great cause as they who followed St. Bernard to Clairvaux. "Show us," they say, "the reality of the values, the genuine claims of the cause which you offer." Religion in a university chapel may not forget the scientific spirit and mistake emotion for intelligent and resolute endeavor, but it will remember also that few great steps forward in human progress have been made without vision and enthusiasm. Often in history it has been the young who have seen this vision and felt the kindling of a passion that breaks new paths.

Finally, the religion of a university chapel may, through worship, unite all the pervasive influences of art to bring in fuller measure joy, enhancement, and harmony. This again is not a distinctive experience unknown and unfelt by scientist and scholar. Each field of nature, each type of language, each monument of the past, each institution of human society, offers material for fascination and for wonder. Quite apart from uses to other ends, there is a delight in discovery, a quickening of spirit when hitherto unrelated facts fall into order and yield new meanings. We work for the joy of working. But the young, especially, find it hard to keep unremittingly at tasks which in later years will become the very habit and structure of body and mind. Indeed, when we consider the conditions under which the human body and mind took form, and then consider the complexity of the culture which is to be mastered and of the morals to which conformity is asked, the wonder is perhaps that the young do not oftener grow discouraged or rebel.

When relief is sought, it is easy to turn to forms of recreation which amuse but give no calm. Perhaps our students need nothing so much as the deeper and ordered rhythms of noble music, the poet's imagery, the conflicts and stresses resolved, and all the influences transmitted through the arts which in such a building will find a fitting home. For these suggest meanings not otherwise perceived; they unite in common feeling; they admit no separation of part and whole, of each and all. Even to those who cannot and will not deny the tragic sense of life they bring broader sympathy and deeper intuition. They at once stir and satisfy the divine discontent; they open a way to the experience of God.

26 Individualism and American Life

It is more or less commonly assumed that the outstanding and even the essential characteristic of American life is individualism. Since the Great War with its extraordinary experiments in collective and unified control of our productive system, the pendulum has swung toward individualistic policies. 'Less government in business, more business in government' has been the popular slogan. The war showed what could be done, even though several millions of the most vigorous men were withdrawn from our productive forces, when the great aim was to produce rather than to make a profit, but the war also opened vistas of more magnificent possibilities in business empire. And undoubtedly war sets a pace too stiff to be easily maintained in time of peace.

Moreover, after a temporary pause, general prosperity seemed to prevail and attain unexampled heights—except, of course, among the farmers. The climax of success seems to have been reached when millions have been added to bank accounts by shrewd speculation without necessity of any productive industry. Prosperity has apparently set its seal upon the policy of noninterference with the individual, particularly upon the unchecked expansion of the profit motive.

The courts have to some degree appeared to sympathize with this return to individualism: After reaching a maximum of control in the Oregon case limiting the working day for women, and in the Oklahoma case upholding the state in requiring banks to guarantee mutually their deposits, the federal Supreme Court refused its sanction to a law restricting child labor in the District of Columbia, to the Kansas Industrial Court Act, and recently to a statute of Tennessee declaring the trade in petroleum to be affected with a public interest.

Legislative bodies have shown a similar trend. Few state legislatures

From *Essays in Honor of John Dewey* (New York: Holt, 1929) 389–401 [1929:01].

have approved the proposed child labor amendment; the railroads have been returned to private management; a resentment against any social control which might threaten a check to prosperity has been frequently in evidence. The Eighteenth Amendment may seem to be an exception, but the opposition to its enforcement voiced by many who cannot be suspected of merely selfish interest is at least in part indicative of impatience with any restriction by government upon the freedom of the individual, no matter what the consequences for social welfare.

Recently individualism has received more distinguished sponsorship than that of academic authority. Mr. Hoover, when Secretary of Commerce, gave the sanction of his great name and prestige to what he called American Individualism.[1] As a candidate for the presidency he reasserted his faith, and his election may seem to imply the acceptance of this doctrine by a large majority of the American people. It is, however, important in the interest of clear thinking to discover just what qualification of individualism is covered by the adjective 'American.' It may be that the magic of the phrase owes more to the association of the term 'American'—standing as it does for a sum of patriotic, religious, and moral institutions, for the adventurous spirit of the pioneer, and the restless creative genius of the inventor, and indeed for a large share in those ties of kin, of place, of tradition, of familiar environment without which life is meager and for ordinary folk scarcely conceivable—than to any very intelligent conviction as to the merits of individualism. Moreover, Mr. Hoover's exposition of the content of individualism seems to include two distinct meanings. On the one hand, self-interest as motive and free competition as social process for selection are approved; on the other hand, the great propelling force of progress is found in "right ideals" by whose growth "through education the selfish impulses become less and less dominant," and of the "impulses which carry us forward none is so potent for progress as the yearning for individual self-expression, the desire for the creation of something." Of these two meanings the first is obviously the historic meaning of individualism. The second is in part an ideal of social as versus selfish nature, and in part the creative spirit—scientific, inventive, or artistic, the 'instinct for workmanship,' which is ordinarily included under 'individuality,' but has no necessary relation either to self-interest or to the opposite. We get additional

1. Herbert Hoover, *American Individualism* (Garden City: Doubleday Page, 1923).

James Hayden Tufts

light upon the importance of the adjective 'American' when we see
that Mr. Hoover contrasts the social system of his choice with 'old-
world individualism' (autocracy), with a system of fixed hereditary
classes, and with bureaucracy. He refuses to identify individualism
with capitalism although economists tell us that the United States is
the most capitalistic country in the world. His dislike of anything
savoring of socialism is a logical consequence of his attachment to
individualism in the first or historic sense of the term.

The ambiguities thus involved in Mr. Hoover's conception of the
actual and the ideal social system and its motivation suggest the two
divisions of this paper: (I) How far and in what respects is the American social system properly termed individualism? (II) Is the greatest
need at present to protect and strengthen the individualistic motive
of self-interest, or on the other hand to encourage the constructive,
scientific interest and the agencies of social solidarity?

I

(1) In its economic phase it may be freely admitted that American
life is individualistic to a great, though by no means exclusive, extent.
The essential character of individualism, so far as its motivation is
concerned, is to center regard in those interests which are exclusive
as contrasted with those that are shareable or social. Material goods
as objects of desire or considered as property are fundamentally exclusive. Acquisitiveness is undoubtedly an active factor in American
business life. True, as Justice Holmes points out, the man of great
wealth cannot consume more than a fraction of what he owns but the
title is his, and to a great extent the power to decide whether goods
shall be consumed and how. Economic power is at present largely
autocratic. Its taxing power, exercised through price and wage, is
seemingly less coercive, but really more omnipresent than that of
government.[2] And insofar as it is gained and administered under the
profit motive, economic power is individualistic. It may or may not be
so exercised as to benefit consumers and workmen. But this is as such
irrelevant. As Professor [Wesley C.] Mitchell puts it, "It is no fault of
the individual business leaders that they take profits as their own
guide. On the contrary they are compelled to do so, for the men who
mix too much philanthropy with business soon cease to be leaders."

2. The price of coal since the war is a good example. Every user who pays
the doubled price has found the pressure as actual as if administered by the
sheriff.

The theory has been that ultimate power rests with the consumer, and that the competition of the market selects as leaders the ablest and those who best supply wants. In some cases this is largely true, but supply of wants need not enter into the motives of the 'leader.' He need only consider profits, and these will sometimes be greatest by making what men need and sometimes by judicious sabotage with a corresponding scarcity price. In the frenzied stock speculation of the past year which a high financial authority has characterized as "incomparably the most gigantic gamble of history," the speculator is obviously guided by the profit motive. No question of contributing to social welfare, or of rendering any equivalent for value received need enter into the process. The motive of something for nothing is thoroughly individualistic, for it aims at adding to the possessions of the individual without requiring any expenditure of possessions or labor.

But while profit serves as a vigorous incentive to business and as a necessary condition if business is to remain solvent, it is far from being the sole actual incentive. Three other motives are active: first, the desire to make a fair return in some form—labor, ideas, useful material things, money—for what is gained or received; second, the adventurous spirit of the inventor and enterpriser, the instinct of workmanship; and third, the sporting interest of rivalry which in the opinion of William James is the principal incentive for getting the hard and disagreeable work of the world done. Of these three, the first—the desire to deal justly—is distinctly social; the second—the scientific or inventive, craftsmanship spirit—is an objective, 'disinterested' motive to achievement, and as such is neither social nor individualistic; the third is mixed, for insofar as it is a desire to win it is individualistic; insofar as it is a desire to win by fair means against an equal opponent it presupposes either a voluntary contest in which both parties share in the agreeable stimulation of the match as in sports and games, or a respect for a fellow being which makes the victor reluctant to press a brave rival too far. In other words it is what Veblen is fond of calling the attitude of live and let live. We wish to examine these three nonindividualistic motives briefly.

As regards the desire to deal justly, to give a fair return, it is doubtless possible to give this a turn by which just dealing is practiced as a means to greater self-interest. 'Honesty is the best policy' is a maxim which reflects such a view. Accounts by economists of the principle of exchange of commodities and services are likely to run in this form: If you want something which another man has, you must either get it by force as under militarism and slavery, or by his consent as in voluntary exchange. And to gain his consent you must offer what he considers a satisfactory equivalent. It cannot be questioned that this is the theory of much of the bargaining or higgling of the market. It could be stretched to justify unconscionable exploitation of native tribes provided their 'consent' was secured to the exchange of furs or lands or gold for glass beads or whiskey. And in modern business it may be said to have found an enlarged sphere in the strategy of 'overcoming sales-resistance' where the salesman aims, not so much at winning consent, as at the more fundamental task of creating desire. But it is needlessly damnatory of human nature, and in particular of American business and industry, to assume that this theory exhausts the meaning of dealing justly. What the law recognizes under the terms 'reasonable' or 'equitable,' what was included under 'honorable,' and later became the ethical standard of many bankers, merchants, and manufacturers, not merely excludes fraud, but forbids taking advantage of the ignorance of the other party; it implies a fair equivalent—fair in the estimation of a reasonable, disinterested third party; it implies under 'honorable dealing' the equality which holds in a group of mutual confidence and goodwill rather than the cautious suspicion of the primitive trader who must be ever alert and on the defensive.

Industry is in its essence more naturally governed by the theory of a fair equivalent than is business. The craftsman makes something. His labor and skill are real and the product is a visible, tangible thing, whereas in business honesty and fairness are less easily tested and departures into the different scheme of speculative values are less subject to any criterion except that of the market. The 'double standard' which the working man resents is that whereas he is expected to give a full equivalent for his wage, the man of business is esteemed shrewd in proportion as he makes large profits with a minimum expenditure of time and effort.

The adventurous, inventive scientific motive which has had a large place in American life is not individualistic except in that sense of the word in which it signifies the disposition to resent dictation and to seek a free field. It has no preference for that meaning of individualism which is identified with reliance upon self-interest. In fact a spirit of adventure, except on the part of chief executives, is likely to find the great business corporation as formidable as a bureaucracy. And the really great inventors, scientists, and creative minds are notoriously neglectful of self-interest. The greatest scientist I have known has said that he has prosecuted his investigations "for fun," and an inventor-manufacturer of my acquaintance, when arranging for the gift to education of a large part of his fortune remarked, "It was fun to make it, but I don't want the bother of it." The scientist wants a comfortable livelihood; the inventor wants means to develop his ideas and place his products before the public, but this is a different matter from making self-interest the chief motive.

Resentment of dictation is undoubtedly a strong force in American life. It had a large place in the restless frontier. It survives in the farmer. It is strong in many captains of industry who resist all government interference except that of a protective tariff. But the sweeping change in American life by which, instead of a nation of self-sufficient, independent farmers, each his own master, we have become a people in which at least two-thirds work for other men or corporations and are therefore in Aristotle's classifications of those who are directed by others, has scarcely favored this aspect of individualism. Indeed those familiar with the labor movement know that it is far from being solely a matter of wages and hours. The laborer of independent spirit resents the military discipline of the factory in which all orders issue from management, and no initiative or participation in determining conditions of work on the part of the employee is welcomed. Against this trend of 'individualistically' conducted industry, union has appeared to be the only defense. In union organization, standardizing labor conditions, setting a more democratically chosen control over against employer control, though often requiring a sacrifice of individual advantage in the common interest, is found at least a measure of what Mr. Sidney Hillman has called "citizenship in industry." The tendency on the part of some to emphasize the free field for the selection of leaders is liable to pass over the case of the rank and file.

As regards the final aspect of business mentioned above, viz., that of rivalry, motives are mixed. There is a well-known difference between cutthroat competition and fair competition. In the first the motive of individual self-interest is unchecked by any scruples. If scruples arise as to the ethics of ruining the competitor or taking his job, they are met by the comforting doctrine of survival of the fittest, nature's method of selecting leaders. In fair competition the motive of self-interest is held in restraint, subject to a regard for the competitor as a fellow human being and to rules of fair play which have come to formulation in the first instance usually as the decent or becoming behavior towards members of the same group and then have become broadened to such ethical principles as the golden rule, and to such legal doctrines as those relating to 'unfair competition.' It was not under the influence of self-interest that these conceptions gained recognition; it was through the legal or judicial premise of the public good, or the moral principle of live and let live, or the sporting principle of fair play among fellows—all social as distinguished from self-interest and individualism.

I conclude this brief survey of motives in business and industry with the summary: Business and industry are carried on from mixed motives of self-interest, of regard for fellow men and for the common weal, and of interest (neither self-interest nor social necessarily) in solving problems by constructive work, and in achievements.

(2) In its political and legal phases also American life combines individualistic with social and even with socialist doctrines. If our Declaration of Independence declares natural rights to be prior to governments, our Constitution emphasizes not only common defense but justice and the general welfare. When we were a nation of farmers individualism was a natural policy of government, but the shift first to slavery as a great commercial system and later to a system of business and industry collective and corporate has compelled a shift in governmental policy. The individual as a person has made way for the impersonal corporation of limited liability and unlimited term of life. Men increasingly live in cities stratified into social groups by the rent they are able to pay. The advance of science has made possible not only governmental control of railroads, banks, and other public utilities, but positive aid in promoting agricultural welfare, in conserving natural resources, in the zoning of cities, in providing parks and playgrounds. Most revolutionary of all, and registering a well-nigh complete abandonment of earlier individualistic views of property was the addition of the income tax amendment to the federal Constitution which embodies at least at least one fundamental principle of socialist doctrine, 'From each according to his ability.' All labor legislation has been in restraint of individualism, and the courts, at least, have upheld the Eighteenth Amendment even though this exercise of police power has been resisted by individualists to the verge of nullification and anarchism. The Fourteenth Amendment has not enacted for the United States Herbert Spencer's *Social Statics*. It is at least probable that as business and industry become more and more nationwide and gigantic in corporate power and resources the American people will dare not merely to control this power in the interest of the common

weal, but themselves as a collective unit to do what cannot be safely entrusted to individual or corporate interest motivated by profit.

(3) The religious consciousness of American life has shown a similar trend from a more individual to a more social point of view. Not that the earlier period was wholly concerned with saving individual souls. The Massachusetts colony was notably regarded by its members as a 'Holy Commonwealth.' The Kingdom of God, the *civitas dei*, the hope of the ages, was here at last to be established. The state was ruled by the clergy as a soviet. Later the presence of increasing numbers in the community who were motivated by secular interest, added to the influence of religious individualists and of religious societies other than those which had sought to establish the commonwealth, brought about a change. The Kingdom of God was again transferred to the other world. The elect, the converted, were here to prepare for heaven. The task of the clergy was to call to repentance. This was the typical conception during the eighteenth century and the early part of the nineteenth. But when slavery became a national problem the churches were forced to take account of a social institution. From that time the churches have never been without a social question. The temperance cause, the labor movement, municipal government, civic duties, social justice, the campaign against child labor—all these in turn have enlisted the sympathies and active philanthropic interest of the churches. The Friends, who were by tradition the most individualistic of all religious groups, were in the Great War foremost in succoring the unfortunate victims. Missionary policies have reflected the changed attitude and have been directed increasingly toward education and improvement of social conditions. Despite contemptuous epithets from the 'hard-boiled,' the churches continue to make their voices felt for humane conditions of labor, for world peace, and for the supremacy of social welfare over individualistic attitudes in the use of alcoholic beverages. The churches represent a very real and vital expression of the American spirit. And what they stand for is not individualism.

(4) The same is true in even higher degree in the activities and point of view of what has come to be called 'social work.' Perhaps the distinctive characteristic of this work is that it combines in a high degree the spirit of humane brotherhood which has been the inheritance of Christianity with scientific method of inquiry and experiment. Finding its beginnings in problems of voluntary charity on the one hand and of public provision for delinquents, defectives, sick, and insane on the other, the scope of inquiry and outlook has widened to

embrace city planning, recreation, race adjustments, immigration, juvenile courts, and indeed the whole field of social relations.[3] Numbers professionally engaged in social work may be relatively few, but the influence of these leaders has been wide. The response of the public in its care of the sick and insane, of the blind and defective, in its provision for parks and playgrounds, in its factory and child labor legislation, and legislation for protection of women in industry, in the establishment of great foundations dedicated to the tasks of preventing disease and otherwise improving social conditions, has been as characteristic of American life as the great development of business and industry.

(5) But neither the spirit of the churches nor that of social work is so peculiarly American as the general interest in education. Amid the extreme inequalities in wealth, in social status, in power and opportunity, produced by our economic individualism, here is at least an approach to that equality which is asserted by Mill to be the only school for true morality. If we have largely escaped the grim bitterness of soul, the sense of injustice in a land of plenty, and the hopeless sodden misery which are equally fatal to a good life and to a healthy society, this is chiefly due to our system of public education. It seems probable that such an institution is the only means of making workable an economic system which produces extremes of inequality and a political system based on equal suffrage. For our educational system is not merely an agency for the selection of 'leaders' through free competition. It is also an agency for giving the common man and woman and child a share in those goods of the mind which are our social inheritance. Those goods—a knowledge of the written word, of the world of nature and of man, of high thought, deep feeling, and noble deeds—are at least not wholly reserved for the few.

Equal opportunity, which Mr. Hoover esteems so highly as tempering the hardness of pure individualism, has had in our educational system much larger scope than in other fields of American institutions—even though it is painfully true that as the child moves on beyond the age of compulsory attendance he finds obstacles in the ignorance or poverty of his parents which too often close the door.

This great educational system, from the elementary grades to the

3. Robert Archey Woods and Albert J. Kennedy, *The Settlement Horizon: A National Estimate* (New York: Russell Sage Foundation, 1922) [cf. 1923:02]; Jane Addams, *Twenty Years at Hull House* (New York: Macmillan, 1910) [cf. 1911:02]; James Hayden Tufts, *Education and Training for Social Work* (New York: Russell Sage Foundation, 1923) [1923:01].

advanced research of the universities is in its conception, its financial support, its personnel, its motivation, social. It is even socialistic rather than individualistic. As carried on by government it violates the canons of Mill and Spencer. It aims to include all children on an equal basis, and relies for support upon all members of the community. In its provision for different classes it exemplifies the maxim 'To each according to his needs.' It bases its claim upon the welfare of the community and the aim to give every child a fair chance. Teachers and scientists give their services with very little profit motive. As members of a profession they feel that they perform a function in the social process, and find their chief reward in the consciousness of making some contribution to the welfare and progress of society. In the case of the more originative minds in the profession the scientific and constructive motive plays an important role.

'The aim to give every child a fair chance' is, it may be said, only another aspect of individualism, and particularly of American individualism. For this means giving every individual his opportunity, equipping him to hold his own, encouraging him to develop his individuality. This, however, is not individualism in the sense of motivation by self-interest. There is a chasm here between each-for-himself and each-for-all, as impassible as the similar chasm in Bentham's utilitarianism. Individualism of a liberal sort would not put a competitor out of the race by fouling or fraud or violence, but it has never regarded it as a duty to pay for the competitor's training or to provide him with the best running shoes.

This brief discussion of American life and institutions may then be summarized in the statement, American business, industry, and government are mixed in their conceptions and motivation; they are in part individualistic as recognizing self-interest and private property, and in part nonindividualistic as recognizing fairness, constructive interest, and the public good; American religious life, social work, and education are decidedly social in purpose and appeal. It is then inappropriate to choose individualism as an adequate term to characterize American life and institutions.

II

Is it desirable, even for the best interests of business, to stress at this time the appeal to self-interest?

The basis of shrinking from socialism—aside from the inappropriateness of a class war to American traditions—is perhaps due chiefly to two causes: (1) the desire by enterprising men of affairs that the fields for capitalistic exploitation of natural resources, of scientific discovery, of inventive genius, and of the concentration of great populations should remain open for private management, private profits, and private property rather than become the property of the commonwealth; (2) unwillingness to allow both economic power and political power to be concentrated in one authority and under one administration. Probably both these motives will continue to operate. The first has been given a longer lease by an increasing disposition on the part of some at least of the great organizations to distribute more widely the surplus profits either by higher wages or by reduced prices or by both. The prodigal wastes of natural resources, and of our distributing and selling systems, can be in part covered up, in part shifted to government or charity account, in part charged to economic reasons, or to interference by government with the economic free hand ('less government in business'). The force of this last plea in avoidance is strengthened by the circumstance that economic power exerted through price is impersonal and therefore seems less coercive than the personal political power exerted by legislatures, sheriffs, and courts, although for the great mass of the working people the economic control over wages and prices touches daily life at a dozen points where the legal and political power touches it at one. Taxation administered through process of rent or food is accepted as if proceeding from laws of an impersonal nature. Hence it seems not worthwhile to waste words upon warning the American people against state socialism.

But is there no evil in the economic motive of profit and self-interest? Mr. Hoover considers that there is danger, but also considers that this is met by public regulation and by the ideal of equal opportunity, which in American society qualifies individualism. I wish to suggest that even on economic grounds the profit motive in its extreme form of 'something for nothing' is suicidal, and that the most needed line of emphasis at present is the scientific and constructive spirit on the one hand, the principle of fairness and an active interest in the common good on the other.

Lest any economic suggestion from an academic source should be regarded as "destructive criticism of minds too weak or too partisan to harbor constructive ideas," the "criticism" of individualism may be taken from one who can scarcely be accused of a "passion for ignorance of its constructive ideals." Mr. Roger Babson writes, "Prosperity cannot last forever in a country where the speculators are making most of the money while the producers of the necessities of life are barely making both ends meet. . . . The weakest factor in the situation today is the growing belief that it is easier to make money in the stock market than at one's legitimate job."[4]

Yet it is hard to see why, on the principles of individualism, each individual should not do what will yield him most profit. Of course, if one asks whether general and sound prosperity can be secured by gambling that is something else. That doubtless depends on producing and distributing useful goods. Efficiency in such production and distribution depends largely on scientific advance and on the human factor, especially the goodwill of labor. If these are fundamental why not aim at them directly? It is not a case of substituting 'altruism' for self-interest. It is rather (1) recognizing and restoring to a normal place the scientific, constructive, or craft interest which is likely to be submerged in the race for profits, and (2) enlarging the range of vision to include not only the individual customers, capitalists, or laborers with whom one bargains or competes, but also society, and the community as a whole, in which there are functions to be performed, duties to be met, and larger ends to be achieved than the competitive process is likely to reckon with. American progress, it is commonly reputed, is due in largest degree to the substitution of machinery for manual labor, but inventors greater and lesser have been notoriously neglectful of pecuniary considerations in comparison with their absorption in working out the solution of a problem. To one who considers the extent to which a high sense of professional honor and public service has replaced the acquisitive motive in the field of government, it does not seem incredible that a similar conception of business as a profession and economic power as a trust because "affected by a public interest" may become increasingly common. Mr. Owen D. Young believes that the shift in responsibility from stockholders to a management which regards itself a trustee to the institution, embracing the interests not only of owners, but of workmen and the public as well, is a forward move towards what is right in business.

If we turn from business to the larger ends of civilization and ask what at the present time we need especially to guard and strengthen in the realm of motives, I should place first the promotion of goodwill between groups, classes, races, and nations. Individualism and the competitive spirit are scarcely adapted to secure this end. The Great War is still too near for us to forget that one factor in the complex situation of mutual fear, competition in armaments, and reaching out

4. Roger Ward Babson, "What about 1929?" *Collier's Weekly* 83 (1929): 8–9.

for markets and natural resources was the individualistic motive of self-interest, whether in its individual or in its national manifestation.

Even for family life, which perhaps ranks second only to international peace and goodwill, the path to good dwellings, to sanitation, hygiene, and protection against the risks of modern industrial society is likely to lie more and more through concerted action in which the state in its administrative functions does for individuals what they cannot well do for themselves. One instance may not prove a general proposition, but one instance made an indelible impression upon the mind of the writer. Traveling across England my eye was caught by a charming little village, with neat stone dwellings of attractive design. Inquiry brought the information that it was a mining village recently rebuilt by the government. I involuntarily compared it with the hideous, dreary, and forlorn mining dwellings which one sees from a train en route from New York to Chicago. In the one it was easy to imagine children growing up with love for home and community. In the other the only agreeable associations would seemingly attach to the public school.

Has not the time come when we may consider on their individual merits in each case methods for solution of the complex problems of a machine age, organized in huge and impersonal corporations, without presuming to settle the matter in advance by epithets of individualism and socialism?

27 Public and Private Morals

We defined social morality as the morality of groups. For certain purposes it is convenient to distinguish two kinds of groups: (1) primary groups, as of family and neighbors; and (2) secondary groups, formed for definite purposes, as in the case of political and economic groups. In common usage a man's relations to his family, his friends, or his neighbors are said to concern his 'private' life; government is clearly 'public'; business and industry are in a transitional position, but under modern conditions are increasingly considered as of public concern. Corresponding broadly to the above distinctions, morals are divided into 'private morals' and 'public morals.' As husband, father, neighbor, friend, a man is in the sphere of private morals. As a government official he has public obligations. As a manufacturer, merchant, banker, employer, employee, he is brought into relations with others which are of public import, especially if the enterprise is a large one. Government and business are therefore classed together as belonging to the field of public morals. Insofar as we are concerned not with the particular conduct or problem of some individual but with the standards set or approved by the group, both private morals (as above defined) and public morals are included under social morality.

I

Certain interesting problems arise when the private and public morals of a people are compared. Some of the moral dilemmas which we have considered may be regarded as resulting from conflicts be-

Excerpt from *America's Social Morality: Dilemmas of the Changing Mores* by James Hayden Tufts, ed. Howard Odum, copyright 1933 by Holt, Rinehart and Winston, Inc. and renewed by Matilda C. Tufts, reprinted by permission of the publisher [1933:01].

tween the standards of the two. One of the clearest statements of the contrasting standards of private and public morals among the American people is that of the late President Hadley. In private morals, he says,

> the typical American citizen bears an excellent character. With the weak he is courteous; with the strong, self-respecting; with all, helpful. He uses his powers and advantages unselfishly. He does not employ his strength to elbow his way to the front through a crowd of women and children. He does not employ cunning to overreach his neighbors and friends. In great emergencies, like fire and flood or railway accidents, it is not the mean and selfish side of human nature which comes prominently to the front in the conduct of our countrymen, but the large and helpful side. We are glad to believe that the heroism shown at these times of crisis is but a manifestation of the ordinary intentions and ideals of our American men and women, which they are showing in thousands of little acts of daily self-sacrifice of which we never hear.[1]

Foreign observers, like Mr. Muirhead, have made comments on American private morals in similarly favorable terms.[2]

But President Hadley points out that with public morals the case is different. Foreign critics have remarked with a mixture of amazement and horror upon our government and our business morals. Our own survey has been chiefly occupied with unpleasant aspects of race and class, with recriminations between business and government and between employers and employed, with lawlessness not of individual offenders but of classes and gangs, with commercial exploitation of the appetites and passions. Brighter lighting has appeared in certain aspects of family life, in the rapid assimilation of immigrants from countries long hostile to each other and in their readiness to forget past grievances in a new environment, in our great democratic system of public education, in the ceaseless movement which prevents the hardening and fixation of class barriers even while it weakens the hold of the mores and indeed is constantly dissolving the older standard and restraints. Yet on the whole the picture of social morality in the United States has shown a good many heavily shaded portions in public morals. Why the contrast between private morals and public morals? Is it a contrast incidental to a certain people, or to a peculiar

1. Arthur Twining Hadley, *Standards of Public Morality* (New York: Macmillan, 1912) 3–4.
2. Ed. note: Cf. 1932:04.

transitional situation, or is there necessarily a contrast between "moral man and immoral society," to use the phrase which Professor Niebuhr has recently set as the title of a discussion of the general situation in Europe as well as in America? Or are there other factors to be considered than those which President Hadley and Professor Niebuhr have put forward?

First let us recall President Hadley's explanation of the contrast. President Hadley was an acute analyst of economic and political institutions as well as by family tradition and public position familiar with many phases of American character. He uses strong terms to express his opinions of our public morality. Ruthless competition against a weaker competitor, snobbishness and servility, selfish deceit instead of heroism, are found in business and politics. And President Hadley wrote before the scandals of the Harding administration and of the Thompson regime in Chicago; before the Seabury investigation and the Insull wrecking of the fortunes of trustful investors. Bad public morals, he insists, are not due to the depravity of the men who manage our business or our politics. This is a popular but superficial view.

> The chief trouble lies in the public standard of morals. . . . The blame for misuse of industrial or political power is . . . ours just as much as theirs. For it is the standards that are at fault, and we as well as they have a share in making the standards. . . . The chief cause of difference between our private and our public morality is that public sentiment is clear in one case and obscure or self-contradictory in the other.[3]

And if we push the inquiry one step further and ask, Why should there be this difference in public sentiment?, Hadley answers, "It is because our experience in the one case has been much longer than our experience in the other." Several thousand years for private morals and a few hundred with our present industrial system, and he might have added, a still briefer term with a political democracy in nations of such great extent, confronted with the new forces set in motion by the Industrial Revolution. When society abandoned the medieval system which defined public as well as private standards in fairly well-understood terms and organized both economics and politics on a system of liberty, it introduced new moral factors. Some have converted the truth of liberty, President Hadley continues—that it is wise to let individuals serve society in their own way—into the falsehood

3. Hadley 5–7.

"we may therefore let them have their own way in everything, with the assurance that they will serve society in spite of themselves; that the selfishness of all men, pulling apart and working for their own interest, can by some occult process be trusted to promote the common interest."[4]

There can be little question that the last sentence points to a fundamental factor in the present situation, but the statement that the reason for the unclear condition of public sentiment is that our experience with the system has been relatively short seems to imply that public sentiment is more rational in its processes than would be admitted by all students of the public mind. Or if it be granted that a considerable degree of agreement in public sentiment may come as a result of longer experience, will this be effective in changing the morals of groups that have strong interests at stake? Will such groups listen to reason? And if they will not, what other methods than scientific demonstration or appeals to reason are necessary and justifiable?

II

It is to these questions that Professor Niebuhr addresses his discussion.[5] Educators, he holds, err in supposing that experimental procedure in the social field can accomplish results similar to its achievements in the physical sciences. In physical science they need only to replace ignorance by knowledge; to dislodge privilege and the collective predatory interest of nationalists or economic groups something more than reason and conscience is needed; "power must be challenged by power." Nor are sociologists and religious idealists less inept. Conference, accommodation, compromise are their methods. They are "unrealistic." They lack "understanding of the brutal character of all human collectives, and the power of self-interest and collective egoism in all intergroup relations."

The three types of collectives or groups selected by Niebuhr as illustrating the thesis are nations, privileged economic classes, and proletarians. The first and third are bound together by strong group loyalty which in itself operates against an impartial and objective—in other words, a rational—attitude toward other groups. Still less can these groups follow the religious ideal of unselfish or self-sacrificing

4. Hadley 23.
5. Reinhold Niebuhr, *Moral Man and Immoral Society: A Study in Ethics and Politics* (New York: Scribners, 1932).

love to others. No nation has been or can be unselfish. Class consciousness, a necessity for effective coherence of the proletarian group,
arrays it against other classes. The German liberal failed to advance
his position by being reasonable; the American Negro had to show
resistance before he could gain a hearing. The second group—that of a
dominant or privileged economic class—has less group consciousness,
except when property interests are threatened; all the more its egoism,
the intensified collective egoism of its members, resists any fair, i.e.,
reasonable views of social situations, to say nothing of sympathy or
altruism. It cannot be changed by any moral suasion.

In view of such inexorable forces as those at work in nationalism,
in privileged classes, and in underprivileged class, Niebuhr foresees
but a modest role for reason and the advance of experimental method.
Group morals is group morals and private morals is private morals.
The industrial age tends to accentuate the sharpness of group conflict.
High ideals and tender emotions of private morals must seem somewhat in the nature of luxuries in an age that suffers from ills which
can be met only by coercion and forcible resistance.

If it were our purpose to consider the merits of Niebuhr's analysis,
it would be pertinent to point out that one fundamental assumption,
namely, that egoism and altruism stand for the ethical poles in conduct, is by no means indisputable. Suicide is not the apex of virtue.
The moral ideal, whether it takes the more intimate mold of personal
relations in the religious conception of love, or the mold of less intimate
affection but no less reverent respect for personal worth in the political
and economic conceptions of *aequum et bonum*, fair, right, and good,
cannot be graded simply in terms of self versus others. It involves a
comprehensive social whole in a kingdom of ends in which persons
stand to each other in many kinds of relation and fulfill various functions. In one situation love may be the transcendent good; in another,
fair dealing; in another, resistance. We do not wish sympathy from
our tradesman—unless he is also a neighbor or associate in some more
personal relation—we wish truth and honesty. We do not, if we are
good citizens, seek benevolence from the government but equality
before the law. We cannot properly think of the position of a nation
as simply that of an independent individual; the nation is rather the
trustee of certain interests of order, justice, and security which it must
guard. The complex character of moral values and duties must be
fundamental in any appraisal. We cannot ignore this fact if we are to
make a thoroughly realistic analysis.

III

Bergson, in his recent essay, looks at group and individual from still a different angle. He seeks primarily to understand moral forces, but throws light upon the relation between social or group agencies and individual initiative.

Bergson distinguishes two sources of morals: social pressure, examples of heroes.[6] From social pressures come the sense of duty, the obligations felt in 'closed' societies, the more impersonal types of moral behavior, in which we observe habits necessary for carrying on the organic social process. From the appeal that heroes make to our imagination and emotion comes an element that is not so much duty as aspiration. It is the morals of an 'open' society, of humanity rather than of a tribe or nation; instead of fixed habits, its spirit is that of 'forward march'; it is creative; it is attended by the feeling of liberation; it is an élan. The morals of pressure embodies what, as it were, nature provides as necessary for the very existence of human society—even as nature provides the bee and the ant with mechanisms necessary for the composite life of the hive and the anthill. The morals of aspiration represent the possibility of advance, the spirit of the 'open' soul. The morals of pressure are relatively easy of formulation; the morals of aspiration are difficult, because, as in the Sermon on the Mount, they are not intended to give rules but to induce a state of the soul. In the development of such a conception as justice the morals of pressure and the morals of aspiration are blended.

As applied to the problem of nationalism, Bergson suggests that "in giving to man the moral conformation necessary for life in a group nature has probably done for the species all that she could do. That men of moral genius have pushed farther the bounds of intelligence and conceived of humanity has been as it were the creation of a new species, achieving what could not be attained at one stroke by all men."

Apart from the Bergsonian metaphysics of the élan, the distinction between the morals of pressure and the morals of aspiration points to a genuine aspect of the relations between individual and public morals. There are certain fundamental necessities of societies, as of individual survival. Protection from hostile attack is one of these. The cruder way is through tribal and national solidarity. A degree of order is also

6. Henri Bergson, *Les Deux Sources de la Morale et de la Religion* (Paris: Alcan, 1932).

necessary. The simplest method of maintaining order is through authority of some sort—elders, chief, king, party boss. Another necessity is food and other material goods. For any variety in these some exchange of goods and services is necessary, and exchange can be carried on only if there be at least a minimum of confidence and fair dealing. In both political and economic society there is a tension between instincts or drives of the individual toward self-preservation or independence, or gain, and social pressure. These drives of individual character may take the form of resisting or evading social power or of capturing and using social power, political or economic. But society never abdicates the authority or the regulations necessary to its own self-preservation. Nature seems to have insured this, even as she insured for all mammals a minimum of parental relationship and parental care.

Progress beyond the minimum has come, in part at least, through moral 'heroes.' Men of vision have imaged and sought better ways of safety than the cruder way of war, or the timid way of isolation. They have seen ways to combine order with liberty and private rights through law. They have found ways to increase mutual confidence and understanding and thereby to increase enormously economic welfare through increased markets and the organization of credit. They have broadened the family and kin attitudes of kindness to the conception of benevolence to all and love of neighbor to love of man. If we compare these examples of the highest and noblest of mankind with the behavior of groups organized, as these are, for some particular necessity and including, as they usually do, many grades of rational and social advance, we must expect unfavorable contrasts such as Niebuhr draws. In fact the same contrasts in principle were found three hundred years ago by the Reformers in their criticism of the Church. It failed to equal the pattern of the Master. In assuming responsibility for mankind instead of remaining a small group of intimate disciples, the Church had necessarily lowered the standard of perfection and has asserted a power that inevitably involved peril.

But it is not through lonely seers of creative genius alone that progress has come. On the one hand, interaction between group interests, on the other, the problems set by conflicts between older mores and new inventions or processes and between individual drives and social requirements, have operated to evoke new adjustments directly or through furnishing the situations that have stimulated the moral genius to his visions and his insights. As instance of the moral value of intergroup conflict may be noted the suppression of family feuds by the courts acting for the king or the state. A present instance is the pressure of economic interests and groups for international trade and goodwill and for modification of the extreme nationalism which, at the instance of other business interests and groups, no doubt, has erected barriers to friendly international relations.

An early instance of the problems, set by a group, which evoked the visions of moral genius, was the increasing wealth and luxury of the city-dwelling commercial class that called out the visions of a higher justice when the herdsman Amos mused upon them. As instances of conflicts in the mores with new inventions, the reflections of Socrates, of the utilitarians, and of the great jurists need no repetition. The point is that the genius both enters into the group and rises above its previous level. His contribution may take the form of that universalizing of the partial which we call reason, or of that concrete image of a better pattern which we call imagination. Socrates and Jesus, in Bergson's phrase, each set a pattern of the 'open soul'; John Marshall, Thomas Jefferson, Abraham Lincoln, Justice Holmes, each confronted a conflict that elicited a new construction which the nation partially, at least, adopted. There is, however, no point in asking whether the whole group is at the level of genius, intellectual or moral. The real point is whether there are certain groups that are so constituted as to make them recalcitrant to moral advance through either appeals to reason or appeals to sympathy and generous cooperation.

IV

We must frankly admit that public morals—nationalism, wars, toleration of crime, unconscionable profit-seeking, maldistribution of wealth, conflicts between employers and employed—present conspicuously difficult problems. As Niebuhr points out, and as our survey has shown, there are genuine dilemmas involved. Under the stress of self-preservation nations, classes, business, labor groups, will resort to desperate measures. And besides this major factor in the problem of moral advance, morals of national and economic groups have a threefold handicap as compared with private morals—the morals of family, neighbor, and friend. (1) Political and economic groups exist for certain special needs and interests which easily tend to assume supreme value and thus distort life; (2) political and economic groups as they increase in size and efficiency tend to become impersonal, whereas family and neighbor morals are more face-to-face; (3) political and economic groups as they gain power acknowledge no superior standard or authority and become a law to themselves.

(1) The tribal or national group exists for protection against enemies without and disturbers of peace and order within. The early means to these ends was through war and despotism. When not at war national groups still regard each other with suspicion and fear, or hold aloof and erect barriers against trade and friendship. Internal attitudes show the survivals of past despotisms in the fear of governmental activities, or disregard of governmental authority, as well as in some of the technicalities of criminal law. Political parties exhibit similar attitudes in a less violent fashion. The party member believes that his party should rule; it must rule if it is to make its policy prevail. To rule it must reward its supporters and destroy, i.e., remove the official heads of, its enemies. The party boss takes Machiavelli for his guide and endeavors to combine the strength of the lion with the cunning of the fox. For him it is not a case of placing party above the common welfare; rather he holds that the only means to public welfare lies through supremacy of his party.

Or if we consider an economic group. Of the two functions of such groups, production and commerce, or in modern terms, industry and business, the productive function soon came under a social ban, partly because of slavery. An artisan could not be a citizen of Aristotle's best city-state. The commercial or trading group was early regarded with suspicion because the very nature of trade invited the trader to make as good a bargain as possible. Success depended upon bargaining skill, restrained only by the thought of keeping open the basis for future trading. Feudal economy subordinated the economic function, but when the modern system of economic freedom in trade and business enterprise reinforced by technological invention came in, the whole perspective of life and society was reversed. The interest that had been either excluded from social and political recognition or subordinated to church and state became the dominating power. It is not surprising if it has showed the excesses of power unrestrained by either inner responsibility or outer control. It has developed efficiently the safeguards essential to orderly and successful business, such as the performance of contracts, and to some extent the guarantees of quality, and of weight and measure; but with the assurance that the wealth of nations is secured through the wealth of individuals and that competition protects the consumer, the laborer, and the public it has gone confidently forward as if released from further obligation to the commonwealth. Public-spirited business men have sought to fulfill these obligations rather through philanthropy—the extension of another type of group morals—than through the conduct of business. Indeed under the system no business can do otherwise than conduct itself according to the rules of business. If it attempts to do business according to principles of family morals it fails—unless its competitors also adopt the same code.

(2) A somewhat similar outcome follows if we consider the relatively impersonal character of government, business, and labor, or, as Niebuhr designates them, proletarian groups. Moral conceptions of right and wrong grew from personal relations, and keep their vigor more easily if still rooted in that soil. Relations might be of status, as between man and wife, parent and child, younger kin and elder kin, chief and tribesman, landlord and tenant, teacher and taught, or of contact, as between buyer and seller, employer and employed. In the case of such private morals as those which President Hadley cites, personal relations are usually involved. The person whom you help or hurt, treat with courtesy and kindness or the reverse, is ordinarily before you. To wrong one who is not only present now but in the natural course of events is likely to be met personally as kin or neighbor or customer, or fellow churchman from time to time, is to go against strong impediments; we wonder that the man 'has the face' to do it. But government in large units—city, state, nation—becomes necessarily official and impersonal. Courts no longer deal with known persons; they know only plaintiffs and defendants; juries, instead of being selected for their knowledge of the facts, are selected because of their impartiality which is often interpreted to imply their ignorance. In modern business the great agency is the corporation. It issues its stock or bonds and sells them 'in the market,' that is, to unknown persons or to other impersonal corporations. It manufactures products and sells them 'in the market,' that is, to unknown consumers. It hires labor, that is, not men and women who in other capacities belong to the same community, attend the same church, and are members of the same social clubs, but strangers, frequently of alien speech, who conform to certain necessary specifications and are known only by a number. A businessman once remarked to the writer, "When one of my customers incorporates, I look out."

In public groups the morals of kindness, helpfulness, consideration feel, and often are, out of place. Public service suffers if jobs are handed out to friends, irrespective of fitness; business suffers in public confidence when blocks of stock are sold to members of the family and others on the 'inside' at prices below the market. Impersonal morals serve certain purposes better than personal morals. But when the check of personal relations and personal morals is removed, a strict standard of impersonal morals is not at once forthcoming. As the preceding chapters have aimed to show, both government and business are confronted with moral dilemmas.

(3) The severest handicap of public morals is that as political and economic groups become powerful they tend to acknowledge no superior standard or authority. The individual is under the control, or at least subject to the influence, of some group; if 'lawless' he is likely to be brought to book. The groups that foster private morals are also subjected to law, and in many cases are influenced by religious ideals.

Even the casual passer would feel the disapproval of casual spectators if he should in President Hadley's phrase "elbow his way through a crowd of women and children." But a state claims 'sovereignty.' It acknowledges no superior, and may even refuse to admit the obligation which "a decent respect to the opinions of mankind" requires. Past traditions are to some extent a standard and restraint, but these are perhaps as often injurious as helpful to confidence and international cooperation. Corporate groups are in theory subject to the law of the land, but as legal persons they are often able to resist successfully restraint by the several states. Charles Francis Adams wrote that when the states first set up commissions to supervise railroads, the government officials were treated with contempt by the roads. No reasonable person would claim that the legal authority of the government insures its moral infallibility. The corporations are entirely within their rights in contending for such powers and guarantees as are properly theirs to enable them to perform their important functions in society. The point is that the possession of great power necessarily renders any group reluctant to submit to control. Group morals control individuals, but what or who shall control groups? *Quis custodiet ipsos custodes?*

If we answer, Public sentiment is all powerful, we encounter another fact that confuses our mores. Those who understand how public sentiment can be manipulated or manufactured are by no means certain that the voice of the people is the voice of God. We cited the explanations of the brewers as to their success in gaining the press, and of the utilities that improved the technique of the brewers by seeking to control not only the press but the teachers and the textbooks. During the World War, propaganda gained recognition as one of the important factors in maintaining national morale and the will to fight. Many good as well as many sinister causes are constantly endeavoring to catch the public ear and bring the pressure of public opinion to bear upon government. Telegrams from thousands of constituents urging him to vote for a particular measure may well coerce a congressman; front page news items in the public press may convey the impression of a popular stampede toward this or that policy. Even a preelection poll may turn thousands and perhaps millions of doubtful voters to vote for what appears to be the winning side. Yet, such as it is, public sentiment is our court of last appeal. The only check that can legitimately be required is that the propaganda for any cause or interest shall be open and that the persons or corporation or group behind it shall announce themselves. A judge listens to attorneys, but he does not consider that the attorney for either side is bound to bring out both sides of the case. The public unfortunately sometimes mistakes the eloquence of the attorney for a judicial decision, when it alone appears on the front page. Disillusionment as to the infallibility of public opinion is a phase of disillusionment that has more justification than some other phases.[7]

Can a democracy control its powerful groups, or must, say, an underprivileged group assert itself and use force, use government as a fulcrum, to get a hearing? Working men distrust the courts; the Negro distrusts a government in which he has no vote. The farmer distrusts Wall Street influence; the city is contemptuous of 'hick towns' and urges its increasing population as giving it the right of majority rule to determine policies of state and nation. The chances for the immediate future do not appear to favor the settlement by calm and reasonable methods of certain of these conflicting claims.

And yet the severe depression through which we are now passing has thus far revealed no evidence in the United States of that 'revolt of the masses' which Ortega has characterized as the great social movement of the time. Why? Perhaps the answer lies in what Ortega styles 'vital integrity' or 'vital tone.' After referring to "the idea, always accepted, never challenged, that the future lies with America," and affirming as its basis "the realization of a higher level of average existence in America, in contrast with a lower level in the select minorities there as compared with those of Europe," Ortega points to vitality as the most important factor in estimating future prospects. "Genuine vital integrity does not consist in satisfaction, in attainment, in arrival." As the proverb has it, 'The road is always better than the inn.' "There

7. Cf. Frederick E. Lumley, *The Propaganda Menace* (New York: Century, 1933). Cf. also Ernest Henry Gruening, *The Public Pays* (New York: Vanguard, 1931); Jack Levin, *Power Ethics* (New York: Knopf, 1931).

is only one absolute decadence; it consists only in a lowering of vitality, and that only exists when it is felt as such."[8]

V

Has America vitality? If so, the outlook for even the underprivileged may be hopeful; the possibility in fuller degree of a democracy, which is also in the old term a commonwealth, lies in the discovery and adoption of new methods to assure the further raising of the level of existence and to secure the 'open society' of Bergson, the 'dream' of opportunity for the average man, of which Adams has written.[9]

The mobility of American society, so adverse to firm, settled mores, is nevertheless a condition favorable to vigorous life, although it is not itself a guarantee of life. When all seems fixed—classes, precedents, laws, economic status, religion, education—when there is no inter-marriage between different stocks, no intermingling of cultures, no facility of transition in economic and social standing, there is more danger of death or of revolt of the masses that see no other way out of their repressed condition.

The criticism of the American scene by the intellectuals, however lacking in perspective for a fair portrait, is an indication of discontent that at least is better than the 'smooth things' spoken by the prophets of a former day. It would be absurd to take the mordant characteriza-tions of Lewis, Dreiser, Mencken, and other realists as a fair sample of American life as a whole, just as it would be absurd to conclude that the average dissenting clergyman in the England of Dickens had the thirst of Mr. Stiggins, or that all nurses were Sairey Gamps. Those who have associated with college men in business would perhaps identify one in a hundred as a Babbitt, and those who know Protestant ministers might find an Elmer Gantry once in a thousand. Social workers and professional women will hardly recognize Ann Vickers as typical. In the Main Streets of the Middle West there are values which Lewis does not choose to see, or at least does not introduce into his picture. Not many Americans have struggled up through such experiences as Dreiser, and Mencken's *Americana* sound as strange and ludicrous to most Americans as they must to Europeans. Nonetheless, bitter medicine has at times been regarded as useful in stimulating sluggish metabolism. We have not yet reached the stage for clear

8. José Ortega y Gasset, *The Revolt of the Masses* (New York: Norton, 1932) 28, 35, 47.
9. James Truslow Adams, *The Epic of America* (Boston: Little, 1931).

vision and grasp of social problems. Our intellectuals have satire for the follies of their countrymen, but lack the humor which implies sympathy with fellow mortals in their weakness. Vision, sympathy, and humor are rare in the interpreters of any culture.

Changes in the means of attaining and securing the ends which the American spirit has prized are more positive signs of vitality. Liberty and equality, independence and opportunity, were the values that brought early colonists and later immigrants, and these values persist, but the content of the terms and the means to the attainment of the values have changed to meet conditions. Liberty in Jefferson's day meant a weak government. Independence, opportunity, and equality were secured chiefly by the abundance of free land. We were a nation of small farmers. We bought few commodities, borrowed little money, and lived largely each on his own. Today economic power which regulates prices and taxes citizens indirectly has far more to do with the citizen's standard of living—with liberty, opportunity, and independence—than the government. To protect citizens against food adulterations, worthless stocks and bonds, irresponsible banks, exorbitant rates by rail, and public utilities requires a strong, not a weak, government. It has brought about a good part of that expansion of government functions which calls out protests from some taxpayers whose wrath would more fitly be directed against the dishonest practices of business that have made such expansion necessary. The doctrines of property affected with a public interest and of the police power are indications of the same change in the conceptions of governmental means to protection of the individual against economic power.

Equality, opportunity, and independence are no longer secured by free land. Most workers now work for an employer, and opportunity to work lies in conditions beyond the worker's control. The industrial system is anything but a system of equality. If it could insure a measure of security, this would be a partial compensation, but it is at present unable to give security. The millions of unemployed all over the industrialized world are a sufficient witness to the combination of political wastage of resources in wars and economic inability to plan wisely. Yet there are two lines in which American society has advanced and in which the working man has shared.

The first and greatest advance has been in the field of public education. The expansion of opportunity to share in one of the highest values of human civilization amounts to a revolution. The increases in the equipment and material now available and the increase in the attendance of pupils in secondary and higher institutions have been noted in previous chapters. Their significance for democracy is profound. Here at any rate, equality, lost in our economic system, is replaced by an equality in access to the goods of the mind. Opportunity to share in the advances of culture is open. Education is an agency of an 'open society.' Educators who take a narrow view of the social process and are impatient at the throngs who seek an education not always wisely adapted to their needs should not forget in their zeal for knowledge for knowledge's sake that education is America's best agency for service to the common man. And economy leagues will do well not to destroy the chief avenue of opportunity now open.

The second advance in which the common man has shared has been the application of science to inventions that add to comfort and enjoyment. Practically all read a daily newspaper, ride in automobiles, listen to radios, see moving pictures, dress in clothes that carry no badge of inferior class, have access to public libraries, and if city dwellers, to public parks. These make for fuller life.

The severest test of a spirit and life that are able to deal with what, measured by European experience, may well be regarded as the most difficult test of modern civilization is the problem of dissolving the barriers of language and deep-seated estrangement or hostile tradition and feeling between racial and national groups. In Europe no demonstration of dangers to civilization, to economic welfare, to life itself, avails to quiet the suspicions and rancors born of age-old conflict and kept alive by repeated wars. It might be thought that such inveterate feelings would continue among the immigrant groups, many of whom in the large cities preserve for years a certain community of cultural tradition and a degree of isolation from the 'native born.' In the World War it was inevitable that before the United States entered as combatant the sympathies of immigrants should be divided. Yet the unanimity of support given to the government was remarkable. It was greater than the unanimity of support to the Union cause in the North during the Civil War, if measured by acceptance of the draft. The writer heard an American general cite as a type of true American a Greek boy in his command who had displayed heroic daring unto death with eager devotion, and many a German family sent its boys to fight against the Fatherland. The story of the Irish youngster who patriotically named George Washington as the 'first man' in answer to the question of the catechism, rejecting the claims to consideration of Adam as a 'furriner' may be mythical, but like all myths it testifies to a real something.

But war is not the best test. The fact that our immigrant groups find their way into all fields of American life, that the second and succeeding generations forget all too soon even the best of their previous traditions and distinctive history, shows at least the vigor of the new life into which they enter so eagerly. Doubtless American life has been modified by the constant stream of immigration. Our cities are as much European in many respects as they are Older American. Washington and Jefferson would scarcely feel at home in Coney Island or Atlantic City, or in the Ford factories or the steel mills. But there is vitality.

A final indication that the heart of America is still active is the spirit in which the unemployment situation of the past four years has been met. In no previous depression has the public responsibility been felt in such an unquestioning temper. The means for dealing with the situation may not have been adequate; the disposition at first was to rely on the older type of private morality, that is, upon charity. But as the situation continued the public responsibility was more and more assumed by public agencies. Public morality is proving the advance that has been made since the legal maxim 'Where the tree falls, there let it lie' expressed the morality of its day. If the gain in sympathy should prove lasting and the attitude of sober consideration of public good become established, it would not be the first instance in history in which moral advance has resulted from adversity.

28 A Social Philosopher's Idea of Good Government

The boundary lines between philosophy and the social sciences, frequently uncertain, are particularly difficult to define in considering good government. If we say that philosophy deals with ends whereas the sciences have to do with means, we have to recognize that the division between ends and means may be at times a convenient tool of analysis but is far from absolute. If one believes that the principles of good for every sphere of life can be derived from pure reason, the method and the task of philosophy are clear. But for one who holds with Plato that knowledge of the human sphere and circle, as well as of the divine circle and sphere, is necessary in the building of a house, it seems impracticable to stay wholly on the side of the line implied in academic allotments of departmental fields. It is significant that of the twenty amendments to the federal Constitution, presumably designed to secure better government, sixteen either were the reflection of a definite philosophy or were advocated on moral as well as on purely political grounds. If, then, I am caught out of bounds, I trust that I may be treated with leniency by the invaded realm.

The first inference that I should draw from Plato's doctrine of house building is that there is no such thing as good government in itself, irrespective of time and place, of race, culture, and education. The human species may or may not be biologically one; it is culturally many. It may assent to common use of number or elemental laws of logic, but emotionally there are many scales of valuation.

Moreover, we live in a changing world, and our own brief national history affords illustration of changing demands upon government. For a nation of farmers, relatively independent, approximately equal

Reprinted by permission of the publisher from James Hayden Tufts, "A Social Philosopher's Idea of Good Government," *Annals of the American Academy of Political and Social Science* 169 (1933), 193–201 [1933:02].

because of land ownership, with little trade, either domestic or foreign, no large cities, of homogeneous stock, accustomed to a common law, and habituated to settled mores, a good government might well be a government of strictly limited powers and few activities. For an industrial people, of all grades of education, of heterogeneous stocks, traditions, and cultures, living in cities and in a machine age, with worldwide trade and high-powered economic organization, a weak government with few functions is a bad government. Automobile traffic demands the traffic policeman, not merely to protect the helpless pedestrian, but also to prevent collisions or blockades of the swift cars and ponderous trucks that crowd the streets.

Yet good government will seek to preserve genuine values in adapting itself to change and new forces. Liberty, independence, and equality appeal to Americans as such genuine values. Good government is then confronted with a primary problem of mediating between stability and change.

A second problem—it might almost be called a dilemma—confronts democracy. On the one hand a stable government in a democracy must have the support of the people, or at least of a majority. It rests, we say, on the will of the people. On the other hand, it seeks certain ends. Now whether these ends are supposed to be determined by reason or by experience as presented in past history, there is bound to be frequent divergence between what the expert in a scientific age believes to be better, and what the mass of people are willing to support; there is equally likely to be divergence between what different groups hold to be right and desirable. Especially in a democracy made up from races and peoples of widely different backgrounds, traditions, and valuations, there is likely to be not only a gap between the ideals of those eminent for enlightened views and the habits of the conservative mass; there are also the clashes between different sections, between city and country, between those who hold with Aristotle that the object of the state is not merely a common life but noble action, and those who emphasize personal liberty or would leave to family, church, school, and the press all efforts to raise moral standards or even to protect those which exist.

Enthusiastic lovers of humanity at the close of the eighteenth century held indeed that there was no conflict between noble ideals and the will of the people. Set man free from oppression, they argued, and the natural goodness of human nature will do the rest. The rise of a power of wealth which has not yet learned the lessons of public responsibility, the rise of the professional criminal who avails himself of the inventions of the age to defy or evade government, the seemingly inescapable conflicts between the rational demands for peace and the inveterate causes of wars, have disillusioned us of the hope of any easy path to progress. They compel more careful consideration of the agencies for forming public opinion, and of education in respect to both the ends and the means of good government.

Instead of attempting to proceed from general principles of ethics to define what is good, it would seem the safer method to look rather at what has commended itself as peculiarly adapted to our conditions. We may not soar so high with this method, but there is much to be said for keeping our feet on the ground. Good government for Americans must build on American traditions, although it need not remain at the level of the Declaration of Independence. To secure rights remains one of the ends of government, even though it leaves out another important end, namely, to develop powers and create new interests in its citizens.

To secure rights, however, is a phrase that is susceptible of two different interpretations. If we understand by 'rights' the claim of persons to be secured in what they have already come to possess, whether through struggle, labor, shrewdness, luck, or inheritance, that is one thing; if we understand it as the claim—necessarily as yet partially unformulated—to have opportunity to develop powers through the heritage of man's past achievement and the resources of present cooperation, that is another and much larger thing. Law tends, perhaps necessarily, to emphasize the first conception; but a philosophy that looks forward rather than backward cannot limit to a static social order the noble words of the Preamble, "to establish justice."

It is not necessary to labor the reasoning that makes rights one fundamental of good government. The forces of modern civilization—religious, political, economic, social—have combined to give worth and dignity to the person who is the subject of rights. To the earlier rights of life, liberty, and property, our government has added the right of public education. Class and race prejudice and poverty partially nullify this right in certain sections, as well as the supposedly elemental right to equality before the law; but few thoughtful persons deny that government should secure to its citizens these rights.

When new forces threaten rights or when new claims to right appear, there is almost certain to be challenge. Irresponsible power is always likely to infringe upon the rights of the less powerful. In our generation, the power of economic organization, which controls the productive process and the application to human welfare of natural forces through the machine, has no doubt been subjected to various attempts at regulation by government, and has itself wavered between attitudes of defiance and of deference to public opinion. Yet economic power is still far from any such degree of responsibility to the public as has come to be demanded of political power by modern democracies.

This irresponsibility is not due chiefly to any deliberate purpose of corporations or individuals to wreck the passengers in their high-powered cars or airships. A primary factor has been the economic philosophy which held that the airship would automatically steer itself and land its passengers in safety at the desired haven of prosperity, and that the pilot in charge need think only of maintaining full speed ahead.

Dropping the figure, the small dealer has found the competition of the great corporation a menace. The farmer has felt his livelihood imperiled by the economic system which compels him to sell in a world market and to buy in a domestic market. The laborer has felt his security of earning power, which once lay in his own skill and diligence, threatened by both the machine and its master, the impersonal employer that knows no individuals but only a labor market. The consumer finds himself at a loss to distinguish qualities of goods which the resources of chemistry can disguise and the persuasions of specious advertising urge upon him. The investor finds himself perplexed by plausible offerings of so-called securities that often turn out to be worthless.

Ruling out practices of intentional deceit, and even such questionable adventures in the grasp for power as those of the Kreugers and the Insulls, there is a gap between the personal responsibility of the old-time merchant or craftsman who was known to his neighbors and could guarantee to them the quality of his goods, and the impersonal attitude of the corporation which buys and sells in the market and is organized for profit, pure and simple.

In the face of such power over the living conditions of the common man, government is forced to interfere to preserve liberty: liberty to the farmer to pay his debts in approximately the same dollars that he borrowed; liberty to the consumer or investor to know what he is buying; liberty to the laborer to associate with other laborers for collective bargaining and against unfair competition from child labor and immigrant labor; liberty to the small firm to engage in business without being crushed by 'unfair competition.' A considerable share of the increased functions of government is due to the necessity for meeting the demands to preserve liberty in the presence of a new power which no one understands—least of all, apparently, those who have wielded it and have credited themselves and been credited with its creation.

Equality was not formally included among the rights mentioned in the Declaration, yet "equal protection of the laws" implied one aspect of equality, and justice has always rested upon a recognition of the person as entitled to some measure of equal consideration. Lincoln was voicing the same deep feeling of Jefferson and of the whole middle class which founded our government when he spoke of our government as "dedicated to the proposition that all men were created equal." Political equality was one phase of this equality, but underlying political equality was an approximate economic equality based on free land. With the disappearance of free land as an actual or potential equalizer, and with the shift from agrarian to industrial economy which involved a shift from relative independence to relative dependence, the measure of equality which prevailed in the beginning was seriously diminished.

Fortunately for the preservation of equality as a principle of democratic government, a new agency of equality was introduced. A system of public education open to all was provided, which has appealed to increasing numbers. In the stress of the present depression the expense of this system has made it the object of attack by some. Proposals to place a part of the cost upon the parent, proposals to limit the scope of public education, or to assign pupils to a certain type of education on the basis of supposedly scientific tests of ability have appeared.

All such proposals must be considered not only from the point of view of the taxpayer, and especially of the wealthy taxpayer who will in any case give his own children all possible advantages; they must be considered also and even more seriously from the point of view of the believer in democratic institutions. To take away from the economically underprivileged their only avenue of equal opportunity while they retain equality in voting power is a course that must give pause to the farsighted statesman. From the viewpoint of good government, public education is not to be tested primarily by its achievements in the production of exceptional scholars or even by its services to the farmer, the inventor, the international trader, the navigator, or the miner, important as these are. Its fundamental importance for government is that it holds out to the common man and his children the one sphere of equality in the conditions that enter into every citizen's life, which is open under our system.

Almost as deeply rooted in American traditions of good government as the Jefferson doctrine of natural rights is the Hamilton doctrine of alliance between government and some influential class for mutual advantage. In Hamilton's view, to give the strong commercial and manufacturing class a stake in the government would lend strength to a somewhat precarious federal adventure. Yet the theory of lending the aid of government to strengthen a class interest must reckon with two perils, both of which have been disclosed by our national experience: the peril of injuring some other class or section, and the peril that the favored class may become so strong as to control the government.

The tariff, designed to aid industry, proved obnoxious to the agrarian South and long was a factor in dividing the nation. More recently it has, in the opinion of economists, aggravated the difficulties of the farmer of the Middle West and the South, who must buy in a domestic market and sell in a world market. Of course, what has commended the class philosophy to such general acceptance as it has from time to time acquired has been the argument that in benefiting industry, the government also benefits the farmer by affording him a larger market for his products, and that in the long run the public gains. And it may be granted that the case is far from simple. Economics is not yet an exact science, much less is it in a position to estimate all the possible social values that may result from an agrarian versus an industrial society. Yet experience certainly shows that a combination of government subventions to industry plus an extreme nationalism is not a guarantee of economic security.

The second peril has repeatedly threatened democratic institutions. For a time, cotton was king. Then the rule passed to Northern manufacturers, or in the West to the railroads. Charles Francis Adams wrote once for all the story of the contempt with which certain railroad officials treated the government. In several states the railroad owned the legislature. At a later period public utilities controlled city governments. The saloon interests owned the police force as well as the board of aldermen. Nor does the fact that New York City prefers to be ruled by a society organized for "patriotic and benevolent purposes" commend the device of handing over government to special and selfish interests as a method of securing good government. Money changers serve useful purposes, but their place, as President [Franklin Delano] Roosevelt reminds us, is not in the temple.

Confronted by the presence of two great institutions, economic organization controlling the forces of a machine age and political organization existing to promote the common good, European peoples are experimenting with subordinating one more or less completely to the other. Thus far we are preferring to keep both. We do not care to try either the Fascist control of the economic by the political power, or the Communist control of the political by the economic class and system. If one chooses to look at the situation distrustfully, one may say that the American people fears to trust either economic organization or political institutions with complete control over both the day's work and the administration of order and justice. If one chooses to look at the situation more hopefully, one may say that the American people believes that both the economic and the political organization may serve the public good instead of exploiting public needs, and is reluctant to abandon the possibility of having two diverse methods of responsible cooperation for public and common ends.

Efforts to control economic power in the public interest have brought about many of the additions to the functions of government which occasion question or disapproval from those whose activities are restricted. Inevitably the greedy or irresponsible practices of some lead to measures of restraint that irk the fairminded and responsible; but until economic power recognizes public welfare as superior to profits, it must expect public supervision and control in increasing rather than decreasing degree.

A second great increase in governmental functions has come through what may be called the assumption of positive tasks of collective action. Government in this case is not attempting to control a rival power, but to serve as an agency for cooperation. Uncertainty still prevails as to whether certain needs are better met by government or by some other agency. It is difficult to lay down any absolute rule to decide which agency works better. Probably for a considerable time to come, the pragmatic test of experiment and testing by results will be the only test that can be applied. In several types of cooperation we have either by custom or by law deliberately selected agencies other than government for important services; in others, we have divided the responsibility.

Until recently, all have agreed that the care of children in their earliest years belongs to the family, subject to the oversight of government in exceptional cases. Religion in our system is for a distinct voluntary body, although government encourages religion to the extent of freeing from taxation property used for religious purposes, and of affording this property protection through its fire and police departments. The dissemination of news and the discussion of public policies are vital functions of social welfare, but these have seemed usually to be better served through the enterprise of a press privately owned, yet subject in varying degree to the influence of professional standards and to public approval, as well as to the commercial ends of profit. The advancement of science has been undertaken, but chiefly in fields where the application to navigation, mining, agriculture, or industry is involved. Pure science has been left largely to private endowment, although the state universities have come to expand their activities in this field.

In the preservation of health, government has limited its work largely to quarantine and protection against epidemics, except in the care of injuries and disease contracted in military service, although workmen's compensation acts may be regarded as in principle protective against accident and occupational diseases. There has, however, been a growing conviction that professional care on a wholly private basis, while giving excellent service to the well-to-do, and much free service to the very poor, is inadequate because out of reach for those of the intermediate class. A recent report of a committee has at least raised the question whether the health as well as the education of the people can wisely be left entirely to private arrangements.

All the above noted fields affect the people in general. The ground on which they are left wholly or in part to other agencies is that other agencies have assumed at least partial responsibility and have more or less adequately met the needs and wishes of the people. The same is true of two other functions which are clearly public, that of general communication and transportation, and that of public welfare in care of those unable to support themselves because of defects in sight, hearing, speech, or sanity, or of age, or other economic disability. Highways and waterways have been provided by government (motor highways have seen an extraordinary increase of governmental expenditure in recent years), railroads by private enterprise with larger and larger measure of public control; postal service by the government, telegraph and telephone under private ownership. Evidently there has been no clearly defined and consistently carried out principle.

In the case of unemployment relief, however, a decided shift has come in the public attitude, and one which discloses a philosophical principle, even though the principle was reluctantly recognized by government. The philosophy on which we have until recently acted limited public relief to certain classes of the unfortunate. It was held that each individual of normal health and faculties was primarily, if not solely, responsible for himself and his dependents, not only in prosperity but also in adversity or old age. We recognized a need of charity and were generous in calamities of fire or flood; but as regards hazards of employment, those individuals who required charity or public aid were generally regarded as inefficient or improvident.

At the outset and for a considerable period during the present depression, the effort was made to continue under this philosophy. Dust was thrown by the epithet 'dole' to characterize public assumption of responsibility. But at last the logic of events forced a change in philosophy. Government could not see its citizens starve because through no fault of theirs the processes of business and industry had ceased to fulfill their normal functions, and the farmer was threatened with ruin. It was not the problem of physical existence merely that must be faced; it was also the problem of maintaining self-respect and morale. And to meet this second need, a change of governmental attitude was necessary.

But the logic of events did not stop with relief. If government finds that the depression has been aggravated if not caused by defects in the policies of business, industry, and finance as hitherto administered, government must investigate and assist in the revision of these policies. If necessary, it must compel such revision. Good government will set up danger signals when people change from horse-drawn vehicles to motor cars. Apparently the enormous speed of the machine age and the huge size of the corporate organizations make the lure of profits and of speculation too strong for self-regulation. The world of business and industry needs a traffic police, and good government finds itself forced to assume the task.

Shall government attempt control of commercial traffic in narcotic drugs, gambling, intoxicants, and prostitution? Some measure of public control seems necessary. Drugs are frequently destructive to moral fiber; gambling is likely to lead to stealing; intoxicants are believed to increase the hazards of a machine age and to aggravate the burdens of poverty upon the community; prostitution degrades its habitués and is the chief agency for the spread of venereal disease. We quarantine against diseases which do not compare in their injurious effects with syphilis and gonorrhea. Why should government expend huge sums on the repression of crime and the education of the young and yet do nothing to check a commercial traffic which, like all lines of business, aims to increase profits by enlarging the number of its patrons and by forming in the young habits which will induce them to contribute to these profits? So reason the advocates of restraint by government.

On the other hand, three groups oppose restriction. The late Mr. Brennan of Chicago, who had a large acquaintance with his fellow citizens, looked with extreme disfavor upon the "projects of 'reformers' to do away with the primary instincts of man—gambling, alcohol, and women." He may be taken as representing the left wing. A 'wide open town' is the policy which commends itself to this group. There is little objection to a moderate license fee, for this does not tend to restrict sales, and even adds to the respectability and the security of the business; but there should be no obstacle that will tend to prevent any resident or visitor from gratifying his appetite at any time or place.

The right wing desires to see appetites controlled by reason, but holds that agencies other than government are better fitted to educate and influence the individual. Family, church, school, economic organization, public opinion, may all be enlisted in the aid of rational control. Government attempts at restriction are more than likely to arouse a feeling of opposition and bravado which defies the law.

The center declines to commit itself either to a wide open policy or to the desirability of securing temperance through agencies other than government. It takes its stand on the principle of personal liberty. What I choose to do in eating or drinking, in sport, in risks, or in sex relations, provided I do violence to no one else, is my own affair. It is no concern of government.

As between the position of restriction by government and that of the three groups opposed to such restriction, it is of course understood that the restrictionist professedly aims not directly at private conduct but at commercial exploitation of the appetites. Nonetheless, restriction of the commercial traffic implies restriction of facilities for gratifying appetite, unless government itself supplies these facilities. Medieval cities did maintain public lupanars to protect the morals of virtuous women, but the prevalence of syphilis finally put an end to the practice. Some governments have undertaken to dispense intoxicants, but there is no general confidence that city governments in the United States could wisely engage in the liquor business, and the cities resent any control by state or national government. There is a considerable trend at present, however, toward public partnership in offering gambling facilities under the form of so-called *pari mutuel* betting. It is argued that since men will gamble anyway, government may as well share in the profits.

So long as we look at the end sought, the restrictionist seems to me to have the better of the argument. Even if we exclude from consideration any so-called 'moral' grounds of action, to prevent disease, to lessen temptations to unnecessary hazards, to prevent accidents in an age when virtually everyone drives a car, to prevent the debauching of police and the control of cities by gambling, liquor, and vice interests, seem to me proper ends of government. But the public is uncertain as to whether government should do any of these things, and still more uncertain as to the best means for accomplishing them in case it make the attempt. We do not repeal the Fifteenth Amendment because it is not obeyed in certain sections, yet we seem likely to repeal the Eighteenth largely, if not wholly, for this reason.

We face a dilemma of democracy under circumstances such as ours. Apparently good government in so large a country, peopled by such diverse stocks with such conflicting cultures, bringing from their native lands such varied traditions, and responding emotionally to skillfully framed appeals must inevitably be a series of compromises if we are to remain a united people and to maintain a cordial support of government.

The practical problem at present appears to be not so much whether we now have good government as whether agencies for making it better are available and active. Broadly speaking, existing agencies in numerous cases are more active in behalf of the Hamilton philosophy of special or class interests than in behalf of the public good as conceived and defined by the wise. The power of propaganda has been shrewdly developed and masked. Formerly, party control over the press presented news and argument after the pattern of an attorney. At present, party control has weakened, but the public is by no means sure that control by a profit-seeking corporation insures abandonment of the attorney's methods.

The attempts of certain public utilities to subsidize teachers in schools and colleges and universities are fresh in the public mind. The further facts that foreign affairs call out ancestral prejudices and that economic problems are increasingly complicated tend to discredit the adequacy of present methods of information and of discussion.

It may also be a fair question whether students of the social and political sciences and of philosophy have done all that the public would permit them to do in the way of presenting facts and principles in forms adapted to enlighten the judgment of the average man. Boys and girls in the schools are not sufficiently matured by doing the day's work to grasp the importance of many aspects of government. The problem of carrying on interest and instruction as experience lengthens is one of the problems that must concern those who desire good government.

29 Equality and Inequality as American Values

"We hold these truths to be self-evident: that all men are created equal"—so declared the Fathers in 1776. A half-century later de Tocqueville when surveying democracy in America fixed upon equality as the fundamental fact from which all other aspects of American society seemed to be derived. Calhoun, indeed, in developing his argument for slavery, repudiated the philosophy of Jefferson. But Lincoln at Gettysburg reaffirmed that this new nation was "dedicated to the proposition that all men are created equal." James Bryce, writing twenty-five years after the close of the Civil War, found the issue not so simple. He considered it necessary to distinguish carefully the different senses of equality before offering any general estimate of its place in the American commonwealth. Yet when on Christmas Eve of 1920 he completed his world-survey of democracy, of which equality is one element, Bryce could speak with confidence of the "universal acceptance of democracy as the normal and natural form of government." "Seventy years ago," he wrote, "the approaching rise of the masses to power was regarded by the educated classes of Europe as a menace to order and prosperity. Then the word Democracy awakened dislike or fear. Now it is a word of praise. Popular power is welcomed, extolled, worshipped."[1]

Today the perspective has changed. In Europe there is reaction against democracy—or at least against democracy as a form of government. How far this means also reaction against democracy as a philosophy of equality is perhaps uncertain. Ortega, the Spanish publicist, thinks that the revolt of the masses has risen to new levels in Europe.

Reprinted by permission of Paul A. Schilpp from James Hayden Tufts, "Equality and Inequality as American Values," *College of the Pacific Publications in Philosophy*, ed. Paul A. Schilpp, vol. 3 (Stockton: College of the Pacific, 1934), 126–137 [1934:01].

1. James Bryce, *Modern Democracies* vol. 1 (New York: Macmillan, 1921) 4.

But even in America, doubtful voices are heard. We have become aware that there is a contrast, if not a conflict, between our political equality and our economic inequality. It seems opportune for the citizen to consider the claims and merits of the rival principles of equality and inequality. All civilized societies, and even uncivilized societies, embody some phase of each principle in their institutions. Their wise adjustment is still a problem unsolved. Our concern tonight is with these principles or values in our own country.

We shall first review briefly the place which both equality and inequality have held in our institutions, then consider the grounds on which these principles claim acceptance, and finally glance at certain present issues which involve new applications of the principles, or perhaps a rethinking of their merits.

I

First, the place of equality in the American system. For although voices through the ages had been lifted in assertion of equality among certain groups of men, or more rarely, among all men, and although courts of justice had long set the balances as their symbol, no other nation had been from birth "dedicated to the proposition that all men are created equal." What did the Fathers mean by this proposition? Its meaning for them must evidently be interpreted in the light of what they were aiming at. They were justifying a declaration of independence from Great Britain. In declaring that men are created equal they laid a foundation for the statements that governments derive their just powers from the consent of the governed, and that whenever any form of government becomes destructive of men's inalienable rights, it is the right of the people to alter or abolish it. What they implied, although they did not here recite what they intended to deny, was that no man or class of men has a divine right to govern other men. God created men *equal*. If governments are instituted it is because equal men choose to form them. Government is a human plan for securing certain inalienable rights. It can be changed. Rights are fundamental and so is equality. To assert a right is to go back to first things. If I claim an inalienable right it is because I am a human being and am claiming for myself only what every human being may claim. In a religious age the strongest and simplest way to affirm this universal basis of rights was to declare that all men are created equal.

That the Fathers were thinking primarily of men as regards their rights to life, liberty, and the pursuit of happiness is further evident from the phrases in which they expressed their ideas. These were not original with Jefferson; they came almost directly from John Locke who a century earlier had likewise been justifying a revolution. Locke was more definitely opposing the divine right of kings on which the Stuarts took their stand. He spoke for an England in which through five hundred years of struggle the right of the common man to equality before the law, to the power over taxation, and to civil and religious liberty had been gradually gaining recognition. Two important forces in this movement had been the emergence of a middle class which wielded with increasing success the power of the purse, and the Christian doctrine, reemphasized by the Reformers, of the worth of the individual soul and the equality of all men before God who is no respecter of persons.

The committee that framed and the Congress that adopted the Declaration of 1776 were then thinking primarily of civil and political equality. They had no notion of proclaiming that all men have equal abilities. They chose Washington to lead their armies and Franklin to represent their cause in France because they deemed these men fitter for those posts than their fellows. Yet they sought to lay the foundations of the new nation in human nature and human rights. When they included among these rights not only life and liberty, which laws protect, but the pursuit of happiness they were foreshadowing the broad assertion of Jeremy Bentham that the test of right in law is, Does the law make for the greatest happiness of the greatest number, every man to count as one? They were declaring for a principle that was bound in time to reach beyond the limited field of government to the conditions of life and society as a whole.

How has this principle of equality fared during the century and a half that has passed since it was set as a national foundation? In government the idea of equality has not only held its own but has made distinct advance. Early restrictions upon white male suffrage were largely removed about the period of Jackson's administration. Abolition of slavery was followed by the Fourteenth and Fifteenth Amendments to the federal Constitution which aimed, so far as law can avail, to extend civil and political rights to the Negro. Inequalities between men and women as regards property and control of children have yielded. The Nineteenth Amendment gave women the suffrage and is unlikely to share the fate of the Eighteenth, adopted in the preceding year.

Membership in Congress, in the Cabinet, and on the Bench has been opened to women. If we look at our government as it stands in constitution and statutes we may well say that equality has gained ground and is not likely to lose what it has gained, unless by violence.

The principle of inequality which prevails in our economic life was not directly affirmed in the Declaration of Independence nor in the federal Constitution, but the Declaration and Constitution named rights which were almost inevitably to lead to inequality. Liberty and the pursuit of happiness were two of the inalienable rights of the Declaration; liberty and private property were guaranteed in the Fifth and Fourteenth Amendments to the Constitution. No doubt to the signers of the Declaration liberty signified primarily civil and religious liberty. But if liberty is affirmed as an absolute right it is not easy to limit its scope to civil and religious fields. Indeed in the very same year of 1776, Adam Smith's *Wealth of Nations* was urging liberty in industry and commerce. The Industrial Revolution soon followed the political revolution and opened a wide opportunity for inventive and organizing ability. In a continent of seemingly inexhaustible land and unlimited natural resources liberty to go where one would, to buy and sell what one pleased, to manufacture what ingenuity could devise, was assumed by the pioneer, the trader, the inventor, the mechanic, and the prospector. The mill owner, the railway builder, the banker assumed and long enjoyed the same liberty. Granted differences in native talent, which no one thought of questioning, and liberty to exploit the resources of a new continent, inequalities were bound to come.

The right of private property was not included among the inalienable rights of the Declaration of 1776, but was so included in other utterances of the day. "Security of right and property" were linked by Samuel Adams as constituting the purpose of government. And in Jefferson's day private property carried little threat to equality. The people were then largely farmers, mechanics, or small merchants. Every man of industrious, steady habits and ordinary thrift could own a farm; few could own so much as to set them sharply apart from their neighbors. Private property among a nation of farmers meant that men were relatively equal and independent. Each lived largely of his own. A century ago in the Vermont town in which my parents were born the account book of the country store shows trade limited for the most part to exchange of butter, cheese, and in winter frozen meat, for salt, calico, and distilled liquors. As the younger generation grew to manhood and was confronted with the necessity of getting an independent living, it moved on to new frontiers.

Forces were soon at work which were to introduce economic inequality on a great scale. During the first half of the nineteenth century the conspicuous developments of inequality appeared in the cotton kingdom. The great planters formed a class superior not only to slaves but also to other whites in their vicinity. They contested the rule of the nation with the industrial North and the agricultural West.

After the Civil War, manufacturing, transportation, commerce, and finance expanded. The number of independent units decreased; the size of those which survived increased enormously. Vast size called for efficient methods of organization. Huge fortunes followed. The system favored inequality both directly by its methods of organization and indirectly through the great wealth accumulated by a relatively small number.

In the modest beginnings the factory, the shop, the bank resembled a patriarchal household. The owner ruled, more or less benevolently; but he knew his men. As employees of a single firm came to number hundreds, thousands, tens of thousands, often of different race and language from those of the employer, personal acquaintance ceased and gave place to rules and orders from above like those of absolute monarchy. Owners no longer resided in the same neighborhood with their workmen, attended the same churches, sent their children to the same schools. A class system based on economic efficiency replaced older class systems based on military prowess or landed ownership.

The rise of the corporation has further contributed to economic inequality. President Nicholas Murray Butler has called the limited-liability corporation the greatest single discovery of modern times. In its conception it has possibilities for democratic equality in that it enables the small adventurer to share in the profits and management of great enterprise. In practice it has lent itself to concentration of capital and control. It has thus increased the power and wealth of the few. When two hundred corporations control more than half the industry of the country and when these two hundred corporations are largely controlled by a relatively small group of individuals, inequality takes on serious proportions.

Accumulation and concentration of wealth in the hands of a few have added to our inequality. Enormous natural resources were ready for exploitation when the inventions of the nineteenth century supplied the tools. Special privileges and grants from government were eagerly grasped by the shrewd. Speculation and other forms of getting something for nothing yielded vast fortunes to some. The comparatively moderate differences in property of a nation of farmers have given place to a condition in which two percent of the population apparently own more than half of the wealth.

Economic power to set prices and wages is a great power. It may be likened to the power of government to lay taxes. But economic power does not always confine itself to the strictly economic field. Frequently it has not only shown itself impatient of control by government but has also sought itself to control government as the simplest method of securing its ends. When at various times this attempt to control government has been measurably successful, the victory of inequality has seemed complete. Fortunately, perhaps, for the survival of equality the economic crash and following depression did much to reduce to more moderate levels the power and prestige of economic leaders.

The logic of the conflict between equality on one side and liberty and private property on the other has been frankly stated by Justice Pitney, speaking for the federal Supreme Court. If contracts are to be just it has seemed desirable to certain legislatures that the parties should be reasonably equal in bargaining power. Kansas passed a law designed to protect the right of laborers to join a union and thus to stand more nearly upon a level with the great corporations. But this law was held by the Court to violate freedom of contract—which has been included by the courts within the broad field of liberty guaranteed by the Constitution. Justice Pitney stated the situation in the following terms:

> No doubt, wherever the right of private property exists, there must and will be inequalities of fortune . . . since it is self-evident that, unless all things are held in common, some persons must have more property than others, it is from the nature of things impossible to uphold freedom of contract and the right of private property without at the same time recognizing as legitimate those inequalities of fortune that are the necessary result of the exercise of those rights.[2]

In other words, when liberty and private property conflict with equality, equality must give way. For constitutional law, liberty and private property have the superior claim because they are explicitly guaranteed by the Constitution. Equality may be claimed as a condition of justice; but how much equality is indispensable to justice is not so much a matter of legal definition as of social philosophy. Three justices of the Court dissented from the decision of the majority.

2. Coppage v. State of Kansas, 236 US 17 (1914).

What has obscured the preponderance of inequality in our economic system has been the phrase 'equality of opportunity,' which we have proudly held to be the glory of America. This has seemed to be a fulfillment of the claim put forward in the Declaration that the "pursuit of happiness" is an inalienable right. The Fathers were more cautious than some moderns. They did not claim a 'right to happiness,' but only a right to its pursuit. Under early conditions, when a continent of vast resources was waiting for the hardy and energetic pioneer, opportunity was a boon. It loosed new energies and kindled new aspirations. But as science, invention, special privilege from government, corporate organization, market manipulation, and inherited wealth increased the opportunities of the shrewd and masterful, and when free land no longer offered opportunity to the less aggressive, the picture changed. The original image was perhaps that of a race down a broad course with plenty of room for each runner. In such a sporting contest, either all start from scratch or the handicaps are so adjusted as to equalize the chances that all contestants will reach the goal at nearly the same instant. But in economic competition the course is frequently so crowded that not only the weaker but the more scrupulous are forced to the wall. And the handicapping is often on the opposite principle of that used in sport.

The extraordinary mobility of American life has also contributed to mislead us as to the true perspective. Striking instances of poor boys making their way to honorable and responsible positions divert attention from a great mass of hardworking men and women who at best get a fair living in prosperous times but are without security or resource when jobs fail or prices fall below costs of production.

Between political equality and economic inequality we have set one institution that has done much to keep a degree of balance in our total outlook. Our educational system has offered increasing opportunities to all without regard to social class or parental wealth. From the old district school and small college to our present generously equipped elementary and secondary schools, and in large measure to our endowed institutions and state universities, the system has kept doors open to students. It has excluded only those who were unable or unwilling to profit by study. In this field equality of opportunity does not mean the possibility of either monopoly or of ruthless competition. The success of A in acquiring knowledge, a broader outlook upon life, and a source of joy or solace throughout changes of fortune does not involve the defeat of B. There is enough knowledge, wisdom, and beauty to go around. The more widely culture is shared, the more each participant profits.

Nevertheless, education is not limited to the schools. As Protagoras long ago pointed out to Socrates, the great public scene is a powerful educative agency. When economic status counts most in the public eye, when economic leaders are eagerly listened to, whether they speak on business, government, religion, or education, the primacy is likely to be with inequality. Before the crash and depression inequality rode high.

II

It is time to look at the merits and values of the rival principles which exist side by side in our institutions. First, then, what can be said for equality? The ultimate grounds for the principle of equality are perhaps intricate, but ordinary experience with human nature suggests both explanations of why we claim equality and reasons why equality is a good principle of society. We may, if we please, call the first the psychological, the second the moral, grounds.

To say that we all are persons and want to be treated as such may seem merely to lug in a new name for ourselves, as though a new name could establish a principle. But the word 'person' stands for three stubborn facts in human nature which mutually support each other. They separate persons from both things and brutes.

Deepest, perhaps, is a fact in our feeling. Everyone not broken in spirit or cowed by fear has some feeling of self-preservation or self-respect which impels to self-defense. Everyone resents, if he dares, being shoved off the sidewalk, crowded out of line, or used as a doormat figuratively or literally. To shove back in turn is almost a reflex act; it is a sort of self-defense. But self-defense is not provoked by physical violence only. An attitude of arrogance or contempt on the part of another which implies a conceit of superiority may be felt as deeply as a blow or a shove. It is, we say, a slap in the face. It means virtually, "You do not count." An arbitrary command which is deemed to arise from mere power without authority arouses similar feeling. Self-defense, the first law of nature, does not permit my self to be ignored or lowered by another without protest.

The second fact of human nature which supports equality is that persons are rational. Men who can converse with one another, understand one another, and reason with one another must have some common basis. If I reason with you I assume that we are equal before the law of thought. Cicero expounded with eloquence this common sharing of mankind in right reason and the Roman jurist Ulpian declared that for natural law all men are equal.

A third fact in human nature which underlies personality is uncovered when we attempt to persuade a fellow being instead of coercing or threatening him. We assume, whatever metaphysicians may allege to the contrary, that he is free to decide, to answer "yes" or answer "no." This means again that he is a person, and on a level with us. If he promises, we hold him responsible to keep his word. If he breaks faith or deceives us, he is, we say, 'letting us down.' No one likes to be let down.

No society can disregard so elementary facts of human nature as are implied in treating all its members as persons and therefore as having some rights to equal consideration. Primitive groups treat fellow members as in some sense equals although they deny equal right to men of other groups whom they kill or enslave. With advancing civilization justice gains clearer definition and equality before the law becomes a distinctive feature. The Roman as he extended his empire humanized his justice by seeking a *jus aequum et bonum*—a law equal and good—as over against the stricter law of past tradition. The justice provided by the older common law of England was similarly broadened by equity, that is, fairness or equality to cover injustices for which the older law offered no remedy. Other moral qualities may be left to the protection of good taste, or public sentiments expressed in praise or blame. Justice is deemed so fundamental that the whole force of government must support it. And the critical test of progress may well be, How high a degree of equality does society through its institutions seek to secure?, provided that equality is sought by securing for the hitherto less-privileged the standards of living gained for the privileged class.

But justice does not stand still at the lowest level. Progress in justice has two stages in its advance: Some gain in living conditions, security, education, culture, is made, usually by a favored few; the sense of justice gradually seeks through institutions to extend this gain as widely as possible. The principle of equality has seldom sought to lower a standard except in cases in which privilege of the few has rested on exploitation of the many.

If the first moral ground of equality has been felt so long and so widely as seemingly to lift justice above all change of time and place, the second ground has as yet scarcely gained general recognition. This second ground is the need of cooperation in our present complex society. In earlier days absolute monarchs could build pyramids by a forced levy upon the people. Feudal lords could compel the labor of their villeins. Even recently sailors were dragged on board ships and made to serve for long voyages. War still resorts to the draft. But these earlier methods for securing concerted action are no longer available for carrying on industry and commerce. Nor does enlightened theory now claim that the lash of poverty is the only substitute for the blows of the whip. The most successful method of securing united effort among intelligent people is the method of cooperation. But cooperation implies that men be treated with the respect and consideration due to persons who are reasonable and free, responsible agents.

What are the springs and values of inequality? Three deeply rooted traits or drives of human nature, almost as universal as the impulse of self-defense, are the urge to power, the zest of rivalry, the response to praise and blame. All may plausibly be regarded as aiding in the struggle for existence and therefore as selected by nature. All three make for inequality.

Few tribes, if any, are without some individual or group that holds superior power. The older men, the medicine man, the patriarchal head of the family, the chief, are simpler types; king, nobility, priest, senate, merchant-prince, founders of industries, leaders of political parties, come with advancing civilization. Few attain conspicuous power, but many at some period of life feel its urge, even though its scope be petty. In older times military prowess, rule in family or state, ecclesiastical rank were natural paths to power. In present society power of wealth and property is both more attractive and seemingly less dependent upon any conditions outside of individual's own efforts. It is less dependent upon popular favor than power of office; it can be handed down to descendants with legal protection.

Rivalry no less than power implies contest and victory. William James's assertion that "nine-tenths of the work of the world is done by it" is very likely an exaggeration, but it is surely a force to be reckoned with in any inventory of human traits. Sports are universal and serve to stimulate strength, skill, endurance, courage. When feudal stability of status gave way to mobility, when the emergence of a middle class opened new fields of opportunity, and above all when competition was acclaimed as supreme economic law and finally as the law of evolution, the scope of rivalry broadened. To some it took the place of God.

Response to praise and blame and love of distinction have likewise firm roots in human nature. Desire of praise is matched by the readiness of men to acclaim and applaud the hero, the athlete, the warrior, the singer, the orator, the lawgiver, the sage, and in Sumner's phrase, the "man-who-can-do-things." It is as if we feel, in recognizing greatness, at least a certain kinship to great spirits, a certain lift in our own level, through the capacity to understand and admire, although we lack ability to achieve what we prize.

General experience as to inequality has been reinforced by certain lines of scientific exploration. It was not reserved for modern science to discover that certain individuals are more highly gifted than others; no one ever questioned it. Nor was it a new assertion that races and peoples differ. Jews looked down upon Gentiles; Greeks upon barbarians; whites upon blacks, Chinese upon all others; early colonists upon later immigrants. But anthropologists explored racial and cultural differences in greater detail. The theory of evolution seemed to point to inequality as a necessary factor in human progress. Intelligence testers found opportunity during the World War to apply their gradings to army recruits. Some enthusiasts have sought to reorganize our educational system on the basis of native capacities as shown by these tests. It is indeed a long step from superiority in certain abilities so tested to such a rating of respective values as would class certain individuals as higher in worth than others. No scientific scale of merit is competent to weigh accurately the value of the type that does the steady work of the world in comparison with the brilliant and erratic, or of the type that makes stable families as versus the type that is restless under fixed conditions. Nor does difference in *kind* of ability constitute inequality in a sense that is opposed to equality of personal worth in social philosophy. A complex society needs many types, and St. Paul long ago pointed out that the hand may be as necessary as the eye, the feet as the head.

As the moral values of equality are justice and cooperation, the moral value of inequality is that it stimulates to achievement and to excellence. It not only appeals to the impulses driving toward power, rivalry, and distinction; it sets conspicuous patterns for imitation. Examples of men who have risen above the mass set marks to aim at. Some men will do their best in the effort to surpass their own previous scores, but for many it is more stimulating to play against a competitor. A society seldom advances with equal front as does a line of troops on parade. More frequently a few push forward and show the way to the rest.

Yet it is instructive to note the perils of excelling, even in intellectual and moral traits. Not only the wise but the common man knows them. A man may be wiser and better than his neighbors, but it is very risky for his own character, as well as for his standing among his neighbors, to admit such superiority, even to himself. Conceit is not an aid to wisdom or moral excellence. 'Let another praise thee' is still good advice.

In case the superiority is one that involves power there is the added danger of pride, of hauteur, if not of arrogance or abuse. The inner moral check to abuse of power is responsibility. But responsibility does not always flower spontaneously. Responsibility to God or to some group has proved almost a necessary means of awakening the inner sense. Societies through the ages have been forced to limit the power of superiors in order to retain liberty for common men. Laws are a device to prevent any one from setting himself and his will in a class apart from other men, and to compel all to submit to equal restraints. Democratic government came largely, not so much as the most efficient method of getting things done, as a method of securing society against the perils of irresponsible power. In the Middle Ages economic power was regulated to some extent by moral considerations, but the modern theory has been that economic ambition needs no restraints. If each seeks his own wealth, the theory of Adam Smith held, all will be profited as if an invisible hand were directing the course of events. Except for the abolition of slavery, American theory has largely adhered to the belief that business, like kings of old, can do no wrong. It is scarcely surprising that business is bewildered and resentful at the present disposition to require truthfulness in advertising, responsibility in stock flotation, reserves for unemployment emergencies, publicity for extravagant salaries and bonuses.

III

Two issues have emerged in the depression and the 'New Deal' which involve problems of balance between equality and inequality. The first is that of cooperation in industry; the second, that of distribution in the national income.

The National Industrial Recovery Act provides that all codes of industries under the act shall be subject to the conditions "(1). That employees shall have the right to organize and bargain collectively through representatives of their own choosing." The purpose of this clause is evidently to place the employee in a more nearly equal position to bargain with the employer. Under present conditions the great employers are chiefly corporations. They act as collective bodies. They have the resources of millions of capital. They choose their own experts and legal advisers. It seems a matter of common fairness that workmen should be allowed to claim a right which the employer has exercised. Whether the courts will now follow Justice Pitney's logic and declare that when equality conflicts with liberty and private property, equality must give way, remains to be seen. Possibly they may conclude that a little equality is not necessarily fatal to liberty—or perhaps that the liberty of the workman is not sufficiently secured by a system of 'take it or leave it.' But in any case it is a landmark of public opinion that the Congress has thus recognized the right of collective bargaining.

Such an act of Congress, like some other laws, may be first nullified by powerful groups and then repealed. The second issue, namely, unequal distribution of incomes, is more stubborn. Extreme inequality in the past distribution of the national income is charged by many economists with being one of the causes of the depression. If it should be maintained that any interference with the present principles of distribution would be in violation of the Constitution, we should have to ask, Does the Constitution require national economic suicide? Chief Justice Hughes evidently thinks it does not. He has recently declared, speaking for the Court, "the State also continues to possess authority to safeguard the vital interests of its people."[3] If the conclusion of the economists is sound it means that such extreme inequality of property and income as that which prevails in the United States defeats itself. The logic appears simple. If industry is to produce, some must consume. The few who are well-to-do can consume only a small part of goods other than luxuries. The great body of goods produced must be consumed by those who are not well-to-do. Increased production can be marketed only if there is a rising standard of living and rising income on the part of the masses. If too large a share of the gains from industry and business goes into the possession of the few, or into idle surplus, or into expansion of plants, and too little into the returns to the farmer and the wages of workmen, the machinery stops. We have poverty in the midst of plenty. Extreme economic inequality breaks down of its own weight when given free scope in modern society.

In his "Gloucester Moors," William Vaughn Moody sees those on

3. Home Building and Loan Association v. Blaisdell, et al., 290 US 434 (1933).

deck in the Ship of Souls resist attempts to relieve the inequality suffered by those below:

> But they said, "Let be:
> Our ship sails faster thus."[4]

It now appears that to sail faster and then crash harder may not be the last word for navigation.

When the importance of equality for cooperation and the social order is receiving such testimony from unexpected quarters it is disconcerting to hear cries of retreat in the field of education. Rural schools have closed to deprive more than a million children of opportunity. This is indeed the result of adhering to the policy of compelling each small locality to provide its own schools, which worked fairly well when distribution of wealth or poverty was not so unequal. More serious in principle is the proposal to restrict secondary and higher education to those who can pay tuition. It is one thing to limit education to those who are diligent; it is quite another to limit opportunities for children by the financial status of their parents. The question is not, as some have stated it, "Has the young man or woman a *right* to a higher education at public cost?" It is rather, "Can the state wisely set up class inequality of opportunity in education, and thus add to the economic inequality which already threatens to overbalance our politic equality?"

4. William Vaughn Moody, *Gloucester Moors and Other Poems* (Boston: Houghton, 1901) 3.

The Institution as Agency of Stability and Readjustment in Ethics

30

I

When the mores are in flux it is natural to seek some firmer basis of moral standards. I need not recount the familiar list—God, Eternal Patterns, Reason, Nature, with capitals. But none of these historic absolutes has been able to remain changeless and at the same time continue to serve as standard. In the concise phrase of [Eugene] Dupréel, "neither nature better known, nor a reason given once for all, not gifts of intuition reserved for a few, can furnish the stability needed."

A recently proposed absolute is that of "essence." "Values," says Hartmann, are essences; "hence can be discerned only a priori. . . . Values do not change but our insight into them changes." Hartmann admits that the individual, as such, could reach no moral values; only when personal entities stand in actional relations to one another can there be any moral value or its opposite. "But," he continues, "the values themselves are neither contained in the relation nor, as it were, derivable from it. They come to it from another source—as standards, something new."[1]

Whether or not are such changeless essences behind the screen it is not my present purpose to inquire. Admittedly, if such essences be, our insight into them is as yet defective, and hence we can have no assurance that any standard within our possession or reach is either absolute or changeless. My inquiry is rather, How can we come by working standards that offer such stability as we crave in a changing

Reprinted by permission of the publisher from James Hayden Tufts, "The Institution as Agency of Stability and Readjustment in Ethics," *The Proceedings and Addresses of the APA* 8 (1934), 138–153. Copyright © 1934 American Philosophical Association [1934:02].

1. Nicolai Hartmann, *Ethics* (New York: Macmillan, 1932) 3 vols.

world? Perhaps Hartmann's "personal entities in actional relations" are a more fruitful source for human standards than his changeless "essences." At any rate, the distinctive character of the several moral standards is due to the concrete actional relations—or group relations—of human association. Kindness derives from kin; justice from conflicting claims; nobility from class-superiority; honesty from exchange of goods or services. Even science, which now sets a standard of truth, had its antecedent in the wisdom that guided and gave security to the social group. Yet civilized man has not been content with the types of group and actional relations which are based on biological origin and nurture or on nearness in space. Nor has he been content merely with mores that conserve the experience and wisdom of the past but resist change with all the strength of habit. A principal factor in moral advance has been that man has formed not only primary groups and mores but also institutions.

A characteristic of an institution is that, while conserving a large measure of what experience has taught, it also faces new situations and conflicting interests or forces under a necessity of partial readjustments. It brings a sense of direction and organizes impulses, habits, and collective strength to deal with the situation or conflict. It is a structure informed more or less consciously by a purpose to be carried through. It gains clearer consciousness of its purpose through the special setup or agency which it has organized. Justice was advanced when special men were appointed to hear disputed claims; when Hammurabi set up his code; when the praetor issued his edicts; and when courts began to record their decisions. Kindness that began with kinship has expanded its range and heightened its claims through agencies of charity and philanthropy. A God-intoxicated Spinoza or Thomas à Kempis might find inspiration in solitude, but the beloved community has been the constant fostering agency of religion. Truth gained in clarity and power through the organization of academies, schools, and universities.

The fundamental role of institutions in human welfare is stressed in the recent decision of the federal Supreme Court in the *Minnesota* case. In view of widespread distress among farmers and owners of small homes who were unable to meet their notes when due and were hence liable to lose their property by foreclosure, the State of Minnesota passed a law providing for the suspension of foreclosure proceedings, subject to an adjustment of payments to be approved by a court. The validity of the law was attacked on the ground that it was in violation of the clause of the federal Constitution which provides that no state shall pass any law impairing the obligation of contract. The Supreme Court in a five-to-four decision upheld the law. Mr. Chief Justice Hughes, speaking for the Court, declared, "The question is no longer merely that of one party to a contract as against another, but of the use of reasonable means to safeguard the economic structure upon which the good of all depends."

The division of the Court with reference to the decision is significant of the twofold purpose of law: It must protect stability; it must adjust to change. The four dissenting justices conceived the function of the Court to be restricted to a literal interpretation of the words of the Constitution. They found stability there. Their statement was, "The Constitution is a written instrument. As such its meaning does not alter. What it meant when adopted it means now." On the other hand, the majority of the Court concurred with the Chief Justice in the opinion, "It is manifest from this review of our decisions that there has been a growing appreciation of public needs and of the necessity of finding ground for a rational compromise between individual rights and public welfare."[2] Evidently the Court, as at present constituted, holds that to adjust institutions to changing needs and conditions is to seek the only kind of stability that is ultimately reliable in a changing world. I can but think that ethics will make greater progress by seeking its stability, as did the Court, in meeting the growing needs of changing man and changing society than in the search for changeless essences.

A further significant suggestion for ethics may be discerned in the phrasing of the Chief Justice previously quoted: "The question is no longer merely that of one party to a contract as against another, but of the use of reasonable means of safeguard the economic structure upon which the good of all depends." The Court holds that the structure is more fundamental than the claims or rights of individuals, which would all be lost if the structure were to be wrecked. An analogous question for ethics would be, Are there moral structures upon which the good of all depends? Examination of such structures, if such there be, may well be held urgent, timely, and even in some respects prior to questions of personal good.

As regards the urgency of such inquiry there is need but to mention the ever-present threat of war manifest in increasing expenditure for armament by all the great powers and not least by our own nation,

2. Home Building and Loan Association v. Blaisdell, et al., 290 US 442 (1933).

and the virtual suspension of free inquiry and discussion in three of the great nations of Europe. Even among us there are less open but nonetheless serious obstacles to free and intelligent formation of public opinion.

As regards timeliness it is pertinent to note that general interest has already shifted from personal character and its virtues to the discussion of the institutional aspects of morals. We do not now concern ourselves so much with the duty of personal kindness as with the question whether society should rely upon private charity to relieve burdens of accident, illness, old age, and unemployment, or whether the appropriate remedy is to be sought in social insurance, public works, or some form of public action which will preserve the morale of the unfortunate and the young. We are thinking of moral structures. All agree that wages should be 'fair,' but the proposal that the laborer through collective bargaining should have a voice assured him by government in a mutual consideration and determination of what is fair arouses determined protest and opposition. It is still prudent for the young man beginning his career to form the habit of paying his debts, but the deeper question presses for answer: What is a reasonable method of dealing with debts when fluctuating money values inevitably work hardship upon one or another class? The arguments for personal sobriety stand as stated by the sages of two thousand years ago, but the proper policy of government as to the sale of intoxicants in an automobile age, confronted by a commercial traffic seeking with all means to extend its sales, is far from settlement. The personal question whether I ought to bear arms in a war declared by my government may be serious to me, but its answer involves weighing nationalism in all its claims and perils. Finally, even the intimate problems of sex and divorce compel consideration of the place of marriage and the family in the process of civilization.

The insignificance of institutions for ethical theory and personal morals may be less obvious; it is no less real. Not all have openly avowed their dependence upon the patterns of social institutions for their categories as did Plato in the *Republic*, but subtle influence is nonetheless present in many of them. Dewey in his *Art as Experience* writes, "Morals are assigned a special compartment in theory and practice because they reflect the divisions embodied in economic and political institutions."[3] It is easy to see certain of these economic and political patterns in their origins. Oldest, perhaps, of all that have

3. John Dewey, *Art as Experience* (New York: Minton Balch, 1934) 348.

come down to us in recorded ethics is the symbol of the balance—an economic instrument—for justice, as we find it already the standard of appeal four thousand years ago in the Tale of the Eloquent Peasant from ancient Egypt. Political institutions, social class, and economic status provided most of the ethical terms of the Greeks and the Romans. Utilitarianism leaned hard on economic concepts. Bentham's units of pleasure have been identified by [John R.] Commons with the subjective use-value of Adam Smith; Bentham's standard for measuring pleasure—if we may trust an unpublished manuscript as revealing his working conception—was frankly the economic unit, money. For comparing two pleasures, two pains, or pain and pleasure, he wrote, "[I]f we would understand one another we must make use of some common measure. The only common measure the nature of things affords is money." Kant on the other hand spoke in legal categories of 'universal law,' and in his concept of autonomy transferred the political concept of democracy to the inner duty of life.

An objection often urged against the ethical values of institutions is that they are conventions. A firmer basis, a more valid standard, has been sought in nature. Dupréel, whom I have previously quoted, would reverse this estimate. Convention, he points out, means agreement. It presupposes minds in relation to one another. It substitutes new reasons founded in agreement for purely mechanical causes of action. The essence of spiritual values, something new, is independence of factual causes. The defect of mores from this point of view is then not that they are conventional, but that they have too little of the element of convention—of agreement between active minds confronting a new need. The superiority of an institution is in just this factor of conscious will and concurrent action which both enables and compels it to make readjustment. Only by such readjustment can it survive. In readjustment lies its stability. A standard for ethics in a changing world must be capable of change if it is to continue as standard.

II

If on the one hand institutions have been an agency through which man has sought stability and progress, and if through institution and convention certain values dimly felt at first have emerged more clearly as men have worked and struggled to secure and maintain them, it is also true that there must be a converse influence of values and principles upon institutions. The very nature of an institution consists in its singling out some special interest, in its selection of some one purpose, for advancement. To secure this advancement it is constantly in danger of disregarding other human needs. It requires correction from the point of view of the total life of person and society, that is, from a moral point of view. At times this moral control over specific institutions comes to be felt as rigorous and constricting. It may then be thrown off. Such was the case when politics and economic activities sought to divest themselves of the moral control exercised through the medieval Church. In the field of government, however, one moral principle, one moral structure, survived and has emerged clearer and stronger than in any previous period. The principle is that power of man over his fellows must be coupled with responsibility. Union of responsibility with power may well be called a fundamental moral structure. To safeguard this structure is a task in which the philosopher may share.

Power is an agency of progress. Human life has lifted and enriched through power over natural forces and through power of association and organization. Religion, government, and more recently science and invention have been conspicuous agencies in discovering or increasing power. Engineers call this the power age, as contrasted with the machine age of yesterday. Some, for example, [Lewis] Mumford, see in this shift the promise of a better day. But neither technology nor the advance of science will necessarily safeguard the moral structure. Increase in sheer power but makes the moral structures more precarious. Experience has shown that only as power is attended with responsibility is its exercise by mortals safe. It has taken six thousand years of struggle and experiment to establish responsibility in government. So late as the period of the American Revolution, as Trevelyn has shown in his *Life of Charles James Fox*,[4] public offices in Great Britain were treated as a means for private enrichment, and public opinion was silently acquiescent. Yet today the principle that the power of government is to be exercised with responsibility to nation or community is generally accepted among civilized peoples. Democracy, fascism, communism differ as to the authority vested with power, but no national ruler declares that he is rightfully entitled to exercise power for his own gain or glory and that he has a right to all that he can get.

Contrast with the political the economic situation. Here is an institu-

4. George Otto Trevelyn, *The Early History of Charles James Fox* (New York: Longmans, Green, 1881).

tion which clearly needs readjustment to meet new conditions. It recognizes responsibilities in the well-established relations of contract but is insensitive to the responsibilities to the public for the new power that has recently come into being. Three facts stand out.

The first fact is that when our national life began and institutions were taking form we were an agrarian people. There was little business in the modern sense; property was mainly in land. In a nation of small farmers a man's holding did not give him a power over his neighbor; it was his home. The long struggle with the Stuarts and that of the colonists against the British government had focused in the defense of property against power of taxation. Property was not so much a power as a right.

The second fact is that with the change from agrarian to industrial culture have come expansion of business, improvement in organization of invention and association, increased interdependence between man and man, vast increase in wealth. Business and property have ceased to be a right only; they have become a power. They assert the prerogative of planning a program for government. Sometimes they attempt to control government through influence upon the press and education; witness the report of the Federal Trade Commission upon the campaign of Public Utilities to enlist newspapers and teachers on their behalf. The corporate method of organization has both increased power and lessened older personal restraints and responsibility. In 1927 more than half of the industry of the nation was controlled by two hundred corporations. Within these great corporations active management is necessarily concentrated. In the phrase of Berle and Means, "The concentration of economic power separate from ownership has, in fact, created economic empires, and has delivered these empires into the hands of a new form of absolutism."[5]

The third fact is that consequences of economic processes are not limited to the economic field. They are seen in the building of factory towns, in the crowding of population into cities with attendant loss of neighborhood relations, in the segregation of social classes on a property basis, in the unequal burden thrown upon the rural population for the rearing and education of children, in the general flux of mores, in the disastrous effects of cycles of depression and unemployment upon large numbers, especially upon the young.

For these far-reaching consequences business and accumulating

5. Adolf A. Berle, Jr., and Gardiner C. Means, *The Modern Corporation and Private Property* (New York: Macmillan, 1933) 124.

property have hitherto taken little if any thought. We have conducted our economic affairs almost like a young and enthusiastic automobilist who is interested so completely in maximum speed that he ignores others and especially pedestrians. Perhaps it would have been too much to ask that industry should hold itself responsible for the larger results of its high-powered machine. And it is far from fair to blame individuals for not setting standards of responsibility which would mean economic ruin unless generally observed. But now that we have been forced to pause and reflect, the saying of St. Paul would seem apposite: "The times of this ignorance God winked at, but now commandeth men to repent." Fascism's method of dealing with the situation is to subordinate business, industry, and personal liberty to national power. Communism abolishes private gain, largely private property, and also a large measure of personal liberty. Can democracy so deal with the situation as to retain the individual initiative that has contributed to our economic advance, and the personal liberty of thought and discussion that has been our just pride? If democracy is to keep economic power, the moral prerequisite is that business and property shall both be held, and hold themselves, responsible, instead of standing wholly upon their rights and letting consequences take care of themselves.

Of course the skirts of philosophy are not wholly clear. Adam Smith's social philosophy seemed to emancipate economic management from moral responsibility. If the very nature of things were such as to ensure that private wealth necessarily made for public good, what need for further concern? And the soundness of the theory seemed to be attested by the extraordinary advances in standards of living made possible by the inventions of the age, the resources of a new country, and the energies of mind that were quick to see the opportunities of the new power. But Smith wrote before the Industrial Revolution.

A recent investigation by a Senate committee brought out two statements which illustrate the uncertain attitude of businessmen engaged in the manufacture and sale of munitions. One such dealer proposed to the committee that, for the future, sales to foreign powers be subject to approval by the government, and that profits in case of war be similarly controlled. The other was content to say, "I am a businessman and my business is to sell munitions." He apparently disclaimed any further responsibility to the public. The efforts of certain firms to wreck a former disarmament conference are notorious. The recent program of the Sulpher Springs Conference of business executives shows little sensitiveness to other than the purely economic bearings of economic policies.

Absolute rights of property have indeed repeatedly been challenged, but usually at the instance of some section or class so that the resulting control has often failed of general acceptance as morally binding. Property in slaves was swept away by war; property in railroads suffered lowered income at the instance of shippers, particularly of farmers; manufacture and sale of intoxicants were limited or prohibited at the demand of 'reformers'; factory legislation and employers' liability were urged by organized labor.

The federal Supreme Court, however, in its epoch-making decision of *Munn vs. Illinois* a half century ago, laid down a principle that definitely recognized the responsibility to the public of "property affected with a public interest." With the increasing interdependence of the members of modern industrial society it is becoming correspondingly difficult to draw a sharp line between property that is so affected and property that is not. The federal Supreme Court itself has until recently been cautious about extending the list of businesses so affected beyond the earlier included classes of transportation and so-called 'public utilities.' Two recent decisions, however, makes it clear that the class of property affected with a public interest is by no means closed. Mr. Justice Roberts, speaking for the Court in the *Nebbia* case, in which the authority of New York State to regulate the price of milk was upheld, declared, "It is clear that there is no closed class or category of businesses affected with a public interest. . . . The phrase 'affected with a public interest' can, in the nature of things, mean no more than that an industry, for adequate reason, is subject to control for the public good."[6] In the *Minnesota* case the Supreme Court affirmed, as against a strict interpretation of one clause in the federal Constitution, the authority of a state under the police power to modify, if not the obligation of contract, at least the ordinary legal remedy of foreclosure for breach of contract. But, the Chief Justice, speaking for the Court, adds significantly, "the State also continues to possess authority to safeguard the vital interests of its people."[7]

Just what the "vital interests" of the people may in the future require in the way of control of government over property and business is then as yet undetermined. J. B. S. Haldane suggests that part of the difficulty in dealing with economic problems is due to our attempt

6. Nebbia v. New York, 291 US 536 (1933).
7. 290 US 434.

to retain an agricultural point of view in dealing with an industrial civilization. In an agrarian economy private ownership of land proved a valuable policy, whereas in an industrial civilization "the idea of absolute ownership which worked well enough for a cow or a field will not work when applied to a public utility," and "the numbers of industries which must be regarded as public utilities is constantly growing."

Undoubtedly the question of the governmental enforcement of responsibility has two sides. For the dialectically minded philosopher it does not lack the charm of the dual between realism and idealism, or of that between absolutism and pragmatism. On the one side is the principle of natural rights with the historic association between religious, civil, and economic liberty, buttressed by the imposing structures of modern civilization built from private initiative. Our leading automobile manufacturer is of the opinion that no help toward better industrial conditions has or can come from governmental interference; advance comes through the laboratory, the workshop, and skilled management. And freedom is justly a power in the sphere of ethics, for it stands for something fundamental to personality. On the other side is the risk, if it may not fairly be called the folly, of committing to irresponsible power, and especially to corporations organized for profit, the decisive voice in the production and distribution of goods and income. Over against the great fortunes and the multiplication of inventions increasingly available for the common man stands the inequality in distribution which not only hampers economic security but is ever a grave threat to social stability in a nation that cherishes political equality.

Whatever the attitude toward governmental enforcement of responsibility on the part of economic power, the grounds for refusing to admit exemption from *moral* responsibility are strong. The consequences of irresponsible power in the economic field have a way of meeting us in areas long recognized as distinctly moral. An experience of the past summer may illustrate the point. When entering Chicago to attend the exposition commemorating a "Century of Progress," I was forcibly reminded of one situation in which the past forty years had seen little or no progress. The train passed through the same region that met my eye when I went to Chicago to live, forty years ago. I saw the same housing, the same dwellings unfit for human habitation, the same squalid surroundings. Approximately similar sights greet the traveler on the elevated roads in New York. It has been estimated that if left to private enterprise it will take two hundred years to replace New York's bad tenements with dwellings fit for human habitation as measured by modern standards. It is a commonplace among social scientists and social workers that such neighborhoods are breeding places and nurseries of criminals. Doubtless not all criminals grow up in city slums and not all children from city slums become criminals. Nevertheless, as agencies of wholesome education city slums leave much to be desired. It is not economically remunerative for owners to rebuild on a decent basis. Even the federal government finds its rebuilding program rendered difficult if not estopped by inability to meet costs of land and construction and provide a standard return to investment, without charging rentals beyond the reach of prospective tenants. Apparently, if economic considerations have the final word, city slums must be indefinitely retained in the richest nation in the world. The situation is not due to the reprehensible conduct of individuals. It is a consequence of making economic return the necessary measure of standards of living and of moral environment and education for the young.

Early environment and family background are not the only points at which economic forces pass over into the moral field. Such depressions as the business cycles have brought are not limited in effects to deficiencies in food and clothing. Those engaged in education are made aware of perils to the morale of young people who find doors of opportunity closed and face not only the evils of idleness and discouragement but postponement of marriage and family life. Simpler agrarian systems gave vocational training of a sort to young people, cared for the aged, and provided subsistence, even though meager, for all. Our industrial system, with notable exceptions, has assumed no responsibility for suitable training for the young, for the care of those past their prime, or for steady employment. The adoption of liability for industrial accidents was an effective incentive to the introduction of safeguards for dangerous machinery. There is reason to believe that similar liability for the issue of securities, for unemployment, for the care of those worn out by the industrial process, might sensibly reduce the present evils. Russia, Italy, Germany are trying to meet certain of these problems in ways that curtail or abolish freedom. If we wish to avoid fascism or communism, is it not more reasonable to apply the democratic principle of responsibility to economic institutions than to ignore responsibility, and hope by shouting loudly enough against communism to drown all complaints?

The increased assumption of responsibility by society, either through government or through voluntary cooperation, is sincerely deplored by some as indicating a lessening of personal initiative and of personal rights. The fact that personal rights were in past years asserted largely in opposition to the class governments of the period led to a sharp antithesis between person and government which easily became the antithesis, if not hostility, of person to state. The conception often held today seems to be that of a fixed number of powers and functions, which are to be divided between person and community but are incapable of increase. Whatever is added to the one is regarded as necessarily subtracted from the other. Every function assumed by the community is believed to leave the person poorer in person and powers. In fact the real purpose of requiring responsibility from economic power is to enlarge the sphere of personal freedom and dignity. It is to claim for the person protection against abuse of economic power similar to that which an earlier day asserted against political power.

Personal rights of the early days were, in fact, very limited. The economic right demanded by pioneer conditions seemed to be the right of property. When every man was on his own there was no need of a right to work. Boundless unoccupied land made further provision by society unnecessary. The aged and helpless had a dubious right to subsistence under the status of pauper which ordinarily carried with it a deprivation of political rights and of self-respect. There was no general right to education. It is reminiscent of that earlier day that the Liberty League, organized to protect rights, in the literature that has come to my attention emphasizes only the right of property and says nothing as to possible responsibilities.

The deeper moral consciousness of the day is feeling its way both toward a widening and deepening of the rights of the person—not merely of the fortunate or gifted few—and toward adequate agencies for securing these rights. In Europe there has been a revolt of the masses against barriers that had shut out the many from the goods of civilization. In America the extraordinary increase of high school and college attendance marks an eager grasp of opportunity by classes that had formerly been content with lower standards of education and more meager development of personality. It is because of the feeling that the community should protect not only bare subsistence but also self-respect and morale against the defects of a too imperfectly responsible economic system—not because a 'brain trust' has fallen in love with an entity called the state—that men who sense reality are not content with the older limits set for personality by the class and scarcity conditions of the past.

The law is often thought to be the most conservative of institutions.

It is necessarily conservative, for it uses compulsion and therefore may well hesitate to move in advance of general moral clarity. Yet its changing emphases may show shifts in moral attitudes, and at times points the way to moral advance. In Dean Pound's account of the ends of law we find the emphasis moving in the ancient world from that of keeping the peace to that of maintaining the status quo of the social order, and in the modern period from natural rights and the greatest possible assertion of individual wills toward a securing as much of the whole body of human wants as we may with the least sacrifice. The self-assertion of individual will is doubtless one phase of personality, but it may, if irresponsible, involve disregard of human wants. It is what many understand by freedom. It is indeed, says Dean Pound, "a philosophy of law for discoverers and colonizers and pioneers and traders and entrepreneurs and captains of industry." He adds, "I am content to see in legal history the record of a continually wider recognizing and satisfying of human wants or claims or desires through social control, a more embracing and more effective securing of social interests, a continually more complete and effective elimination of waste." And finally Mr. Chief Justice Hughes in the decision already cited affirms a similar twofold process of personal security and social control. After summarizing the changes in our economic and social conditions he declares that these changes "have inevitably led to an increased use of the organization of society to protect the very bases of individual opportunity."[8]

The bases of opportunity, the meaning of personality and its potential growth, the implications of responsibility for the exercise of power—these are surely among what the late Professor Calkins called the "persistent problems of philosophy."[9] The new aspirations, hopes, powers of mankind offer new themes for reflection. They invite and challenge philosophy to contribute toward their clarification and interpretation.

It remains to note two theories of natural and social forces, either of which, if valid, would reduce the philosopher's function to that of observer merely. Two years ago on my weekly trips to Westwood I used to pass on the boulevard the elderly Indian who stood on the sidewalk at an intersecting street and went through all the motions of a traffic officer directing the stream of hurrying cars. He is said to have

8. 290 US 442.
9. Mary Whiton Calkins, *The Persistent Problems of Philosophy* (New York: Macmillan, 1907).

fancied that his gestures stopped or released the flow. No one thought it worthwhile to deter him; he did no harm. But the drivers of cars watched the signals controlled by the automatic mechanism. Is the position of the philosopher similar to that of the elderly Indian? Is the determining force of civilization not ideas and words or gestures, but mechanism?

A second ground for regarding ideas as futile is seen by some in the resistless strength of collectives desperate from repression or entrenched by the combined power of prestige and possessions. The united proletariat, the armed Fascists, the organized property-holding class with virtual control over government—what reck they of liberal ideas? They set up their own institutions; they create and impose their own standards.

To ignore the tremendous role in civilization of the cosmic forces which have placed man here and fashioned his makeup as a 'going concern,' or to deny that seemingly irrational drives of mob action, revolution, and counter mass-movements at times burst all bounds and defy rational control would indeed be silly. But it is late in the day to ignore or belittle the power of ideas. An earlier generation might well dread the lightning, but electric energy has become a useful and for the most part an obedient servant. What more immovable than continents, yet we converse across the ocean. Gravitation long defied ideas of flight, but the conquest of the air has been achieved. Impounded waters have often broken all bounds in roaring torrents, but we do not hesitate to dam the Colorado, the Tennessee, the Columbia. The individual dies, but man builds institutions that live on, superior to nature's limits. Natural drives may furnish the raw stuff of human activities—drives for food, for sexual satisfaction, for power, for self-defense—but it is ideas that shape these into institutions, domestic, political, economic. Nor is it the ideas of the masters only—of a Locke, a Rousseau, an Adam Smith, a Marx. Many minds contribute to shape and reshape our fundamental structures. And it was of an American philosopher that Turgot said, "Eripuit caelo fulmen, sceptrumque tyrannis." I venture to think that William James would say that the philosopher of today who looks at his world confronts a live option.

31 Reunion Letter

Fifty years means something, even to an institution which is constantly renewing its youth. But to the class of '89 Divinity, fifty years means a working lifetime! Some of the best among them have finished their work—of these, two bore names honored in Yale history, Theodore Bacon and Frank Shipman. Some because of distance from New Haven cannot be present today. Those of us who are here salute the young men who stand with courage and high hope where we stood fifty years ago. We salute also those of the middle years who are day by day making the decisions that shape history. Finally, and to us most important, we rejoice to renew contact with the institution which sought to give us open minds and courageous hearts.

For the individual's span at best is short. His working years are soon counted. He can accomplish little alone. But man has learned to build institutions. Through these he gives cumulative strength and enduring life to aims and ideals of generations and ages. Justice would be fragmentary without courts. Religion would be a lonely struggle without the church. Science and education would advance with halting step were there no university. The university not only hands on the torch but also brings successive generations into quickening contact with living men who embody the spirit of inquiry and the purpose to help mankind.

We of '89 Divinity studied with some of the great scholars and teachers of the older generation—Samuel Harris, George Park Fisher, Timothy Dwight. We found a new Old Testament and a new ancient

From *After Fifty Years: A Report of the Class of '89, Yale Divinity School*, ed. James Gibson Robertson (Cambridge, NY: Press of the Washington County *Post*, 1939) 52–55 [1939:01].

world under the inspiring enthusiasm of William Rainey Harper. A few caught glimpses of a new field opening in anthropology and sociology in the classroom of William Graham Sumner. But in the regular curriculum of the Divinity School there was no mention of social problems or labor movements. As no teacher of that day foresaw the automobile, the airplane, the radio, so none could anticipate the changes in the intellectual and social worlds which we were to experience.

Changes in the intellectual world affecting religious conceptions and beliefs have been far more fundamental than those brought about by the Reformation. Shifts from country to city, from farm to shop, the crumbling of the family, the disappearance of Sunday as a distinctive day of rest and worship generally observed have set hard tasks for the preacher. Social classes have become class conscious. Hopes which fifty years ago were widely cherished of a peaceful evolution toward justice and general well-being have been dashed by wars. The Christian teaching that "God has made of one all nations" has been repudiated by a masterful government.

Such issues are not settled in one generation. It does not suffice to repeat the old answers. Our religious symbols must interpret a different universe. The Good News of Judea does not afford ready-made solutions for our industrial conflicts. Still less will an appeal to Sinai command peace or secure justice. We realize, perhaps even more clearly than the apostle, that we know in part. Yet our generation has not suffered moral and spiritual defeat. It may count at least three gains in the religious field. They are not spectacular, as are the advances in science and invention. But we think they are real.

(1) The profound change which has come in our conceptions of the universe has not seen the leaders of religious thought fighting the leaders of science nor fearing the truth; the Gladstone-Huxley duel has not been repeated.

(2) If studies in evolution and psychology have disclosed deeper roots for the lusts and passions which used to be charged conveniently to the wiles of Satan, religion in turn has not failed to deepen its own foundations in human nature. As scholars have studied sympathetically the religions of the world and of the ages, they have found religion rooted deep in the needs and aspirations of humanity.

(3) As science and invention have been bringing men nearer together we have seen a growing sense of social responsibility. We are giving a broader answer to the question, Who is my neighbor? The

common people in nearly all countries have come not merely to fear, but to abhor war.

Amid the changes which our generation has seen these gains are evidence that there abide faith in truth and right, hope for a better order, love for fellow men. And the greatest of these still is love.

Annotated Bibliography: The Writings of James Hayden Tufts

Index

Annotated Bibliography: The Writings of James Hayden Tufts

1889:01 "A Word to '89."
Amherst Literary Monthly 4.3 (1889): 145–146.

In this letter to the class of 1889—many of whom he had taught mathematics during his years as instructor at Amherst (1885–1987)—JHT, who had just completed his divinity studies at the Yale Divinity School, calls on them to live lives of service to the community.

1892:01 *The Sources and Development of Kant's Teleology.*
Chicago: U of Chicago P, 1892. ii + 48 pp.

In his doctoral dissertation, completed at the Albert-Ludwigs-Universität in Freiburg, JHT examines the topic of final causes. The text itself is in English, although it cites numerous passages in German, French, and Latin. In the first chapter, he discusses teleology in modern philosophy prior to Kant, with special reference to Leibniz. Chapter 2 explores Kant's thought up to 1762, demonstrating his general support for the recognition of final causes in his early work and the beginnings of Hume's influence; chapter 3 considers Kant's development through the first *Kritik*. In chapter 4, JHT considers the development of Kant's understanding of final causes after 1781 and suggests the continued importance of Kant's inquiry.

1893:01 Translator and editor of Wilhelm Windelband, *A History of Philosophy, with Especial Reference to the Formation and Development of Its Problems and Conceptions.*
New York: Macmillan, 1893. xiii + 659 pp.

In this translation of Windelband's 1892 *Geschichte der Philosophie*, JHT offers (1) the Translator's Preface that emphasizes the importance of the history of philosophy and the special value of the Windelband text, and some comments on particular German-English equivalencies; (2) numerous bibliographical additions to the original that indicate sources in English; (3) occasional elaborations on the translation of key terms; (4) occasional textual clarifications; and (5) a brief interpolation on David Hume (pp. 475–476). (JHT later translated the second edition [1901:01].)

1895:01 Review of Albion Woodbury Small and George Edgar
Vincent, *An Introduction to the Study of Society*;
Gabriel Tarde, *Les Transformations du droit*, 2ème ed.;
R. Berthelot, "L'Imitation et la logique sociale";
Georg Simmel, "Le Problème de la sociologie"; and
Emile Durkheim, "Les Règles de la methode
sociologique."
Psychological Review 2.3 (1895): 305–309.

A discussion of recent sociological literature organized around the questions of the province of sociology, its relationship to psychology, and the methods proper to the study of society.

1895:02 Review of Alois Riehl, *Introduction to the Theory of Science
and Metaphysics*.
Philosophical Review 4.4 (1895): 432–435.

In this discussion of a translation of part of a work by his dissertation director, JHT praises Riehl for his insightful Kantian contributions to the philosophy of science. JHT concludes with some remarks on the translation of philosophical German into English.

1895:03 Review of Marcel Bernès, "La Sociologie: ses conditions
d'existence, son importance scientifique et
philosophique," and "Sur la méthode de la sociologie."
Psychological Review, 2.4 (1895): 407–408.

A highly favorable account of two recent articles on social psychology.

1895:04 Review of Charles Douglas, *John Stuart Mill: A Study of His
Philosophy*.
Philosophical Review 4.5 (1895): 572–573.

A brief but highly favorable review of an attempt to save Mill from charges of inconsistency.

1895:05 Review of M. Lapie, "L'Année sociologique, 1894," and
Gabriel Tarde, *La Logique sociale*.
Psychological Review 2.6 (1895): 616–618.

A discussion of recent writing on the growth of the psychological approach to the study of society and on the social factors that make society possible.

1896:01 Recent Sociological Tendencies in France."
American Journal of Sociology 1.4 (1896): 446–456.

In this article, reconsidering the material reviewed in 1895:01, 1895:03, and 1895:05, Tufts discusses the recent work of Tarde, Berthelot, Simmel, Durkheim, Bernès, and Lapie. His general theme is the inadequacy of biological categories and metaphors (like 'organism') and the superiority of psychological categories and metaphors (like 'person') for the study of society.

1896:02 "Refutations of Idealism in the *Lose Blätter*."
Philosophical Review 5.1 (1896): 51–58.

This discussion of aspects of idealism found in the two volumes of Kant's manuscripts (JHT reviewed volume two in the same number of *Psychological Review* [1896:03]) suggests the importance of the study of the six refutations of idealism for understanding Kant's philosophical development, especially as they are related to the question of the "thing-in-itself."

1896:03 Review of Rudolph Reicke, ed., *Lose Blätter aus Kant's Nachlass. Zweites Heft;* and Erich Adickes, *Kant-Studien.*
Philosophical Review 5.1 (1896): 64–69.

JHT's discussion of Reicke's second volume of selections from Kant's manuscripts is a general survey of the contents. His discussion of Adickes's study of the development of Kant's thought supports Adickes's rejection of Benno Erdmann's chronology.

1896:04 Review of Max Apel, *Kants Erkenntnisstheorie und seine Stellung zur Metaphysik: Eine Einführung in das Studium von Kants "Kritik der Reinen Vernunft".*
Philosophical Review 5.3 (1896): 326.

JHT finds Apel's discussion of Kant's epistemology inadequate either as an introduction, since it presumes too much, or as an advanced study, since it relies too heavily on familiar material.

1896:05 Review of Georg Albert, *Kants transcendentale Logik mit besonderer Berücksichtigung der schopenhauerschen Kritik der kantischen Philosophie.*
Philosophical Review 5.3 (1896): 327.

A brief critical note.

1897:01 Review of Gédéon Gory, *L'Immanence de la raison dans la connaissance sensible.*
Philosophical Review 6.3 (1897): 297–301.

A mildly favorable discussion of a generally Kantian attempt to analyze the use and misuse of intellectual abstractions.

1897:02   Review of Gustave Le Bon, "Psychologie du socialisme."
          Psychological Review 4.3 (1897): 316–317.

A summary of a discussion of socialism understood as a collective belief in conflict with inherited sentiments of conservatism.

1897:03   Review of Bernard Bosanquet, "Sociology and Philosophy."
          Psychological Review 4.3 (1897): 317–318.

A brief summary of a discussion of the relationship of social science to social psychology.

1897:04   Can Epistemology be Based on Mental States?"
          Philosophical Review 6.6 (1897): 577–592.

JHT opens with a consideration of the value of inquiry into the theory of knowledge, especially when an idea or thought is seen as a 'copy' of reality. Any such theory, he suggests, is inadequate because of the problems of evaluating the accuracy of the copy and because of the implications of passive mind. JHT's response is to present such judgments as the interpretation of one part of reality by another and to use as the criterion of judgment its social workability. In this way, JHT believes, truth can be integrated with beauty and goodness, and the moral and spiritual values of nature can be integrated with the intellectual values of the scientist. (Cf. 1898:04.)

1897:05   Review of Franklin Henry Giddings, *The Principles of
          Sociology* and *The Theory of Socialization;*
          and James Mark Baldwin, "The Genesis of Social
          Interests."
          Psychological Review 4.6 (1897): 660–664.

In his discussion of two volumes by Giddings, JHT focuses on his contribution to the advance of social psychology, a contribution that he considers to be substantial in spite of Giddings's lingering Spencerian rather than Jamesian psychology. The favorable discussion of Baldwin summarizes the article, emphasizing the importance of the *socius*.

1898:01   *The Individual and His Relation to Society as Reflected in
          British Ethics.*
          Part 1. *The Individual in Relation to Law and Institutions*
          (with Helen B. Thompson).
          University of Chicago Contributions to Philosophy, no. 5
          Chicago: U of Chicago P, 1898. 53 pp.

In this little volume, JHT considers aspects of the development of individualism in modern British thought prior to Shaftesbury. He begins with a consideration of the social background—the rise of communication and manufacturing, colonization, the nation state, individual conscience, and freer thought and speech—that contributed to the growth of individualism. The second section considers thought about the nature and importance of individualism. JHT begins with the growing recognition of private interest as a rational force in economic reality, and with the theological recognition of the individual's direct access to Scripture and to reason as means to determining the Divine Will. In his consideration of political theory, JHT emphasizes the growing importance of the claims of sovereignty of the people as presented by religious thinkers like Richard Hooker, Richard Mather and John Milton, and by Thomas Hobbes. JHT then turns to developments in ethical thought considering Francis Bacon and Hobbes. (Thompson's contribution [pp. 27–45] examines Cumberland, emphasizing the relationship between the individual and the group through reason and benevolence.) Finally, in his consideration of John Locke, JHT emphasizes Locke's role as a bridge between the past and the future who turned the growth of individuality into rights. (JHT's examination of the development of British ethics is continued in 1904:01.)

1898:02 "The Relation of Philosophy to Other Graduate Studies."
Graduate Courses, 1898–99: A Handbook for Graduate Students, ed. George Wyllys Benedict.
Chicago: U of Chicago P, 1898. xix–xxxi.

In this address to the Annual Convention of Graduate Clubs, JHT discusses several aspects of graduate education centering on the relationship of specialized doctoral study to the broader aspects of college teaching. In the spirit of Emerson's address, "The American Scholar," JHT advocates that potential teachers develop a sense of the broad historical and intellectual context of their particular specialties. The role of philosophy is to criticize the assumptions and proceedings of the particular sciences and to emphasize the importance of the unity of knowledge and the unity of life. Philosophy is also of value itself as an instrument of the advance of truth.

1898:03 Review of James Mark Baldwin, *Social and Ethical Interpretations in Mental Development: A Study in Social Psychology*.
Psychological Review 5.3 (1898): 313–321.

JHT offers a highly favorable discussion that summarizes Baldwin's account of the development of the self as an essentially social entity and considers aspects of ethics, the emotions, intelligence, and so on. In addition to occasional interpolations, JHT concludes with a series of questions about Baldwin's use of such concepts as the social self, the will, and imitation.

1898:04 "A Reply [to John Edward Russell]."
Philosophical Review 7.4 (1898): 396–397.

In this brief response to a criticism of 1897:04, JHT rejects the claim that his view as presented there results in idealism since he denies a break between experience and reality. He then repeats his call that we consider the less than absolute levels of truth, beauty, and goodness to be an incentive for future efforts.

1898:05 Review of Otto Willmann, *Geschichte des Idealismus.* Dritter Band. *Der Idealismus der Neuzeit.*
Philosophical Review 7.5 (1898): 523–526.

JHT criticizes this Thomistic history of idealism in modern philosophy for its scholastic narrowness and for its failure to recognize that the truly idealistic elements in modern thought are to be found in the ideals of freedom and individuality.

1899:01 Review of Simon Nelson Patten, *The Development of English Thought: A Study in the Economic Interpretation of History.*
Philosophical Review 8.5 (1899): 518–524.

A markedly critical discussion of a volume that offers, in place of JHT's ideal of grounding philosophical ideas in the activities of life, various psychological and materialistic reductions. (cf. 1903:07).

1899:02 Review of Franklin Henry Giddings, *The Elements of Sociology.*
Psychological Review 6.5 (1899): 533–536.

A mildly critical examination of an attempt to elaborate a social psychology from the point of view of Spencer and associationist psychology.

1899:03 Review of Cyrille Blondeau, *L'Absolu et sa loi constitutive.*
Philosophical Review 8.6 (1899): 657–658.

A critical discussion of a combination of Spinoza and Pascal with modern psychology and physiology.

1899:04 Review of Ludwig Goldschmidt, *Kant und Helmholtz: Populärwissenschaftliche Studie.*
Philosophical Review 8.6 (1899): 658.

A brief critical notice.

1899:05 Review of Gustav Wolff, *Zur Psychologie des Erkennens:*
Eine biologische Studie.
Philosophical Review 8.6 (1899): 659.

A brief descriptive review of a criticism of natural selection.

1900:01 [Report of the Dean of the Senior Colleges.]
The President's Report, 1898–1899.
Chicago: U of Chicago P, 1900. 27–34.

In this report on the conditions of the Senior Colleges for 1898–1899, JHT
discusses developments in enrollments and degree requirements.

1900:02 Review of George Frederick Stout, *A Manual of Psychology.*
Biblical World 16.3 (1900): 228–230.

This favorable discussion of a genetic elaboration of psychology by the editor
of *Mind* finds the book helpful to those, especially teachers and preachers, who
would understand the development of character, self-organization, coherent
thought, and so on.

1901:01 Translator and editor of Wilhelm Windelband, *A History of*
Philosophy, with Especial Reference to the Formation and
Development of Its Problems and Conceptions. 2d ed., rev.
and enl.
New York: Macmillan, 1901. xv + 726 pp.

In this translation of Windelband's 1900 "completely revised and expanded
edition" of his *Geschichte der Philosophie*, JHT offers, in addition to his contributions to the first edition [1893:01] and the translation of Windelband's changes
from the first edition (which consist primarily in a rewritten chapter on the
nineteenth century and an appendix containing modifications of his earlier
text) (1) a brief translator's note on the second edition, (2) occasional improvements in his translations and bibliography, and (3) an interpolated section on
British ethics in the nineteenth century that considers briefly the thought of
Jeremy Bentham, S. T. Coleridge, Thomas Carlyle, J. S. Mill, Herbert Spencer
and T. H. Green (pp. 663–670). (Cf. 1904:17.)

1901:02 Contributor to *Dictionary of Philosophy and Psychology.* Ed.
James Mark Baldwin. Vol. 1.
New York: Macmillan, 1901.
JHT's entries: "Absolutism (aesthetic)," p. 4;
"Admiration," p. 17; "Aesthetic" and "Aesthetics," pp.
20–21; "Aesthetic Standard," p. 21; "Algedonic
Aesthetics," p. 33; "Art" and "Art Theories," pp. 69–73;
"Art Impulse," p. 73; "Association (in aesthetics)," pp.

77–78; "Balance (in aesthetics)," p. 100; "Baroco (Barocco, Baroque)," p. 101; "Beauty" and "The Beautiful," pp. 104–109; "Caricature," p. 155; "Catharsis," pp. 161–162; "Characteristic" (with James Mark Baldwin), pp. 173–174; "Classification (of the fine arts)," pp. 186–188; "Comic" (with James Mark Baldwin), pp. 198–199; "Criterion (aesthetic)," p. 245; "Criticism (aesthetic)," p. 246; "Decorative Art," p. 258; "Figure" and "Figurative (in aesthetics)," p. 382; "Fitness (in aesthetics)," pp. 384–385; "Form" and "Formalism (in aesthetics)," pp. 390–391; "Grace," pp. 418–419; "Grotesque" (with James Mark Baldwin), p. 431; "Humour" and "Humorous," p. 488; "Ideal (in aesthetics)," pp. 499–500; "Idealism (in aesthetics)" (with Karl Groos), pp. 503–504; "Ideality," p. 504; "Idealization (aesthetic)" (with James Mark Baldwin), p. 504; "Impressionism," pp. 526–527; "Intellectualism (aesthetic)," p. 559; "Irony," p. 574.

In these many entries, JHT offers variously definitions; translations of equivalent terms in Greek, Latin, German, French and Italian; discussions of the positions, historical overviews, examinations of contemporary controversies, cross-references, and bibliographies in various languages. Of particular interest are "Aesthetic" and "Aesthetics," "Art" and "Art Theories," and "Beauty" and "The Beautiful." (JHT's contributions to the *Dictionary* continue in 1902:02.)

1901:03   Review of Alexander Thomas Ormond, *Foundations of Knowledge.*
                Philosophical Review 10.1 (1901): 57–62.

A mildly favorable discussion of an attempt to integrate a kind of Kantian critical epistemology with intuitionism and mysticism.

1901:04   Review of Léon Brunschvicg, *Introduction à la vie de l'esprit.*
                Psychological Review 8.1 (1901): 96.

A highly favorable notice of an introductory philosophy text.

1901:05   Review of Henri Bergson, *Le Rire, essai sur la signification du comique.*
                Psychological Review 8.1 (1901): 98–99.

A brief review of a study that locates the comic in the failure of the individual to adapt to society and that considers laughter to be a tool of socialization.

1901:06   Review of Johannes Ziegler, *Das Komische*.
            Psychological Review 8.1 (January 1901): 99.

A brief notice of an attempt to locate the comic in the contrast between mechanical processes and human purposes.

1901:07   Review of William Graham, *English Political Philosophy from [Thomas] Hobbes to [Henry] Maine*.
            American Historical Review 6.2 (1901): 360–362.

A favorable discussion of an account of aspects of the thought of Hobbes, Locke, Burke, Bentham, J. S. Mill, and Maine that downplays its philosophical weaknesses and emphasizes its more general benefits.

1901:08   Review of Benno Erdmann, *Immanuel Kant's Kritik der reinen Vernunft*, and *Beiträge zur Geschichte und Revision des Textes von Kant's Kritik der reinen Vernunft*.
            Philosophical Review 10.2 (1901): 221–222.

A brief but favorable review of Erdmann's fifth edition of Kant's *Critique of Pure Reason* and his appended volume of explanatory materials.

1901:09   Review of Benjamin Rand, ed., *The Life, Unpublished Letters and Philosophical Regimen of Anthony, Earl of Shaftesbury, Author of the "Characteristics"*.
            American Historical Review 6.3 (1901): 609–610.

A brief descriptive review that discusses the philosophical and historical aspects of the volume.

1902:01   Contributor to and editor of *James Tufts: A Memorial*.
            Chicago: U of Chicago P, 1902. 145 pp.

In this loving biography of his father, JHT begins with a discussion of the history of the Tuffs/Tufts family through James Tufts's parents: the Reverend James Tufts (1764–1841) and Submit Flagg Hayden (1777–1870). Chapter 2 examines JHT's father's early years in Wardsboro, Vermont, especially the religious influence on this parson's son, his early efforts at teaching school, and his religious conversion. Chapter 3 considers JHT's father's higher education at Burr Seminary, Yale College, and Andover Theological Seminary; the partial loss of his voice that made a preaching career impossible; and his return to the teaching profession. In chapter 4, JHT details his father's brief career as principal of the Monson [Massachusetts] Academy; his marriage in 1855 to Mary Elizabeth Warren (1823–1910); his private teaching; the brief life of JHT's older brother, James Frederic Tufts (April 28–December 1, 1860); and his own birth (July 9, 1862). Chapter 5 considers his father's semiretirement to public affairs, preaching, personal friendships, and occasional publications.

1902:02   Contributor to *Dictionary of Philosophy and Psychology*. Ed.
James Mark Baldwin. Vol. 2.
New York: Macmillan, 1902.
JHT's entries: "Line of Beauty," p. 8; "Naive," p. 127;
"Naturalism (in art)" (with John Dewey and Karl Groos),
p. 138; "Perfection (in aesthetics)," p. 278; "Picturesque,"
p. 301; "Power," pp. 318–319; "Pre-Socratic Philosophy,"
pp. 334–337; "Psyche," pp. 374–375; "Quality" and
"Quantity (aesthetic)," p. 409; "Rationalism (in
aesthetics)," p. 416; "Realism (in aesthetics)" (with Karl
Groos), p. 424; "Repose," p. 464; "Romantic," p. 479;
"Schools of Greece," pp. 495–498; "Sensualism (in
aesthetics)," p. 520; "Socratic Philosophy," pp. 549–552;
"Solipsism," pp. 553–554; "Sophistry" and "Sophists," pp.
556–557; "Style," pp. 605–606; "Sublime," p. 611; "Symbol
(and Symbolic)," p. 640; "Sympathy (aesthetic)" (with
James Mark Baldwin), p. 653; "Tragic," p. 709; "Type"
and "Typical (in aesthetic)," p. 721; "Unity in Variety,"
pp. 736–737; "Utility (in aesthetics)," pp. 745–746; "World-
ground," p. 822; "World-soul," p. 822.

In this continuation of 1901:02, JHT again offers variously definitions; translations of equivalent terms in Greek, Latin, German, French and Italian; discussions of the positions, historical overviews, examinations of contemporary
controversies, cross-references, and bibliographies in various languages. Of
particular interest are "Pre-Socratic Philosophy," "Schools of Greece," "Socratic Philosophy," and "Solipsism."

1902:03   "On the Genesis of the Aesthetic Categories."
Decennial Publications of the University of Chicago, First Ser.,
vol. 3, part 2.
Chicago: U of Chicago P, 1902. 10 pp.

In this article JHT considers aesthetic categories in the light of social psychology, suggesting an essential role for the social conditions under which the
categories develop. He begins with an enumeration of some of the marks of
aesthetic consciousness in terms of an objectivity of judgment, contempla-
tiveness or detachment, and an apprehension of broad significance. He then
turns to a consideration of their genesis. His view is that the aesthetic attitude
is initially connected with art rather than nature; the production of art is prior
to the appreciation of art, the cause rather than the effect; and art is social in
nature, and thus aesthetic categories are rooted in the social consciousness of
a group. As a result, JHT maintains, objectivity, detachment, and apprehension of broad significance as marks of aesthetic consciousness can be better
understood.

1902:04 Review of Paul Monroe, *Source Book of the History of*
Education, for the Greek and Roman Period.
American Journal of Sociology 7.5 (1902): 709.

A favorable notice of a volume of translated excerpts from ancient writers on
education.

1902:05 Abstract of "Aesthetic Categories from the Standpoint of
Social Psychology."
Psychological Review 9.2 (1902): 147–148.

The outline of a paper, drawing upon JHT's "On the Genesis of the Aesthetic
Categories" (1902:03), that was presented to the American Psychological Association.

1902:06 Review of Joseph McCabe, *Peter Abélard.*
American Historical Review 7.3 (1902): 598–599.

A brief review that finds the book useful for the general public but unsatisfactory for the philosophical audience.

1903:01 "Notes on the Bibliography of the History of Philosophy."
Year-Book of the Bibliographical Society of Chicago, 1902–1903.
Vol 4.
Chicago: Bibliographical Society of Chicago, 1903. 20–31.

In this piece, JHT offers an examination of the current status of bibliographical
resources, primarily in English and German, available for the study of the
history of philosophy, and a consideration of the role that the history of
philosophy has played in the Western philosophical tradition.

1903:02 [Report of the Dean of the Senior Colleges.]
The Presidents' Report: Administration.
University of Chicago Decennial Publications, First Ser.,
vol. 1.
Chicago: U of Chicago P, 1903. 64–96.

In this largely statistical report on conditions in the Senior Colleges at the end
of the University of Chicago's first decade, JHT considers enrollment, transfer
and graduation rates, various qualities of the students, the effect of the quarter
system on the length of residence, and the impact of some recent changes in
the curriculum.

1903:03 "On the Genesis of the Aesthetic Categories."
Philosophical Review 12.1 (1903): 1–15.

A reprinting of 1902:03 with only minor stylistic changes.

1903:04 Review of Gabriel Tarde, *Psychologie économique*. 2 vols.
Psychological Review 10.2 (1903): 179–180.

A critical discussion of an attempt to revise the notion of 'economic-man'
through the introduction of the perspective of social psychology that fails
because of an inadequate social psychology and an outdated conception of
economics.

1903:05 Review of Charles Horton Cooley, *Human Nature and the
Social Order*.
Psychological Review 10.3 (1903): 329–331.

A highly favorable discussion of an attempt to understand the individual as
a thoroughly social being. (Cf. 1909:16.)

1903:06 [Remarks at the Correspondence-Study Conference]
University [of Chicago] Record, 8.4 (1903): 93–94.

JHT, as dean of the senior colleges, considers the advantages and disadvantages of correspondence and residence study and maintains that correspondence work is not an easier or less desirable way to complete college work.

1903:07 Review of Simon Nelson Patten, *Heredity and Social
Progress*.
Psychological Review 10.5 (1903): 574–575.

A highly critical discussion of a study of the course of human progress.

1903:08 Review of Guillaume Leonce Duprat, *Le Mensonge: étude de
psycho-sociologie pathologique et normale*.
Psychological Bulletin 10.6 (1903): 674–676.

A favorable discussion of a study for parents and educators of the various
types of deception and their apparent causes.

1903:09 Review of Émile Tardieu, *L'Ennui, étude psychologique*.
Psychological Bulletin 10.6 (1903): 676.

A favorable notice of a classificatory study.

1903:10 Review of Ch. Ribéry, *Essai de classification naturelle des
caractères*.
Psychological Review 10.6 (1903): 676–678.

A discussion of a study of character that emphasizes physical temperament,
sensibility, and will over intellect.

1904:01   *The Individual and His Relation to Society as Reflected in*
British Ethics.
Part 2. *The Individual in Social and Economic Relations.*
University of Chicago Contributions to Philosophy, no. 6.
Chicago: U of Chicago P, 1904. iv + 58 pp.

In this continuation of his survey of the development of British ethics begun
in 1898:01, JHT turns to the eighteenth century. Section 1 is a general consideration of life and thought in Britain, especially the shift from religious and
political issues to economic ones; the impact of this shift on class structure
and inherited patterns of authority; and the growth in science, communication, and freer thought. Section 2 introduces the 'moral sense' as a means to
ground the moral life that Cumberland and Locke had earlier freed from
authority. In section 3, JHT discusses Shaftesbury's assemblage of the following strands: that in morality feeling is primary; that goodness and virtue
are fundamentally subjective; that the individual is naturally social, innately
inclined to herding and associating; that intellectual pleasures are more fulfilling than hedonistic ones, and that virtuous affections are pleasurable; and
that ultimately 'right taste' must be cultivated. Section 4 considers Bernard
Mandeville's analysis of the individual that emphasizes paradoxical relationships like those between private vice and public good, between honor and the
respect of others, between sociableness and individual desires, and between
morality and economic prudence. In Section 5, JHT considers Francis Hutche-
son's emphasis upon the moral sense as a source of pleasure, the ideal nature
of honor, and the possibility of disinterested benevolence. Sections 6 and 7
survey the contribution of Joseph Butler (the integration of reflective thought
into the discussion of the role of moral sense, the individual as the source of
moral authority), John Clarke, John Gay, and David Hartley. Section 8 contains
JHT's discussion of David Hume's ethics in which he considers the conflicting
aspects of Hume's thought—his analytical philosophical method versus his
broader sense of human experience—that give rise to antithetical accounts of
good and virtue, of sympathy, justice, and benevolence. In section 9, JHT
discusses the social character of the moral self in the work of Adam Smith.
After reminding us of the primacy of self-interest in Smith, JHT emphasizes
our evaluation of the propriety and the merits of particular actions in terms
of a conscience that is a social self, the element of reasonableness in morality
that gives rise to the 'impartial spectator,' the inadequacy of sympathy as a
socializing agent, and the difference between agent and spectator as one of
degree. JHT suggests that Smith is the best interpreter of the social life of his
time.

1904:02   *The Individual and His Relation to Society as Reflected in the*
British Ethics of the Eighteenth Century.
Part 2. *The Individual in Social and Economic Relations.*

Psychological Review: Monograph Supplements 6.2 (1904).
New York: Macmillan, 1904. iv + 58 pp.

A reprint of 1904:01.

1904:03 "The Practical and the Liberal in Education."
Centennial Souvenir: Monson Academy Centennial Jubilee,
1804–1904.
Palmer, Mass: n.p., 1904. 12–18.

JHT begins with a consideration of the importance of the contribution of
education between the primary school and the university or professional
school: the academy, the high school, and the college. He then turns to his
main theme: the dual task of keeping education practical (developing mind
and soul with the aim of a contributing and fulfilling relationship to the
physical world) and liberal (the development of free, broad-minded and serious men and women). His final topic is the continued role of education in
social advance.

1904:04 Review of Léon Bourgeois and Alfred Croiset, eds., *Essai*
d'une philosophie de la solidarité.
American Journal of Sociology 9.4 (1904): 584–586.

A favorable discussion of a series of addresses on the topic of social solidarity.

1904:05 Abstract of "The Chief Factors in the Formation of the
Moral Self."
Journal of Philosophy, Psychology and Scientific Methods 1.1
(1904): 21–22.

An abstract of a paper examining the physical, social, and individual elements
of the developed moral self that JHT presented to the American Philosophical
Association. This material later appeared in an expanded form in 1906:01.

1904:06 Abstract of "Note on the Idea of the Moral Sense in
British Thought Prior to Shaftesbury."
Psychological Bulletin 1.2 (1904): 54.

An abstract of 1904:08.

1904:07 Abstract of "The Chief Factors in the Formation of the
Moral Self."
Psychological Bulletin 1.2 (1904): 55.

A shorter version of 1904:05.

1904:08   "Note on the Idea of a 'Moral Sense' in British Thought
Prior to Shaftesbury."
Journal of Philosophy, Psychology and Scientific Methods 1.4
(1904): 97–98.

A brief account of the concept of 'moral sense' that was operative in the
thought of John Tillotson (1630–1694) and Isaac Barrow (1630–1677), drawn
from 1904:01 and presented to the American Philosophical Association.

1904:09   "The Social Standpoint."
Journal of Philosophy, Psychology and Scientific Methods 1.8
(1904): 197–200.

After an elaboration of earlier considerations of the social aspects of life, JHT
explores the impact of the growing social standpoint on economics, ethics,
psychology, law, labor questions, justice, religion, aesthetics, and metaphysics.

1904:10   Review of Lester Frank Ward, *Pure Sociology: A Treatise on
the Origin and Spontaneous Development of Society.*
Philosophical Review 13.3 (1904): 347–351.

A long and mostly descriptive discussion of an attempt to analyze the nature
of society in which JHT emphasizes the potential gains from this volume for
readers from philosophy and psychology.

1904:11   Review of Ernst Victor Zenker, *Die Gesellschaft.* Erster
Band: *Natürliche Entwicklungsgeschichte der Gesellschaft*; and
Zweiter Band: *Die sociologische Theorie.*
Psychological Bulletin 1.11 (1904): 394–397.

A mildly favorable discussion of a study of factors in the evolution of society.

1904:12   Review of Thorstein Veblen, *The Theory of Business
Enterprise.*
Psychological Bulletin 1.11 (1904): 398–403.

A highly favorable discussion of an attempt to present business enterprise as
it is understood by those who engage in it and emphasize pecuniary success
over all other factors, and to demonstrate the conflict between the industrial
processes and business practices, which JHT sees as just a bit oversimplified.

1904:13   Review of Paul Bergemann, *Ethik als Kulturphilosophie.*
Psychological Bulletin 1.11 (1904): 403–404.

A descriptive discussion of a comparison of the development of ethics in
matriarchal and patriarchal societies.

1904:14 Review of René Worms, *Philosophie des sciences sociales*: I.
Objet des sciences sociales.
Psychological Bulletin 1.11 (1904): 404.

A brief note on a study of the nature of social facts.

1904:15 Review of Dudley Kidd, *The Essential Kaffir*.
Psychological Bulletin 1.11 (1904): 404–406.

A favorable discussion of a survey of aspects of African society prepared for
the general public. (Cf. 1907:14 and 1909:17.)

1904:16 Review of Theodor Lipps, *Ästhetik: Psychologie des Schönen
und der Kunst*. Erster Teil: *Grundlegung der Ästhetik*.
Philosophical Review 13.6 (1904): 677–681.

A favorable discussion of a treatment of aesthetics from an individualistic
psychological point of view that emphasizes *Einfühlung* or 'sympathy' as the
essence of aesthetic feeling. (Cf. 1908:04.)

1904:17 Review of Wilhelm Windelband, *Lehrbuch der Geschichte der
Philosophie*. Dritte, durchgesehene Auflage.
Philosophical Review 13.6 (1904): 706–707.

A favorable notice of the appearance of the third edition of Windelband's
History of Philosophy, the first two of which JHT had translated into English
(1893:01 and 1901:01).

1904:18 Review of Charles Alexander Eastman, *Indian Boyhood*.
Psychological Bulletin 1.13 (1904): 474–476.

A favorable discussion of an account of growing up as a Native American.

1905:01 [Report of the Dean of the Senior Colleges.]
The President's Report, 1902–1904.
Chicago: U of Chicago P, 1905. 77–84.

In this report for the academic years 1902–1904, JHT discusses the changes
caused by the founding of the College of Education and general statistical
information about the student body in the senior colleges.

1905:02 Abstract of "The Significant and the Non-Essential in
Kant's Aesthetics."
Psychological Bulletin 2.2 (1905): 66.

An abstract of a paper examining aspects of Kant's work on the aesthetic judgment, the aesthetic attitude, and the relation of aesthetics to philosophy presented to the American Philosophical Association.

1905:03 Summary of *The Individual and His Relation to Society as Reflected in the British Ethics of the Eighteenth Century.* *Psychological Bulletin* 2.3 (1905): 114–115.

JHT offers a brief account of his essay 1904:02 that emphasizes that the focus of the work is social psychology rather than ethics.

1905:04 Review of George Stuart Fullerton, *A System of Metaphysics.* *Journal of Philosophy, Psychology and Scientific Methods* 2.7 (1905): 187–191.

A descriptive discussion of a Berkeleyan account of the self and the external world.

1905:05 Review of Johannes Volkelt, *System der Ästhetik.* Erster Band. *Philosophical Review* 14.6 (1905): 717–720.

A highly favorable discussion of a study of aesthetics that JHT believes demonstrates great acuity in both philosophic and psychological analysis. (The second volume is discussed in 1910:07.)

1905:06 "Social Psychology in [Albion Woodbury] Small's *General Sociology.*" *Psychological Bulletin* 2.12 (1905): 393–398.

In this review essay, JHT concentrates on three aspects of the work: the six interests as the elements of the social process, the nature of the social process as conflictive and cooperative, and the province of social psychology as distinct from biology and individual psychology.

1905:07 Review of Adolphe Louis Cureau, "Essai sur la psychologie des races nègres de l'Afrique tropicale." *Psychological Bulletin* 2.12 (1905): 420.

A descriptive account of a study that contrasts various African groups with each other and compares them invidiously with whites.

1905:08 Review of Francis Galton, et al., *Sociological Papers.* *Psychological Bulletin* 2.12 (1905): 422–423.

A brief description of a volume of papers and communications.

1906:01 "On Moral Evolution."
Studies in Philosophy and Psychology by Former Students of Charles Edward Garman. Ed. James Hayden Tufts, et al.
Boston: Houghton, 1906. 3–39.

In this article, JHT uses recent developments in anthropology and psychology in an attempt to outline the development of the moral self. He discusses first his sense of human nature, both with regard to the material and the goal of a moral self. Next he considers the relative contributions of the various causal agencies in moral evolution: the natural or heredity component, the social or learned component, and the individual or volitional component. JHT then explores various instances of how social or personal and rational or theoretical controls contribute to the development of such values as 'honor,' 'right,' 'justice,' 'law,' 'responsibility,' 'sincerity,' and 'sympathy.' Finally, he considers how problematic factors have led to more recent developments in ethics by challenging old habits and methods. (Cf. 1907:08; 1909:01.)

1906:02   [Report of the Head of the Department of Philosophy.]
            The President's Report, 1904–1905.
            Chicago: U of Chicago P, 1906. 113–114.

In this report, JHT discusses developments in the philosophical and educational work of the department over the last year. Primary among them was the departure of John Dewey.

1906:03   "General Policy of the *School Review.*"
            School Review 14.1 (1906): 65.

JHT, as a new editor, offers a reaffirmation of the journal's focus on the broad range of issues related to secondary education.

1906:04   "President [William Rainey] Harper."
            School Review 14.2 (1906): 153.

A brief obituary for the recently deceased president of the University of Chicago.

1906:05   "The New Editorial Staff."
            School Review 14.3 (1906): 227.

A brief explanation of the allocation of duties among the members of the editorial staff.

1906:06   "Needed School Legislation."
            School Review 14.4 (1906): 307–308.

A discussion of possible measures to draw more men into education and to decrease teacher turnover.

1906:07 "Meeting of the N.E.A. Postponed."
School Review 14.5 (1906): 383.

A brief announcement that the National Education Association would not be meeting in San Francisco that summer due to the disastrous earthquake of April 18.

1906:08 "Editorial Notes."
School Review 14.6 (1906): 438.

A brief introduction to extensive excerpts from a recent report by the Massachusetts Commission on Industrial and Technical Education.

1906:09 Review of E. Morselli, "Società e Ideale Etico."
Psychological Bulletin 3.6 (1906): 213–214.

A brief summary of an article advocating the ongoing necessity for both communal and personal contribution to the moral life.

1906:10 "Some Contributions of Psychology to the Conception of Justice."
Philosophical Review 15.4 (1906): 361–379.

In his presidential address to the Western Philosophical Association, JHT considers the need for our sense of justice to be grounded in an adequate understanding of human nature. Of the factors of human nature, JHT considers complexity, habitualness and adjustment, situatedness, and sociality to be especially important here. He then applies this broadened sense of human nature to three contemporary issues: the abstractness of the narrow focus of criminal justice intended to eliminate 'extraneous' factors, the inadequacy of our system of distributive justice to satisfy any principle of justice, and the need for broader distribution of the goods of education.

1906:11 Review of Alfred William Howitt, *The Native Tribes of South-east Australia*; and Baldwin Spencer and F. J. Gillen, *The Northern Tribes of Central Australia*.
Psychological Bulletin 3.7 (1906): 237–238.

A favorable notice of two anthropological studies of interest to the social psychologist.

1906:12 Review of Inazo Nitobe, *Bushido, The Soul of Japan*; and Lafcadio Hearn, *Japan: An Interpretation*.
Psychological Bulletin 3.7 (1906): 238.

A favorable notice of two studies of Japanese life and customs of interest to the social psychologist.

1906:13   Review of Georges Dumas, *Psychologie de deux messies positivistes, Saint-Simon et Auguste Comte.*
Psychological Bulletin 3.7 (1906): 239.

A brief discussion of an interpretation of the two positivists using what JHT considers to be the crude category of messianism.

1906:14   "Dr. [Susan Myra] Kingsbury's Investigation of the Relation of Children to the Industries."
School Review 14.7 (1906): 535–537.

A discussion of a report on the causes and results of dropping out of school and of possible educational reforms to minimize this.

1906:15   "The Williamstown Conference."
School Review 14.10 (1906): 760–761.

A report on a recent conference about standardizing college entrance requirements.

1906:16   "Some Contributions of Psychology to the Conception of Justice."
Michigan Law Review 5.2 (1906): 79–93.

A reprint of 1906:10.

1906:17   "[Edward] Westermarck on the Origin of Moral Ideas."
Psychological Bulletin 3.12 (1906): 400–403.

A review-essay of the first volume of *The Origin and Development of the Moral Ideas* that emphasizes the inadequacy of Westermarck's understanding of the origin of moral ideas and calls for a better integration of the study of morals with economic and industrial conditions.

1906:18   Review of Ernest Solvay, *Note sur les formules d'introduction à l'énergétique physio- et psycho-sociologique;*
Emile Waxweiler, *Esquisse d'une sociologie;*
Raphael Petrucci, *Les Origines naturelles de la propriété;*
Louis Wodon, *Sur Quelques Erreurs de methode dans l'étude de l'homme primitif;*
Emile Houze, *L'Aryen et l'anthroposociologie;*
Charles Henry and Emile Waxweiler, *Mesure des capacités intellectuelle et énergétique. Avec une remarque additionnelle: sur l'interprétation sociologique de la distribution des salaires;*

and Raphael Petrucci, *Origine polyphylétique, homotypie, et non-comparabilité des sociétés animales.*
Psychological Bulletin 3.12 (1906): 404–408.

A discussion of a series of sociological monographs by the Solvay Institut de Sociologie of Brussels.

1906:19 Review of Alexander Pilcz, *Beitrag zur vergleichenden Rassen-Psychiatrie.*
Psychological Bulletin 3.12 (1906): 419–420.

A descriptive discussion of a European study of mental disorder among Germans, Northern Slavs, Hungarians, and Jews.

1906:20 Review of Karl Lamprecht, "Grundzüge des modernen Seelenlebens in Deutschland."
Psychological Bulletin 3.12 (1906): 420.

A brief summary of a study of recent trends in Germany.

1907:01 [Report of the Head of the Department of Philosophy.]
The President's Reports, 1905–1906.
Chicago: U of Chicago P, 1907. 115.

A brief listing of the research work in progress from the eleven members of the department. (Such reports, increasingly sketchy in nature, continue to appear over JHT's signature in the next nine presidential reports.)

1907:02 "European Editors and Correspondents."
School Review 15.1 (1907): 95–96.

The introduction of five European educators who had joined the staff as advisory editors.

1907:03 Review of Charles Franklin Thwing, *A History of Higher Education in America.*
School Review 15.3 (1907): 239.

A brief discussion of a study of higher education that emphasizes the older colleges.

1907:04 Review of Samuel F. Hamilton, *The Recitation.*
School Review 15.3 (1907): 239–240.

A notice of a plan for Herbartian education that JHT finds too rigid.

1907:05 "Are College Entrance Requirements Too High?"
School Review 15.4 (1907): 302–303.

JHT examines a recent report than answers the title question in the affirmative, and offers some suggestions about revising the exclusively intellectual nature of college requirements.

1907:06   "Address [at the Memorial Service for Wilbur Samuel
Jackman, Principal of the University Elementary School]."
University [of Chicago] Record 11.4 (1907): 153–154.

While noting that individuals cannot be accurately evaluated independent of their situation, JHT emphasizes the importance of Jackman's personal contribution to teacher education and to the advancement of education in the natural sciences.

1907:07   "The Significance of Mr. [Wilbur Samuel] Jackman's
Work."
Elementary School Teacher 7.8 (1907): 443–446.

A reprint of 1907:06.

1907:08   "[Charles Edward] Garman as a Teacher."
Journal of Philosophy, Psychology and Scientific Methods 4.10
(1907): 263–267.

A loving obituary for Garman (1850–1907), JHT's former teacher and colleague at Amherst College for whose festschrift he had prepared 1906:01. JHT discusses Garman's conception of philosophy and his dedication to teaching, and his teaching methods and extensive use of homemade pamphlets. (These remarks are expanded in 1909:01.) JHT also offers along the way pieces of a picture of higher education in New England in the 1870s and 1880s.

1907:09   "The Teachers and the Hague Conference."
School Review, 15.7 (1907): 550–551.

JHT emphasizes the importance of the international movement toward arbitration and jurisprudence over warfare and the role that teachers might play in advancing the movement.

1907:10   "Two Types of Educational Administration."
School Review 15.8 (1907): 618–619.

JHT considers two approaches to organizing school systems, one based in efficiency of operation from the top down and the other based in adapting to student needs by the teacher, and the relative values of each.

1907:11   "The Boston Schools."
              School Review 15.9 (1907): 693–694.

A report on recent developments.

1907:12   "On the Psychology of the Family."
              Psychological Bulletin 4.12 (1907): 371–374.

In this rewritten section from chapter 26, "The Family," of the forthcoming
Dewey and Tufts's *Ethics* (1908:01), JHT examines the psychological strains
that contemporary middle-class family life imposes on the wife.

1907:13   Review of William Graham Sumner, *Folkways: A Study of
              the Sociological Importance of Usages, Manners, Customs and
              Morals.*
              Psychological Bulletin 4.12 (1907): 384–388.

A favorable discussion of a volume, full of illustrative examples, on the nature
and role of customary morality by one of JHT's former teachers at Yale. (Cf.
1915:06 and 1919:17.)

1907:14   Review of Dudley Kidd, *Savage Childhood: A Study of Kafir
              Children.*
              Psychological Bulletin 4.12 (1907): 397–398.

A brief descriptive discussion of an examination of the development of self-
consciousness and its various aspects. (Cf. 1904:15 and 1909:17.)

1908:01   *Ethics* (with John Dewey).
              New York: Henry Holt, 1908. xiii + 618 pp.

In the preface, JHT and Dewey discuss and defend the general shape of the
volume and specify the contributions of each. In the introduction (chapter 1),
they offer an initial definition of 'ethics,' a sense of the general context in
which they are undertaking their inquiry into morality, and their reasons for
adopting the genetic method. They then consider the search for a criterion of
morality and offer 'growth' as such a criterion, and explore moral growth
as a process of developing greater rationality and greater sociality and of
consciously seeking the right and good.

   In part 1, "The Beginnings and Growth of Morality," JHT traces the process
of moral development in the history of the West. Chapter 2 begins the consideration of the life of the early group with a collection of moral events culled

from various moments in human experience. He then considers the economic, political, religious, and sexual aspects of various types of groups and the moral import of these groups. Chapter 3 begins with a distinction between customary and reflective morality. JHT then discusses various premoral rationalizing and socializing agencies like occupations, war, and art. Next he considers the moral impact of family life, and he closes with a focus on these premoral agencies as the foundation for the growth of morality. In chapter 4, JHT discusses customs as the sanctified habits of the group that draw their authority from, and that are enforced by, the ongoing life of the group. He then considers the difference between these mores as living codes and mere habits, and the values and defects of customary morality. In chapter 5, JHT discusses the movement from group morality to personal morality, or from custom to conscience, as the triumph of progress and individuality over order and authority. He then considers various social factors (the shift from hunting to agriculture and commerce, the growth of science and the arts, military power and new religions) and psychological factors (self-assertive instincts and impulses for sex, for private property, for various kinds of liberty, and for esteem) in this movement. Finally, JHT explores the need for this movement from custom to conscience to create a reconstructed society with reconstructed individuals. In chapter 6, JHT examines the Hebrew contribution to Western morality as fundamentally religious in nature, being based on the prophets' call for righteousness that raised their morals out of the customary. JHT then examines the moral meaning of a voluntary covenant with a personal lawgiver as an advance over inherited custom and as the means for the replacement of bad luck with punishment and for the introduction of the problem of evil. Finally he considers the meaning of various moral terms—'righteousness,' 'sin,' 'responsibility,' 'sincerity,' 'life,' and 'community'—from the Hebrew perspective. In chapter 7, JHT discusses the contribution of the Greeks, beginning with the distinction between nature and convention, and their conception of order and justice. Next, he discusses the intellectual force of individualism: in reasoned challenges to religion and custom; in the commercial life, class privilege, the challenges to class law; and in movement from the customary to the good in its various guises. JHT then discusses the response of Plato and Aristotle, who emphasize the human's social nature and the importance of rational control of passion. Finally, he considers the importance for Greek thought of the contrast between the real and the ideal and the building of responsible moral character. Chapter 8 surveys development in moral life since the Greeks. JHT begins with a consideration of the medieval duality of the military ideals of the warrior tribes and the religious ideals of the Church. Next is a consideration of the development of individualism in the discussions of natural rights and of duty, and a consideration of the advancement of individualism through the effects of industry, commerce, and art. Finally, JHT considers the development of intelligence—both in the sense of thought freed from the restrictions of authority and in the sense of the advance of learning—through the Renaissance and the Enlightenment and into the nineteenth century. In chapter 9, JHT offers a comparison of customary and reflective morality that suggests the ongoing need for the study of our moral inheritance. He explores elements of continuity (especially the persistence of group morality in all the various groupings and the dependence of moral conceptions upon group relations) and contrast (the differentiation of the moral from other factors, the introduction of intelligence for custom and principles for rules, the processive nature of reflection) between customary and reflective morality. JHT next discusses the possible opposition inherent between individuals and society when no value is to be found in the inherited ways. Finally, he considers the various positive and negative effects of the reflective stage of morality upon individualism and society.

(Dewey's contribution comprises all of part 2, "Theory of the Moral Life," and the first two chapters of part 3, "The World of Action," that explore general social and political themes.)

In chapter 22, JHT begins his consideration of the economic aspects of the world of action with a general examination of the issues of the complex relationship between the economic realm and human well-being, the influence of the productive process and property upon character, and the effects for society of economic activity. He then turns to the special problems of the new economic situation—largeness and impersonality—and their fundamental impact on moral thinking. Next JHT examines the moral import of the various aspects of industry and commerce: corporations and unions, employers and employees, the public, and the law. Finally, he considers production, exchange and valuation, and the social requirement that large and impersonal organization be brought under moral principles. In chapter 23, JHT states seven principles that should underlie the economic order: (1) People are more important than money; (2) wealth should depend upon working; (3) wealth should depend upon public service; (4) collective production requires collective morality; (5) personal responsibility must be reimposed upon corporations; (6) there should be more publicity and more explicit laws; and (7) all should share in the wealth of society. Chapters 24 and 25 consider in great detail the various aspects of the conflict between individualism (the belief that each can best secure his or her own welfare through voluntary associations and contracts) and socialism (the belief that society should secure citizens' well-being) and the intermediate view of 'equal opportunity' that comprises all sorts of attempts at combining the two. In addition to this theoretical discussion, he also considers some current tendencies to advance public welfare, and three problems: the open versus the closed shop, corporate capitalization, and the unearned increment. (Chapter 25 is followed by a brief outline of social legislation by Henry R. Seager presented as an "Appendix.") In chapter 26, JHT discusses the moral problems of the modern family, beginning with some historical antecedents and influences. Next he considers the family from a psychological point of view as a relationship between husband and wife, parents and children, and as a relationship with inherent strains. Finally he considers some current conditions and problems of family life: the removal of much of work from the home, the role of women in society, authority within the home, and divorce. (Cf. 1932:01.)

1908:02   Review of Boris Sidis, *Studies in Psychopathology.*
              School Review 16.1 (1908): 65.

A descriptive notice of a study of the potentially lasting impact of negative
childhood experiences.

1908:03   "Appointive or Elective Boards of Education."
              School Review 16.2 (1908): 136–138.

In the light of recent events in Chicago, JHT reports on an informal survey
that he undertook to determine the views of a number of school superintendents on questions of the proper relationship between school boards and city
governments.

1908:04   Review of Theodor Lipps, *Ästhetik: Psychologie des Schönen
              und der Kunst.* Zweiter Teil: *Die ästhetische Betrachtung und
              die bildende Kunst.*
              Philosophical Review 17.2 (1908): 199–202.

A mildly critical discussion of the second volume of Lipp's *Aesthetics* (the first
volume was reviewed in 1904:16) that focuses upon the plastic and spatial
arts.

1908:05   Review of Antoine Wylm, *La Morale sexuelle.*
              Psychological Bulletin 5.3 (1908): 95.

A descriptive notice that emphasizes the work's psychological themes.

1908:06   "The Adjustment of the Church to the Psychological
              Conditions of the Present."
              American Journal of Theology 12.2 (1908): 177–188.

In this examination of the current intellectual climate, JHT criticizes the widespread failure of religion to challenge its traditional thinking and recognize
adequately the importance of the economic and scientific aspects of contemporary life. Preachers should use these elements to recover key aspects of the
religious perspective that have been submerged in the modern world, such
as personal worth, justice, the inquiring spirit, and faith as a prerequisite of
work for possible future betterment.

1908:07   "Educational Problems as Seen by University Presidents."
              School Review 16.6 (1908): 412–415.

A discussion of issues of the college curriculum: the relationship of liberal
education to training for the professions, the beginnings of professional educa-

tion for business and consular service, methods of instruction to present to student teachers, and the nature and scope of higher education for women.

1908:08 "Is There a Place for Moral Instruction?"
School Review 16.7 (1908): 475–477.

While emphasizing that the school—along with the family, the arts, and so on—is one of the institutions of moral education in society, JHT rejects direct instruction in morality unless it recognizes that morality is more than intellectual and attempts to find and evaluate principles for conduct that aim not at conformity or obedience but at developing students' judgment.

1908:09 "Ethical Value."
Journal of Philosophy, Psychology and Scientific Methods 5.19 (1908): 517–522.

In this paper, presented to the Western Philosophical Association, JHT discusses ethical value as both rational and social. On the *volitional* side, ethical valuing is a choosing activity of a unified self that is responsible and seeking a moral order. On the *affective* side, although some emotion is necessary, ethical valuing requires no particular emotion. JHT concludes with a discussion of the development of ethical values from elemental biological needs, from groups, from values like honor, and from aversion.

1908:10 "How Far Is Formal Systematic Instruction Desirable in Moral Training in the Schools?"
Religious Education 3.4 (1908): 121–125.

In this brief essay, related to 1908:08 and 1908:11 and written in the spirit of 1908:01, JHT considers the indirect, customary, and reflective agencies of moral development and advocates that moral instruction emphasizing the reflective agencies be delayed until secondary school. (Cf. 1909:12.)

1908:11 "Two Standpoints For Moral Instruction."
School Review 16.8 (1908): 551–553.

The first standpoint is the personal one that emphasizes developing individual conscience and character; the second, that which emphasizes developing the recognition of the mutual interdependence between society and its members. JHT advocates the latter.

1908:12 "Industrial Education in the Cleveland Platform."
Elementary School Teacher 9.2 (1908): 108–110.

An editorial, related to 1908:14, attacking the recently adopted stance of the National Education Association on industrial education for advocating the goal of 'trained and skilled labor' rather than 'intelligent and cultured' workers.

1908:13 "Professor Charles H[ubbard] Judd Coming to Chicago." *School Review* 16.9 (1908): 615.

A brief announcement of changes at the University of Chicago that will have an as yet undetermined effect on the journal.

1908:14 "The Springfield Tests Again." *School Review* 16.9 (1908): 615–618.

JHT offers an extended condemnation of the drill and memory method of schooling, related to 1908:12, based in part on our inability to know what exactly to drill the students in and in part on some documentary evidence of the failure of that method when it was used in 'the good old days.'

1908:15 "Dr. [Adolph] Meyer on the Dangers of Knowing Things without Doing Things." *Elementary School Teacher* 9.3 (1908): 153–155.

A commentary on a recent article on *dementia praecox* in which JHT points to the importance of not making the life of the imagination more attractive to children than the life of doing.

1908:16 Review of Edgar James Swift, *Mind in the Making: A Study in Mental Development.* *Elementary School Teacher* 9.3 (1908): 162–163.

A highly favorable discussion of a study of aspects of intellectual growth that suggests educational changes to achieve social progress.

1908:17 "President [Charles William] Eliot and the Teaching Profession." *School Review* 16.10 (1908): 683–685.

JHT offers an appreciation on the occasion of Eliot's retirement from Harvard University by considering his impact on secondary education.

1908:18 Review of Frank Chapman Sharp, *A Study of the Influence of Custom on the Moral Judgment.* *Psychological Bulletin* 5.12 (1908): 391–394.

A critical discussion of a study which purports to show the lack of influence of custom in moral conduct.

1908:19 Review of Josiah Royce, *The Philosophy of Loyalty.*
Psychological Bulletin 5.12 (1908): 394–396.

A discussion that is not unfavorable to Royce's attempt to reduce the virtues to one, although JHT advocates justice as the primary one.

1908:20 Review of George Chatterton-Hill, *Heredity and Selection in Sociology.*
Psychological Bulletin 5.12 (1908): 398–399.

A mildly critical discussion of a study that finds social progress possible only through the adoption of religious sanctions on conduct.

1908:21 Review of Magnus Hirschfeld, *Le Troisième Sexe. Les Homosexuels de Berlin.*
Psychological Bulletin 5.12 (1908): 400.

A descriptive note on a sociological study.

1908:22 Review of Paul Eltztasche, "L'Esprit de l'Allemagne moderne."
Psychological Bulletin 5.12 (1908): 403.

A descriptive note on a sociological study.

1909:01 Contributor to and editor of *Letters, Lectures and Addresses of Charles Edward Garman: A Memorial Volume.*
Prepared with the cooperation of the Class of 1884, Amherst College, by Eliza Miner Garman.
Boston and New York: Houghton, 1909.

In the preface, written with Walter F. Wilcox and William S. Rossiter, JHT details the history of this volume (pp. vii–x). The introduction (pp. 1–53), which JHT wrote in collaboration with Mrs. Eliza Miner Garman, begins with a consideration of Garman's family background. He then turns to Garman's education at Amherst College and Yale Divinity School and his return to Amherst to teach, initially as instructor of mathematics and eventually as professor of mental and moral philosophy. Next to be considered, in an expansion of 1907:08, is Garman's understanding of philosophy and his extraordinary success as a teacher, in part due to his ongoing use of homemade philosophy pamphlets. Finally, an introduction is given to the philosophical writings of Garman that follow. JHT also reproduces his glowing address at the presentation of the commemorative volume of 1906 (pp. 593–595). (Cf. 1906:01.)

1909:02   [Report of the Dean of the Senior Colleges.]
              The President's Report, 1907–1908.
              Chicago: U of Chicago P, 1909. 83–88.

In this report on the conditions of the senior colleges for 1907–1908, JHT discusses the different perceived burdens of strictly academic and preprofessional work, and suggests that the amount of and the standards for academic work should be raised.

1909:03   "Feminization."
              School Review, 17.1 (1909): 55–58.

In this response to charges that the personnel and the subject matter of the schools are 'feminizing,' JHT reminds readers that in the recent past the study of Greek and Latin were thought to render women 'masculine.' The real issue, JHT continues, is that the new economic situation takes the father out of the role of adult male companion, and he suggests that a renewal of this positive relationship is what the introduction of more men into schools might accomplish.

1909:04   Review of William Lee Howard, *The Protection of the
              Innocent.*
              School Review 17.1 (1909): 66.

A favorable notice of a call for sex education in high schools.

1909:05   "The Need of Educational Investigation."
              School Review 17.2 (1909): 129 131.

An editorial that calls for further scientific inquiry into educational topics and a brief survey of the current field of educational research.

1909:06   "American College Education and Life."
              Science ns 29 (1909): 407–414.

In this examination of American education and society, JHT begins with the view that college and life had earlier been integrated when the structure of education was fixed and its goal was the preparation of students for largely deductive careers in the ministry, law, and medicine. However, as society became less fixed, as science developed, as technical and graduate schools proliferated, as courses of study become more fragmented and individual, the college has become detached from the larger social life. JHT calls for a reconstruction of the ideal of a liberal culture prevalent in the college by means of emphasizing the experimental method and the social standpoint to reintegrate the college experience into the life of the society. JHT closes with some comments on the importance of these educational changes for women.

1909:07 "Darwin and Evolutionary Ethics."
Psychological Review 16.3 (1909): 195–206.

As part of a symposium on the impact of Darwin on intellectual life on the occasion of the fiftieth anniversary of *The Origin of Species*, JHT discusses Darwin's effect on ethics. After a survey of the history of ethics from the evolutionary point of view—considering such topics as the relationship between the validity of an ethical standard and its perceived survival value, the relationship between ethics and the natural world, and the nature and ethical role of moral sense and sympathy—JHT turns to a consideration of Darwin's contribution, which he takes to be an emphasis upon human continuity with the natural world and upon the social nature of humans out of which morality developed. Finally, JHT rejects a number of interpretations of 'Darwinism' for failing to recognize the contribution of human rationality to moral progress and for failing to offer a broad enough conception of the common good.

1909:08 "President [James Burrill] Angell and Secondary Education."
School Review 17.6 (1909): 437–438.

A celebration of the contribution of President Angell to secondary education and to the teaching profession on the occasion of his retirement from the University of Michigan.

1909:09 Review of Edward Alsworth Ross, *Social Psychology: An Outline and Source Book*.
Journal of Philosophy, Psychology and Scientific Methods 6.13 (1909): 357–361.

A mildly critical discussion of a study that too narrowly construes the topic.

1909:10 Abstract of "Some Features of the Social Aspects of Hegelianism."
Journal of Philosophy, Psychology and Scientific Methods 6.15 (1909): 407.

An abstract of a paper presented to the Western Philosophical Association that considers Hegel's views on science and social progress. (Cf. 1910:01.)

1909:11 Review of Michael Ernest Sadler, ed., *Moral Instruction and Training in Schools*. 2 vols.
School Review 17.7 (1909): 506–507.

A favorable discussion of a study on the current state of ethical instruction.

1909:12 "The School and Modern Life: The Problem of Moral Education in the Public Schools as Affected by the

Changed Conditions in Industry and Home Life."
Religious Education 4.5 (1909): 343–348.

Continuing along lines previously explored in 1908:10, JHT elaborates on the way in which schools previously fit into a social situation in which the family was a cooperative working unit, and he contrasts this situation with the contemporary urban situation. JHT concludes with a call for a fundamental reorganization of school life—including changes in content, methods, and personnel—based in the demands of social justice.

1909:13 "Housing in Illinois Cities."
Chicago Medical Recorder (1909): 758–769.

In this examination of the housing situation outside of Chicago, presented to the Illinois State Conference of Charities and Correction, JHT offers a detailed discussion of problems in Alton, East St. Louis, Joliet, Peoria, Quincy, and Springfield. He argues that such cities are sufficiently different from Chicago to deserve stronger zoning rules and housing codes.

1909:14 "William T[orrey] Harris."
School Review 17.10 (1909): 717.

A eulogy for the educational administrator and Hegelian philosopher whom JHT recalls again in 1935:01.

1909:15 Review of William Isaac Thomas, *Source Book for Social Origins: Ethnological Materials, Psychological Standpoint, Classified and Annotated Bibliographies for the Interpretation of Savage Society.*
Psychological Bulletin 6.12 (1909): 417–418.

A brief but favorable account of a volume that JHT hopes will serve to help organize the position of social science in higher education.

1909:16 Review of Charles Horton Cooley, *Social Organization, A Study of the Larger Mind.*
Psychological Bulletin 6.12 (1909): 418–420.

A highly favorable discussion of an attempt to understand the nature and development of social organization. (Cf. 1903:05.)

1909:17 Review of Dudley Kidd, *Kafir Socialism and the Dawn of Individualism.*
Psychological Bulletin 6.12 (1909): 420.

A brief descriptive notice of the third in a series of volumes. (Cf. 1904:15 and 1907:14.)

1910:01   "The Present Task of Ethical Theory."
International Journal of Ethics 20.2 (1910): 141–152.

In this paper, JHT sets out to indicate some of the reconstructions that are necessary in our fundamental ethical conceptions if they are to be useful in the current social situation. Seen in the light of the ongoing scientific attempts to advance human welfare and the increasing impact of social organization on individuals, our outdated understandings of 'reason,' the 'self,' 'freedom,' 'happiness,' and the 'state' stand in need of revision to make them useful in dealing with social problems.

1910:02   "The Ultimate Test of Religious Truth: Is It Historical or Philosophical?"
American Journal of Theology 14.1 (1910): 16–24.

In this paper, presented at the 1909 graduation of the Yale Divinity School (from which he had graduated in 1889) JHT maintains that religion deals with facts like need, community, change, and morality. The test of religious truth cannot be historical because such an approach would commit us to a literal and inerrant interpretation of Scripture. The test can, however, be philosophical, if by 'philosophical' is understood the experimental and social organization of interpretations of the four kinds of facts that will transform the natural into the spiritual.

1910:03   Review of Clarence Frank Birdseye, *The Reorganization of Our Colleges.*
School Review 18.2 (1910): 133–134.

A discussion of a proposal that links many of the problems of undergraduates with their styles of life and suggests the creation of a department within the college to supervise their lives.

1910:04   Contributor to "Building Ordinances of the City of Chicago."
City Club [of Chicago] Bulletin 3.16 (1910): 189–203.

JHT chaired this session of the City Club at which a proposed revision of the Chicago building code was discussed, offering a brief introduction and a few comments. His comments emphasize the important influence of the housing situation on the development of children and the growing realization that architects and engineers must be seen as professionals with social responsibility.

1910:05   Review of Ralph Barton Perry, *The Moral Economy.*
International Journal of Ethics 20.3 (1910): 358–361.

In this mildly critical discussion of an attempt to discover the nature of morality in the direct analysis of life, JHT regrets the focus on the lives of the cultured few rather than on the social problems of the many.

1910:06   Review of Jane Addams, *The Spirit of Youth and the City Streets.*
School Review 18.6 (1910): 428–429.

A highly favorable discussion of an examination of how modern society undermines the chances of the young for fulfilling lives and of what might be done. (Cf. 1911:02.)

1910:07   Review of Johannes Volkelt, *System der Ästhetik.* Zweiter Band.
Philosophical Review 19.5 (1910): 548–550.

In this highly favorable discussion of Volkelt's second volume (the first was discussed in 1905:05), JHT considers the author's presentation of the various species of the aesthetic.

1910:08   "Present Problems of Instruction in the University of Chicago" (with other members of the Committee on Instruction).
University of Chicago Magazine 3.2 (1910): 58–86.

JHT, as chair of the Committee on Instruction and a member of the reporting sub-committee, took part in the writing of this report based on a survey conducted among instructors, students, and alumni of the University of Chicago on questions of teaching methods, amount of required study times for various courses, reasons for unsatisfactory courses, student cheating, etc. A series of nine proposed changes are then offered.

1910:09   "Recent Literature on Social Psychology."
Psychological Bulletin 7.12 (1910): 406–412.

A wide-ranging survey of eleven articles and books of interest to the social psychologist that appeared during the year.

1911:01   [Letter to Classmates.]
Class of 'Eighty-Four, Amherst College, Twenty-seventh Annual Reunion (December 30, 1910).
N.P.: n.p., 1911. 57–59.

In this letter to his fellow graduates of 1884, JHT compares his life at the University of Chicago with their shared life at Amherst. In spite of the obvious differences, he focuses on the similarities between the two academic environments: the respect for science and learning, the struggle to get an education, the democratic spirit, and so on. Missing at Chicago, however, is the comrade-ship of the small college that JHT recalls with great fondness.

1911:02   Review of Jane Addams, *Twenty Years at Hull House.*
          School Review 19.3 (1911): 207–208.

A brief but highly favorable discussion of her life and her work at the Chicago settlement house. (Cf. 1910:06.)

1911:03   "Authority in Ethics."
          American Journal of Theology 15.1 (1911): 148–151.

A favorable review-essay of Thomas Cuming Hall's *History of Ethics within Organized Christianity* that explores the struggles of Christianity with the legal-istic approach to morality inherent in institutionalization. (Cf. 1911:04.)

1911:04   Review of Thomas Cuming Hall, *History of Ethics within
          Organized Christianity.*
          Philosophical Review 20.3 (1911): 317–320.

A highly favorable discussion of a study of the various ethical writers within the Christian tradition with an emphasis upon the role that institutional authority played in moral theorizing. (Cf. 1911:03.)

1912:01   *Mary Warren Tufts.*
          Chicago: University of Chicago Press, 1912, 27 pp.

JHT's mother (1823–1910), born in Wardsboro, Vermont, as was JHT's father, was the daughter of a physician. JHT's account begins with a consideration of her childhood, discussing in part her remembrances of church services; her future father-in-law, the Reverend James Tufts; her education at Mt. Holyoke Seminary and Castleton Seminary; her years of teaching school; and her wedding to JHT's father, James Tufts, in 1855. The second chapter recounts her housekeeping life beginning at age thirty-six, a long, undiagnosed illness and eventual recovery, and her activities before and after her husband's death in 1901. Chapter 3 briefly considers some of her personality traits, especially her vividness of memory and imagination.

1912:02   "The Characteristic of the American College."
          Amherst Monthly 26.9 (1912): 265–269.

In this paper, JHT explores the proper social function of the college as distinct from the university's goals of research and public service. Historically, the key elements were three: comradeship, the classical curriculum, and the chapel. In the modern, democratic age, the college can contribute by fostering a broader sense of human fellowship, by developing a curriculum that includes the study of the scientific method, and by instilling a desire to pursue the

Kingdom of God on earth through social reconstruction. JHT closes with a consideration of the difficulty that colleges have in competing with universities for faculty, a difficulty mitigated by the possibility of measurable influence upon students that college professors have.

1912:03 "Recent Discussions of Moral Evolution."
Harvard Theological Review 5.2 (1912): 155–179.

In this survey, JHT examines recent works in ethics by Edward Westermarck, Leonard T. Hobhouse, William Graham Sumner, Dewey and JHT (1908:01), Edward A. Ross, William McDougall, Charles Horton Cooley, Josiah Royce, Hugo Münsterberg, Dewey, Addison Webster Moore, and others from the point of view of the following four topics: the origin of the idea and feeling of moral obligation in custom, the stages of moral evolution, the reasons for changes in moral standards, and whether there is some absolute standard of moral progress against which we may judge our efforts.

1912:04 Abstract of "The New Individualism."
Journal of Philosophy, Psychology and Scientific Methods 9.13 (1912): 351–352.

An abstract of a paper presented to the Western Philosophical Association that responds to Warner Fite's recently published *Individualism*. (Cf. 1917:02.)

1912:05 Review of Robert Clarkson Brooks, *Corruption in American Politics and Life.*
International Journal of Ethics 22.4 (1912): 485–488.

A favorable account of an attempt to examine, in a cool and systematic way, the evils of American life that the muckrakers had sensationalized.

1912:06 "The Use of Legal Material in Teaching Ethics."
Journal of Philosophy, Psychology and Scientific Methods 9.17 (1912): 460–462.

In this paper, presented to the Western Philosophical Association, JHT advocates the introduction of material from the legal life of the community as a backdrop for teaching ethics: Should moral rules or constitutions change, and if so how? Should rules be enforced in the absence of harm? Should we emphasize motives or intent or results in our evaluations? To what extent is there a common good? (Cf. 1913:05 and 1915:04.)

1912:07 Review of Charles Abram Ellwood, *Sociology in Its Psychological Aspects.*
Psychological Bulletin 9.12 (1912): 461–465.

A favorable discussion of a study of sociology that calls for a starting point in social psychology.

1913:01   "History [of the Class of '84]."
         Class of 'Eighty-Four, Amherst College, Thirty-Fifth Reunion
         (December 31, 1912).
         N.P.: n.p., 1913. 23–47.

In this history of the class of 1884, JHT focuses upon the professions that his classmates have followed for the twenty-eight years since graduation and that have shaped their lives. Based on correspondence with several of his classmates, he discusses continuities and changes in the professions of the ministry, medicine, law, farming, business, and teaching. His general themes are the growth and integration of the economic sphere, the greater levels of preparation necessary for the various fields, and the types of public service possible in each area.

1913:02   Review of Fritz Berolzheimer, *The World's Legal
         Philosophies.*
         Harvard Law Review 26.3 (1913): 279–280.

A mixed review that praises the volume's elaboration of the central chapters of human progress but complains about its overly minute focus.

1913:03   "The Study of Public Morality in High Schools."
         Religious Education 7.6 (1913): 631–636.

JHT discusses the importance of instruction in public morality in high school—including topics like the conduct of public officials rather than acts that concern only the family—because such an approach to ethics emphasizes finding solutions to problems rather than following preset standards, because it does not interfere with private life, and because improvements in public morality are so necessary. He closes with a consideration of three themes to be emphasized: Business and industry should be presented as a system of service; government should be presented as an established system of ordered freedom; and the reality of change and the ongoing necessity for social reconstruction should be presented as central elements of an adequate morality. (Cf. 1914:04; 1914:05; 1918:01.)

1913:04   "The University and the Advance of Justice."
         University of Chicago Magazine 5.6 (1913): 186–198.

In this convocation address at the University of Chicago, JHT presents justice as the fundamental human requirement and as being grounded in the social nature of man. After indicating that conceptions of justice have changed relative to conditions, he suggests that our sense of justice must change as well to a more social one and that the university can play a major role in this process. The role that JHT sees for the university is diverse: to help develop a scientific approach different from our ineffectual system of criminal justice, to help develop an adequate system of protecting citizens from the direct and indirect harmful results of our industrial system, to help develop an integrated system of judicial and legislative efforts to address social problems, to help develop a high level of intelligent public opinion on the issues of the day, and to help develop a spirit of public service in all of its members.

1913:05   Abstract of "The Criteria of Social Ends."
         Journal of Philosophy, Psychology and Scientific Methods 10.19
         (1913): 517–519.

Although this report was actually written by William Ernest Hocking, it details the contents of a paper JHT read at the Conference on the Relation of Law to Social Ends. The paper itself discussed two methods for attempting to determine when public actions should be undertaken to advance 'the common good.' JHT rejected any attempt to decide by deduction from a fixed definition or from precedent, and suggested the need to determine the proper role for public action hypothetically in particular cases by examining public need. (Cf. 1912:06 and 1913:06.)

1913:06   [Letter on Oliver Wendell Holmes, Jr.]
         Journal of Philosophy, Psychology and Scientific Methods 10.22
         (1913): 615–616.

In this brief note, JHT corrects a misinterpretation contained in Hocking's report on his recent paper (1913:05).

1914:01   Review of Frank Chapman Sharp, *Success: A Course in
         Moral Instruction for the High School.* 2d ed.
         International Journal of Ethics 24.2 (1914): 239–241.

An initially favorable discussion of a volume on the art of living that questions whether 'success,' because it has so many possible interpretations, should be taken as primary.

1914:02   Review of Mrs. A. L. [Susan Miller] Quackenbush, *Social
         Forces: A Topical Outline, with Bibliography.*
         Elementary School Teacher 14.6 (1914): 296.

A favorable notice of a source book for citizenship education.

1914:03   Review of Eugene Dupréel, *Le Rapport social: essai sur
         l'objet et la mèthode de la sociologie.*
         Philosophical Review 23.2 (1914): 221–222.

A descriptive discussion that considers the usefulness of Dupréel's central concept of 'social rapport.'

1914:04   "The Teaching of Ideals."
             School Review 22.5 (1914): 326–333.

In this paper, JHT considers the content and methods of teaching moral ideals in secondary education. The ideals themselves must be ones proper to the future citizens in a democracy, capable of development over time, and grounded in the realities of our social situation. The means that can be used are the recognition of group life; the imagery of art and literature; and primarily deliberate, hypothetical inquiry. JHT closes with a discussion of the role that such ideals could play in contemporary business life and politics, and a brief coda on the importance of the teacher.

1914:05   "Ethics in High Schools and Colleges: Teaching Ethics for Purposes of Social Training."
             Religious Education 9.5 (1914): 454–459.

After indicating some differences between college and high school ethics instruction, JHT considers two similarities of purpose: the common emphasis upon standards of public morality, and the common focus upon intelligence rather than habit or sentiment. He then discusses themes that need to be emphasized in high school ethics teaching: the students' future role in a democracy, the dynamic nature of modern society, the need to focus upon the common good, and the complexities of a class society. Our overall aim, JHT writes, ought to be to develop high school graduates who are appreciative of the development of the institutions of society and prepared for the more critical ethical work of college.

1914:06   Review of Fritz Berolzheimer, *Moral und Gesellschaft des 20. Jahrhunderts.*
             International Journal of Ethics 25.1 (1914): 121–122.

A brief but favorable review of a volume that attempts to integrate moral, legal, and social questions.

1914:07   Review of Rufus Matthew Jones, *Spiritual Reformers in the 16th and 17th Centuries.*
             International Journal of Ethics 25.1 (1914): 124.

A mildly favorably notice of a study of a number of religious thinkers who influenced Quakerism.

1914:08   "The Present Significance of Scholarship."
             Washington University Record 10.2 (1914): 1–12.

In this Phi Beta Kappa address at Washington University, JHT discusses the role of a scholar in a democracy. Noting that formerly the scholar was seen as a man of learning and culture in a world that was completed and displayed for our contemplation, he advocates that in our processive world the scholar's task must be that of an investigator and reconstructor of human institutions—especially in the fields of religion, law, and urban problems.

1914:09   Review of Elias Hershey Sneath and George Hodges,
Moral Training in the School and Home: A Manual for Teachers and Parents; and Elias Hershey Sneath, George Hodges, and Edward Lawrence Stevens, *The Golden Deed Book: A School Reader*.
Elementary School Teacher 14.4 (1914): 188.

A notice of two volumes advocating moral training for children through the use of stories.

1914:10   Review of Charles Keen Taylor, *The Moral Education of School Children*.
Elementary School Teacher 14.4 (1914): 188–189.

A notice of a study on the role of the school in moral education.

1914:11   Review of Hermann Weimer, *The Way to the Heart of the Pupil*.
Elementary School Teacher 14.4 (1914): 189.

A notice of a volume on teaching methodology.

1915:01   "The Test of Religion."
University of Chicago Sermons. Ed. Theodore Gerald Soares. Chicago: U of Chicago P, 1915. 89–104.

In this sermon, JHT briefly examines the various tests that have been applied to religion over the ages: in magical times, military victory and natural success; in more intellectual eras, rational consistency; in times of self-denial, purification; when God is a judge, assurance of forgiveness; in individualistic periods, a personal relationship with God; and, to the Kantian, the recognition of duty. As the modern test of religion, JHT offers cooperation and loyalty to the cause of creating the Kingdom of God.

1915:02   "The Ethics of the Family."
Proceedings of the National Conference of Charities and Correction, 1915.
Chicago: Hildmann, 1915. 24–37.

In this address, JHT maintains that we must move beyond the negative morality of taboos and proscriptions to develop a positive morality that emphasizes freedom for women, the importance of full opportunities for children, the value of sexuality and motherhood, and eugenics. He also discusses the nature of married love, children's need for the guidance of two parents, and family life as an institution of moral growth. (Cf. 1915:03 and 1916:02.)

1915:03 "The Ethics of the Family."
The Family.
New York: Russell Sage Foundation, 1915. 5–20.

A reprint of 1915:02.

1915:04 "Why Should Law and Philosophy Get Together?"
International Journal of Ethics 25.2 (1915): 188–195.

After a consideration of a series of differences between law and philosophy, JHT notes that every attempt of philosophers to address concrete problems brings them into the legal realm where legislative and constitutional limits on potential actions must be recognized and dealt with (Cf. 1912:06.)

1915:05 "Ethics of States."
Philosophical Review 24.2 (1915): 131–149.

In this presidential address to a joint meeting of the American Philosophical Association and the Western Philosophical Association, JHT examines, in the context of the recently begun European War, the paradox of the state's power to draw out the loftiest and the worst in human conduct. Rejecting the easy claims of self-styled 'realists' and blind patriots, he attempts to understand the basis of the paradox. JHT sees the ethical tradition of the combatants as a collection of five different codes; those of self-interest, honor, law, family, and ideals. States are currently organizations driven by self-interest and inspired by honor. He mentions, however, that as peoples come to recognize the difference between military success and righteousness, and the futility of having states act as judges of the morality of their own causes, there is a good chance that they will recognize the need for justice toward and friendly intercourse with their international neighbors.

1915:06 Review of William Graham Sumner, *The Challenge of Facts and Other Essays.*
International Journal of Ethics 25.3 (1915): 427–428.

A critical notice of a volume of papers by JHT's respected former teacher. (Cf. 1907:13 and 1919:17.)

1915:07 Review of Louis Dembitz Brandeis, *Business, A Profession.*
International Journal of Ethics 25.3 (1915): 428.

A favorable notice of Brandeis's attempt to develop a third way between capitalism and socialism.

1915:08   Review of *The Confessions of Frederick the Great*; with
Heinrich von Treitschke, *The Life of Frederick the Great*.
International Journal of Ethics 25.3 (1915): 428.

A notice of a book that JHT believes will aid in understanding modern Prussia.

1915:09   Review of Benedetto Croce, *Philosophy of the Practical,
Economic and Ethic.*
Philosophical Review 14.3 (1915): 321–325.

While JHT admits that this volume is a notable contribution to idealistic ethics, he indicates that he finds the general approach fully inadequate because of its rejection of the experiential element in ethics.

1915:10   "The Services of Present-Day Philosophy to Theological
Reconstruction."
Biblical World 46.1 (1915): 9–14.

Because both philosophy and theology attempt to see the world from the broadest perspective, JHT considers a series of elements found in modern, nonidealistic philosophy to see what they might contribute to contemporary theology. The philosophical elements are the radical empiricism of William James and the important range of social experience, discussions of evolution and emergence, the theme of voluntarism and its impact on understandings of reason and belief, analyses of the social self, and the quest for social justice.

1915:11   Review of John Dewey, *German Philosophy and Politics.*
International Journal of Ethics 26.1 (1915): 131–133.

A highly favorable review of Dewey's attempt to trace the intellectual roots of Prussian militarism back to Kant's emphasis upon duty, and his view that we need to strive for a world of positive human interaction rather than simply nonwar.

1916:01   Introduction to *The Philosophy of Wang Yang-Ming*. Trans.
Frederick Goodrich Henke.
Chicago: Open Court, 1916. vii–ix.

In this brief introduction to a translation of the thought of the Chinese administrator and philosopher Wang Shou-Jen (1472–1529), JHT emphasizes the need of Western thinkers to study the thought of the East, which he believes will be found to contain congenial ideas.

1916:02   "The Ethics of the Family."
International Journal of Ethics 26.2 (1916): 223–240.

A reprint of 1915:02.

1916:03   Review of Edward Page, *Trade Morals, Their Origin, Growth, and Promise.*
International Journal of Ethics 26.2 (1916): 305.

A descriptive notice of the interplay of conflicting systems of morals in society.

1916:04   Review of William Howard Taft, *Ethics in Service.*
International Journal of Ethics 26.2 (1916): 305.

A descriptive notice of a series of lectures by the former president on legal and social topics.

1916:05   Review of Upton Sinclair, ed., *The Cry for Justice: An Anthology of the Literature of Social Protest.*
International Journal of Ethics 26.2 (1916): 305–306.

A favorable notice of a survey from ancient Egypt to the present.

1916:06   Review of Albert Kocourek and John Henry Wigmore, eds., *Evolution of Law: Select Readings on the Origin and Development of Legal Institutions.* Vol. 2.
International Journal of Ethics 26.2 (1916): 306.

A favorable notice of a study for lawyers and for others who would understand legal systems.

1916:07   Review of Walton Hale Hamilton, *Current Economic Problems.*
International Journal of Ethics 26.2 (1916): 306–307.

A favorable notice of a large collection of short selections that discuss industrial and economic issues in the modern world.

1916:08   Review of James MacKaye, *The Happiness of Nations: A Beginning in Political Engineering.*
International Journal of Ethics 26.2 (1916): 307–308.

A descriptive notice of an attempt at justifying a more utilitarian social order.

1916:09   Review of Henry Jones Ford, *The Natural History of the State: An Introduction to Political Science.*
International Journal of Ethics 26.3 (1916): 438

A descriptive review of an evolutionary version of naturalistic ethics.

1916:10   Review of Elsie Clews Parsons, *Fear and Conventionality.*
              International Journal of Ethics 26.3 (1916): 438.

A favorable study of the history and current status of social customs believed
to be rooted in fear.

1916:11   Review of Arnold Bennett Hall, *Outlines of International
              Law.*
              International Journal of Ethics 26.3 (1916): 438–439.

A descriptive notice of a volume for the general public.

1916:12   Review of Frances Alice Kellor, *Out of Work, A Study of
              Unemployment.*
              International Journal of Ethics 26.3 (1916): 439.

A favorable notice of a study of aspects of the unemployment situation that
closes with a stinging condemnation of intermittent responses to an ongoing
problem.

1916:13   "Professor [Robert Franklin] Hoxie's Work."
              University of Chicago Magazine 8.9 (1916): 440–441.

A eulogy for the social scientist whose work focused on the problems of an
industrial society.

1916:14   Review of William T. Whitney, *Moral Education, An
              Experimental Investigation*
              International Journal of Ethics 26.4 (1916): 570.

A descriptive notice of an attempt to correlate religious training, home training, and school behavior with later success.

1916:15   Review of Arthur Twining Hadley, *Undercurrents in
              American Politics.*
              International Journal of Ethics 26.4 (1916): 570–571.

A favorable notice of a volume containing two series of lectures on democratic
themes.

1916:16   Abstract of "Reshaping our Philosophy."
              Journal of Philosophy, Psychology and Scientific Methods 13.14
              (1916): 378–379.

In this abstract of a paper presented to the Western Philosophical Association,
JHT advocates the reconstruction of our conceptions of 'liberty,' 'union,' and

'democracy' to fit our current situation in which the new economic power has not yet been tamed for the common good. (This material later appeared in part 4 of 1918:01.)

1916:17   Review of Edwin Leavitt Clarke, *American Men of Letters, Their Nature and Nurture.*
International Journal of Ethics 27.1 (1916): 123–124.

A descriptive notice of an attempt to determine the influence of inheritance and the environment on social progress.

1917:01   *Our Democracy: Its Origins and Its Tasks.*
New York: Henry Holt, 1917. vi + 327 pp.

In this volume, completed in September 1917, JHT attempts to make clear for general readers, young and old, the principles for which the United States stands and for which it had recently entered the World War. The volume itself is divided into two parts, "The Beginnings of Cooperation, Order, and Liberty" and "Liberty, Union, Democracy in the New World," which appear with only minor changes as parts 1 and 4 of *The Real Business of Living* (1918:01). Treating the latter volume, on which JHT had worked for several years, as the primary text, the substantial differences between this volume and it are the omission of parts 2 and 3 of *The Real Business of Living* in this volume; the compression of material from chapters 15–16 and 32 of *The Real Business of Living* into chapter 15 of this volume; and the compression of material from chapters 18–20 and 23–26 from this volume into chapters 35 and 38 respectively of *The Real Business of Living*.

1917:02   "The Moral Life and the Construction of Values and Standards."
John Dewey, et al. *Creative Intelligence: Essays in the Pragmatic Attitude.*
New York: Henry Holt, 1917. 354–408.

In this interpretation of the moral life, JHT attempts to give an outline of ethics that uses the valuable aspects of the evolutionary and the conceptual approaches. He begins with a consideration of four factors essential to morality: the centrality of embodiment, our common life with others, the ongoing role of intelligence and reason, and the creative and self-creative aspects of judgment. In the second section, JHT analyzes the concepts of 'good' and 'right,' with an emphasis upon the social and processive elements in their meanings: The 'good' of any situation is objectively a value and human valuing can improve with experience; there is a social factor to moral judgments that renders them more objective than economic judgments; 'right' means more than the means to the 'good,' and it plays its own role in moral consciousness; the ideal order of 'right' actions is modified over time; and 'right' is not purely a rational matter, but is more a reasonable blending of the intellectual and the emotional. In the third section, he contrasts his view with the view of Warner Fite, which he considers to be insufficiently processive and excessively rationalistic (cf. 1912:04). Finally, JHT suggests the possibility of progress in the physical, social and intellectual aspects of living through an ongoing creative reconstruction of our moral situation.

1917:03   "Ethics in the Last Twenty-Five Years."
            Philosophical Review 26.1 (1917): 28–45.

JHT focuses in this essay upon two central developments during the quarter-century life of the *Review*: the impact of the evolutionary method and genetic study on ethical thought, and the return of ethical interest in the broad range of public issues. Under the first heading, he considers (1) ethical evaluations of the evolutionary process and (2) evaluations of the moral significance of the study of the evolution of ethical standards in the context of the life of the group and its customs. His second theme is the ethical impact of various fundamental changes that call for a social sense of justice adequate to a democracy burdened with racial, imperial, and industrial problems, and for answers to problems of family life and sexuality.

1917:04   "Social Legislation for 1917."
            Woman's City Club [of Chicago] Bulletin 5.7 (1917): 1–4.

In this piece, JHT discusses briefly the reasons for the formation of the Illinois Committee on Social Legislation (of which he was the chairman), some past successes, and an overview of legislation under consideration for 1917 dealing with such matters as loan sharking, conditions of imprisonment, children, labor conditions, charitable organizations, and health insurance.

1917:05   [Statement on Social Legislation in Illinois].
            City Club [of Chicago] Bulletin 10.1 (1917): 21–23.

A reprint of 1917:04, with some omissions.

1917:06   Review of Floyd James Melvin, *Socialism as the Sociological
            Ideal: A Broader Basis for Socialism.*
            International Journal of Ethics 27.2 (1917): 269.

A descriptive notice of an attempt to clarify the meaning of the term.

1917:07   Review of Henry Schaeffer, *The Social Legislation of the
            Primitive Semites.*
            International Journal of Ethics 27.3 (1917): 404.

A mildly favorable notice of a survey of laws organized by topic.

1917:08   Review of George Thomas White Patrick, *The Psychology of Relaxation*.
International Journal of Ethics 27.3 (1917): 407.

A favorable notice of a broad study of physical well-being.

1917:09   Review of Joseph Edward Davies, *Trust Laws and Unfair Competition*;William Harrison Spring Stevens, *Unfair Competition*; and Homer Blosser Reed, *The Morals of Monopoly and Competition*.
International Journal of Ethics 27.4 (1917): 534.

A favorable notice of a trio of volumes that examines aspects of the problem of unfair competition.

1917:10   Review of Edith Abbott and Sophonisba Preston Breckinridge, *Truancy and Non-Attendance in Chicago Schools: A Study of the Social Aspects of the Compulsory Education and Child Labor Legislation of Illinois*.
International Journal of Ethics 27.4 (1917): 535.

A highly favorable notice of a well-documented study whose significance reaches beyond Chicago.

1917:11   Review of Alfred Hoyt Granger, *England's World Empire*.
International Journal of Ethics 27.4 (1917): 541.

A descriptive notice of a study mildly critical of England.

1917:12   Abstract of "Ethics and International Relations."
Journal of Philosophy, Psychology and Scientific Methods 14.26 (1917): 720–721.

An abstract of 1918:05.

1918:01   *The Real Business of Living.*
New York: Henry Holt, 1918. vii + 476 pp.

This volume, completed by JHT in February of 1918 after over five years of work, is aimed at students in the final years of high school. In accordance with the view that JHT had expressed in 1913:03, 1914:04, and especially 1914:05, the purpose of the volume is to develop in these students a better sense of the nature of public morality and civic duty and a greater appreciation for the long process of social progress. In this way, he hoped to prepare them for more critical work in college. Parts of this volume had previously appeared in 1917:01.

In part 1, JHT offers a historical introduction to the American experience through a speculative account of the growth of our social institutions. After a brief introductory chapter that emphasizes the need to learn cooperation and create liberty and democracy, chapter 2 examines early human life as a process of the consolidation of the simple physical tools of existence to be followed by the great social gains of social progress. Chapter 3 considers the role of the clan or tribe in protection and in establishing a customary social order and the modest amount of progress it made possible through its limited amounts of cooperation and liberty. Chapter 4 begins a consideration of agriculture as an advance over nomadism and the creation of class societies by conquest. Chapter 5 continues with a consideration of warriors and the military imposition of a royal state and of the growth of this state as a political and economic power. JHT considers the advances of the early state in chapter 6: peace, order, common law, and private property in land. Chapter 7 considers the power of the ideals of the dominant warrior class—honor, courage, loyalty, and chivalry—as unified group standards, and their later evolution into the ideals of the gentleman. In chapter 8, JHT introduces the town, handicrafts and trade, and, between the gentry and the peasants, the middle class of merchants and craftsmen who made possible a new kind of cooperation through exchange of goods and ideas. He examines the results of town life—increases in wealth and comfort, knowledge and skill, freedom through privileges—in chapter 9. Chapter 10 discusses the rise of some middle-class virtues: honesty, fairness, dignity of labor. In chapter 11, JHT turns from the consideration of cooperation to that of liberty, and explores initially a series of senses in which 'liberty' is used. Chapter 12 explores the process of the expansion of liberties from privileges only for the few to rights for larger segments of the general populace. Chapter 13 discusses the role of ideas in the progress of liberty and democracy through the efforts of writers, philosophers, and religious prophets. Chapter 14 ends part 1 with a brief summary that concludes that the full democratic life is one of freedom and responsibility.

In part 2, JHT considers the role of cooperation and freedom in the economic realm. Chapter 15 examines the impact of the Industrial Revolution with an emphasis upon changes in industry—machines, steam power, factories, division of labor, working in larger groups—and in business under the name of capitalism. In chapter 16, JHT considers the corporation as a cooperative institution with advantages and dangers, especially its blurring of the lines of responsibility. He discusses the reasons for the tendency of economic organization toward centralization in chapter 17. A series of effects of the Industrial Revolution—including increases in population, wealth and education, the growth of the factory labor class, and the wage system—are examined in chapter 18. Chapter 19 introduces the topic of the moral principles of business and industry necessary to control the desire for gain. The first of these principles—responsibility and good faith to live up to legitimate contractual agreements—and particular relationships of responsibility, like agent or trustee, are the topics of chapters 20 and 21. The second fundamental principle is that business and industry are organized for service to the common good. This principle is discussed in chapter 22, largely in terms of nonproductive means of making money; in chapter 23, in terms of the use of regulatory controls; and in chapter 24, in terms of theories justifying private property and its relationship to the common good. The third fundamental principle of business and industry is that of fairness or justice in prices (chapter 25), wages (chapter 26), and competition (chapters 27–28).

In part 3, JHT explores the problems and possibilities of urban and rural America. Chapter 29 examines the economic and other factors behind the development of the problems of the modern city, especially those related to factories and housing. In chapter 30, JHT considers the proper role of urban government in protecting the populace from the indirect ills of poor water or food, of sewage, fire, crime, or disease, and in providing for services like education. Chapter 31 discusses the values of contemporary country living— independence, equality, health, and so on—and ways of dealing with its problems, especially isolation and limitations on opportunities through greater applications of science and more cooperative activities.

In part 4, JHT explores the problems of liberty, union, and democracy in the modern world. Chapter 32 details four significant historical factors in the American experience: the fact that the majority of immigrants came from middle and lower classes, the abundance of free land, the democratizing influence of frontier life, and the advantages and disadvantages of the impact of the Industrial Revolution as a new kind of cooperation. Chapter 33 discusses the origin of the American conception of liberty in the various 'natural' rights that free people from obedience to attempts at oppression by the government; chapter 34, such current problems of liberty as the need for education for better citizenship and better health and the inability of the majority to protect itself from the misuse of liberty by the few. Chapter 35 considers the American movement after liberation toward a stronger union—favored by statesmen, property owners and the commercial classes, and opposed especially by the poor majority—and the particular checks and balances form of constitution adopted as a compromise. In chapter 36, JHT explores two current problems of union: ethnic and racial problems in the North and South, and capital and labor problems. Democracy is his next major theme. In chapter 37, he considers 'democracy' in its political meaning as a form of self-government and the various historical justifications for self-government; in chapter 38, the obstacles to self-government presented by the system of checks and balances, invisible government through powerful unelected forces like the railroads, the long ballot, and attempted reforms. Chapter 39 considers 'democracy' in its moral meaning of equality and full participation in the goods of life, rejects a series of attempts to justify inequality, and offers a defense of equality. In chapter 40, JHT discusses the areas of legal, civil, social, economic, and educational equality, and the kinds of contemporary efforts needed to make equality more of a reality in each. Chapter 41 considers in general terms the current relationship between the United States and other nations in the light of our historical nonintervention in European politics, the Monroe Doctrine and our general interest in peace, four recent issues of international conflict, and the new possibilities for international cooperation inherent in the modern world. In chapter 42, JHT considers the morality of warfare, admitting that it is an evil but maintaining that it is not as bad as permitting the destruction of liberty and justice.

1918:02   *The Ethics of Cooperation.*
           Boston: Houghton, 1918. 73 pp.

In his Weinstock Lecture at the semicentenary celebration of the University of California, JHT initially considers three forms of social organization—dominance, competition, and cooperation—the last of which he equates with attempts to secure common ends, the promotion of equality, and the sharing of decision making and power. JHT discusses next the different interpretations of 'liberty,' 'power,' and 'justice' in each form of organization, with an emphasis upon how in a cooperative situation all three reinforce efforts toward equality and shared participation. Then JHT considers the historical process of the roles of dominance, competition, and cooperation in the institutions of government, religion, commerce, and industry, emphasizing the gradual growth of cooperation. Next, JHT considers two defects in our economic order from the point of view of cooperation. The first is that the participants do not primarily intend to cooperate—they intend to get what they desire—whereas JHT thinks that successful mutual benefit must be deliberate rather than accidental, and that such a standard can be enacted in the economic realm as it was in the political. The second defect of our current economic system is that the unequal distribution of wealth, and consequently of power and opportunities for a better life, persists even though it is counteracted somewhat by our governmental agencies, especially the schools. Finally, JHT considers the need for the postwar world to choose the method of cooperation in the face of the anticipated challenges to internationalism by attempts at political dominance, predatory economic competition, and destructive nationalism, itself the most dangerous because it is rooted in a kind of cooperation. In a brief concluding section, JHT offers a statement of faith that with increased human interaction, mutual understanding and cooperation will grow. (Cf. 1919:04.)

1918:03   Review of Robert Mark Wenley, *The Life and Work of George Sylvester Morris.*
           International Journal of Ethics 28.2 (1918): 280–281.

A highly favorable discussion of both the volume and the work of Morris.

1918:04   Review of Walter Franklin Robie, *Rational Sex Ethics.*
           International Journal of Ethics 28.2 (1918): 289–290.

A descriptive notice of a physician-therapist's study of contemporary sexuality.

1918:05 "Ethics and International Relations."
International Journal of Ethics 28.3 (1918): 299–313.

In this paper, presented to the American Philosophical Association, JHT explores the connection between morality and national frontiers in three areas. As to whether nations are freed from all moral responsibility, JHT examines and rejects a series of claims that they are, and he suggests the moral need for intelligence to seek international cooperation. The topic of a standard of justice for evaluating any international situation admittedly brings into conflict defenders of the status quo and those who believe their needs are unsatisfied; but JHT suggests the establishment of legal institutions, rather than war, as a means of resolving imbalances. His third theme is the contrast between systems built on aristocracy and on democracy, and here he maintains that the future should be one that aims not at class rule but at equality.

1918:06 Review of Felix Adler, *An Ethical Philosophy of Life.*
International Journal of Ethics 29.1 (1918): 100–103.

A favorable discussion of an intellectual autobiography by the founder of the Society for Ethical Culture and a cofounder of the *Journal* itself.

1919:01 "Why Social Workers Should Study the Need of Health Insurance."
Proceedings of the National Conference of Social Work, 1918.
Chicago: Rogers and Hall, 1919. 407–416.

In this paper read before the National Conference of Social Work in May 1918, JHT proposes that social workers push for a system of social insurance to make available to all citizens the benefits of modern medical science. The likelihood of such a complicated system actually succeeding is demonstrated by the evidence of the administrative capabilities of the American organization for the World War. The fact that the populace has not yet called for such insurance should not be an indication, JHT writes, that they do not need it; rather, it is only an indication that they have not yet fully grasped the possibilities.

1919:02 "Wartime Gains for the American Family."
Proceedings of the National Conference of Social Work, 1919.
Chicago: Rogers and Hall, 1919. 326–332.

A shortened version of an address before the National Conference on Social Work in June 1919. For the full text, see 1919:03.

1919:03 "Wartime Gains for the American Family."
New York: Russell Sage Foundation, 1919. 20 pp.

In this paper, JHT examines the direct and indirect effects of the war on family life in America. He begins with a consideration of the impact of the war and other factors like economic status and levels of education on family size, reproduction rates, and so on. JHT sees some benefits likely to result from the income tax and the possibility of efforts to improve the health of future mothers. He then turns to a consideration of non-eugenic gains like advances in public health, especially in combatting venereal disease; the national movement for the prohibition of alcoholic beverages; improvements in the standard of living; increased employment for women outside the home and the call for maternity leave and child care; and increased equality between men and women.

1919:04 "The Ethics of Co-operation."
The Semicentenary Celebration of the Founding of the University of California [1868–1918], with an Account of the Conference on International Relations.
Berkeley: U of California P, 1919. 215–236.

A reprint of 1918:02.

1919:05 [Letter on Aid for the Peoples of Jugoslavia.]
Journal of Philosophy, Psychology and Scientific Methods 16.4 (1919): 92.

In this brief statement, written in response to a Serbian call for aid in articulating a national democratic perspective (pp. 89–90), JHT calls on philosophers to turn for a time from the problems of past philosophy to the problems affecting the fundamental values of living in the current situation, a turn that he thinks might help American students as well as the people in Jugoslavia.

1919:06 "George Burman Foster."
University [of Chicago] Record 5.2 (1919): 180–185.

A respectful eulogy for a professor of religion for whom religion was primarily an attitude of personal companionship.

1919:07 Review of Mary Parker Follett, *The New State: Group Organization the Solution of Popular Government.*
International Journal of Ethics 29.3 (1919): 374–377.

A mildly negative discussion of a proposal to base the state on the local unit, the neighborhood group, a plan that JHT believes suffers from the current morbidity of neighborhoods. (Cf. 1925:02.)

1919:08 Review of Edward Gleason Spaulding, *The New Rationalism: The Development of a Constructive Realism upon*

the Basis of Modern Logic and Science, and through the
Criticism of Opposed Philosophical Systems.
International Journal of Ethics 29.3 (1919): 383–384.

A mildly critical discussion of one of the statements of new realism in which JHT's focus is ethical claims and problems.

1919:09 Review of Robert Franklin Hoxie, *Trade Unionism in the*
United States.
International Journal of Ethics 29.3 (1919): 391.

A highly favorable notice of a posthumous volume on the philosophy of trade unionism. (Cf. 1916:13.)

1919:10 Review of William Lyon Mackenzie King, *Industry and*
Humanity: A Study in the Principles Underlying Industrial
Reconstruction.
International Journal of Ethics 29.3 (1919): 391–392.

A favorable notice of a study of the current industrial situation.

1919:11 Review of Ordway Tead, *Instincts in Industry: A Study of*
Working-Class Psychology.
International Journal of Ethics 29.3 (1919): 392.

A descriptive notice of a study of the lives of workers.

1919:12 Review of Westel Woodbury Willoughby, *Prussian Political*
Philosophy: Its Principles and Implications.
International Journal of Ethics 29.3 (1919): 393–394.

A favorable notice of a study on German political theory.

1919:13 Review of Morrison Isaac Swift, *Can Mankind Survive.*
International Journal of Ethics 29.4 (1919): 509.

A descriptive notice of a volume that answers the question negatively.

1919:14 Abstract of "The Function of Philosophy in Social
Reconstruction."
Journal of Philosophy, Psychology and Scientific Methods 16.17
(1919): 465–466.

In this abstract of a paper drawing upon material published in part 2 of 1918:01 and presented to the Western Philosophical Association, JHT suggests that because capital and labor have attained greater social power, it is now necessary to expect of them increased responsibility and cooperation and that philosophy has a role to play in this process.

1919:15 "Wartime Gains for the American Family."
International Journal of Ethics 30.1 (1919): 83–100.

A reprint of 1919:03.

1919:16 Review of Irving Babbitt, *Rousseau and Romanticism*.
International Journal of Ethics 30.1 (1919): 101–105.

In this critical discussion of a study of the ethics of romanticism that condemns it for a lack of rationality and decorum, JHT points to Babbitt's failure to understand romanticism as part of the historical struggle against unjustified authority.

1919:17 Review of William Graham Sumner, *The Forgotten Man and Other Essays*.
International Journal of Ethics 30.1 (1919): 106–108.

In this discussion of another edition of Sumner's work (cf. 1907:13 and 1915:06), JHT shows again his respect for his former teacher, *in spite of* his ideas.

1919:18 Review of The National Municipal League, *National Municipal Review*.
International Journal of Ethics 30.1 (1919): 117.

A favorable notice of various changes in the *Review*.

1919:19 "The Community and Economic Groups."
Philosophical Review 28.6 (1919): 589–597.

In this paper JHT presents the view that in the contemporary world, economic power has outdistanced the political. The main cause of this growth of economic power, he suggests, is the changing nature of property. In the form of widely held small farms, property had been a means of security against want; but, in the form of narrowly controlled industrial capital, property had become a means to control the lives of others. JHT believes that the common good is most likely to be attained neither by enforcing stronger political controls over the economic realm, nor by abandoning a concern with the common good, but by attempting to draw the competing economic groups into long-term agreements to negotiate responsibly and cooperatively for the common good, as he was then doing with the clothing industry in Chicago. (Cf. 1920:02 and 1921:09.)

1919:20   Abstract of "The Community and Economic Groups."
              Journal of Philosophy, Psychology and Scientific Methods 16.26
              (1919): 718–719.

An abstract of 1919:19.

1920:01   Contributor to and editor of *Cynthia Whitaker Tufts*.
              Chicago: U of Chicago P, 1920. 83 pp.

In the foreword, JHT offers a brief account of the origins of the various parts
of this memorial volume for his wife, Cynthia Hobart Whitaker Tufts (1860–
1920). After Cynthia's own account of various memories in "My Life" (pp. 7–
54), which ends with their marriage on August 25, 1891, JHT discusses in
"The Later Years" her family background and personal traits. He then considers their year in Germany (1891–1892), the first years at the University of
Chicago, caring for aged parents, and her final illness. JHT closes with a
discussion of her sense of good judgment.

1920:02   "Board of Arbitration for the Agreements Between the
              Amalgamated Clothing Workers of America and Chicago
              Industrial Federation of Clothing Manufacturers."
              *The Hart, Schaffner and Marx Labor Agreement: Industrial Law
              in the Clothing Industry*. Ed. Earl Dean Howard.
              Chicago: n.p., 1920. 56–63.

The text of a decision rendered on December 22, 1919, by JHT, in his capacity
as chairman of the Board of Arbitration. The substance of the decision was
that the clothing workers covered by the agreement were to receive wage
increases ranging from five to twenty percent to compensate them for increases in the cost of living and to take account of the increased demand for
clothing workers. (This volume also contains a number of fragments of other
related decisions rendered by JHT.) (Cf. 1919:19 and 1921:09.)

1920:03   Review of Frank Chapman Sharp, *Education for Character:
              Moral Training in the School and Home*.
              School Review 28.3 (1920): 227–228.

A favorable discussion of an introduction to the topic of moral education, an
area of instruction that JHT believes might be given another chance in the
wake of the World War.

1920:04   Review of John Moffatt Mecklin, *Introduction to Social
              Ethics: The Social Conscience in a Democracy*.
              International Journal of Ethics 31.1 (1920): 111–112.

A favorable discussion of a study of the various aspects of social ethics in
which JHT focuses on its consideration of the role of organized religion in

social reform, and its omission of any discussion of the possibilities of the income tax to redistribute the burdens of society.

1920:05   Review of William John Fielding, *Sanity in Sex*.
          International Journal of Ethics 31.1 (1920): 117.

A descriptive note about a study of the modern movement for bringing more rationality to sexual practices.

1920:06   Review of Clement Richard Attlee, *The Social Worker*.
          International Journal of Ethics 31.1 (1920): 117.

A favorable notice of a study of the training and activities of social workers in Britain.

1921:01   Contributor to *A Dictionary of Religion and Ethics*. Eds.
          Shailer Mathews and Gerald Birney Smith.
          New York: Macmillan, 1921.
          JHT's entries: "Aesthetics," p. 6; "Ethics," pp. 152–155;
          "Ethics of Capitalism," pp. 68–70; "Ethics of [the] Labor
          Movement," pp. 249–250; "Ethics of Politics," pp. 341–
          342; "Justice," p. 241; "Right," p. 378; "Romanticism," p.
          386; "Social Ethics," pp. 415–416.

In these entries, JHT offers definitions of the terms, overviews of the aspects of the topics, and brief historical surveys. Of particular interest are "Ethics of Capitalism," "Ethics of [the] Labor Movement," "Ethics of Politics," and "Social Ethics."

1921:02   Review of Richard Henry Tawney, *The Acquisitive Society*.
          International Journal of Ethics 31.2 (1921): 237–238.

A highly favorable notice of a volume that compares the acquisitive society invidiously with the functional or service society.

1921:03   Review of Frederick Jackson Turner, *The Frontier in
          American History*.
          International Journal of Ethics 31.2 (1921): 238.

A highly favorable notice of a volume of essays on the role of the Frontier in the development of American democracy.

1921:04   [A Letter on Country Life.]
          Survey 45.26 (1921): 933.

A brief letter strongly supporting Joseph K. Hart's article, "What's Wrong with Gopher Prairie?" (in the March 21 issue), in which Hart had contended that the meaning of Sinclair Lewis's *Main Street* should not be seen as the destructive effects of small town life, but rather as the destruction of small town life by contemporary civilization and higher education.

1921:05   Review of Joseph Kinmont Hart, *Community Organization*.
              International Journal of Ethics 31.3 (1921): 343–344.

A highly favorable notice of an examination of the development and life of the community.

1921:06   Review of Bertrand Russell, *Bolshevism: Theory and Practice*.
              International Journal of Ethics 31.3 (1921): 344.

A mildly favorable notice of a critical discussion of Soviet Russia that emphasizes the importance of the democratic introduction of reforms.

1921:07   Review of Zechariah Chafee, Jr., *Freedom of Speech*.
              International Journal of Ethics 31.3 (1921): 345.

A favorable notice of a discussion of free speech in the context of the postwar hysteria.

1921:08   Review of Durant Drake, *Shall We Stand by the Church? A Dispassionate Inquiry*.
              International Journal of Ethics 31.3 (1921): 346.

A mildly favorable notice of a collection of essays examining the problem of decreased church involvement.

1921:09   "Judicial Law-Making Exemplified in Industrial Arbitration."
              Columbia Law Review 21.5 (1921): 405–415.

In this account of the importance and the possibilities of industrial arbitration, JHT, based upon his own experience as an arbitrator (cf. 1920:02), summarizes the working process of such a board of arbitration. He then discusses the semi-permanent aspects of the process and the quasi-professional status of the representatives as instances of similarities between industrial arbitration and our legal system. Next he turns to a consideration of four fundamental problems that need to be kept in mind during such arbitration: (1) the tension between the arbitrators' abstract sense of justice in evaluating complaints and proposals and the demonstrated balance of power between the two parties, (2) the need to decide between a literalistic interpretation of particular agreements or a more broad interpretation of them in light of the general aims of the arbitration process, (3) the issue of maintaining traditional work practices or of allowing labor-saving improvements, and (4) the question of the role to be played in industrial arbitration by the notion of a 'fair wage.' (cf. 1919:19 and 1920:02.)

1921:10 "The Legal and Social Philosophy of Mr. Justice Holmes."
American Bar Association Journal 7.7 (1921): 359–363.

In this review-essay of Holmes's *Collected Legal Papers* (1920), JHT compares him to William James as an opponent of absolutism. JHT then explores four topics: (1) the relationship between logic and law, and Holmes's view that any conclusion can be rendered logical in a narrow sense but that more important for deciding issues is not the abstract law but the judge's social theory; (2) the role of courts in a democracy to resist the majority's will as expressed through legislation and Holmes's ultimate criterion of the common good; (3) the view of the law as predictive, suggesting that Holmes was not advocating the study of law solely from the viewpoint of the evil person since he remains committed to social life; and (4) Holmes's view on the value of the life of activity over that of the scholar. (Cf. 1921:15 and 1932:02.)

1921:11 Review of Goldsworth Lowes Dickinson, ed., *Handbooks on International Relations.*
International Journal of Ethics 31.4 (1921): 453–454.

A favorable notice of a series of handbooks on various aspects of international relations for the general public.

1921:12 Review of Frederic Clemson Howe, *Denmark: A Co-operative Commonwealth.*
International Journal of Ethics 31.4 (1921): 454.

A descriptive notice on a study of recent social changes in Denmark with a consideration of what changes might work in America.

1921:13 Review of the *Proceedings of the International Conference of Women Physicians.* 6 vols.
International Journal of Ethics 31.4 (1921): 454.

A favorable notice of a series of volumes that explores various aspects of the health of women and children.

1921:14 Review of Henry James, *The Letters of William James.* 2 vols.
Journal of Philosophy 18.14 (1921): 381–387.

In this review of James's letters edited by his son, Henry, JHT celebrates the various aspects of James's personality and suggests that the study of the letters will help undermine various misinterpretations of James: that he had a narrow sense of the practical, or that he was a subjectivist, or that he had come late to philosophy.

1921:15 "Reply [to Everett Pepperrell Wheeler]."
American Bar Association Journal 7.8 (1921): 433–434.

In this defense of his claim in 1921:10 that sixty percent of the wealth of the country was in the hands of two percent of the population, JHT repeats that his point was not about income, which he grants is not so unequally distributed, but about wealth.

1921:16 "Dr. [James Rowland] Angell, the New President of Yale."
The World's Work 42 (1921): 387–400.

As an admitted longtime friend of Angell, JHT, who had earned his B.D. from Yale in 1889, introduces the new president. He discusses Angell's life and academic career, and suggests that Angell will bring the spirit of democracy and public service found in higher education in the West with him to Yale.

1921:17 Review of Irwin Edman, *Human Traits and Their Social Significance*.
International Journal of Ethics 32.1 (1921): 115–116.

A favorable notice of a textbook on human nature.

1921:18 Review of Leo Pasvolsky, *The Economics of Communism*.
International Journal of Ethics 32.1 (1921): 116.

A descriptive notice of an unfavorable account of the 'Soviet Experiment.'

1921:19 Review of Gustave Le Bon, *The World in Revolt: A Psychological Study of Our Times*.
International Journal of Ethics 32.1 (1921): 116.

A mildly favorable notice of a study of the European situation in the immediate postwar period.

1921:20 "Limitation of Armament, the American Policy."
American Federationist 28 (1921): 926–927.

In this brief article condemning high levels of arms spending as provocative and wasteful, JHT suggests that the United States should return to the suggestions of Washington, Madison, and Monroe and limit its international military presence.

1922:01   Review of Horatio Hackett Newman, *Readings in Evolution,*
              Genetics and Eugenics.
              International Journal of Ethics 32.2 (1922): 232.

A mildly favorable notice of a volume of historical and contemporary readings.

1922:02   Review of Samuel Jackson Holmes, *The Trend of the Race.*
              A Study of Present Tendencies in the Biological Development of
              Civilized Mankind.
              International Journal of Ethics 32.2 (1922): 233.

A mildly favorable notice of a volume on eugenics.

1922:03   "Religion's Place in Securing a Better World-Order."
              Journal of Religion 2.2 (1922): 113–128.

In this examination of the role that religion might play in contemporary social reconstruction, JHT calls first for religion to transcend its historical fixation with ritual, personal mysticism, and individual salvation. It would then be possible, he believes, for religion to emphasize other of its traits: its power to transform society, its recognition of the role of faith in the possibilities of human nature and in the benevolence of nature, its recognition of the possibility of regeneration, and its emphasis upon the importance of community and justice. JHT closes with a brief restatement of the intellectual bankruptcy of religion and the view that the religious spirit is still alive in the efforts of the university and the world of arts and letters.

1923:01   *Education and Training for Social Work.*
              New York: Russell Sage Foundation, 1923. xii + 240 pp.

This study, based upon research that JHT began while at Columbia University in late 1920 and continued through all of 1921, is an attempt to survey the current system of preparing social workers. In part 1, JHT examines the general field of social work. In chapter 1, he considers a series of different definitions of 'social work,' finally settling on a conception of it that emphasizes both that it must supplement the other, narrower professions—educators, lawyers, physicians, and so on—and that it must maintain flexibility in light of humanity's changing needs. Chapter 2, following upon this contextual sense of 'social work' just developed, explores the complexity of the relationship between the central concerns of the social worker and its more tangential relationships to architecture, medicine, law, education, and so on. (An essay by George W. Kirchwey on the relationship of social work to juvenile delinquency is on pp. 41–54.) In chapter 3, JHT rejects the view that social work is a women's profession. Although he recognizes certain specific valuable contributions of women, he maintains that both the profession and society's goals will be best advanced if the profession contains a considerable number of men, and he then considers how more men might be attracted. Chapter 4 examines the intrinsic appeal of social work, which JHT considers to be primarily the opportunity to be useful, especially if social work is to emphasize undertaking efforts to advance social reconstruction.

Part 2 examines problems of education and training for the field of social work. Chapter 5 considers the relationship between the need for technique, which requires 'training,' and for sensitivity, grounded in 'education,' both of which are necessary to the social worker. In chapter 6, JHT discusses the dual task of professional schools of preparing students and of advancing research, and suggests why the preparation of social workers is better in the professional school setting rather than through simply a cluster of interrelated courses. The location of the professional school for social work is the topic of chapter 7, and JHT advocates its placement within the university context rather than as an independent school, especially in those areas with strong state university systems. In addition, JHT notes that rural social work requires at least some rural preparation as well. Chapter 8 considers whether social work is properly a graduate or undergraduate course of study, a question that JHT answers by suggesting that preparation be made at the highest level that is practical. He considers the related theme of the level of education required for entrance into programs in social work in chapter 9. Chapter 10 examines the question of requiring as prerequisites for the professional study of social work specific topics like biology, psychology, social psychology, history, economics, political science, sociology, and philosophy. Problems of the curriculum—a vocational versus an academic emphasis, the length of the course of study, a unified or a diversified course of study—are JHT's topics in chapter 11. Problems of instruction—the case study method versus an examination of broader theoretical sweep, and the integration of field work—are examined in chapter 12. The final chapter suggests conditions under which it is advisable to give economic aid to desirable candidates interested in social work. In two appendices, JHT surveys current salary levels for social workers and the attendance levels at various institutions of preparation for social work. (Cf. 1923:04.)

1923:02   Review of Robert Archey Woods and Albert Joseph Kennedy, *The Settlement Horizon: A National Estimate.* *International Journal of Ethics* 33.2 (1923): 221–223.

A highly favorable review of a volume that explores the motives, aims, methods, and achievements of the settlement movement.

1923:03   Review of Arthur Kenyon Rogers, *English and American Philosophy since 1800: A Critical Survey.* *International Journal of Ethics* 33.3 (1923): 344.

A mildly favorable notice of a polemical history of recent Anglo-American philosophy.

1923:04 "Some Larger Aspects of Social Work."
            Journal of Social Forces 1.4 (1923): 359–361.

In this essay, JHT considers three contemporary features of the situation of
social work. The first is the impact of the giant foundations—Rockefeller,
Carnegie, Russell Sage, and others—and their proper role in the field of
social work. The second contemporary feature is the different approaches to
preparation for social work at the original schools and at the large state
universities. The third is the contemporary situation in the field of social work
itself and its attempts to make its efforts more scientific. In this situation of
confusion and opportunity, JHT proposes that social workers take as their
professional concern the broad question of how well our social life is satisfying
the needs of human society. (Cf. 1923:01.)

1923:05 "The Future of the *Journal*."
            International Journal of Ethics 34.1 (1923): 1–5.

At the start of its thirty-fourth year of publication, JHT offers a brief survey
of the origin and history of *The International Journal of Ethics* that he had been
leading for the last nine years, along with a statement of certain management
changes now that the publication of the journal was to be taken over by the
University of Chicago Press.

1924:01 "Ella Adams Moore."
            Ella Adams Moore: 1864–1924.
            Chicago: n.p., 1924. 5–15.

In this memorial piece for the late wife of Addison Webster Moore, JHT
discusses aspects of her life in the context of the situation of women in the
Midwest.

1924:02 [Report of the Dean of Faculties.]
            The President's Report, 1923–1924.
            Chicago: U of Chicago P, 1924. 3–7.

In his first report as the newly created dean of faculties, JHT discusses a series
of issues of educational administration at the University of Chicago.

1924:03 Review of Roscoe Pound, *Interpretations of Legal History.*
            American Bar Association Journal 10.5 (1924): 328–330.

In this favorable review of a study that attempts to turn the question of legal
justification from an examination of history to a consideration of results, JHT
disputes only the author's willingness to accept expressed desires over needs
in his calculation of results.

1924:04 Review of James Edward Geoffrey de Montmorency, *Law and the Humanities*.
American Bar Association Journal 10.5 (1924): 330.

A favorable notice of a study advocating the closer integration of legal and humanistic studies.

1924:05 [Letter about the Importance of Truth Telling.]
Survey 52.4 (1924): 254.

In this brief letter, JHT notes the conflicting requirements of veracity and confidentiality, and suggests restraint in entering into obligations with individuals that are likely to conflict with other obligations.

1924:06 "Richard Green Moulton, Charles Zueblin, and Edwin Erle Sparks."
University [of Chicago] Record 10.4 (1924): 297–301.

In this largely biographical eulogy for three former colleagues who worked in literature, sociology, and American history respectively, JHT praises especially their efforts for the university's extension programs.

1925:01 "General Statement of the Vice-President and Dean of Faculties."
The President's Report, 1924–1925.
Chicago: U of Chicago P, 1925. ix–xix.

In this report JHT, as acting-president of the university, discusses a number of issues: the administration of the late Ernest DeWitt Burton, the procedures to be followed during the selection of the next president, and various other university matters.

1925:02 Review of Mary Parker Follett, *Creative Experience*.
International Journal of Ethics 35.2 (1925): 189–190.

A mildly favorable discussion of a volume in which the author brings to bear certain philosophical and psychological ideas to address social conflict and the role of expertise in a democracy. (Cf. 1919:07.)

1925:03 Review of Harry Elmer Barnes, *The New History and the Social Studies*.
International Journal of Ethics 36.1 (1925): 108.

A mildly negative notice of a volume that surveys the contemporary situation in the various social sciences.

1925:04 Review of Monroe Nathan Work, *The Negro Year Book.*
International Journal of Ethics 36.1 (1925): 109.

A descriptive notice of a volume of history, statistics, and other information.

1926:01 "A University Chapel."
Journal of Religion 6.5 (1926): 449–456.

In this eloquent address at the laying of the cornerstone for the University
Chapel at the University of Chicago, JHT discusses the relationship between
religion and science. He emphasizes that the chapel is not to be a church, but
rather a focus of spirit and feeling, a place where the connections of man and
nature will be recognized. As such, the chapel can help supplement science's
craving for truth with religion's goal of service to humankind. The chapel,
JHT notes, is especially important for the young to foster open-mindedness,
a recognition of the great issues, and an appreciation of the need for inner
harmony.

1926:02 Review of John Maurice Clark, *Social Control of Business.*
International Journal of Ethics 37.1 (1926): 101–102.

In this favorable discussion of a statement of economic and political philosophy, JHT praises Clark's attempts to explore the possible role that science
might play in the advance of our economic situation toward democracy and
fuller human life.

1926:03 Review of Julius Seelye Bixler, *Religion in the Philosophy of
William James.*
International Journal of Ethics 37.1 (1926): 107–108.

A favorable notice of a study on James's attitude toward religion.

1926:04 Review of *Philosophical Essays Presented to John Watson.*
International Journal of Ethics 37.1 (1926): 109–110.

A favorable notice of a festschrift celebrating Watson's half-century of service
at Queen's University in Kingston, Ontario.

1926:05 Review of William Carlson Smith, *The Ao Tribe of Assam.*
International Journal of Ethics 37.1 (1926): 110.

A descriptive notice of a study of the effects of external contact on the customs
of the tribe.

1927:01 "Ethics" (with Matilde Castro Tufts).
Edgar Dawson, et al. *Teaching the Social Studies.*
New York: Macmillan, 1927. 186–209.

In this piece, JHT and his wife consider five topics: the general field of ethics and the purposes of ethical inquiry; the historical sources of our moral codes; some of the major figures in the history of ethics, divided into the inspirational and the systematic; the relationship between ethics and the various social sciences; and the value of ethical study for the teacher and the pre-high school and high school student. (There is also a bibliography, suggested by the authors, to be found on pp. 390.) (Cf. 1913:02, 1914:04, 1914:05, and 1918:01.)

1927:02   Review of John Stanislaus Zybura, ed., *Present-Day Thinkers and the New Scholasticism: An International Symposium.*
International Journal of Ethics 37.2 (1927): 219.

A descriptive notice of a volume that considers neo-scholasticism and responses to it.

1927:03   Review of Ralph Barton Perry, *Philosophy of the Recent Past: An Outline of European and American Philosophy since 1860.*
International Journal of Ethics 37.2 (1927): 219.

A favorable notice of a volume that surveys leading trends in recent philosophy.

1927:04   Review of Arthur Fisher Bentley, *Relativity in Man and Society.*
International Journal of Ethics 37.2 (1927): 220.

A mildly favorable notice of an attempt to apply the gains of relativity thinking to social life.

1928:01   Review of Arthur Kenyon Rogers, *Morals in Review.*
International Journal of Ethics 38.2 (1928): 234–235.

A mildly favorable discussion of a study of the history of ethics that presents the ideas of the leading ethics thinkers well, but divorced from their lives and times.

1929:01   "Individualism and American Life."
Essays in Honor of John Dewey on the Occasion of His Seventieth Birthday.
New York: Henry Holt, 1929. 389–401.

In this contribution to the Dewey festschrift, JHT explores the current social situation, especially as it demonstrates a resurgence of individualism after the Great War. President Herbert Hoover's *American Individualism* (1923) serves as a backdrop throughout. JHT's first theme is to consider in what respects the American social system is properly termed individualistic; and he suggests that business, industry, and government are partly but not exclusively individualistic, while religion, social work, and education are fundamentally social. JHT's second theme is to consider whether American society will benefit from a continued emphasis upon self-interest, and he suggests rather that the active promotion of the common good will achieve better results for the vast majority of individuals.

1929:02   "John Dewey Asks Philosophy [to] Follow Science."
                Daily Tribune [Chicago], December 14, 1929: 14.

A brief but highly favorable review of *The Quest for Certainty, Characters and Events, Sources of a Science of Education,* and *Essays in Honor of John Dewey on the Occasion of His Seventieth Birthday.*

1930:01   "What I Believe."
                Contemporary American Philosophy: Personal Statements. Eds.
                George Plimpton Adams and William Pepperell
                Montague.
                New York: Macmillan, 1930. Vol. 2. 333–353.

In this credo, JHT ranges widely. Some of his discussion is autobiographical: his New England family history, his own upbringing, his undergraduate education at Amherst College in a time of intellectual change (A.B., 1884), his two year instructorship in mathematics at Amherst, his two years at the Yale Divinity School (B.D., 1889), his call to Michigan (1889–1891) and to the new University of Chicago in 1892, and his doctoral study in Germany in between (Ph.D., 1892). JHT also discusses the old and the new (as in the case of established religion in the modern world) and the city of Chicago: its life, power and economic disparity, the role of the new university, and the intellectual and moral role of reform in Chicago. The theoretical portion of the article contains the skeleton of a genetic class morality and its application to the capitalism and communism of his day. JHT closes with a discussion of three related themes: the importance of teaching in higher education in addition to research, the importance of art, and the symbolic nature of and importance of religion.

1930:02   "The Graduate School."
                Higher Education in America. Ed. Raymond Asa Kent.
                Boston: Ginn, 1930. 350–366.

In this general survey of the philosophy and practice of graduate education, JHT begins with a consideration of the dual and sometimes conflicting aims of graduate school: the advancement of knowledge and the advanced education of students. He next considers the complex issues of preparing teachers for various teaching situations and the impact of graduate education on the university as a whole. He next considers the conditions and facilities necessary for successful graduate education and the standards that should be applied to graduate work. JHT's final themes are the relationship of graduate and undergraduate work and the advisability of providing financial assistance for graduate students.

1930:03 "In A Seminary—Forty Years Ago and Now."
Chicago Theological Seminary Register January 1930: 3–8.

In this essay, JHT, the acting-president of the Chicago Theological Seminary, offers a brief sketch of the social, industrial, and intellectual situation when he graduated from the Yale Divinity School in 1889. He then surveys some key positive and negative factors of the present situation: the domination of society by the economic realm, increasing international consciousness, the scientific mentality and the growth of social science, and some aspects of current theology. Finally, JHT considers some of the current changes in seminaries in response.

1930:04 "In A Seminary—Forty Years Ago and Now."
Religious Education 25.3 (1930): 230–234.

A reprint of 1930:03 with some omissions.

1930:05 "Recent Ethics in Its Broader Relations."
University of California Publications in Philosophy 12.2 (1930): 181–201.

In this examination of ethical thought since the Great War, JHT considers first the international and domestic problems resulting from close integration of lives combined with the failure to develop mutual understanding. He then considers the destructive impact of the comparative study of group relations upon certain classic ethical theories that overemphasize individuality, tradition and authority, and considers the general moral situation of a materialistic and freedom-seeking culture. JHT next critically explores the moral thought of some representative thinkers—Bertrand Russell, Ralph Barton Perry, G. E. Moore, Benedetto Croce, and others—as their thought addresses this climate, and follows with a favorable consideration of John Dewey's approach as a way to overcome tradition without surrendering the possibility of the criticism of desires. He concludes with a reminder of the importance of science to both ethical theorizing and the popular mind, and of the ongoing need for institutions to foster human values.

1931:01 [Memorial Address for George Herbert Mead.]
George Herbert Mead.
Chicago: n.p., 1931. 24–30.

A loving eulogy for Mead (1863–1931), JHT's friend, in-law, and colleague at the University of Chicago since 1894, that includes a discussion of their first encounter in Berlin in 1891, Mead's childhood and education, his influence as a lecturer and writer, and his various social involvements in Chicago. (Cf. 1931:11.)

1931:02 "Doctor [Addison Webster] Moore as Student and Teacher."
University [of Chicago] Record 17.1 (1931), pp. 45–47.

In these excerpts from his remarks at the memorial service for Addison Webster Moore (1866–1930), JHT discusses Moore's career—from his early work with Dewey at Chicago in 1894 through his retirement in 1929—and offers a few personal reminiscences.

1931:03 Review of Edwin Robert Anderson Seligman, ed.,
Encyclopedia of the Social Sciences. Vol. 1–2.
International Journal of Ethics 41.2 (1931): 234–236.

A highly favorable discussion of the first two volumes of a fifteen volume work.

1931:04 Review of Herbert Wallace Schneider, *The Puritan Mind.*
International Journal of Ethics 41.2 (1931): 256–257.

A highly favorable discussion of an attempt to understand the Puritan system of thought, especially as it is related to the attempts to establish an ideal society.

1931:05 Review of Leo Markun, *Mrs. Grundy, A History of Four Centuries of Morals.*
International Journal of Ethics 41.2 (1931): 270.

A mildly favorable notice of a survey for the general public of four hundred years of European and American ethical conduct.

1931:06 Review of Caroline Hadley Robinson, *Seventy Birth Control Clinics.*
International Journal of Ethics 41.2 (1931): 272.

A descriptive notice of a study of the workings of various clinics and of the social implications of birth control.

1931:07 Review of Benjamin Willard Robinson, *The Sayings of Jesus.*
International Journal of Ethics 41.2 (1931): 277.

A mildly favorable notice of an attempt to free the message of Christianity from the accretions of the ages.

1931:08   Review of Daniel Essertier, ed., *Philosophes Savants Francais du XXe siècle*. Vol. 5. *La Sociologie*.
International Journal of Ethics 41.2 (1931): 280.

A mildly favorable notice of a volume of readings of recent French sociologists.

1931:09   Review of Harry James Carman, *Social and Economic History of the United States*. Vol. 1. *From Handicraft to Factory, 1500–1820*.
International Journal of Ethics 41.2 (1931): 280.

A brief descriptive notice.

1931:10   Review of Harry Best, *Crime and the Criminal Law in the United States*.
International Journal of Ethics 41.3 (1931): 365–366.

A favorable discussion of a survey of criminal activity and our ineffective social responses.

1931:11   "Extracts from the [Memorial] Address [for George Herbert Mead] by James H. Tufts."
University [of Chicago] Record 17.3 (1931): 177–178.

A reprint of parts of 1931:01.

1932:01   *Ethics* (with John Dewey). Rev. ed.
New York: Henry Holt, 1932. xiii + 528 pp.

In the "Preface to the 1932 Edition," JHT and Dewey consider some of the changes in the book, and in society, in the twenty-four years since the first edition (1908:01). In the "Preface to the First Edition," they discuss and defend the general shape of the volume and specify the contributions of each. In the Introduction (chapter 1), they offer an initial definition of 'ethics,' a sense of the general context in which they are undertaking their inquiry into morality, and their reasons for adopting the comparative and genetic methods. They then consider the process of growth through greater levels of rationality, socialization, and the deliberate seeking of the rational and social, i.e., morality.

In part 1, "The Beginnings and Growth of Morality," JHT traces the process of moral development in the history of the West. Chapter 2 begins the consideration of the life of the early group with a collection of moral events culled from various moments in human experience. He then considers the economic, political, religious, and sexual aspects of various types of groups and the moral import of these groups. Chapter 3 discusses various premoral agencies—biological ones like child rearing, rationalizing ones like various occupations, and socializing ones like language and cooperative activities—that contribute a foundation for the growth of morality. In chapter 4, JHT discusses customs as the sanctified habits of the group that draw their authority from, and that are enforced by, the ongoing life of the group. He then discusses the difference between these mores as living codes and mere habits, and the values and defects of customary morality. In chapter 5, JHT considers the movement from group morality to personal morality, or from custom to conscience, as the triumph of progress and individuality over order and authority. He then considers various social factors (the shift from hunting to agriculture and commerce, the growth of science and the arts, military authority and new religions) and psychological factors (self-assertive instincts and impulses for sex, for private property, for various kinds of liberty, and for esteem) in this movement. Finally, JHT explores the need for this movement from custom to conscience to create a reconstructed society with reconstructed individuals. In chapter 6, JHT examines the Hebrew contribution to Western morality as fundamentally religious in nature, being based on the prophets' call for righteousness that raised their morals out of the customary. JHT then examines the moral meaning of a voluntary covenant with a personal lawgiver as an advance over inherited customs and as the means for the replacement of bad luck with punishment and for the introduction of the problem of evil. Finally, he considers the meaning of various moral terms—'righteousness,' 'sin,' 'responsibility,' 'sincerity,' 'life,' 'community'—from the Hebrew perspective. In chapter 7, JHT discusses the contribution of the Greeks, beginning with the distinction between nature and convention, and their conception of order and justice. Next, he discusses the intellectual force of individuality and individualism in reasoned challenges to religion and custom; in the commercial life, class privilege, the challenges to class law; and in the movement from the customary to the good in its various guises. JHT then discusses the relationship between the individual and the social order, maintaining the social nature of man and the importance of the rational control of passion in Plato and Aristotle. Finally, he considers the importance for Greek thought of the contrast between the real and the ideal and the building of a responsible moral character. Chapter 8 considers the Roman contribution to our moral history, centering around the law. JHT begins with a consideration of Roman society as essentially administrative and divided by class and economic inequality. The central moral ideas were Stoic in origin: universal and rational natural law, human equality, political justice and duty. In chapter 9, JHT surveys developments in moral life since the Romans. The medieval period he sees as unified by the wideranging authority of the universal Church. He discusses the Renaissance and the Reformation as periods of nationalism, civil and religious liberty, economic change, exploration and science, and so on, all of which affected morality. He then discusses the political revolution in America and France as democratic in an egalitarian sense, the Industrial Revolution, and the revolutionary developments in the natural and social sciences. Finally, he briefly discusses the dependence of moral conceptions upon group relations and the four pre-Darwinian attempts to systematize the changes he has surveyed: those of Hobbes, the 'moral sense' writers, Kant, and the utilitarians.

(Dewey's contribution comprises all of part 2, "Theory of the Moral Life," and the first two chapters of part 3, "The World of Action," that explore general social and political themes.)

Chapter 18 contains a general discussion of ethical problems in economic life beginning with an exposition of the centrality of the economic realm to modern living and of the nature of the capitalist economic system. JHT then addresses some ethical problems of industry: the well-being and security of workers, the size and the potential harm of a national economy run on impersonal cycles. In chapter 19, JHT considers the labor problem as one of conflicting interests between employers and the employed that can be settled only by determining a fair system of bargaining to decide issues like the ratio of wages to profits, a fair rate of working, control of the shop, who should bear the burden of risks, and the means available to keep bargaining power reasonably equal. Chapter 20 discusses the moral problems of business: the relationship of the profit motive to the public good, the question of distributive justice, and conflicts among various conceptions of 'justice.' In chapter 21, JHT surveys past efforts at the social control of business and industry by legislative means, and chapter 22 looks to the future. Here JHT considers current trends that might lessen the evils of American capitalism, the Italian Fascist and Soviet Communist alternatives, and some changes that are necessary if capitalism is to continue: the rejection of laissez-faire; improvements in equality and justice; increased productivity with decreased waste; increased job security and protection of workers' well-being; increased consumer demand for quality in housing, products, and leisure; and a more just distribution of the social surplus. JHT concludes with a general questioning of the moral quality of a society that is fundamentally economic in outlook. In chapter 23, JHT discusses the moral problems of the family, beginning with some historical antecedents and influences. Next, he considers economic, political, and religious changes in the modern period that affect the family, with an emphasis upon more casual sexuality and divorce as aspects of a flight from responsibility. JHT then compares the individual perspective on marriage (considering whether the satisfaction of the needs for sex and friendship are best achieved together or separately, casually or in long-standing relationships) with the social perspective (considering marriage as an institution of cooperation, growth in personality, and the education of children). Finally, JHT examines economic and political attitudes as sources of friction: whether women should work outside the home, the locus of family authority, sexuality and birth control.

1932:02 "A Philosopher-King: Justice [Oliver Wendell] Holmes."
University of California Chronicle 34.2 (1932): 168–183.

JHT's highly favorable account of the philosophical perspective of Holmes (1841–1935), who was celebrating fifty years of service on the bench, is in two parts. The first is JHT's recognition of the practical value of thinking and a statement of his view that a good judge does not and cannot simply *apply* the law, but must *interpret* it to take account of social and institutional changes over time. JHT's second part is a demonstration of why he believes Holmes is such a judge through a survey of his writings that offer an experimental philosophy of law. (Cf. 1921:10.)

1932:03   Contributor to "A Symposium: The Aim and Content of Graduate Training in Ethics."
International Journal of Ethics 43.1 (1932): 62–64.

While recognizing that social, educational, and political issues had slipped in importance relative to topics of epistemological and metaphysical interest in philosophic graduate education, JHT assumes that the pendulum will swing back. The graduate student should begin with a fundamental inquiry into the history of ethics that explores the Hebrew-Christian, the Roman, and the Kantian approaches to morality. JHT then considers four fundamental issues that should be addressed in graduate education: (1) problems surrounding the definition of the field of ethics, (2) the nature of moral consciousness, (3) some consideration of specific problems of the day, and (4) a consideration of the importance of ethical inquiry.

1932:04   Review of John Henry Muirhead, *The Platonic Tradition in Anglo-Saxon Philosophy.*
International Journal of Ethics 43.1 (1932): 65–66.

A favorable discussion of a study of British and American idealism that puts to rest the long-standing charge that British and American philosophy is essentially empiricist.

1933:01   *America's Social Morality: Dilemmas of the Changing Mores.*
New York: Henry Holt, 1933. × + 376 pp.

In this volume, JHT offers a moral portrait of his country by examining the strains and tensions on the institutions of American life. Chapter 1 considers the question of the nature of *social* morality—how group standards develop and change, the role they play in personal moral growth, conflicting mores, and so on—rather than *individual* morality, which he sees as dealing with a person's relationship to a moral standard. He also offers a brief survey of the conditions awaiting the American settlers, the streams of immigrants with their various traditions and cultures, and some of the changes in American mores since settlement. In chapter 2, JHT examines what Americans value, especially the progression from religious to political to economic values, and the role that education has played. Chapter 3 analyzes Americans at work and at play, surveying the development and current situation of their activities. In chapter 4, JHT discusses the reality of economic, ethnic, and especially racial classes in the context of the professed American value of equality. Chapter 5 considers briefly the causal factors behind suicide. In chapter 6, JHT explores issues of sex, marriage, and family: our obsession with sexuality versus its repression, the conflict between sexual maturity and socially delayed marriage, the basing of marriage on emotion or on reason, and the relationship of personal freedom and divorce to family responsibility. Chapters 7 and 8 consider the realm of American business. Here JHT explores in sequence six problems that result from the challenge of capitalist business practice to American traditional mores: (1) consumers' inability to evaluate products in the light of their complexity and of advertising, (2) prices set by a marketplace that is not fully honest and that does great harm to classes like farmers, (3) the abuse of laissez-faire and the necessary profit motive to harm the common good, (4) the inherent instabilities of a competitive system, (5) the growth of economic power without social responsibility, and (6) speculation as a source of wealth not based in social service. In chapter 9, JHT discusses moral problems in the relationship between industry and its employees—the ratio between profits and wages, the length of the work week, the responsibility for injury and old age, and the control of the workplace—and the roots of such problems in the distribution of bargaining power. Chapter 10 discusses wealth as a moral issue, considering such topics as the various limitations on the power of property holders and the role of charity. In chapter 11, JHT examines two central governmental problems: the conflict between the need for continuity and the need for adaptation, and the conflict between those who emphasize rights and freedoms and those who emphasize equality and the common good. JHT then takes up a series of topics related to the use of law as an agency of control: in chapter 12, he considers the problem of those organizations that are economically powerful enough to endanger the common good; in chapter 13, the various factors involved in the criminality of young offenders and of organized professionals; and in chapter 14, the lawlessness and excesses of law enforcement officers and the question of majoritarian statutes versus 'higher' laws with regard to conscientious objectors. In chapters 15–18, JHT considers society's efforts to protect and educate by restraining or eliminating highly commercialized activities that it takes to be vices: gambling, the consumption of alcohol, and prostitution. Chapter 19 addresses the issue of international relations and the dilemma of nationalism as a social force for good and evil, with a special consideration of the American Indians. In chapter 20, JHT explores the topic of private morals (the morals of family, neighbors, and friends) and public morals (the morals of business and government) insofar as they involve group standards or social morality. He considers various claims about the unmodifiable fundamental differences between private and public morals, such that a privately moral person could be publicly immoral, and that principles like discussion and cooperation, applicable to one, might not fit the other. He suggests that the explanation lies in the effects of largeness, impersonality, and institutional inertia, which are remediable by continued educational and scientific advance and by the continued growth of public responsibility.

1933:02   "A Social Philosopher's Idea of Good Government."
               Annals of the American Academy of Political and Social Science
               169 (1933): 193–201.

While rejecting the possibility of a single type of government that is good in
all places and at all times, JHT advances the view that a good government
must mediate between stability and change, play a role in public education
and the formation of public opinion, and attempt to balance individual rights
and social justice. As an example, JHT considers the problem of irresponsible
economic power victimizing small dealers, farmers, laborers, consumers, and
investors, and defending itself with platitudes about the rights of property.
The solution JHT offers is governmental intervention—at least through public
education—to preserve some semblance of equality. Government is also justified in advancing many cooperative activities to promote the common good,
especially with regard to unemployment relief, and in restricting commercialized vices. JHT concludes by pointing to the foundation of governmental
improvement in better education.

1933:03   Review of Morris Raphael Cohen, *Law and the Social Order;*
               and Felix S. Cohen, *Ethical Systems and Legal Ideals: An*
               Essay on the Foundation of Legal Criticism.
               Journal of Philosophy 30.23 (1933): 628–631.

In his highly favorable discussion of the first volume, JHT focuses on such
themes as the author's call for the integration of law and ethics and his
rejection of the 'phonograph' theory of law—the theory that judges find the
law, but do not make it. In his less favorable discussion of the second volume,
JHT favors the author's call for the integration of law and ethics but has
considerable trouble with his hedonism and his reading of the history of recent
ethical thought.

1934:01   "Equality and Inequality as American Values."
               College of the Pacific Publications in Philosophy. Ed. Paul
               Arthur Schilpp. Vol. 3.
               Stockton, CA: College of the Pacific, 1934. 126–137.

In light of recent European and American doubts about democratic government, JHT considers the place of equality and inequality in a democracy. He
begins with a consideration of civil and political equality, grounded in the
Declaration of Independence and the Constitution, and of the economic inequality that necessarily followed from the absolute guarantees of freedom.
He sees the basic inequality of American life to be modified only by occasional
individual successes and by the efforts of the educational system. JHT then
discusses the psychological basis of equality found in human nature and the
moral basis found in appeals to justice and cooperation, and attempts to justify
inequality either by appeals to human nature or as stimuli to achievement

and excellence. Finally, he discusses two early instances of the New Deal's attempts to foster greater social equality: the National Industrial Recovery Act of 1933 that allowed collective bargaining, and the reemphasis upon the common good that might advance efforts toward the redistribution of income and wealth.

1934:02 "The Institution as Agency of Stability and Readjustment in Ethics."
Proceedings and Addresses of the American Philosophical Association 8 (1934): 138–153.

In this presidential address to the Pacific Division of the American Philosophical Association, JHT discusses the need for moral stability in society and suggests that this stability most likely will be found not in rigid absolutes but in social institutions that can adapt to new social situations. The second theme of the paper is a defense of the adoption of such a flexible stance toward the institution of property. Growing in power since the earlier agrarian period, the rights of property have not been restrained by increased responsibility to advance the common good. By means of the institutions of equality, however, restraints can be improved. JHT closes with a brief coda on the power of ideas and on the need for contributions by philosophers in this task of advancing equality. (Cf. 1935:02.)

1935:01 "William Torrey Harris—A Personal Impression."
International Education Review 4 (1935): 235–236.

In this brief article, JHT narrates a series of personal encounters with Harris and praises him for his regard for younger colleagues, students, and children. (Cf. 1909:14.)

1935:02 "The Institution as Agency of Stability and Readjustment in Ethics."
Philosophical Review 44.2 (1935): 138–153.

A reprint of 1934:02.

1935:03 Review of John Rogers Commons, *Myself.*
International Journal of Ethics 45.3 (1935): 367–368.

A highly favorable discussion of an autobiographical volume by the writer on labor relations who attempted to develop a third alternative between continued capitalistic exploitation and communistic revolution.

1935:04 Review of Edgar Frederick Carritt, *Morals and Politics: Theories of Their Relation from Hobbes and Spinoza to Marx and Bosanquet.*
International Journal of Ethics 45.4 (1935): 448–450.

424 Annotated Bibliography

A mildly favorable discussion of a study of the relationship between political duty and self-interest that JHT finds valuable but unenlightening with regard to the current European political situation.

1935:05 Review of John Elof Boodin, *Three Interpretations of the Universe*; and *God: A Cosmic Philosophy of Religion*.
International Journal of Ethics 45.4 (1935): 466–468.

A favorable discussion of a pair of studies that attempt to interpret scientific data about the nature of the order of the universe through a theological perspective.

1935:06 Review of Arthur Hazard Dakin, Jr., *Von Hügel and the Supernatural*.
International Journal of Ethics 45.4 (1935): 494–495.

A favorable notice of a broad exploration of the supernatural.

1935:07 "[Vilfredo] Pareto's Significance for Ethics."
Journal of Social Philosophy 1.1 (1935): 64–77.

In this review-essay of the belated English translation of Pareto's *Trattato di Sociologia Generale* (1916), JHT examines his belief that, although ethical theory cannot claim to be true, morality is socially useful. JHT rejects his view that ethical theories cannot claim to be true either because they involve absolute standards, since not all ethical theories do, or because they make use of terms that are not precisely and rightly defined, since even the sciences that Pareto respects make use of such terms as well. JHT also rejects Pareto's view that morality is a useful tool of social control since he rejects the Machiavellian view of democracy upon which such a role for morality is based. JHT finds Pareto's reminder of the nonlogical factors in human action to be his greatest significance for ethics, although in his work he finds nothing to help us in our attempts to move forward.

1936:01 "Liberal Movements in the United States—Their Methods and Aims."
International Journal of Ethics 46.3 (1936): 253–275.

In the midst of doubts about the effectiveness of liberalism inspired by communism and fascism, JHT compares the libertarian and communitarian senses of 'liberalism.' He then examines in detail six liberal reform movements: (1) the remarkable growth of public education; (2) the movement for women's rights in the face of ignorance, general conservatism, the common law, and religious authority; (3) the emancipation and racial equality movement and (4) the labor movement, both of which have operated in the face of deeply-entrenched economic power; (5) the embattled agrarianism movement of recent years; and (6) the broad social work and social justice movement. JHT closes with a statement of his belief that gains made by means of liberal action are slow but sure, and a call for a press that is not the voice of the economically powerful.

1936:02   Review of Ralph Barton Perry, *The Thought and Character of William James, As Revealed in Unpublished Correspondence and Notes, Together With His Published Writings.* 2 vols.
International Journal of Ethics 46.4 (1936): 504–507.

A highly favorable discussion that initially praises Perry for his efforts and then turns to a celebration of James's thought and character.

1938:01   Review of Ralph Waldo Nelson, *The Experimental Logic of Jesus.*
International Journal of Ethics 48.2 (1938): 254–257.

A favorable discussion of a volume that advocates the rejection of authoritarianism by religious groups and its replacement by an experimental method of evaluating beliefs by their consequences.

1938:02   "Forty Years of American Philosophy."
International Journal of Ethics 48.3 (1938): 433–438.

In this review-essay of *Nature and Mind* (1937), JHT discusses the philosophic work of Frederick James Eugene Woodbridge in the context of four decades of fundamental social changes throughout which academic philosophy has continued to wonder whether knowledge is possible. While pointing to Woodbridge's interest in the theory of knowledge and the realism question, JHT is more interested in discussing his naturalistic metaphysics and the implications for ethics of his view that moral situations are fundamental parts of the cosmos.

1939:01   [Official Letter for Fiftieth Reunion.]
After Fifty Years: A Report of the Class of '89, Yale Divinity School. Ed. James Gibson Robertson.
Cambridge, NY: Press of the Washington County *Post*, 1939. 52–55.

In this piece, JHT stresses that because human life is short, we need institutions like courts and churches and universities to carry forward human gains. He follows with a summary of social changes over the past half-century and a call for religious reconstruction in response. He concludes with a listing of three favorable changes that the last half-century has witnessed: the end of the conflict between religion and science, a more accurate picture of human nature in religion, and a growing sense of social responsibility. (Cf. 1939:02 and 1939:05.)

1939:02   [Personal Letter for Fiftieth Reunion.]
*After Fifty Years: A Report of the Class of '89, Yale Divinity
School.* Ed. James Gibson Robertson.
Cambridge, NY: Press of the Washington County *Post*,
1939. 56–60.

In this autobiographical message to his fellows, JHT discusses aspects of
his academic, publishing, and personal life over the last half-century. (Cf.
1939:01.)

1939:03   "Sixty-One Years Ago in Monson Schools."
Monson *Register* 30 March 1939.

In this brief essay, JHT discusses his experiences teaching for two years in the
Monson school district before his eighteenth birthday.

1939:04   Review of Edwin Arthur Burtt, *Types of Religious
Philosophy.*
Philosophical Review 48.3 (1939): 332–336.

A highly favorable discussion of a volume that examines the thought of several
religious bodies and the religious philosophy of several contemporary thinkers
in which JHT praises the author's impartiality of presentation.

1939:05   "Looking Back after Fifty Years."
Yale Divinity News November 1939: 5–6.

A reprint of 1939:01.

1940:01   Review of *The Philosopher of the Common Man: Essays in
Honor of John Dewey to Celebrate His Eightieth Birthday.*
Journal of Philosophy 37.12 (1940): 332–334.

In this highly favorable discussion of the festschrift for Dewey's eightieth
birthday, JHT examines each of the essays briefly. He then focuses on Edwin
W. Patterson's consideration of a Pragmatic philosophy of law, emphasizing
that it means neither ignoring the wisdom of the past nor divorcing law and
morality. JHT concludes with a loving consideration of the Dewey contribution—"Creative Democracy: The Task before Us"—in which Dewey calls for
a reconstruction of our democratic life.

1940:02   "[Jonathan] Edwards and [Isaac] Newton."
Philosophical Review 49.6 (1940): 609–622.

In this consideration of the influence of Newton on Edwards that he had begun
at Columbia University nearly two decades before, JHT offers a comparison of
their conceptions of the universe as law-governed and an examination of their

understandings of the interrelated physical concepts of 'atom,' 'solidarity,' and 'gravitation.' He concludes with a brief discussion of Edwards's 'idealism' and its relation to natural science.

1942:01   Contributor to *James Hayden Tufts*.
Chicago: n.p., 1942. 68 pp.

JHT's account of his own life, selected from autobiographical notes, begins with his childhood, his father's 'home school,' and his manual activities around the farm. Then he turns to family history, which leads him back to his own early education. His account of Amherst College in the 1880s follows: student life, studies, football, the ideas in the air, and so on. The concluding sections are a brief statement by JHT on the possibilities of social advance and a discussion of the life of the teacher that he sees as a life of learning. (Cf. 1943:02.)

1943:01   "Ethics."
Twentieth Century Philosophy: Living Schools of Thought. Ed. Dagobert David Runes.
New York: Philosophical Library, 1943. 11–37.

In this survey of the contemporary moral situation, JHT begins with a statement of three fundamental moral facts—we recognize duties, we seek the good in living, and we approve of virtue—and of the present importance of the moral problems set by groups and institutions. He then considers the origin of moral theorizing in conflicts between static mores and changing social pressures. JHT next examines some themes in recent individualistic ethics: the attempt to ground duty in the social nature of man, the recognition of creative activity as essential to the moral life, and the emphasis upon the distinctive character of moral language. He then considers the relationship between four fundamental moral values—effective freedom, welfare, equality, and peace—and the modern social situation. Finally, JHT critically examines communism and national socialism as philosophies that reject these four fundamental moral values, and he suggests that we can preserve our democratic way of life only if we preserve our pluralistic society and our spirit of moral growth.

1943:02   "Amherst College in the 'Eighties."
Amherst Graduates' Quarterly 32.3 (1943): 209–217.

A reprint of a portion of 1942:01.

UNPUBLISHED MATERIALS

Extensive archival materials of Tufts's writings can be found at the following locations:

1. Archives and Special Collections
   Amherst College Library
   Amherst College
   Amherst, MA 01002

(Includes family papers and genealogical material, personal and professional correspondence, memoirs, copies of published materials, his college scrapbook and photo album, and his unpublished master's thesis: "The Growth of the Love of Nature in English Poetry.")

2. Special Collections
   Regenstein Library
   The University of Chicago
   Chicago, IL 60637

(Includes manuscripts of class notes and lectures, professional correspondence, memoirs, materials related to his social and political activities, photos.)

3. Special Collections
   Morris Library
   Southern Illinois University
   Carbondale, IL 62901

(Includes copies of published works and manuscripts, family papers and genealogical materials, professional and personal correspondence, newspaper clippings and photos.)

Index

Specific writings of James Hayden Tufts are referred to throughout by listing the year followed by the publication number as given in the Annotated Bibliography.

James Campbell is associate professor of philosophy at the University of Toledo. After undergraduate study at Temple University, he earned his doctorate at SUNY/Stony Brook. He taught previously at the University of Maine and the University of Kentucky, and has recently spent a year as a Fulbright Lecturer at the University of Innsbruck in Austria. Professor Campbell is the author of numerous essays on American philosophy and culture, as well as *The Community Reconstructs: The Meaning of Pragmatic Social Thought* (1992).